# PROPHECY WARS

# PROPHECY WARS

## THE BIBLICAL BATTLE OVER THE END TIMES

### GARY DeMar

A Biblical Worldview Ministry
AmericanVision.org

Powder Springs, Georgia

# Contents

# Preface

On February 23, 2013, I participated in "Revelation: An Evangelical Symposium" in Reno, Nevada, with Sam Waldron (Academic Dean and Resident Professor of Systematic Theology at the Midwest Center for Theological Studies and author of *The End Times Made Simple*) and James Hamilton (Associate Professor of Biblical Theology at The Southern Baptist Theological Seminary and author of *Revelation: The Spirit Speaks to the Churches*.)

The Symposium was hosted by Sierra Bible Church and moderated by Brian Borgman, founding pastor of Grace Community Church in Minden, Nevada.

We barely scratched the surface in the presentation of our respective positions since each of us only had 55 minutes to present our views with almost no time allotted for cross examination. A great deal was left unsaid and unchallenged. That's to be expected.

Because there was not an opportunity to respond to a number of claims and charges made by Mr. Hamilton, who holds a historic premillennial position, and Mr. Waldron, who advocates for amillennialism, I decided to respond in print with this short book.

*Prophecy Wars* covers topics related to (1) the time texts, audience reference (the use of the second person plural), and prophetic signs that are described by Jesus in the Olivet Discourse (Matt. 24; Mark 13; Luke 21), (2) the claim made by James Hamilton that preterism is based on the historical works of first-century Roman-Jewish historian Flavius Josephus (AD 37-100), an eyewitness to the destruction of Jerusalem that occurred in AD 70, (4) the meaning of Jesus' use of "this generation," and (5) John Murray's (1898-1975) interpretation of Matthew 24-25, a position that Mr. Waldron follows.

For a more complete discussion of prophetic topics, especially related to the Olivet Discourse, see my books *Last Days Madness, Is Jesus Coming Soon?*, and *Wars and Rumors of Wars*.

For a discussion of other prophetic topics, see my books *New Testament Eschatology: What the Early Church Believed about Bible Prophecy* (with Francis X. Gumerlock), *The Gog and Magog End-Time Alliance,*

*10 Popular Prophecy Myths Exposed and Answered*, *Left Behind: Separating Fact from Fiction*, and *Identifying the Real Last Days Scoffers*. Also see Francis X. Gumerlock's *The Day and the Hour: Christianity's Perennial Fascination with Predicting the End of the World* and *Revelation and the First Century: Preterist Interpretations of the Apocalypse in Early Christianity*.

Something needs to be said about the definition of preterism. If you believe Old Testament prophecies were fulfilled in the person and work of Jesus as the Christ and numerous New Testament passages were fulfilled in that first-century generation, then you are to some degree a preterist because you believe the fulfillment of those prophecies are in the *past*.

> The term preterism comes from the Latin *praeter* which refers to something that is "past." Christian preterism as it relates to the New Testament contends that most prophecies were fulfilled in events leading up to and including the events surrounding the destruction of Jerusalem that took place in AD 70 as prophesied by Jesus in Matthew 23-25, Mark 13, and Luke 17, 19, and 21.

For example, as *Prophecy Wars* will show, the Olivet Discourse is Jesus' prophecy about the destruction of Jerusalem that took place in AD 70. Its fulfillment, therefore, is in our past.

In addition, I have added chapters that deal with the speculative nature of prophetic thinking today that always seems to arise in troubled and uncertain times. There is some repetition in the following chapters because many of the chapters were originally articles that often covered the same ground because the same arguments keep coming up.

# Introduction

My first introduction to the topic of Bible prophecy came by way of Hal Lindsey's *Late Great Planet Earth*. That was in 1973 when I was in my final year at Western Michigan University. Having very little knowledge of the Bible, I was intrigued with the argument and the seemingly incontrovertible evidence that we were living in the last days. The signs, I was told, were all around us. It all seemed to make sense; until I read the Bible. As I began to read the New Testament, I came across numerous passages that did not fit Lindsey's *Late Great Planet Earth* paradigm. Here are three from the Gospel of Matthew that immediately caught my attention:

- "But whenever they persecute you in one city, flee to the next; for truly I say to you, you will not finish going through the cities of Israel until the Son of Man comes" (Matt 10:23).
- "For the Son of Man is going to come in the glory of His Father with His angels, and WILL THEN REPAY EVERY MAN ACCORDING TO HIS DEEDS. Truly I say to you, there are some of those who are standing here who will not taste death until they see the Son of Man coming in His kingdom" (Matt. 16:28).
- "Truly I say to you, this generation will not pass away until all these things take place" (Matt. 24:34; see 12:39, 41, 42; 23:36).

I was perplexed, since Jesus was obviously addressing a first-century audience about His coming. Not being able to reconcile these verses with the popular prophecy works of the day, I put the study of eschatology on hold until I had a better working knowledge of the Bible. About a year later, the issue again became a topic of discussion. By then I was a student at Reformed Theological Seminary where I had access to a theological library. I picked up William Hendriksen's commentary on Matthew from his multi-volume New Testament Commentary series published by Baker Book House. Hendriksen's comments on these passages were not much help.

In his more than two pages of explanation as to why "this generation" does not mean the generation of Jesus' day, Hendriksen did not reference a single verse in the synoptic gospels where the same phrase is used (Matt. 11:16-19;[1] 12:39,[2] 41,[3] 42;[4] 16:4;[5] 17:17;[6] 23:36;[7] Mark 8:12; Luke 7:31; 11:29, 30, 31, 32, 50, 51; 17:25; 21:32). Here's what he wrote:

> By no means has it been established that the term "this generation" must be limited to contemporaries. It can also refer to "this kind of people"; for example, the Jews, at any time or in any age. Worthy of the consideration in this connection are such passages as Deut. 32:5, 20; Ps. 12:7; 78:8; etc., where the LXX uses the same word as is here rendered "generation," but evidently with a meaning that goes beyond "group of contemporaries."[8] Thus even in the New Testament (see Acts 2:40; Phil. 2:15; Heb. 3:10), though the starting point may well be a reference to the people of that particular day, this may not be the entire meaning. So also probably here in Matt. 24:34.[9]

With this interpretation, Hendriksen and others indicated that Jews throughout history were culpable for the death of Jesus when the Bible clearly condemns a single generation (and not even all of that

---

1. "But to what shall I compare **this generation**?" (Matt. 11:16).

2. "An evil and adulterous generation craves for a sign; and yet no sign will be given to it but the sign of Jonah the prophet" (Matt. 12:39). That sign was given to that generation.

3. "The men of Nineveh shall stand up with **this generation** at the judgment, and shall condemn it because they repented at the preaching of Jonah; and behold, something greater than Jonah is here" (Matt. 12:41; cf. Luke 11:29). Jesus could only have meant that current generation since it was the only generation that could be condemned because Jesus is the Someone who is "greater than Jonah," and Jesus was in their presence in the same way Jonah was in the presence of the Ninevites.

4. "The Queen of the South shall rise up with **this generation** at the judgment and shall condemn it" (Matt. 12:42).

5. "An evil and adulterous generation seeks after a sign; and a sign will not be given it, except the sign of Jonah." (Matt. 16:4).

6. "And Jesus answered and said, 'You unbelieving and perverted generation, how long shall I be with you? How long shall I put up with you?...'" (Matt. 17:17). Note the use of "you."

7. "Truly I say to you, all these things will come upon **this generation**" (Matt. 23:36).

8. I believe Hendriksen is wrong on this point. The Bible is referencing a specific generation, the generation that was in the wilderness, not the Jewish race throughout history or during a distant period of "great tribulation" (Deut. 32:5, 20). The same is true of Psalm 78:8: "And not be like their fathers, a stubborn and rebellious generation, a generation that did not prepare its heart and whose spirit was not faithful to God."

9. William Hendriksen, *Exposition of the Gospel According to Matthew* (Grand Rapids, MI: Baker Book House, 1973), 868.

generation) (John 19:15; Acts 2:36, 49). Consider this comment from amillennialist Anthony Hoekema that is similar to that of Hendriksen:

> By "this generation," then, Jesus means the rebellious, apostate, unbelieving Jewish people, as they have revealed themselves in the past, are revealing themselves in the present, and will continue to reveal themselves in the future.[10]

Peter restricts the historical parameters of judgment by reciting the charge (Acts 2:23)[11] and identifying the generation that was guilty of the charge (2:39-40).[12] The judgment upon Jerusalem and the destruction of the temple was the end point of that generation's judgment.

In his attempt to back up his weak exegetical argument, Hendriksen writes: "Jesus does not necessarily mean that his disciples shall see all that has been predicted and is going to take place" even though in Matthew 24:33 Jesus says, "**you** too, when **you** see all these things, recognize that He is near, right at the door."[13] If Jesus wanted to refer to a future generation, He mostly likely would have used the distant demonstrative "that" instead of the near demonstrative "this."[14]

---

10. Anthony Hoekema, *The Bible And The Future* (Grand Rapids, MI: Eerdmans, 1979), 117.

11. "This [Jesus], delivered over by the predetermined plan and foreknowledge of God, you nailed to a cross by the hands of godless men and put Him to death."

12. "For the promise is for you and your children and for all who are far off, as many as the Lord our God will call to Himself. And with many other words he solemnly testified and kept on exhorting them, saying, 'Be saved from this perverse generation!'"

13. Hendriksen, *Exposition of the Gospel According to Matthew*, 868. "In Lk. xxi. 28 it is said 'your redemption draweth nigh' and in verse 31 'the kingdom of God is nigh.' The corresponding expression in Matt. and Mk. is 'he (or it) is nigh.' 'He' or 'it' has no word corresponding to it in the Greek. It is supplied from the verb. Now all four of these expressions are not what we should expect to find in connection with the second coming but are more easily applied to the destruction of Jerusalem. The disciples had been warned to flee to the mountains to be saved from the terrible destruction whose days had been shortened 'for the elect's sake.' This may account for the expression 'your redemption.' 'The kingdom of God is near' is parallel to if not explanatory of expression 'your redemption.' It is the common phrase with which the Lord introduced his preaching and hence is not a special phrase describing the second coming." Edgar M. Wilson, "The Second Coming in the Discourse of the Last Things," *The Princeton Theological Review* (January 1928), 77.

14. "Greek grammars and lexicons recognize two demonstratives: near and distant. The near demonstrative, as the name denotes, points to someone or something 'near,' in close proximity. They appear as the singular word 'this' and its plural 'these.' The distant demonstratives, as their name suggests, appear as 'that' (singular), or 'those' (plural)." Cullen I. K. Story and J. Lyle Story, *Greek To Me: Learning New Testament Greek through Memory*

Hendriksen's comments on Matthew 24:14 are weak. He does not mention that Jesus used the Greek word *oikoumenē*, a word that refers to a limited geographical area (Luke 2:1; 4:5; 21:26; Acts 11:28; 17:6, 31; 19:27; Rom. 10:18; Heb. 1:6; 2:5; Rev. 3:10; 16:14).

James Hamilton follows a similar line of argument: "Jesus explains that there will be birth pains until the gospel has gone through the whole world (24:4-14)."[15] Michael Horton also, following a mixed futurist approach to the Olivet Discourse similar to the position taken by Sam Waldron, writes: "Since the gospel was obviously not preached to all the nations by AD 70, it is impossible to conclude with preterists that the 'end' to which Jesus refers is a past event."[16] He must have missed 1 Timothy 3:16d and Romans 16:26.

Jack Lewis, among with many other commentators, disagrees with Horton's and Hamilton's conclusions:

How often this passage has been applied to the final end of the world! Some, seeing much of the world unevangelized, take comfort that the end is not near. However, most of the empire was evangelized before AD 70 (1 Thess. 1:8; Rom. 1:5, 8; Col. 1:6, 23).[17]

The "end" to which Jesus refers, as will be pointed out in greater detail, is not the end of the world (*kosmos*), as some translations have it, but the "end of the age" (*aiōn*) (Matt. 24:3). For a detailed study of how

*Visualization* (New York: Harper, 1979), 74. "Sometimes it is desired to call attention with special emphasis to a designated object, whether in the physical vicinity of the speaker or the literary context of the writer. For this purpose the demonstrative construction is used.... For that which is relatively near in actuality or thought the *immediate* demonstrative [*houtos*] is used.-... For that which is relatively distant in actuality or thought the *remote* demonstrative [*ekeinos*] is used." H. E. Dana and Julius R. Mantey, *A Manual Grammar of the Greek New Testament* (New York; Macmillan, 1957), 127-128, sec. 136. Similarly, "*This*, referring to something comparatively near at hand, just as *ekeinos* [that] refers to something comparatively farther away." William F. Arndt and F. Wilbur Gingrich, *A Greek-English Lexicon of the New Testament and Other Early Christian Literature*, 4th ed. (Chicago, IL: The University of Chicago Press, 1952), 600.

15. James H. Hamilton, *God's Glory in Salvation through Judgment: A Biblical Theology* (Wheaton: IL: Crossway, 2010), 377.

16. Michael Horton, *The Christian Faith: A Systematic Theology for Pilgrims on the Way* (Grand Rapids, MI: Zondervan, 2011), 937.

17. Jack P. Lewis, *The Gospel According to Matthew: The Living Word Commentary* (Austin, TX: Sweet Publishing Company, 1976), 2:124.

*oikoumenē* is used in the New Testament, see chapter 8 of my book *10 Popular Prophecy Myths Exposed and Answered.*

More recent commentaries, as well as those with a long history (e.g., Henry Hammond, John Gill, Adam Clarke, Philip Doddridge, John Lightfoot, Thomas Newton, Milton Terry, and Thomas Scott) acknowledge that Jesus' use of "this generation" refers to His own generation and not an unspecific generation in the future. For example, contemporary commentator Grant Osborne summarizes the argument quite well:

> "This generation" (ἡ γενεὰ αὕτη) in the gospels always means the people of Jesus' own time (11:16; 12:41-42; 23:36) not, as some have proposed, the generation of the last days in history, the Jewish people, the human race in general, or the sinful people.[18]

A list of other commentators who hold the same view on the interpretation of "this generation" can be found in chapter 3 of this book and in my book *Wars and Rumors of Wars.*

## Marcellus Kik's *Matthew 24*

While I was a student at Reformed Theological Seminary, the light came on. The RTS librarian had put out some books to sell that came from his personal library. My eyes focused on a faded red hardback with "Matthew XXIV" stamped on the spine. It was J. Marcellus Kik's brief commentary on Matthew's version of the Olivet Discourse. In the Preface to the second edition, Kik wrote:

> The first edition of this work was published in 1948 and it is indeed gratifying that the demand for it has necessitated a second edition. The particular interpretation represented in this book found slow acceptance but in recent years approval has multiplied, especially with the decline of the dispensational position.[19]

---

18. Grant R. Osborne, *Matthew: Exegetical Commentary on the New Testament* (Grand Rapids, MI: Zondervan, 2010), 899-900.

19. J. Marcellus Kik, *Matthew Twenty-Four: An Exposition* (Philadelphia: Presbyterian and Reformed, [1948]), vii.

In time, I learned that Kik's interpretive approach was not new or unique to him. His little book forever changed the way I studied the Bible because it used the Bible to interpret the Bible, the very methodology I was learning in my seminary classes. Kik expressed in his first edition how I felt after reading his verse-by-verse exposition of Matthew 24:

> It is with a thrill that one suddenly discovers the key which unlocks the meaning of a difficult portion of Scripture. Matthew Twenty-four is difficult to understand. It is made more difficult by commentaries which speak of "double meanings," "prophetic perspectives," and "partial and complete fulfillments."

## Jesus and His Mistaken Prophecy

There is a history of skeptics turning to Bible prophecy to claim that Jesus was wrong about the timing of His coming at "the end of the age" (Matt. 24:3) and the signs associated with it. Noted atheist Bertrand Russell (1872-1970) wrote the following in his book *Why I Am Not a Christian*, a lecture he delivered on March 6, 1927 to the National Secular Society:

> I am concerned with Christ as he appears in the Gospel narrative as it stands, and there one does find some things that do not seem to be very wise. For one thing, He certainly thought that His second coming would occur in clouds of glory before the death of all the people who were living at that time. There are a great many texts that prove that and there are a lot of places where it is quite clear that He believed that His coming would happen during the lifetime of many then living. That was the belief of His earlier followers, and it was the basis of a good deal of His moral teaching.[20]

It's obvious that Russell was not aware of or ignored the mountain of scholarship that was available to him that showed that the prophecy given by Jesus was fulfilled in great detail just as He said it would be before the generation of His day passed away.

---

20. Bertrand Russell, *Why I Am Not a Christian* (New York: Simon and Schuster, 1957), 16.

There have been others. C. S. Lewis noted the supposed problem in Jesus' statement in Matthew 24:34 that He would return before that first-century generation passed away. After dealing with critics who maintain that Jesus was just another Palestinian seer, Lewis confronts the more serious objection:

> But there is worse to come. "Say what you like," we shall be told, "the apocalyptic beliefs of the first Christians have been proved to be false. It is clear from the New Testament that they all expected the Second Coming in their own lifetime. And, worse still, they had a reason, and one which you will find very embarrassing. Their Master had told them so. He shared, and indeed created, their delusion. He said in so many words, "this generation shall not pass till all these things be done." And He was wrong. He clearly knew no more about the end of the world than anyone else. It is certainly the most embarrassing verse in the Bible.[21]

Two examples of how the predictions by Jesus about the "end" and how they affect biblical reliability and veracity come to mind. In his best-selling book *Misquoting Jesus*, Bart Ehrman describes how he struggled to reconcile what he had been taught about the inerrancy of the Bible with what he believed to be predictive errors made by Jesus. His road toward skepticism and unbelief includes what he describes as "one of the most popular books on campus" that was being read while he was a student at Moody Bible Institute in the 1970s, Hal "Lindsay's [sic] apocalyptic blueprint for our future, *The Late Great Planet Earth*."[22] Ehrman writes that he "was particularly struck by the 'when'" of Lindsey's prophetic outline of Matthew 24.

Lindsey followed a futuristic paradigm that assured his readers that Jesus would return within forty-years of 1948 (1948 + 40 = 1988), because, according to him, the re-establishment of the nation of Israel

---

21. C. S. Lewis, *The World's Last Night and Other Essays* (New York: Harcourt, Brace and Company, 1960), 97-98. Also see Gerald A. Larue, "The Bible and the Prophets of Doom," *Skeptical Inquirer* (January/February 1999), 29; Michael Shermer, *How We Believe: The Search for God in an Age of Science* (New York: W. H. Freeman and Company, 2000), 1-7; Tim Callahan, *Bible Prophecy: Failure or Fulfillment?* (Altadena, CA: Millennium Press, 1997), 204-229.

22. Bart D. Ehrman, *Misquoting Jesus: The Story Behind Who Changed the Bible and Why* (New York: Harper Collins, 2005), 12.

was the prophetic key to Bible prophecy. As anyone who reads the New Testament can see, there is not a single word said about Israel becoming a nation again. Ehrman writes that "this message proved completely compelling to us. It may seem odd now—given the circumstances that 1988 has come and gone, with no Armageddon—but, on the other hand, there are millions of Christians who still believe that the Bible can be read literally as completely inspired in its predictions of what is soon to happen to bring history as we know it to a close."[23]

Instead of questioning the exegetical work of Lindsey and other prophecy writers, Ehrman rejected the Bible. As the chairman of the Department of Religious Studies at the University of North Carolina at Chapel Hill, and someone who is described as "an authority on the history of the New Testament, the early church, and the life of Jesus," Ehrman should have known that the interpretation made popular by Lindsey, Tim LaHaye, and other prophecy writers is a recent interpretive system when compared to the great Bible expositors of the past.

In his 2008 debate with Douglas Wilson, the late Christopher Hitchens charged that Jesus was wrong because He predicted that His coming would take place within the time span of their generation (Matt. 24:34).[24] This, of course, would make Jesus a false prophet and the New Testament unreliable if Hitchens' claim was true. If Jesus was wrong about what generation would be alive when the destruction of Jerusalem was to take place, then why should anyone trust Him on anything He said? In just a few sentences in his response, Wilson showed that Jesus was referring to a more near-term judgment that in fact did take place before that first-century generation passed away. It's the only way to read the Olivet Discourse. Hitchens did not know how to answer Wilson.

The skeptics are reading the Olivet Discourse in the right way. Jesus predicted that He would return within the time period of that generation. Unfortunately, too many Christians are giving the wrong answer when skeptics claim Jesus was mistaken. All of what Jesus said *would happen* before that generation passed away *did happen*.

---

23. Ehrman, *Misquoting Jesus*, 13.

24. See the 2009 film *Collision*: https://en.wikipedia.org/wiki/Collision_(2009_film) Also see Joel McDurmon, *Collision: The Official Study Guide* (Powder Springs, GA: American Vision, 2010), chap. 8.

# CHAPTER 1

# The Exegetical Gerrymandering of the Time Texts

A s with all debates and symposiums, there is no way to respond to everything someone says. But it was rather frustrating that neither of the opponents of preterism tried to explain how the crucial time texts of Revelation should be understood even though it is a significant part of the preterist position. I began my presentation with Revelation 22:10, compared it to Daniel 12:4, and then went back to Revelation 1:1 and 1:3. While it wasn't the only point I made, it was obvious that it was an important point.

In Daniel 12:4, Daniel is told to "seal up the book until the end of time" (also see Dan. 8:17, 19; 11:27, 35, 40; 12:9, 13). The "end" referenced in these passages is an end of an era, a period of covenantal time, not the end of the cosmos (Heb. 1:1-2). "The book [of Daniel] is sealed, and most commentators believe that the opening of the sealed book by Jesus in Revelation 5-6 alludes partly to Daniel's prophecy. Revelation takes up where Daniel leaves off, and deals mostly with the Apostolic Age and the death and resurrection of the Church."[1]

Unlike Daniel, John is told, "Do not seal up the words of the prophecy of this book, for the time is near" (Rev. 22:10). Daniel's prophecy is sealed until Jesus breaks the seals in Revelation 6. The events of Revelation were to take place "soon" (1:1) for the "time is near" (1:3), that is, soon and near for those who first read Revelation since that's what the words "soon" and "near" mean in the Bible.

In preparing for the Symposium, I noted that James Hamilton's commentary on Revelation did not spend much time on the meaning of these time words. He cites portions of verses 1 and 3 in the first

---

1. James B. Jordan, *The Handwriting on the Wall: A Commentary on the Book of Daniel* (Powder Springs, GA: American Vision Press, 2007), 621.

chapter of Revelation (31), but he does not wrestle with what "soon" and "near" mean. In fact, he obfuscates by declaring:

> The revelation is given so that the servants of God and Christ will know "the things that must soon take place" (1:1). No matter how many millennia pass before these events occur, in the light of eternity they will soon come to pass. These events could happen at any moment. Are you ready? (32)

Revelation does not say these events "could happen at any moment" over thousands of years. The revelation given to John is clear:

> The Revelation of Jesus Christ, which God gave Him to show to His bond-servants, the things which **must soon take place**; and He sent and communicated it by His angel to His bond-servant John, who testified to the word of God and to the testimony of Jesus Christ, even to all that he saw. Blessed is he who reads and those who hear the words of the prophecy, and heed the things which are written in it; **for the time is near** (1:1-3).

Hamilton describes the phrase in verse 3, "for the time is near," as "pregnant words." What does it mean "that reality is soon to break into this world where things are not as they seem"? (34). Hamilton does quote Revelation 22:10—"I am coming soon"—but no comment is forthcoming (415). He quotes a portion of 22:10 again (418), but leaves out the word "soon." Near the conclusion to his commentary, he writes: "Once again Jesus validates this teaching with the announcement that he is coming in 22:20: 'He who testifies to these things says, "Surely I am coming soon."'[2] But he does not explain how "Surely I am coming soon" fits in with a position that has Jesus' "soon coming" being nearly two millennia away and counting.

## The Things Which Must Soon Take Place

Revelation begins with a statement about when the revealed events were to take place:

> The Revelation of Jesus Christ, which God gave Him to show to His bond-servants, the things which **must soon [τάχει] take**

---

2. James M. Hamilton, Jr., *Revelation: The Spirit Speaks to the Churches* (Wheaton, IL: Crossway Books, 2012), 419.

**place**; and He sent and communicated *it* by His angel to His bond-servant John, who testified to the word of God and to the testimony of Jesus Christ, *even* to all that he saw. Blessed is he who reads and those who hear the words of the prophecy, and heed the things which are written in it; **for the time is near** [ἐγγύς] (Rev. 1:1-3).

J. Dwight Pentecost, a noted dispensational futurist, comments, "It is to be observed that the time element holds a relatively small place in prophecy."[3] Let's put Pentecost's claim to the test. The words "soon" and "near" are always used in the New Testament for events that are close in terms of time. For example:

- John 11:29: "And when she heard it, she arose quickly [ταχὺ], and was coming to Him."
- John 11:31: "The Jews then who were with her in the house, and consoling her, when they saw that Mary rose up quickly [ταχέως] and went out, followed her, supposing that she was going to the tomb to weep there."
- John 13:27: "And after the morsel, Satan then entered into him. Jesus therefore said to him, 'What you do, do quickly [τάχιον].'"
- John 2:13: "And the Passover of the Jews was at hand [ἐγγὺς], and Jesus went up to Jerusalem."
- John 6:4: "Now the Passover, the feast of the Jews, was at hand [ἐγγὺς]."
- John 7:2: "Now the feast of the Jews, the Feast of Booths, was at hand [ἐγγὺς]."
- John 11:55: "Now the Passover of the Jews was at hand [ἐγγὺς], and many went up to Jerusalem out of the country before the Passover, to purify themselves."[4]

In all the examples I've read, quickly is not only about the speed of the action but the immediacy of the action. According to Grant S. Osborne

---

3. J. Dwight Pentecost, *Things to Come: A Study in Biblical Eschatology* (Grand Rapids, MI: Zondervan/Academie, [1958] 1964), 46.

4. See Appendix B of this book for further examples.

in his commentary on Revelation, the Greek word *taxu* "does not mean Christ is coming 'quickly' but 'very soon' (as in 1:7; 22:7)."[5]

Thomas Ice writes that "the terms 'quickly' and 'near' are more properly interpreted as *qualitative indicators* describing how Christ will return. *How* will He return? He will come back 'quickly' or 'suddenly.'"[6]

The problem with Ice's analysis is that "quickly" does not anticipate much of a delay in any of the verses where the word is used (e.g., Matt. 5:25; 28:7; Luke 15:22; 16:6; John 11:29, 31; 13:27; Acts 22:18), certainly not nearly 2,000 years! With "quickly" the action happens soon after. In fact, Ice uses Acts 22:18 as "descriptive of the manner in which the action takes place: 'I saw Him saying to me, "Make haste, and get out of Jerusalem *quickly*, because they will not accept your testimony about Me."'"

If we apply Ice's understanding of "quickly" to this verse, it would read this way: "When you decide to get out of Jerusalem, do it *quickly*." But this makes no sense since Jesus' words were a warning for Paul to "make haste" in leaving the city, that is, to do it "quickly" because he had enemies in the city. If he waited and only acted speedily when he decided to leave, then Jesus' warning was inconsequential.

Ice contrasts Acts 22:18 with 1 Timothy 3:14, a verse he describes as a "timing passage": "I am writing these things to you, hoping to come to you **before long** [*en tachei*]." If 1 Timothy 3:14 is a timing passage, then so is Revelation 1:1 since both use the same Greek construction (*en tachei*) that's identical in all three verses (Acts 22:18; 1 Tim. 3:14; Rev. 1:1). So let's use "before long" in Revelation 1:1 and see how it reads: "The Revelation of Jesus Christ, which God gave Him to show to His bond-servants, the things which must take place **before long** [*en tachei*]." "Before long" does not have the meaning of an unspecified time going on for millennia!

In Revelation 1:1, John was shown "the things which must shortly take place." Why must they "shortly take place? Because the reader is

---

5. *Revelation: Baker Exegetical Commentary on the New Testament* (Grand Rapids, MI: Academic, 2002), 194, note 24.

6. Thomas Ice, "Preterist 'Time Texts,'" *The End Times Controversy: The Second Coming Under Attack*, eds. Tim LaHaye and Thomas Ice (Eugene, OR: Harvest House, 2003), 102. "Suddenly" is a completely different word in Greek (Mark. 13:36; Luke 2:13; 9:39). Another Greek word expresses a similar idea (Luke 21:34; 1 Thess. 5:3).

told "the time is near" (Rev. 1:3). Jesus defines "near" to mean "at the door" (Matt. 24:33). James writes that "the coming of the Lord is at hand," and he defines "at hand" to mean "right at the door" (5:8-9).

If the purpose of Revelation was to demonstrate that the events of the book were a prophetic certainty that could occur at any time, John could have been told to write, "The Revelation of Jesus Christ, which God gave Him to show His bond-servants the things which *must* take place." This wording would have had the effect of expressing necessity without committing to any time parameters, the very thing dispensationalists claim the Bible teaches. Revelation uses this construction in several places (4:1; 10:11; 17:10; 20:3). But by adding "shortly," Jesus is telling Revelation's first readers that not only are these coming events a certainty, they will happen quickly because "the time is near."

Let's allow Milton Terry, author of *Biblical Hermeneutics*, to put the debate over time words into perspective:

> When a writer says that an event will shortly and speedily come to pass, or is about to take place, it is contrary to all propriety to declare that his statements allow us to believe the event is in the far future. It is a reprehensible abuse of language to say that the words *immediately*, or *near at hand*, mean *ages hence*, or *after a long time*. Such a treatment of the language of Scripture is even worse than the theory of a double sense.[7]

Terry is a good judge in this matter since he is respected by futurists and those who believe that the majority of events described in Revelation have already been fulfilled. He is to the point—near means near all the time!

Charles L. Feinberg writes in his commentary that the phrase "things which must shortly come to pass" in Revelation 1:1 "gives no basis for the historical interpretation of the book. Events are seen here from the perspective of the Lord and not from the human viewpoint (cf. II Pet 3:8). The same Greek words appear in Luke 18:7-8 (Gr *en tachei*), where the delay is clearly a prolonged one."[8] He continues with this

---

7. Milton S. Terry, *Biblical Hermeneutics: A Treatise on the Interpretation of the Old and New Testaments* (New York: Phillips & Hunt, 1883), 495-496.

8. Luke 18:78: If the unrighteous judge will give justice to the widow because of her

line of argument in his comments on "The time is at hand" (Rev. 1:3): "These words (Gr *ho kairos engus*) appear only twice in the Revelation. Neither reference indicates the possible length involved. Again, all is seen from the perspective of God."[9]

John Walvoord argues that "must shortly come to pass" in Revelation 1:1 does not mean "that the event may occur soon, but when it does, it will be sudden (cf. Luke 18:8; Acts 12:7; 22:18; 25:4; Rom. 16:20)." A similar interpretation is given to "for the time is near [at hand]" (Rev. 1:3): "The expression 'at hand' indicates nearness from the standpoint of prophetic revelation, not necessarily that the event will immediately occur."[10] How does this view compare with other passages?

- Jesus said, "My time is at hand [lit., near]" (Matt. 26:18). Does Walvoord's method apply here? Was Jesus' time chronologically near or are we still waiting for it to happen? (cf. Matt. 3:15; Mark 1:15).

- "Now learn the parable from the fig tree: when its branch has already become tender, and puts forth its leaves, you know that summer **is near**" (Matt. 24:32). How far away is summer? The analogy makes it evident that "near" means close: appearance of leaves = nearness of summer.

- "Even so you too, when you see all these things, recognize that He is near, right at the door" (24:33). Here we find a brief commentary on what "near" means—"right at the door": signs = nearness of Jesus' return.

John Walvoord's comments on Revelation 11:14, where the word "quickly" is used, demonstrate how exegetical gerrymandering takes place: "The third woe contained in the seventh trumpet is announced as coming quickly. *The end of the age is rapidly approaching,*"[11] but

---

persistence, can we expect anything less from God? The widow received justice *in her lifetime!* God is not like the unrighteous judge, "He will bring about justice for them speedily" (v. 8).

9. Charles L. Feinberg, "Revelation," *Liberty Bible Commentary,* eds. Edward E. Hindson and Woodrow Michael Kroll (Lynchburg, VA: The OldTime Gospel Hour, 1982), 2:790.

10. John F. Walvoord, *The Revelation of Jesus Christ* (Chicago, IL: Moody Press, [1966] 1987), 35, 37.

11. Walvoord, *The Revelation of Jesus Christ,* 183.

not when it refers to Jesus' coming. How is it possible that the word "quickly" in Revelation 11:14 can mean "the end of the age is rapidly approaching" but Jesus' use of coming "quickly" cannot mean "rapidly approaching" in 1:1, 2:16, 3:11, 22:7, 12, and 20? In fact, Walvoord's comments on Revelation 22:7 demonstrate how shaky his position is: "The thought seems to be that when the action comes, it will be sudden."[12] For a dispensationalist it may seem to be that way, but the Bible doesn't mean it that way.

Nowhere does Jesus say, "When I come it will be fast." He says, "I am coming quickly." Robert Thomas argues in a similar way: "A major thrust of Revelation is its emphasis upon the shortness of time before fulfillment."[13] How is nearly 2000 years and counting a "shortness of time"?

These commentators are obscuring the obvious to protect a prophetic system. How are these words used in everyday speech? For example, you find that your son's room is a mess. You give the following instructions: "Clean up your room, and do it quickly. I'll be back soon to check on it." Two hours later you return and examine your son's progress and find things as they were when you gave him the work order. You ask him why he didn't clean his room as he was told to do, reminding him that you wanted it done *quickly* and that you would return *soon* to check on the progress. He says, "Dad, you said you would be back 'soon.' As you know, the time element holds a relatively small place in room cleaning. Besides, when I start to clean it, I'll do it quickly! I could clean it today or next week, but I'll be fast when I do it!"

Premillennialist George Eldon Ladd's comment on the time words and phrases in Revelation are equally off base:

These events are "soon to take place" (cf. 11:18; 22:10). These words have troubled commentators. The simplest solution is to take the preterist view and to say that John, like the entire Christian community, thought that the coming of the Lord was near, when in fact they were wrong. Our Lord himself seems to share this error in perspective in the saying: "This generation will not pass away before all these things take

---

12. Walvoord, *The Revelation of Jesus Christ*, 333.

13. Robert Thomas, *Revelation 1-7: An Exegetical Commentary* (Chicago: Moody Press, 1995), 55.

place" (Mark 13:30).... However, the simple meaning cannot be avoided. The problem is raised by the fact that the prophets were little interested in chronology, and the future was always viewed as imminent.[14]

Robert Thomas, like Ladd, rejects the "plain and normal" interpretation because such an interpretation would mean

> nearness of fulfillment for the events predicted. The objection is that such an alternative is impossible because a futurist approach to the book would require the events to have taken place in John's lifetime. As the matter stands, it has been almost nineteen hundred years since the prediction and much of what the book predicts still has not begun to happen. The response of this view to the seeming difficulty raised by the delay of more than nineteen hundred years is not that John was mistaken but that time in the Apocalypse is computed either relatively to the divine apprehension as here and in 22:10 (cf. also 1:3; 3:11; 22:7, 12, 20) or absolutely in itself as long or short (cf. 8:1; 20:2). When measuring time, Scripture has a different standard from ours (cf. 1 John 2:18) (Lee). The purpose of *en tachei* [soon] is to teach the imminence of the events foretold, not to set a time limit within which they must occur (Johnson). It must be kept in mind that God is not limited by considerations of time in the same way man is (cf. 2 Pet. 3:8).[15]

Thomas continually begs the question when it comes to the timing of prophetic events. He begins with the premise that the events prophesied in Revelation have not taken place and then adjusts the meaning of the time texts to fit his futurist position. If the time texts

---

14. George Eldon Ladd, *A Commentary on the Revelation of John* (Grand Rapids, MI: Eerdmans, 1972), 22.

15. Thomas, *Revelation 1-7*, 55-56. Earlier in his commentary, Thomas insists on a literal hermeneutic (29-39). This principle is cleverly avoided when it comes to the plain meaning of the time texts. Compare what Thomas writes about Scripture using a "different standard from ours" when "measuring time" with these verses: "She arose quickly, and was coming to him" (John 11:29); "Mary rose up quickly and went out" (11:31); "'What you do, do quickly'" (13:27); "I am coming quickly" (Rev. 3:11); "The second woe is past; behold, the third woe is coming quickly" (11:14). What does "quickly" mean in these texts? The dispensationalist wants us to believe that Revelation 3:11 reads something like this: "When I come, it will be fast." This is impossible given how "quickly" is used elsewhere in Scripture. Consider Revelation 11:14. When the second woe is past, the third woe will follow soon after.

are taken in their "plain sense," then there are only two possible meanings: (1) God was mistaken and the Bible is filled with unreliable information, or (2) the events described therein came to pass soon after the prophecy was given.

Earlier in his commentary on Revelation, Thomas writes that "The futurist approach to the book is the only one that grants sufficient recognition to the prophetic style of the book and a normal hermeneutical pattern on interpretation based on that style. It views the book as focusing on the last period(s) of world history and outlining the various events and their relationships to one another. *This is the view that best accords with the principle of literal interpretation.*"[16] All agree that Revelation is about the future. The question is, how far in the future does the prophecy go?

Thomas uses 1 John 2:18 in an attempt to prove that "Scripture has a different standard from ours" when it comes to measuring time. This can only be true if one begins with the unproven premise that John was not describing some near eschatological event. John's readers had heard that antichrist was coming. John corrects them by stating that "many antichrists have arisen." This was evidence that it was the "last hour." For Thomas, "last hour" is nearly two thousand years. Is this what dispensationalists mean by the "principle of literal interpretation" and the "plain sense" method?

> In the original text, the Greek word used is *taxu*, and this does not mean "soon," in the sense of "sometime," but rather "now," "immediately." Therefore, we must understand Rev. 22:12 in this way: "I am coming now, bringing my recompense." The concluding word of Rev. 22:20 is: "He who testifies to these things says, 'surely I am coming soon.'" Here we again find the word *taxu*, so this means: I am coming quickly, immediately. This is followed by the prayer: "Amen. Come, Lord Jesus!"... The Apocalypse expresses the fervent waiting for the end within the circles in which the writer lived—not an expectation that will happen at some unknown point $X$ in time (just to repeat this), but one in the immediate present.[17]

---

16. Thomas, *Revelation 1-7*, 32. Emphasis added.
17. Kurt Aland, *A History of Christianity: From the Beginnings to the Threshold of the*

Revelation is introduced by time words, and it concludes with the same time words. Jesus says, "And behold, I am coming quickly [ταχὺ]. Blessed is he who heeds the words of the prophecy of this book" (22:7, 12, 20). Then John is told by the angel in Revelation 22:10, "'Do not seal up the words of the prophecy of this book, for the time is near [ἐγγὺς].'" Notice the use of "quickly" in the middle portions of Revelation (2:16; 3:11; 11:14). In what way would a soon return be a threat to Pergamum and Philadelphia if quickly meant "it will be fast when I come"?

While the time indicators do not tell us when Revelation was written, they do indicate that events had to have taken place within a time period that was relatively close. To argue that what was revealed to John was nothing more than a claim that the events could happen at any moment over a period of thousands of years does not fit how "near" and "shortly" are used elsewhere by John and the other New Testament writers. If these verses do not mean that Jesus' return in judgment was chronologically near to Revelation's first readers, then what words could He have used if He wanted His first readers to know that these events were chronologically near for them and not chronologically near for some distant future generation? How would Jesus have said it?

If near, shortly, soon, and quickly don't mean what they mean in ordinary speech, then how can we know anything about what the Bible says? Up is down, down is up, near is far, and far is near in the mad, mad, mad world of prophetic dissonance.[18]

---

*Reformation*, trans. James L. Schaaf (Philadelphia, PA: Fortress, 1985), 1:88.

18. For further study of the topic of timing, see chapter 14 and Appendix B of this book.

CHAPTER 2

# "It Doesn't Matter if Jesus Uses 'This' or 'That'"

During the round-table discussion phase of the Reno Symposium, each of us was asked what there is about the two competing positions that we could say is a positive feature. When premillennialist James Hamilton was asked about preterism, you could tell he had a hard time coming up with something positive. Preterism is the biggest threat to premillennialism. To say anything positive opens the door to legitimacy. Even so, he could not have said anything more positive when he declared that preterists pay attention to "the text." Amen!

Before any worthwhile discussion can take place about the Bible, the first question I always ask is, "What does the text say?" The tempter approached Eve with a question about the text: "Indeed has God said, 'You shall not eat from any tree of the garden?'" (Gen. 3:1).

> The serpent intentionally misconstrues the command of God by formulating the question designed to get the woman to express the command in her own words.[1]

The devil does a similar thing in the wilderness temptation of Jesus (Matt. 4:1-11; Luke 4:1-13). Paul makes a necessary distinction between "seed" and "seeds" (Gal. 3:16). The particulars of the text matter. An interpreter can't move on to what a text means until he nails down what the text says.

It matters that Jesus said "this generation" rather than "that generation," just like it matters that He mostly uses the second person plural "you" and not the third person plural "they" (Matt. 24:30, 33) throughout the Olivet Discourse.

Let's look at some examples of prophecy writers who add words that aren't present, dismissing words that are in a text, or giving unusual

---

1. John H. Walton, *The NIV Application Commentary: Genesis* (Grand Rapids, MI: Zondervan, 2001), 204.

19

definitions to commonly used words that don't comport with how those words are used elsewhere in the Bible.

Tim Demy and Gary Stewart reject the obvious biblical meaning of "this generation" and argue that "Jesus must be speaking of a future generation. Jesus is stating that a future generation will experience the events described in Matthew 24:4-33—'these things.' These future people will not die until all the events are literally fulfilled."[2] As we've seen, "this generation" never refers to a future generation. Moreover, Jesus does not say "a future generation." Finally, we are told by Jesus what generation will see "these things": "You," those in Jesus' audience, "too, when **you** see all these things, recognize that He is near, right at the door" (24:33). The "you" referred to them!

To further misread Scripture at this point, Henry Morris, a dispensationalist and one of the founding fathers of the modern-day six-day creationist movement, turns "this" into "that" without any support. The following comments are taken from his *Defender's Study Bible* which was first published in 1995:

> The word "this" is the demonstrative adjective and could better be translated "that generation." That is, the generation which sees all these signs (probably starting with World War I) shall not have completely passed away until all these things have taken place (1045).

He wrote something similar on Matthew 24:34 in his book *Creation and the Second Coming*:

> In this striking prophecy, the words "this generation" has the emphasis of "*that* generation." That is, that generation—the one that sees the specific signs of His coming—will not completely pass away until He has returned to reign as King.[3] Now if the first sign was, as we have surmised, the first World War, then followed by all His other signs, His coming must indeed by very near[4]—even at the doors! There are only a few people still living

---

2. "Tim Demy and Gary Stewart, *101 Most Puzzling Bible Verses: Insight into Frequently Misunderstood Scriptures* (Eugene, OR: Harvest House, 2006), 106.

3. There is nothing in Matthew 24 that says Jesus is going to return to earth to reign as king.

4. Why does "near" mean "even at the doors" for Morris in the twentieth century, but it did not mean "near" in the first century? Compare the use of "near" in Matthew 24:33 with James 5:8-9.

from that[5] generation. I myself was born just a month before the Armistice was signed on November 11, 1918. Those who were old enough really to know about that first World War—"the beginning of sorrows"—would be at least in their eighties now. Thus, we cannot be dogmatic, we could very well now be living in the very last days before the return of the Lord.[6]

Morris' comments demonstrate that he understands the distinction between "this" and "that" and how "that" is needed to support his distant future interpretation. That First World War generation is long gone.[7] The same can be said for most of the Second World War generation.

Matthew 24:33 tells us what audience Jesus said would see "these things," and it wasn't the World War I generation: "so, **you** too, when **you** see all **these** things, recognize that He is near, right at the door." It is obvious, and without any need for debate, that the first "you" refers to those who asked the questions that led to Jesus' extended remarks (Matt. 24:2-4). Jesus identifies those who will "see all these things" by again using "you." If Jesus had a future generation in mind, He could have eliminated all confusion by saying, "when they see all these things, recognize that He is near, right at the door. Truly I say to you, **that** generation will not pass away until all these things take place." Instead, Morris and, as we'll see, James Hamilton, have to massage the text to gain support for a future tribulation period and thereby obscure the meaning of the passage.[8]

Hamilton declared in his critique of my interpretation of the Olivet Discourse that it doesn't matter if the demonstrative adjective "this" or the far demonstrative "that" is used in Matthew 24:34. I was shocked

---

5. Notice how Morris uses the far demonstrative "that" to refer to a generation in the past. How would Morris have described the generation in which he was living? Obviously with the near demonstrative "this" to distinguish it from "that" *past* generation.

6. Henry Morris, *Creation and the Second Coming* (Green Forest, AR: Master Books, 1991), 183. Morris died on February 25, 2006 at the age of 87.

7. Frank Buckles, the last American surviving veteran from World War I died February 28, 2011. He was 110.

8. Demy and Stewart argue that there is no mention of an audience reference in Matthew 24:33, just that "The phrases 'this generation' and 'these things' are linked together by context and grammar in such a way that Jesus must be speaking of a future generation." This is the height of obfuscation. Jesus clearly identifies the audience in verse 33: "when YOU see all these things."

when I heard him say this. But it only demonstrates the lengths some interpreters will go to defend a faltering position.

Greek grammars and lexicons seem to think it's important to note whether "this" or "that" is being used, otherwise why bother having entries for these near and far demonstrative adjectives? For example:

> Greek grammars and lexicons recognize two demonstratives: near and distant. The near demonstrative, as the name denotes, points to someone or something "near," in close proximity. They appear as the singular word "this" and its plural "these." The distant demonstratives, as their name suggests, appear as 'that' (singular), or "those" (plural).[9]

Consider these comments from a leading New Testament Greek grammar:

> Sometimes it is desired to call attention with special emphasis to a designated object, whether in the physical vicinity or the speaker or the literary context of the writer. For this purpose the demonstrative construction is used.... For that which is relatively near in actuality or thought the *immediate* demonstrative [*houtos*] is used.... For that which is relatively distant in actuality or thought the *remote* demonstrative [*ekeinos*] is used.[10]

Or this from a leading New Testament lexicon: "*This*, referring to something comparatively near at hand, just as *ekeinos* [that] refers to something comparatively farther away."[11]

The texts that govern the timing of the Olivet prophecy— Matthew 23:36 and 24:34—make it clear that Jesus was speaking of events leading up to and including the destruction of the temple that took place in AD 70. I suggest that Hamilton consult a concordance and note how "this" and "that" are consistently used throughout the gospels.[12]

---

9. Cullen I. K. Story and J. Lyle Story, *Greek To Me: Learning New Testament Greek Through Memory Visualization* (New York: Harper, 1979), 74.

10. H. E. Dana and Julius R. Mantey, *A Manual Grammar of the Greek New Testament* (New York; Macmillan, 1957), 127-128, sec. 136.

11. William F. Arndt and F. Wilbur Gingrich, *A Greek-English Lexicon of the New Testament and Other Early Christian Literature*, 4th ed. (Chicago, IL: The University of Chicago Press, 1952), 600.

12. David Alan Black, *Learn to Read New Testament Greek*, 3rd ed. (Nashville: Broadman & Holman, 2009), 80.

Dispensational premillennialist Thomas Ice tries to discount the use of the near demonstrative "this" by appealing to Daniel B. Wallace's *Greek Grammar Beyond the Basics*. Wallace notes that the near demonstrative "οὗτός [*houtos*] regularly refers to the *near* object ('this'), while ἐκεῖνος (*ekeinos*) regularly refers to the *far* object ('that')." Note his use of "regularly." Wallace goes on to state that "this" and "that" "can refer either to that which is near/far in the (1) context, (2) in the writer's mind, or (3) in space or time of the writer's audience."[13] In a footnote, Wallace mentions Zerwick's *Biblical Greek* and his comment that "the proximateness or remoteness may be not grammatical ... but psychological."[14] The example that Zerwick and Wallace use for this principle is found in Acts 4:10-11:

> Let it be known to all of you and to all the people of Israel, that by the name of Jesus Christ the Nazarene, whom you crucified, whom God raised from the dead—this [οὗτος/*houtos*] *man* stands here before you in good health. This [οὗτός/*houtos*] is the STONE WHICH WAS REJECTED by you, THE BUILDERS, but WHICH BECAME THE CHIEF CORNER stone.

The use of "this" (οὗτός/*houtos*) in Acts 4:11 refers back to 4:10 where "Jesus Christ" is mentioned ("this is the stone") but is not physically present in the way "the name" and the healed man were at the time the events described by Luke took place. Wallace writes: "θεος is the nearest noun and οὗτός (referring to the healed man) is the nearest substantive. But sinceἸησοῦ Χριστοῦ is the 'nearest *psychologically*,—was more vividly present to [the writer's] mind than any other,' it is the antecedent."[15] Note what Mounce writes: Jesus "was more vividly present." "This" refers to what is near, either physically or psychologically.

The use of the near demonstrative "this" used in Matthew 24:34 fits the context: (1) "this generation" repeatedly means the generation contemporary with Jesus (Matt. 11:16; 12:39, 41-42; 16:14; 23:36; Mark 8:12; 13:30; Luke 7:31; 11:29, 30, 31, 32, 50, 51; 17:25; 21:32), (2) the use of the second person plural throughout the chapter identifies

13. Daniel B. Wallace, *Greek Grammar Beyond the Basics: An Exegetical Syntax of the New Testament* (Grand Rapids, MI: Zondervan, 1996), 325.

14. Maximilian Zerwick, *Biblical Greek Illustrated by Examples* (Rome, Italy: Pontificii Instituti Biblici, 1963), 68. Wallace, *Greek Grammar*, 325, note 26. Wallace uses "proximity" for Zerwick's "proximateness."

15. Wallace, *Greek Grammar*, 326.

Jesus' present audience, (3) Jesus' statement in verse 33 that His present audience would be the ones to see the signs ("when **you** see all these things"), and (4) "οὗτός regularly refers to the *near* object ('this')."

The burden of proof, therefore, is on Ice to show that "the grammatical use of 'this' allows Jesus to speak in the first century but prophetically look ahead to a distant time." What Ice has to prove is that Jesus actually is using "this generation" to refer "to a distant time" and not just that "this" **can** be used this way.

To support his claim that Jesus is referring to a distant time, Ice writes, "The phrase 'all these things' governs the meaning of 'this generation.'" If this is true, then the debate is over since Jesus tells His then present audience that they will be the ones to see "all these things" (24:33). Ice is so committed to this position that he has to maintain that "the evidence demonstrates that none of those things were fulfilled in the AD 70 destruction of Jerusalem."[16]

We only need to find one of the signs Jesus mentioned as being fulfilled and Ice's argument is refuted. We know from the Bible and secular histories of the period that wars and rumors of wars, earthquakes (Matt. 27:4; 28:2; Acts 16:26), famines (Acts 11:28), false prophets (1 John 4:1; 2 Peter 2:1), tribulation (Rev. 1:9), and the gospel preached throughout all the then-known world (Rom. 1:8; 16:27-28; Col. 1:6, 23; 1 Tim 3:16) took place before the Romans sacked the city of Jerusalem and tore down the temple stone by stone, just what Jesus predicted would happen (Matt. 24:2) before that Apostolic generation passed away (24:34). Consider this recent archeological discovery:

> Archaeologists may have discovered evidence of a dire famine that gripped Jerusalem during a Roman siege nearly 2,000 years ago.
>
> Cooking pots and a ceramic lamp were found in an ancient cistern near the Western Wall, the Israel Antiquities Authority (IAA) announced. Excavators believe these artifacts were left in the underground chamber by Jewish residents who were trying to eat what little food they had in secret during the war.

---

16. Thomas Ice, "This Generation," *The Popular Encyclopedia of Bible Prophecy*, eds. Tim LaHaye and Ed Hindson (Eugene, OR: Harvest House Publishers, 2004), 117.

"This is the first time we are able to connect archaeological finds with the famine that occurred during the siege of Jerusalem at the time of the Great Revolt," Eli Shukron, excavation director for the IAA, said in a statement. The Great Revolt was the first of several Jewish uprisings against Roman rule that began in AD 66. The revolt was ultimately unsuccessful. The Romans eventually took back Jerusalem from the Jewish rebels and destroyed much of the city, including the Second Temple.

*****

The historian Flavius Josephus provided the seminal account of the Roman siege of Jerusalem—and the desperate hunger that accompanied it—in his book "The Jewish War" (Simon & Brown, 2013). He wrote about how residents in the city concealed their food and ate in secret, fearing it would be stolen by the rebels.

"For as nowhere was there corn to be seen, men broke into the houses and ransacked them," Josephus wrote. "If they found some they maltreated the occupants for saying there was none; if they did not, they suspected them of having hidden it more carefully and tortured them."[17]

Another way to get around the biblical meaning of "this generation" is to claim that Jesus was saying, "the *Jewish* race will not pass away until all these things take place."[18] There are three problems with this interpretation that's found in *The Scofield Reference Bible*. First, it's the wrong Greek word. If Jesus wanted to refer to the Jewish race, He would have used *genos* instead of *genea*. *Genea* is always translated as "generation" in the New Testament (e.g., Matt. 1:17; Luke 1:48, 50; 16:8; Acts 2:40).

Second, turning "generation" into "race" makes no logical sense. Jesus would have argued that when all the things He just outlined take place, the Jewish race would then pass away.

---

17. Megan Gannon, "Traces of Wartime Famine Unearthed in Jerusalem," Live Science (June 27, 2013): https://bit.ly/3BlPBKl

18. William Hendriksen, *Exposition of the Gospel According to Matthew*, New Testament Commentary (Grand Rapids, MI: Baker Book House), 868-869. Hendriksen does not make a single comparison with how "this generation" is used in Matthew's gospel. Instead he appeals to the Greek translation of the Hebrew Old Testament.

Third, try using "race" where "generation" appears (Matt. 1:17; 11:16; 12:39, 41, 42, 45; 16:4; 17:17; Mark 8:12, 38; 9:19; 13:30; Luke 1:48, 50; 7:31; 9:41; 11:29, 30, 31, 32, 50, 51; 16:8; 17:25; 21:32). "Race" does not fit.

Some claim that "this generation" actually means "the generation that sees the signs."[19] In order to get this translation, "this" has to be replaced with "the" and four words have to be added. This is not the way to interpret the Bible. In addition, we are told in Matthew 24:33 who will see the signs: "even so **you** too, when **you** see all these things, recognize that He is near, right at the door." The "you" is them, not us.

## This Kind of Generation

A popular attempt at an interpretive solution is to claim that Jesus was referring to a certain type or kind of generation.[20] This is the view proposed by Hamilton and others like Neil D. Nelson, Jr. Nelson argues that "this generation" (11:16; 12:41, 42, 45; 23:36; 24:34):

> reveals that the kind of people referred to are characterized as those who reject Jesus and his messengers and the salvific message they preach, who remain unbelieving and unrepentant, who actively oppose Jesus and his messengers through testing and persecution, and who will face eschatological judgment. The pejorative adjectives given to "this generation" (evil, adulterous, faithless, perverse; cf. 12:39, 45; 16:4; 17:17) throughout the gospel are qualities that distinguish those who are subjects of the kingdom from those who are not....The opponents of Jesus' disciples in Matthew 24-25 share similar traits with "this generation" as characterized in these ... chapters.[21]

Of course, Jesus doesn't use the phrase "this kind of generation" or "this type of people" in Matthew 24:34. Jesus does use the phrases "evil and adulterous generation" (Matt. 12:39; 16:4), "evil generation" (12:45), and "unbelieving and perverted generation" (Matt. 17:17), but

---

19. John MacArthur, *The MacArthur New Testament Commentary* (Chicago: Moody Press, 1989), 64.

20. Richard C. H. Lenski, *Interpretation of St. Matthew's Gospel* (Minneapolis: Augsburg Publishing House, [1943] 1961), 952.

21. Neil D. Nelson, Jr., "'This Generation' in Matt. 24:34: A Literary Critical Perspective," *Journal of the Evangelical Theological Society* 38:3 (September 1995), 376.

"evil," "adulterous," "unbelieving," and "perverted" are in the texts. Even so, Jesus referred to that first-century generation, not some future generation that might be evil or adulterous (Matt. 12:38-45).

Matthew 23:39 and 24:34 do not include any of the above adjectives; therefore, the burden of proof rests with those who claim that Jesus has a "kind of people" or a "type of generation" in mind rather than the generation of His day. In fact, the first time Jesus uses "this generation," the adjectives "evil" and "adulterous" are not used:

> "But to what shall I compare **this generation**? It is like children sitting in the market places, who call out to the other *children,* and say, 'We played the flute for you, and you did not dance; we sang a dirge, and you did not mourn.' For John came neither eating nor drinking, and they say, 'He has a demon!' The Son of Man came eating and drinking, and they say, 'Behold, a gluttonous man and a drunkard, a friend of tax collectors and sinners!' Yet wisdom is vindicated by her deeds" (Matt. 11:16).

It's obvious that Jesus was referring to that particular generation because He mentions John the Baptist and Himself (Son of Man). "By this phrase," John Nolland writes, "Jesus means his own contemporaries as the generation in whom the eschatological events, beginning with the ministry of John the Baptist, are being played out."[22] Grant Osborne is even more emphatic that *"generation"* refers to Jesus' present audience:

> Whenever Jesus uses "generation" (γενεά), it is always describing his contemporaries (the nation, not just the leaders) in a context of wickedness, unbelief, and rejection (cf. 12:39-41-42, 45; 16:4; 17:17; 23:36; 24:34).[23]

Ardent dispensationalist Arno C. Gaebelein (1861-1945) agrees. "The words which follow [Matt. 11:16] are a true description of the generation which was privileged to see the King, Jehovah, manifested in the earth.

---

22. John Nolland, *The Gospel of Matthew: A Commentary on the Greek Text* (Grand Rapids, MI: Eerdmans, 2005), 461.

23. Osborne, *Matthew*, 426.

'But to whom shall I liken this generation?...'"[24] Unfortunately, he redefines "this generation" in Matthew 24:34.

> The wrong interpretation of the word "generation" is responsible for the erroneous conception so prevalent in our days. It is said that "this generation" must mean the very generation the people who lived then upon the earth when the Lord spoke these words. It is easily seen how if this is the meaning of this generation the events predicted by our Lord *must* have been fulfilled within the life time of the people living then. What other event could be meant than the destruction of Jerusalem in the year 70? Thus the wrong interpretation of these two words, "this generation," has led the large numbers of Bible teachers and readers of this discourse astray. But let us get the right meaning of generation and all will be clear. The word *genea* means not necessarily the same persons living but it has also the meaning of *race*.[25]

D. A. Carson, Louis A. Barbieri, Jr., and Robert H. Gundry also maintain that the use of "this generation" in Matthew 24 refer to that Apostolic generation. Words do matter when it comes to the biblical text. It matters whether Jesus said "you" and not "they" and "this generation" and not "that generation."

The next chapter will continue the study of how the Gospels use the phrase "this generation" and how commentators interpret the phrase.

---

24. Arno C. Gaebelein, *The Gospel of Matthew: An Exposition, 2 vols.* (New York: Gospel Publishing House, 1907), 1:226

25. Gaebelein, *The Gospel of Matthew*, 2:214-215.

# CHAPTER 3

# What Commentators Say About "This Generation"

James Hamilton took issue with my argument that the phrase "this generation" refers to the generation to whom Jesus was speaking. During the critique phase of the Symposium, Hamilton argued that "this generation" in Matthew 24:34 and elsewhere in the gospels means a "type of generation" rather than a particular generation. Of course, Jesus doesn't say "this type of generation will not pass away until all these things take place." He said, "this generation will not pass away."

Past generations may have been evil, adulterous, and perverse, and future generations may exhibit similar moral atrophy, but it was the generation that was alive during Jesus' ministry that would fall under God's judgment. There's no other way to interpret "this generation." Consider Matthew 12:41-42:

> The men of Nineveh will stand up with **this generation** at the judgment, and will condemn it because they repented at the preaching of Jonah; and behold, one [πλεῖον] greater than Jonah is here. *The* Queen of *the* South will rise up with **this generation** at the judgment and will condemn it, because she came from the ends of the earth to hear the wisdom of Solomon; and behold, one [πλεῖον] greater than Solomon is here.

The "one greater" is Jesus Christ. Jesus is not describing a type of generation that could refer to any generation. He says the "one greater ... is **here**." Jesus is present with His audience in the same way that Jonah and the Queen of the South were present with their generational audiences as Grant R. Osborne writes makes clear:

> The people of Nineveh repented after Jonah preached judgment to them (Jonah 3:5). They will condemn (i.e., be a legal witness against) the Jewish generation of Jesus' day, which has refused to

repent after Jesus has proclaimed both salvation and judgment to them.[1]

Notice the audience reference when Jesus encounters unbelief. He's not describing a distant future of unbelief, but the unbelief that was staring Him in the face and denying His messianic mission (John 16:13):

> "And Jesus answered and said, '**You** unbelieving and perverted generation, how long shall I be with **you**? How long shall I put up with **you**? Bring him here to Me'" (Matt. 17:17).

Is there any doubt that Jesus was referring to that generation and that generation alone? "Jesus speaks of his contemporaries in very negative terms: they are not only faithless but also morally crooked or depraved (cf. 11:16; 12:39, 45; Deut. 32:5, 20)."[2] There may be unbelief in the future among other generations, but Jesus clearly identifies the people of His day as being part of a "perverted generation." Why use "you" if Jesus didn't mean them? Is there any indication in Matthew 17:17 that Jesus does not mean the generation that was before Him and that had decision-making power to accept or reject Him? R. T. France notes:

> Jesus' surprising outburst is addressed not to a man ... but to the whole "generation." For similar characterizations of "this generation" as unbelieving and unresponsive cf. 11:16; 12:39, 41-42, 45; 16:4; it is a Matthean theme which will reach its culmination in the charge in 23:34-36 that "this generation" has reached the point of no return in its rejection of God's messengers."[3]

## What the Commentators Say

Following the biblical evidence, many Bible commentators have interpreted Jesus' use of "this generation" in the Olivet Discourse as the generation of Jesus' day. Here are some examples:

---

1. Grant R. Osborne, *Matthew: Exegetical Commentary on the New Testament* (Grand Rapids, MI: Zondervan, 2010), 486.

2. David L. Turner, *Matthew: Baker Exegetical Commentary on the New Testament* (Grand Rapids, MI: Baker Academic, 2008), 424.

3. R. T. France, *The Gospel of Matthew* (Grand Rapids, MI: Eerdmans, 2007), 660.

- **Henry Hammond** (1653): "I now assure you, that in the age of some that are now alive, shall all that has been said in this chapter [Matt. 24] be certainly fulfilled."[4]
- **John Lightfoot** (1658): "Hence it appears plain enough, that the foregoing verses [Matt. 24:1-34] are not to be understood of the last judgment, but, as we said, of the destruction of Jerusalem. There were some among the disciples (particularly John), who lived to see these things come to pass. With Matt. xvi. 28, compare John xxi. 22. And there were some Rabbins [sic] alive at the time when Christ spoke these things, that lived until the city was destroyed."[5]
- **Philip Doddridge** (1750): "And *verily I say unto you;* and urge you to observe it, as absolutely necessary in order to understand what I have been saying, *That this generation* of men now living *shall not pass away until all these things be fulfilled,* for what I have foretold concerning the destruction of the Jewish state is so near at hand, that some of you shall live to see it all accomplished with a dreadful exactness."[6]
- **Thomas Newton** (1755): "It is to me a wonder how any man can refer part of the foregoing discourse to the destruction of Jerusalem, and part to the end of the world, or any other distant event, when it is said so positively here in the conclusion, *All these things shall be fulfilled in this generation.*"[7]
- **John Gill** (1766): "This is a full and clear proof, that not any thing that is said before [v. 34], relates to the second coming of Christ, the day of judgment, and the end of the world; but that

4. Henry Hammond, *A Paraphrase, and Annotations Upon all the Books of the New Testament, Briefly Explaining all the Difficult Places Thereof* (London: Printed for John Nicholson, at the King's-Arms in Little Britain, 1702), 102.

5. John Lightfoot, *A Commentary on the New Testament from the Talmud and Hebraica,* 4 vols. (Oxford: Oxford University Press, [1658-1674] 1859), 2:320.

6. Philip Doddridge, *The Family Expositor; or, A Paraphrase and Version of the New Testament; with Critical Notes, and a Practical Improvement of each Section,* 6 vols. (Charlestown, MA.: Ethridge and Company, 1807), 1:377.

7. Thomas Newton, *Dissertations on the Prophecies, Which Have Remarkably Been Fulfilled, and at This Time are Fulfilling in the World* (London: J.F. Dove, 1754), 377.

all belongs to the coming of the son of man in the destruction of Jerusalem, and to the end of the Jewish state."[8]

- **Thomas Scott** (1817): "This absolutely restricts our primary interpretation of the prophecy to the destruction of Jerusalem, which took place within forty years."[9]

- **John J. Owen** (1857): "*This generation.* See N[ote] on 1:17. The men now living. *Shall not pass* (*away* Luke [21:32]). The destruction of Jerusalem by Titus took place only about 40 years after this prediction was uttered. This limits the preceding calamities and commotions to the destruction of Jerusalem, and the end of the Jewish persecuting power. No language could make this plainer than that here used. How it can be so lost sight of by interpreters is truly wonderful. With these words of the Lord Jesus himself, limiting the foregoing predictions to that very generation, we do not see how any one can dream of referring them, except in the way of accommodation, to the judgment of the great day. *These things.* The pronoun here employed in the Greek, refers to what immediately precedes, and must therefore include vs. 29-31, in the events which were to take place, before the men of that generation should pass way. Unless this verse is deprived of all its force, it must refer, beyond all doubt, the foregoing prediction to the coming of Christ to destroy Jerusalem. Olshausen sees and acknowledges the force of this, and seemingly forgetful that portions of the preceding prediction he has declared to be referable to nothing short of the final appearance of Christ, he makes this remarkable concession: 'The only way of explaining these difficulties [i.e. such as arise from the closing of the preceding predictions by such a positive affirmation on the part of Christ, that they all shall take place before the generation then on earth should pass away], is to view the prophecy with reference to the immediate present, but in such a manner that every thing includes a further reference to the future.' So convenient is it to fall upon

---

8. John Gill, *An Exposition of the New Testament*, 3 vols. (London: Mathews and Leigh, 1809), 1:296.

9. Thomas Scott, *The Holy Bible Containing the Old and New Testaments*, 3 vols. (New York: Collins and Hannay, 1832), 3:111.

the *double sense*, when pressed by a passage like this.... Our Lord had predicted in general terms his coming to destroy Jerusalem [24:35]. It was to be soon. The race of men then living, were not all to pass away before its accomplishment. But the precise day and hour was known only to Him, with whom the future was as the past. The disciples were not, therefore, to expect any more definite revelation in respect to the precise time, than what had just been given in v. 34."[10]

- **Henry Cowles** (1881): "Some interpreters have construed the words—'this generation'—to mean this sort of people, *i.e.,* the Jews, or the wicked, etc., seeking to set aside its only legitimate sense, viz., the men then living. Such wresting of Christ's words cannot be reprobated too severely."[11]

- **Milton Terry** (1883): "The significations which, apparently under the pressure of an assumed exegetical necessity, have been put upon the words ... *this generation,* may well seem absurd to the unbiased critic. To put upon them such meanings as 'the human race' (Jerome), or 'the Jewish race' (Clarke, Dorner, Auberlan), or 'the race of Christian believers' (Chrysostom, Lange), may reasonably be condemned as a reading whatever suits our purpose into the words of Scripture. The evident meaning of the word is seen in such texts as Matt. i, 17; xvii, 17; Acts xiv, 16; xv, 21 (by-gone generations of old), and nothing in New Testament exegesis is capable of more convincing proof than that γενεα is the Greek equivalent of our word *generation*; i.e., the mass or great body of people living at one period—the period of average lifetime. Even if it be allowed that in such passages as Matt. xi, 16; or Luke xvi, 8, the thought of a particular race or class of people is implied, it is beyond doubt that in those same passages the persons referred to are conceived as contemporaries."[12]

---

10. John J. Owen, *Commentary on Matthew and Mark* (New York: Leavitt & Allen, 1857), 324.

11. Henry Cowles, *Matthew and Mark, with Notes: Critical, Explanatory, and Practical, Designed for Both Pastors and People* (New York: D. Appleton & Co., 1881), 219.

12. Milton Terry, *Biblical Hermeneutics* (New York: Phillips & Hunt, 1883), 443, note 1.

- **John Broadas** (1886): "Verily, I say unto you (see on 5:18), calling attention to something of special importance. **This generation**, as in 23:36, also 11:16 12:41f.; and compare Luke 17:25 with 21:32. The word cannot have any other meaning here than the obvious one. The attempts to establish for it the sense of race or nation have failed. There are some examples in which it might have such a meaning, but none in which it must, for in every case the recognized meaning will answer, and so another sense is not admissible. (Comp. on 3:6) Some of the Fathers took it to mean the generation of believers, *i. e.*, the Christians, etc., after the loose manner of interpreting into which many of them so often fell. We now commonly make the rough estimate of three generations to a century. The year in which our Lord said this was most probably AD 30, and if so, it was forty years to the destruction of Jerusalem. The thought is thus the same as in 16:28; and comp. John 21:22f. **Till all these things be fulfilled**, or, more exactly, take place, 'come to pass,' see on 5:18. The emphasis is on 'all.' All the things predicted in v. 4-31 would occur before or in immediate connection with the destruction of Jerusalem."[13]

- **G. R. Beasley-Murray** (1957): "Despite all the attempts to establish the contrary, there seems to be no escape from the admission that here [in Mark 13:30] [*hē genea hautē*] is to be taken in its natural sense of the generation contemporary with Jesus."[14]

- **Robert G. Bratcher and Eugene A. Nida** (1961): "[T]he obvious meaning of the words 'this generation' is the people contemporary with Jesus. Nothing can be gained by trying to take the word in any sense other than its normal one: in Mark (elsewhere in 8:12, 9:19) the word always has this meaning."[15]

---

13. John A. Broadus, "Matthew," *An American Commentary of the New Testament*, ed. Alvah Hovey (Philadelphia: The American Baptist Publication Society, 1886), 491-492.

14. G.R. Beasley-Murray, *A Commentary on Mark Thirteen* (London: Macnillan & Co. Ltd., 1957), 100. Also see Beasley-Murray's comments in *Jesus and the Last Days: The Interpretation of the Olivet Discourse* (Peabody, MA: Hendrickson Publishers, 1993), 444.

15. Robert G. Bratcher and Eugene A. Nida, *A Translator's Handbook of the Gospel of Mark* (New York: United Bible Societies, 1961), 419.

- **William L. Lane** (1974): "The significance of the temporal reference has been debated, but in Mark 'this generation' clearly designates the contemporaries of Jesus (see on Chs. 8:12, 38; 9:19) and there is no consideration from the context which lends support to any other proposal. Jesus solemnly affirms that the generation contemporary with his disciples will witness the fulfillment of his prophetic word, culminating in the destruction of Jerusalem and the dismantling of the Temple."[16]

- **Jack P. Lewis** (1976): "The meaning of **generation** *(genea)* is crucial to the interpretation of the entire chapter. While Scofield, following Jerome, contended that it meant the Jewish race, there is only one possible case in the New Testament (Luke 16:8) where the lexicon suggests that *genea* means race.[17] There is a distinction between *genos* (race) and *genea* (generation). Others have argued that *genea* means the final generation; that is, once the signs have started, all these happenings would transpire in one generation (cf. 23:36). But elsewhere in Matthew *genea* means the people alive at one time and usually at the time of Jesus (1:17; 11:16; 12:39,41,45; 23:36; Mark 8:38; Luke 11:50f.; 17:25), and it doubtlessly means the same here."[18]

- **F. F. Bruce** (1983): "The phrase 'this generation' is found too often on Jesus' lips in this literal sense for us to suppose that it suddenly takes on a different meaning in the saying we are now examining. Moreover, if the generation of the end-time had been intended, 'that generation' would have been a more natural way of referring to it than 'this generation.'[19]

- **D. A. Carson** (1984): "[This generation] can only with the greatest difficulty be made to mean anything other than the generation living when Jesus spoke."[20]

---

16. William L. Lane, *Commentary on the Gospel of Mark* (Grand Rapids, MI: Eerdmans, 1974), 480.

17. The New American Standard translates *genea* in Luke 16:8 as "kind," but "generation" is equally valid.

18. Jack P. Lewis, *The Gospel According to Matthew, Part 2;* Living Word Commentary: Sweet Publishing, 1976), 128.

19. F. F. Bruce, *The Hard Sayings of Jesus* (Downers Grove, IL: InterVarsity Press, 1983), 227.

20. D. A. Carson, "Matthew, *The Expositor's Bible Commentary*, gen ed. Frank E. Gaebelein,

- **William Sanford LaSor** (1987): "If 'this generation' is taken literally, all of the predictions were to take place within the life-span of those living at that time."[21]

- *New Bible Commentary* (1994): "Christ's use of the words 'immediately after' [in Matthew 24:30] does not leave room for a long delay (2,000 years or more before his literal second coming occurs), neither does the explicit time-scale given in Matthew 24:34. The word 'parousia' does not occur in this section but is prominently reintroduced in the new paragraph which begins at Matthew 24:36, where its unknown time is contrasted with the clear statement that the events of this paragraph will take place within 'this generation' (Matthew 24:36). This section is therefore in direct continuity with what has gone before, the account of the siege of Jerusalem. Here we reach its climax. The language ... is drawn from Daniel 7:13-14, which points to the vindication and enthronement of Jesus (rather than his second coming ['parousia']).... In this context, therefore, this poetic language appropriately refers to the great changes which were about to take place in the world, when Jerusalem and its temple were destroyed. It speaks of the 'Son of Man' entering into his kingship, and 'his angels' gathering in his new people from all the earth. The fall of the temple is thus presented, in highly allusive language, as the end of the old order, to be replaced by the new regime of Jesus, the Son of Man, and the international growth of his church, the new people of God.... The NIV margin offers 'race' as an alternative to 'generation.' This suggestion is prompted more by embarrassment on the part of those who think Matthew 24:30 refers to the 'parousia' (second coming) rather than by any natural sense of the word 'genea'!"[22]

- **Donald A. Hagner** (1995): "[T]hose listening there and then to the teaching of Jesus (ἡ γενεὰ αὕτη, "this generation," is used consistently in the Gospel to refer to Jesus' contemporaries;

---

12 vols. (Grand Rapids, MI: Zondervan, 1984), 8:507.

21. William Sanford LaSor, *The Truth About Armageddon: What the Bible Says About the End Times* (Grand Rapids, MI: Baker Book House, 1987), 122.

22. *New Bible Commentary: 21st Century Edition*, eds. Gordon. J. Wenham, J. A. Motyer, D. A. Carson, R. T. France (Downers Grove, IL: InterVarsity Press, 1994), 936, 937.

cf. 11:16; 12:41-42, 45; 23:36). The attempt to explain ἡ γενεὰ αὕτη, "this generation," as the generation alive at the time of the parousia or more generally as the human race or people of God goes against the natural meaning of the phrase and makes the words irrelevant both to Jesus' listeners and to Matthew's readers. The fact that, as Lövestam has shown, the expression clearly alludes to a sinful generation, one ripe for judgment, fits the fall of Jerusalem (and not merely the end of the age, which is Lövestam's conclusion).[23]

- **N.T. Wright** (2004): "All this is spoken to Jesus' disciples so they will know when the cataclysmic events are going to happen. Watch for the leaves on the tree, and you can tell it's nearly summer. Watch for these events, and you'll know that the great event, the destruction of the Temple and Jesus' complete vindication, are just around the corner. And be sure of this, says Jesus (and Matthew wants to underline this): it will happen within a generation. That is an extra important reason why everything that has been said in the passage so far must be taken to refer to the destruction of Jerusalem and the events that surround it. Only when we appreciate how significant that moment was for everything Jesus had said and done will we understand what Jesus himself stood for."[24]

- **John Nolland** (2005): "Matthew uses *genea* here for the tenth time. Though his use of the term has a range of emphases, it consistently refers to (the time span of) a single human generation. All the alternative senses proposed here [in 24:34] (the Jewish people; humanity; the generation of the end-time signs; wicked people) are artificial and based on the need to protect Jesus from error. 'This generation' is the generation of Jesus' contemporaries."[25]

23. Donald A. Hagner, *Matthew 14-28*, Word Biblical Commentary (Dallas: Word, Incorporated, 1995), vol. 33B, 715.

24. Tom Wright, *Matthew for Everyone*, Part 2: Chapters 16-28 (London: Society for Promoting Christian Knowledge, 2004), 123-124.

25. John Nolland *The Gospel of Matthew: A Commentary on the Greek Text* (Grand Rapids, MI: Eerdmans, 2005), 988-989.

- **R. T. France** (2007): "'This generation' has been used frequently in this gospel for Jesus' contemporaries, especially in a context of God's impending judgment; see 11:16; 12:39, 41-42, 45; 16:4; 17:17, and especially 23:36, where God's judgment on 'this generation' leads up to Jesus' first prediction of the devastation of the temple in 23:38. It may safely be concluded that if it had not been for the embarrassment caused by supposing that Jesus was here talking about his *parousia*, no one would have thought of suggesting any other meaning for 'this generation,' such as 'the Jewish race' or 'human beings in general' or 'all the generations of Judaism that reject him' or even 'this kind' (meaning scribes, Pharisees, and Sadducees). Such broad senses, even if they were lexically possible, would offer no help in response to the disciples' question 'When?'"[26]
- **Paul Copan** (2008): "In these passages, the 'coming' (the Greek verb is *erchomai* = '[I] come') is expected *within* Jesus' own 'adulterous and sinful generation.' Something dramatic will apparently take place in the near future."[27]
- **Grant R. Osborne** (2010): "'This generation' ([*hē genea hautē*]) in the gospels always means the people of Jesus' own time (11:16; 12:41-42; 23:36) not, as some have proposed, the generation of the last days in history, the Jewish people, the human race in general, or the sinful people."[28]

Even with all this evidence, there are still those who try their best to make "this generation" into any generation but the generation to whom Jesus addressed. The Biblical evidence, however, is against them.

---

26. France, *The Gospel of Matthew*, 930.

27. Paul Copan, *When God Goes to Starbucks: A Guide to Everyday Apologetics* (Grand Rapids, MI: Baker Books, 2008), 163. See the full contents of chapters 15 and 16.

28. Osborne, *Matthew*, 899-900.

# CHAPTER 4

# Sam Waldron, John Murray, and the Olivet Discourse

During the Question and Answer session at the Reno Symposium on Revelation, Sam Waldron said that he followed John Murray's interpretation of Matthew 24 and 25. Since there was no time for cross examination, I was not able to respond (we were all put in this position). So I have taken some time to work my way through some of Murray's exposition.[1] For a comprehensive study of the Olivet Discourse, see my books *Last Days Madness* and *Is Jesus Coming Soon?*

Waldron writes that "the best rebuttal for deficient views of Matthew 24 is the presentation of the proper view. These faulty views [futurist, double fulfillment, preterist] will be best refuted by simply presenting the interpretation of Professor Murray...."[2] As I hope to show in this chapter, John Murray's exegesis on Matthew 24 does not fix the context. The preterist interpretation best fits the context, the time parameters, and audience reference when Scripture is compared with Scripture.

When I began my study of the Olivet Discourse while a student at Reformed Theological Seminary, I remember looking at John Murray's exegesis on Matthew 24-25 when it was first published in the second volume of his *Collected Works*. It raised more questions than it attempted to answer. Murray argues that there are a number of divisions in the Olivet Discourse that address different periods of prophetic time. For example, "In verses 4-14 Jesus deals with certain outstanding features

---

1. John Murray, "The Interadventual Period and the Advent: Matthew 24 and 25," *Collected Writings of John Murray (2): Select Lectures in Systematic Theology* (Carlisle, PA: The Banner of Truth Trust, 1977), 2:387-400.

2. Samuel E. Waldron, *More of the End Times Made Simple* (Calvary Press Publishing, 2009), 103.

of the interadventual period" (2:388), the time between Jesus' first coming and His physical Second Coming, an event he maintains is still in our future. For Murray, "the end" [τέλος] (Matt. 24:3, 6, 13, 14) is a yet future end that will commence with certain prophetic events and the return of Jesus in glory.

While this is a popular position, a study of the Olivet Discourse will show that what Jesus described was the end of the Old Covenant age that is shown outwardly with the destruction of the temple in Jerusalem in AD 70. The "coming" [παρουσία] of Jesus mentioned in Matthew 24:27 (also vv. 3, 37, 39) is a judgment coming reminiscent of judgment comings that were common in the Old Testament.

The "coming" [ἐρχόμενον] of Jesus in Matthew 24:30, quoting from Daniel 7:13, is a coming up to the Ancient of Days not a physical coming of Jesus to earth to set up a millennial kingdom. "The 'son of man' figure 'comes' to the Ancient of Days. He comes *from* earth *to* heaven, vindicated after suffering."[3]

These and other themes related to Murray's position will be fleshed out in this chapter.

## Jesus and the "End of the Age"

Peter states that "the end [τέλος/*telos*] of all things has come near" (1 Peter 4:7). "While modern readers may immediately think of the end of the world, the semantic range of the word *telos* suggests more than mere termination and may refer to the last state of a process as well as to it outcome or goal."[4] We use "the end" in similar ways. Context determines what's coming to an end. The biblical process of "end" is the close of the Old Covenant era that is laid out in great detail in the book of Hebrews. The New Testament writers' use of "end" is not necessarily an indicator that the end of prophetic history is in view. It's most likely an end of an identifiable era. "In six or seven years from the time of [Peter] writing [his first letter]," Jay E. Adams argues, "the overthrow of Jerusalem, with all its tragic stories, as foretold in the book of Revelation and in the Olivet Discourse upon which that part

---

3. N. T. Wright, *Jesus and the Victory of God* (Minneapolis: Fortress Press, 1996), 360.

4. Karen H. Jobes, *1 Peter: Baker Exegetical Commentary on the New Testament* (Grand Rapids, MI: Baker Academic, 2005), 275.

is based, would take place.... 'So,' says Peter, 'hold on; **the end is near.**' The full **end** of the O.T. order (already made defunct by the cross and the empty tomb) was about to occur.'"[5]

Other passages use similar language without indicating that the Second Coming is in view (Rom. 13:11; Heb. 1:1-2; 9:26; James 5:7-8; 1 Peter 1:20; 1 John 2:18). In Hebrews 9:26, we read about "the end of the ages" that were a reality for first-century Christians. Similar language is found in 1 Peter 1:20: "For He was foreknown before the foundation of the world, but has appeared in these last times for the sake of you." The "you" was them.

The use of a temporal and specific "the end" is rooted in the Old Testament. Ezekiel repeatedly warns of "an end" that is coming that is very similar to what Jesus indicates in the Olivet Discourse:

> "And you, son of man, thus says the Lord GOD to the land of Israel, 'An end! The end is coming on the four corners of the land. Now the end is upon you, and I will send My anger against you; I will judge you according to your ways and bring all your abominations upon you.... An end is coming; the end has come! It has awakened against you; behold, it has come! Your doom has come to you, O inhabitant of the land. The time has come, the day is near—tumult rather than joyful shouting on the mountains'" (Ezek. 7:2-3, 6-7).

Ezekiel's prophecy is not about a distant eschatological end that some in Ezekiel's day believed was to happen to a future generation (12:21-25). "[T]he end envisioned here is not a chronological end of time or the end of cosmic history; it is the end of a city's existence."[6]

## The Age to Come

The "age to come" most often refers to the new covenant age and not the eternal state. This is why Paul could tell the Christians at Corinth that "the ends [τέλη] of the ages [αἰῶνω] have come" (1 Cor. 10:11). In Matthew 12:32 we find Jesus saying the following:

5. Jay E. Adams, *Trust and Obey: A Practical Commentary on First Peter* (Phillipsburg, NJ: Presbyterian and Reformed, 1978), 130. Emphasis in original.

6. Daniel I. Block, "Gog and Magog in Ezekiel's Eschatological Vision," *Eschatology in the Bible & Theology: Evangelical Essays at the Dawn of a New Millennium*, eds. Kent E. Brower and Mark W. Elliott (Downers Grove, IL: InterVarsity Press, 1999), 86.

"And whoever shall speak a word against the Son of Man, it shall be forgiven him; but whoever shall speak against the Holy Spirit, it shall not be forgiven him, either in this age, or the age [about to: μέλλοντι/*mellonti*] come."

The use of *mellō* indicates that the next age—"the age to come"—was "about to" come; it was not an event far in the future. Why does the "age to come" in this passage have to refer to the eternal state? No one will be speaking against the Holy Spirit in heaven. The verse could just as easily be read this way: "And whoever shall speak a word against the Son of Man, it shall be forgiven him; but whoever shall speak against the Holy Spirit, it shall not be forgiven him, either in this age [the growing old ... ready to disappear covenant age], or the age to come [the new covenant age about to dawn]." In either age, speaking against the Holy Spirit will not be forgiven.

Consider Matthew 13:39-40, a passage that Waldron[7] says refers to Jesus' Second Coming:

"And the enemy who sowed them is the devil, and the harvest is the end of the age; and the reapers are angels. Therefore just as the tares are gathered up and burned with fire, so shall it be at the end of the age."

Once again, we are left with determining what age and what end Jesus is describing. I believe the "end of the age" is the end of the Old Covenant era that the writer of Hebrews tells us was "growing old ... ready [near: ἐγγύς/*engus*] to disappear" (Heb. 8:13).

Later in Matthew we read: "For the Son of Man is going [lit. about to/*mellō*] come in the glory of His Father with His angels; and WILL THEN RECOMPENSE EVERY MAN ACCORDING TO HIS DEEDS. Truly I say to you, there are some standing here who shall not taste death until they see the Son of Man coming in His kingdom" (Matt. 16:27-28).[8] This coming of the Son of Man had to be far enough in the future where nearly all of Jesus' disciples were dead but not so far in the future that every disciple was dead. The event that fits the time parameter of this prophecy is the destruction of Jerusalem in AD 70 not a distant yet-to-take-place coming.

---

7. Waldron, *More of the End Times Made Simple*, 101.
8. See chapter 17 of this book.

Jesus expands on this theme when He tells the parable of the Landowner (Matt. 21:33-46). "And when the chief priests and the Pharisees heard His parables, they understood that He was speaking about them" (21:45). Jesus then expands His indictment of them by telling one more parable about how the king's son was mistreated by the invited guests, Jesus' fellow-Jews. "But the king was enraged and sent his armies and destroyed those murderers, and set their city on fire" (22:7), which brought an end to the Old Covenant age. These are the tares. They have all the outward and covenantal appearances that should grant them entry into the kingdom (wedding), but it's not enough. Outwardly they "appear righteous to men, but inwardly [they] are full of hypocrisy and lawlessness" (23:28).

This ingathering of the wheat and the burning of the tares can only take place when the harvest is mature. Separating believing Jews from unbelieving Jews was easily made during the time leading up to the destruction of Jerusalem at the hands of the Romans. Those who believed Jesus' prophecy fled to the mountains outside of Judea and were saved from the conflagration (Matt. 24:16; see vv. 13 and 22). Those who did not (tares) were caught in the judgment events surrounding Jerusalem's demise and the temple's destruction.

Matthew 24:31 is a reflection of what we find in the parable of the wheat and the tares: "And He will send forth His angels with A GREAT TRUMPET and THEY WILL GATHER TOGETHER His elect from the four winds, from one end of heaven to the other." The trumpet, like so much of the language used by Jesus in the Olivet Discourse, is taken from the Old Testament. When Israel was in captivity, we are told that "a great trumpet" was blown and those "who were perishing in the land of Assyria and who were scattered in the land of Egypt will come and worship the LORD in the holy mountain at Jerusalem" (Isa. 27:13). Did the people in these far off regions actually hear a trumpet?

## It's Not the End of the World as We Know It

Like a number of commentators, Murray argues that the disciples were confused about the "end of the age" (Matt. 24:3), believing that when the temple was destroyed, it would also mean a final eschatological end. Murray writes:

In view of the terms of the parallel verses in Mark and Luke— 'when will these things be, and what will be the sign when all these things come to pass' (Mark 13:4)—we should most probably regard the disciples as thinking of the destruction of the temple and the coming (παρουσία) as coincident, and the sign, in their esteem, would be the sign of all three events specified in Matthew 24:3—destruction of the temple, the coming, and the consummation of the age (2:387).

Waldron also believes the disciples were mistaken in combining the three events. If they were mistaken, why didn't Jesus say so? He had corrected the disciples on a number of occasions (Matt. 8:23-27; 16:21-23; Mark 9:30-33; Luke 9:37-56; John 12:15-17; 13:7-13; 16:18; 20:9; Acts 1:6-8), but not on this very significant point. Murray and Waldron assume what must be proved. They heard Jesus apply what was about to happen to them: "**You** will be hearing ... they will deliver **you** to tribulation, and will kill **you**, and **you** will be hated by all nations because of My name ... when **you** see" (Matt. 24:6, 9, 15, 33).

As we'll see, language about the end of this or that is common, and did not often if ever refer to the end of planet Earth, the cosmos, or temporal history. Anyone familiar with the Old Testament prophets would know this:

The word of the Lord which came to Zephaniah son of Cushi, son of Gedaliah, son of Amariah, son of Hezekiah, in the days of Josiah son of Amon, king of Judah: "I will completely remove all things from the face of the earth," declares the Lord. "I will remove man and beast; I will remove the birds of the sky and the fish of the sea, and the ruins along with the wicked; and I will cut off man from the face of the earth," declares the Lord. "So I will stretch out My hand against Judah and against all the inhabitants of Jerusalem. And I will cut off the remnant of Baal from this place, and the names of the idolatrous priests along with the priests" (Zeph. 1:1-4).

This opening section of Zephaniah reads like the end of "everything from the face of the earth." In fact, the passage says as much. But it was a description of a local judgment—"against Judah and all the inhabitants of Jerusalem." Nearly identical language is found in Jeremiah 4:19-31. Micah 1:1-4 describes something similar:

> The word of the Lord which came to Micah of Moresheth in
> the days of Jotham, Ahaz and Hezekiah, kings of Judah, which
> he saw concerning Samaria and Jerusalem.
> Hear, O peoples, all of you;
>     Listen, O earth and all it contains,
> And let the Lord GOD be a witness against you,
>     The Lord from His holy temple.
> For behold, the Lord is coming forth from His place.
>     He will come down and tread on the high places of the earth.
> The mountains will melt under Him
>     And the valleys will be split,
> Like wax before the fire,
>     Like water poured down a steep place.

The end of the world? An end-time catastrophic judgment that will engulf the world so that billions will die? Not quite:

> All this is for the rebellion of Jacob
>     And for the sins of the house of Israel.
> What is the rebellion of Jacob?
>     Is it not Samaria?
> What is the high place of Judah?
>     Is it not Jerusalem? (1:5)

Psalm 18 is about the deliverance of David, one man, against the pursuit of Saul, and yet it is "as graphic as anything we find in the Olivet Discourse."[9] The New Testament is not any different when it describes an end and uses language that is earth-shattering (Heb. 12:25-29).

A similar "end" phrase is used by the author of Hebrews: "But now once at the **consummation of the ages** He has been manifested to put away sin by the sacrifice of Himself" (Heb. 9:26). Jesus was manifested, not at the beginning, but "at the consummation of the ages" (συντελείας τοῦ αἰώνων). The period between AD 30 and 70 is, as the apostle Peter

9. David J. Palm, "The Signs of His Coming: An Examination of the Olivet Discourse from a Preterist Perspective," A Thesis Submitted to the Faculty in partial fulfillment of the requirements for the degree of Master of Arts Concentration in New Testament at Trinity Evangelical Divinity School (June 1993), 57.

describes it, "these last times" (1 Peter 1:20). As time drew near for Jerusalem's destruction, Peter could say that "the end of all things was at hand" (1 Peter 4:7). Milton Terry offers the following as a summary of the meaning of the "end of the age."

> It is the solemn termination and crisis of the dispensation which had run its course when the temple fell, and there was not left one stone upon another which was not thrown down. That catastrophe, which in Heb. xii, 26, is conceived as a shaking of the earth and the heaven, is the end contemplated in this discourse; not "the end of the world," but the termination and consummation of the pre-Messianic age.[10]

The numerous New Testament time indicators demonstrate that Jesus did not have a distant "end" in mind when He spoke of the "end of the age." Charles Wright, in his commentary on Zechariah, offers the following helpful discussion of the meaning of the "end of the age" that is similar to Terry's remarks:

> The passing away of the dispensation of the law of Moses, which as limited in great part to Israel after the flesh, might well be called the Jewish dispensation, was justly regarded as "the end of the age" (συντελείας τοῦ αἰῶνος, Matt. xxiv. 3). The Messiah was viewed as the bringer in of a new world. The period of the Messiah was, therefore, correctly characterised by the Synagogue as "the world to come." In this signification our Lord used that expression when he uttered the solemn warning that the sin against the Holy Ghost would be forgiven "neither in this world [lit: αἰῶνι = age] (the then dispensation), neither in the world [lit: *one*, that is, age] to come" (Matt. xii. 12:32), or the new dispensation, when, "having overcome the sharpness of death," Christ "opened the kingdom of heaven to all believers."[11]

The "age to come" is a designation for the post-Old Covenant era—the Christian age—an age that was long ago prophesied by the prophets.

---

10. Milton S. Terry, *Biblical Apocalyptics: A Study of the Most Notable Revelations of God and of Christ* (Grand Rapids, MI: Baker Book House, [1898] 1988), 225.

11. Charles Henry Hamilton Wright, *Zechariah and His Prophecies* (Minneapolis, MN: Klock and Klock, [1879] 1980), 449.

Abraham, for example, "rejoiced in order to see [Jesus'] day; and he saw it, and was glad" (John 8:56). The old covenant with its attendant animal sacrifices and earthly priesthood passed away when God's lamb, Jesus Christ, took away the sins of the world. Murray continues:

> Verses 15-28 comprise another section of the discourse. This section cannot be a continuation, because verse 14 had brought us up to the end. It must be, to some extent, recapitulation (2:388).

Of course, it doesn't have to be a continuation to fit in the context of "this generation." Unlike Murray and Waldron, I contend that Jesus is covering the same time period throughout the discourse. The "end of the age" of 24:3 is the same "end" of 24:13. So if verses 15-28 refer to events leading up to the dismantling of the temple, which Murray and Waldron assert, then the same is true of verses 3-14. Both sections describe the same "end" that other verses in the New Testament describe (1 Cor. 10:11; Heb. 1:1-2; 9:26; 10:25; 1 Peter 4:7; 1 John 2:18; Jude 17-18).

## The "Tribulation of Those Days"

There is then a third section Murray says begins at Matthew 24:29. It's here that he says "we encounter some difficulty" (2:389):

> For "the tribulation of those days" might appear to refer to the "great tribulation" of verse 21 which is associated particularly with the desolation of verse 21. And we ask: How could it be said that, immediately after 70 AD, the events specified in verses 29-31 took place? (2:389).

The words "immediately after the tribulation of those days" don't leave room for a gap in time. If verses 15-28 refer to the lead up to the destruction of the temple that took place in AD 70, then "immediately after" means just that. This means that at least everything up through 24:35 had to have been fulfilled before that particular generation passed away, including the events of 24:29-33 and verses 4-28. In addition to having trouble with "immediately after," Murray also has trouble with "this generation" because it nullifies his argument that there are different time periods, some before "this generation" and some after:

> Ostensibly the expression "this generation" would suggest the generation then living, the period, commonly designated

"generation," in which Jesus spoke these words. And the question would then arise: Did all the things spoken of in the preceding context actually occur? (2:391-392).

On a positive note, Murray dismisses the notion that the Greek word translated "generation" (*genea*) means "race," that is, the Jewish race, a favorite explanation made popular by the *Scofield Reference Bible*. Even most dispensationalists have stopped arguing that *genea* means "race." But this hasn't stopped them from trying to make it mean any generation *except* the generation of Jesus' day. Here's Murray's conclusion:

> Usage in both Testaments requires, therefore, that 'generation' in Matthew 24:34 be understood in the sense of the living generation (2:393).

Murray is still left with the difficulty of explaining how some of the events preceding 24:35 were not fulfilled when he admits that "this generation" refers to "the living generation" of Jesus' day, and Jesus says "this [living] generation will not pass away until ALL these things take place." Since Jesus lists specific events from verses 3 through 34, the "all" must refer to all of them not just the ones in verses 15-34. Note verse 33: "when **you** see," referring to those in Jesus' audience, "all these things, recognize that He is near, right at the door." It's obvious that Jesus addressed His present audience not audiences down through history or a yet future end-time generation.

Murray (2:389) and Waldron believe the solution to their problem is found by going to Luke's version of the Olivet Discourse, specifically Luke 21:24, a verse that does not appear in Matthew's version:

> And they will fall by the edge of the sword, and will be led captive into all the nations; and Jerusalem will be trampled under foot by the Gentiles until the times of the Gentiles are fulfilled.

I don't see how this solves Murray's problem since Luke 21:24 follows immediately after verse 23, a verse that is parallel to Matthew 24:19, a verse that Murray and Waldron agree refers to the events of Jesus' own generation:

Murray contends that "until the times of the Gentiles are fulfilled" applies to a time "extended far beyond the destruction of Jerusalem and the events immediately associated with it" (2:389). He assumes what must be proved. The "time of the Gentiles," a period of time the book of Revelation maintains was "forty-two months" (Rev. 11:2), resulted in the destruction of the temple, the sacking of the city, and the captivity of Jews who survived the Roman siege. Milton Terry writes:

> "The statement of Luke xxi, 24, that 'Jerusalem shall be trodden down by the Gentiles until the time of the Gentiles be fulfilled,' is supposed to involve events which did not take place in that generation. The 'times of the Gentiles' (καιροὶ ἐθνῶν [kairoi ethnōn]) are assumed to be the times of the opportunities of grace afforded to the Gentiles under the Gospel. But to understand the words in this sense would be, as Van Oosterzee observes, to interpolate a thought entirely foreign to the context. 'The times of the Gentiles,' says Bengel, 'are the times allotted to the Gentiles to tread down the city;' but there is nothing in the passage or context to authorize his further remark that 'these times shall be ended when the Gentiles's conversion shall be full consummated,' and that the treading down by Romans, Persians, Saracens, Franks, and Turks is to be understood. These καιροὶ [times] are manifestly times of judgment upon Jerusalem, not times of salvation to the Gentiles. The most natural and obvious parallel is Rev. xi. 2, where the outer court of the temple is said to be 'given to the Gentiles,' by whom the holy city shall be trodden down forty-two months, a period equivalent to the 'time and times and half a time' of Rev. xii, 14, and of Dan. vii, 25; xii, 7. This is a symbolical period of judgment (see above, p. 384 [in *Biblical Hermeneutics*], but does not denote ages and generations. It is three and a half—a divided seven, a short but signal period of woe. The 'times of the Gentiles,' therefore, are the three and a half times (approximating three and a half years) during which the Gentile armies besieged and trampled down Jerusalem."[12]

Luke and John use the Greek word πατέω (*pateō*), "trodden down" or "trodden under foot," a common way of portraying defeat and dominion over an enemy (Josh. 10:24; 2 Kings 7:17, 20; 9:33; Isa. 14:19; Deut. 11:24;

---

12. Milton S. Terry, *Biblical Hermeneutics*, unabridged ed. (Grand Rapids, MI: Zondervan, n.d.), 445.

Judges 20:43; 1 Kings 5:3; Joshua 14:9; Ps. 18:38; 47:3; 74:21; 110:1; Lam. 1:15; 3:34; Isa. 14:25; 41:2; 63:6; 66:1; Jer. 25:30; Dan. 8:7; Joel 3:13; Amos 2:6-7; 4:13; Micah 1:3; 5:5-6; Mal. 4:3; Matt. 7:6; Mark 12:36; Luke 20:43; Acts 2:35; Rom. 16:20 [notice the word "soon"]; 1 Cor. 15:25; Eph. 1:22; Heb. 1:13; 2:8; 10:13; Rev. 19:15).

Like Matthew and Mark's version of the Olivet Discourse, "this generation" still governs the time parameters of the chapter (Luke 21:32). This would mean that "the times of the Gentiles" had to fit within the time period of "this generation." And it did, as Revelation 11:2 makes clear.

## So Much That's Missing

I'm surprised that Murray does not make reference to J. Marcellus Kik's work or that of so many other expositors and commentators who have written on the Olivet Discourse and see everything up through verse 34 as a reference to the AD 70 destruction of Jerusalem. Murray's article was first delivered as "an address at a School of Theology convened in London in September 1968." (2:387). Kik's *Matthew Twenty-Four: An Exposition* was first published in 1948. Murray was surely aware of it since they both shared the same publisher and the same theological tradition. Waldron is familiar with Kik's work. He references it in two endnotes but does not interact with his arguments.

### AUDIENCE REFERENCE

Murray does not mention Jesus' use of the second person plural (you) throughout the discourse. Jesus' use of the second personal plural beginning with Matthew 21 leaves no doubt that He had that audience in view: "When the chief priests and the Pharisees heard His parables, they understood that He was speaking about **them**" (21:45). The uses of "you" continues through chapter 24. The Pharisees understood what Jesus was saying: "Then the Pharisees went and counseled together how they might trap Him in what He said" (23:15). Why? Because Jesus was describing what was going to happen to them and their generation.

Jesus described them as "sons of those who murdered the prophets" (23:31; cf. Heb. 11:32-38; 1 Kings 19:10; 2 Chron. 16:10; 1 Kings 22:27;

Jer. 26:23). It was their generation that would "fill up" the measure of the guilt of their fathers (Matt. 23:32; cf. Gen. 15:16; 1 Thess. 2:16).

> Therefore, behold, I am sending **you** prophets and wise men and scribes; some of them **you** will kill and crucify, and some of them **you** will scourge in **your synagogues**, and persecute from city to city, so that upon **you** may fall the guilt of all the righteous blood shed on earth, from the blood of righteous Abel to the blood of Zechariah, the son of Berechiah,[13] whom **you** murdered between the temple and the altar. Truly I say to **you**, all these things will come upon **this generation** (23:34-36).

The second person plural is used repeatedly throughout the chapter. Neither Waldron nor James Hamilton commented on the audience reference. This was surprising since Hamilton spent a good amount of his time during his opening statement commenting on Matthew's version of the Olivet Discourse.

In his commentary on Revelation, Hamilton includes a chart showing the parallels between the Olivet Discourse and Revelation 6[14] (page 119). Not once does Hamilton mention the audience reference. In fact, in commenting on Matthew 24:9-12, he uses the phrase "believers put to death" when the text says, "Then they will deliver you to tribulation, and will kill you, and you will be hated by all nations because of My name" (24:9). It's not just "believers" in general, but a group of believers at that time and place. Compare with Matthew 10:16-23.

Matthew 24 begins the same way in terms of audience reference: "See to it that no one misleads **you** ... And **you** will be hearing of wars and rumors of wars; see that **you** are not frightened ... Then they will deliver **you** up to tribulation, and will kill **you**, and **you** will be hated by all nations on account of My name" (vv. 4, 6, 9). There is nothing in these verses that would have led Jesus' audience to conclude that He was speaking about a different group of people.

---

13. For a study of the identity of "Zechariah, the son of Berechiah," see Gary DeMar, *Identifying the Real Last Days Scoffers* (2012), Appendix B and *Wars and Rumors of Wars* (2023), 18-27.

14. James M. Hamilton, *Revelation: The Spirit Speaks to the Churches* (Wheaton, IL: Crossway, 2012), 166-167.

## FAMINES, EARTHQUAKES, AND WARS

In addition to a contemporary audience, Jesus mentions famines (Matt. 24:7). The book of Acts mentions that there was "a great famine all over the world [οἰκουμένην: see Matt. 24:14; Luke 2:1]" that "took place in the reign of Claudius" (Acts 11:28; see Josephus, *Antiquities* iii.xv.3, Tacitus, *Annals* 12:43; Suetonius, *Claudius* 18), earthquakes (Matt. 27:51-54; 28:2; Acts 4:31; 16:26; Laodicea in AD 61 and at Pompeii in AD 62). The same is true of wars and rumors of wars during that time.

Three earthquakes shook Rome after Jesus' Olivet prophecy and prior to Jerusalem's destruction: AD 51 (Tacitus, *Annals* 12.43.1.), 53 (Syncellus, P 336C), and 57 (Hieron, *Chronicles*, p. 182). A later earthquake destroyed the city of Laodicea around AD 60. Tacitus (*Annals*, 14:27) notes: "One of the famous cities of Asia, Laodicea, was that same year overthrown by an earthquake, and, without any relief from us, recovered itself by its own resources." In AD 62, an earthquake rocked Pompeii. The New Testament mentions a number of "great earthquakes" (Matt. 27:51, 54; 28:2; Acts 4:31; 16:26).

Of course, this is not to say that there will never be any wars, famines, earthquakes, or tribulation after that generation passed away. Actually, these events are common to every era, both before (see the Old Testament) and after the end of that generation. The context of these events, however, concerns the destruction of the temple (Matt. 24:2) that did take place before that first-century generation passed away.

Some will argue that global wars are what Jesus had in view. "[R]ather than the local war in Judea, the account in Matthew depicts something on a much broader scale. In the words of Craig Evans, 'the expectation of global warfare and chaos.... However, there were no major wars prior to the Jewish revolt.'"[15]

First, there is nothing in the text that Jesus has anything more in mind than wars in that generation's immediate future. For those of that generation, the wars they encountered were "global," if by global we

---

15. Craig A. Evans, "Mark 8:27-16:20," *Word Biblical Commentary*, Vol. 34B (Dallas: Word Books, 2001), 307. Quoted in H. Wayne House, "Josephus and the Fall of Jerusalem: An Evaluation of the Preterist View on Jerusalem in Prophecy, Pre-Trib Study Group" (December 8, 2008).

mean the nation-states they were familiar with. Paul had plans to go to Spain (Rom. 15:24-28).

Second, Jesus is clear about His audience: "**you** will be hearing of wars and rumors of war." Jesus identifies the audience that would hear about these wars, both real and rumored. He couldn't be any clearer.

Third, it's important not to read modern-day definitions of war and how ancient peoples understood and used the terms "nations" and "kingdoms." Even though Rome "kept the peace" (*Pax Romana*), wars or "battles" among subjected peoples were still going on. Wars during a time of peace are signs, not during times of war. There's more.

> In AD 40 there was a disturbance at Mesopotamia which (Josephus says) caused the deaths of more than 50,000 people. In AD 49 a tumult at Jerusalem at the time of the Passover resulted in 10,000 to 20,000 deaths. At Caesarea contentions between Jewish people and other inhabitants resulted in over 20,000 Jews being killed. As Jews moved elsewhere, over 20,000 were destroyed by Syrians. At Scythopolis, over 13,000 Jews were killed. Thousands were killed in other places, and at Alexandria 50,000 were killed. At Damascus, 10,000 were killed in an hour's time. These were not wars of a world-wide scope as we know the world today. They were in Galilee, and in Syria, and in the areas east and south of Judaea. And Judaea was in revolt against Rome, "while the armies of Spain, Gaul and Germany, Illyricum and Syria, converged upon Italy, to decide who should succeed to Nero's purple."[16]

If these numbers are accurate, then these conflicts certainly qualify as "wars." The Roman historian Tacitus (AD 56-117) (*Histories*, 1.2) writes of the period: "I am entering on the history of a period rich in disasters, frightful in its wars, torn by civil strife, and even in peace full of horrors.... There were three civil wars; there were more with foreign enemies; there were often wars that had both characters at once.... There were disturbances in Illyricum; Gaul wavered in its allegiance; Britain was thoroughly subdued and immediately abandoned; the tribes of the Suevi and the Sarmatae rose in concert against us; the Dacians had the

---

16. John Bray, *Matthew 24 Fulfilled* (Powder Springs, GA: American Vision, [1996] 2008).

glory of inflicting as well as suffering defeat; the armies of Parthia were all but set in motion by the cheat of a counterfeit Nero."

Even though Tacitus describes these conflicts as "wars," "civil strife," and "civil wars," H. Wayne House argues "the conflicts within the Roman Empire were not really wars between kingdoms and nations in the first century AD, as described in the Olivet Discourse.[17] Nations dominated by Rome still considered themselves to be national entities as well as kingdoms (Matt. 27:11, 37, 42). It's not any different today. Nations within the former Soviet orbit thought of themselves as particular nations as they are today.

## PREACHING THE GOSPEL IN THE 'WHOLE WORLD'

The gospel was preached "in the whole world" (οἰκουμένη) (Matt. 24:14) in the same way that the "whole world" (οἰκουμένην) was taxed during the reign of Caesar Augustus (Luke 2:1) and a famine occurred "all over the world" (οἰκουμένην) during the reign of Claudius (Acts 11:28). These events were Roman Empire-wide not world (κόσμος) wide.[18]

On Matthew 24:14, Murray notes that "the world-wide preaching of the gospel for a witness to the nations" is a Roman Empire-wide event and not a distant global event (Rom. 1:8 [κόσμος]; 16:25-26; Col. 1:6, 23; 1 Tim. 3:16d). (2:388). Hamilton is mistaken when he writes, "In the Olivet Discourse, Jesus says the gospel has to be proclaimed to the whole world, 'then the end will come' (Matthew 24:14)."[19] Like Murray, he does not mention that Matthew uses οἰκουμένη and not κόσμος. Murray's comments surprised me because in his Romans commentary, he wrote the following about Romans 1:8:

> "Throughout the whole world" [kosmos] has been regarded as hyperbole. This is not perhaps the most felicitous way to expressing the apostle's thought. Paul did not mean, of course, that the whole world distributively, every person under heaven, had heard of the faith of the Roman believers. His terms could not be pressed into that meaning even if most literally understood. But the expression here witnesses to the extensive

17. House, "Josephus and the Fall of Jerusalem."

18. Megan Gannon, "Traces of 2,000-year-old wartime famine unearthed in Jerusalem," Fox News (July 1, 2013: http://fxn.ws/13ZmDtY

19. Hamilton, *Revelation*, 166.

diffusion of the gospel throughout the known world during the apostolic age (*cf.* Col. 1:23; Acts 17:30, 31).[20]

If *kosmos* can be used in a way that applies to a limited geographical area and time, as Murray and other commentators argue, can't the same be said for Jesus' use of the more restrictive *oikoumenē* in Matthew 24:14?

Murray's argument rests on the unproven assumption that "the end" (24:13-14) refers to an end that is still in our future. In reality, Jesus was addressing the very specific "end of the age" that would come before that generation passed away (24:3, 34). The expression "end of the age," to repeat, refers "to the end of the 'Jewish age,' *i.e.,* the time of transference from a national to an international people of God,"[21] what the Apostle Paul describes as the "ends of the ages" (τέλη τῶν αἰώνων) that had come upon that generation (1 Cor. 10:11). Matthew is the only gospel writer to use the phrase "the end of the age" (Matt. 13:39, 40, 49; 24:3; 28:20).

A similar use of *telos* (end) is used by Jesus in Matthew 10:22: "You will be hated by all because of My name, but it is the one who has endured to the end who will be saved." The disciples are in a shortened localized time period. Jack P. Lewis comments:

**He who endures to the end will be saved** is parallel to Luke 21:19: "By your endurance you will gain your lives." ... It does not signify "to the end of time" (cf. [Matt.] 24:13; 1 Cor. 13:7; Rev. 3:11).[22]

Jesus is not using "saved" to mean saved from eternal judgment but saved from death during that first-century period of tribulation. Just a few verses later, Jesus explains how anyone who escapes the doomed city will be saved by retreating to the local mountains (Matt. 24:15-22).

By escaping this "great tribulation," they would be "saved" in a physical sense (24:22). Henry Hammond writes "that σωθήσεται ['will be saved'] is not always to be interpreted of eternal salvation, but of temporal escaping (any more than σωτηρία [*sotēria*] does ... where it is clearly the deliverance of the *Israelites* out of *Egypt* by *Moses* [Acts 7:25;

---

20. John Murray, *The Epistle to the Romans*, 2 vols. (Grand Rapids, MI: Eerdmans, 1959), 1:19. The one-volume edition was published in 1968.

21. R. T. France, *The Gospel According to Matthew: An Introduction and Commentary* (Grand Rapids, MI: Eerdmans, 1985), 337.

22. Jack P. Lewis, *The Gospel According to Matthew*, 2 vols. (Austin, TX: Sweet Publishing Co., 1976), 1:152. Also see his comments on Matthew 24:13-14 in volume 2 of The Gospel According to Matthew (124-125).

see Gen. 19:19]."[23] Most translations translate σωτηρία in Acts 7:25 as "deliverance," that is, physical deliverance by Moses from the oppression of the Egyptians. This meaning of "saved" is common in Matthew's gospel: "[F]or she was saying to herself, 'If I only touch His garment, I will get well [using a form of σῴζω].' But Jesus turning and seeing her said, 'Daughter, take courage; your faith has made you well. At once the woman was made well" (Matt. 9:21-22; also 8:25; 14:30; 24:22; 27:40, 42, 49).

The use of "saved" in Matthew 24:13, 22 describes saved or rescued from physical calamity because Jesus uses the same phraseology in Matthew 10 when He sends out the twelve "to the lost sheep of the house of Israel" (10:5-6). The audience is identified by Jesus. It's very specific and reads very much like what we find in the Olivet Discourse. For example: "You will be hated by all because of My name, but it is the one who has endured to the end who will be saved [σωθήσεται from σῴζω]" (Matt. 10:22; cf. 24:13). Even dispensational commentator John Phillips acknowledges that "[t]he word translated 'shall be saved' [in 10:22] can also be translated 'shall escape' or 'shall be delivered.'"[24]

Jesus commissioned them only to go those in Israel: "But whenever they persecute **you** in one city, flee to the next; for truly I say to **you**, **you** will not finish going through the cities of Israel until the Son of Man comes" (10:23). The audience reference is self-evident, and so is the timing. If this were a description of events that impacted a future generation. Jay Adams writes:

As Jesus said, there was no need to linger in a city that refused to hear; there were plenty more cities to cover before it was too late and Jesus would come in judgment on Israel (70 AD).[25]

The 1995 edition of the *New International Version Study Bible* notes that in Matthew 10:23 "Jesus' saying here is probably best understood

---

23. Henry Hammond, *A Paraphrase and Annotations Upon the Books of the New Testament, Briefly Explaining all the Difficult Places thereof*, 7th ed. (London: 1702), 47.

24. John Phillips, *Exploring the Gospel of Matthew: An Expository Commentary* (Grand Rapids, MI: Kregel Publications, 1999), 192.

25. Jay E. Adams, The Christian's *Counselor's Commentary: The Gospels of Matthew and Mark* (Woodruff, SC: Timeless Texts, 1999), 94. Also see D.A. Carson, "Matthew, *The Expositor's Bible Commentary*, gen ed. Frank E. Gaebelein, 12 vols. (Grand Rapids, MI: Zondervan, 1984) 8:250-253.

as referring to his coming in judgment on the Jews when Jerusalem and the temple were destroyed in AD 70."

It's evident that without identifying the audience Jesus was addressing, all types of speculative interpretations are possible. I've been amazed how some interpreters try to get around what is obvious to any reader of the Olivet Discourse. That's why liberals have claimed Jesus was mistaken. Jesus had His present audience of that generation in view. If the audience reference of "you" did not refer to the audience that first heard Jesus' words, then what audience reference could Jesus have used if He had wanted to single out that generation? If "you" did not mean them, then how else could He have said it to refer to them?

## THE TRANSITION TEXT?

Murray hopes to solve the dilemma he had placed himself in by an appeal to Matthew 24:35-36 (2:394): "Heaven and earth will pass away, but My words will not pass away. But of that day and hour no one knows, not even the angels of heaven, nor the Son, but the Father alone." It's here that Murray believes there is a shift in focus to a yet future physical coming of Jesus.[26]

> This would have made clear to the disciples the distinction between the destruction of Jerusalem and correlative events on the more proximate horizon [the destruction of Jerusalem], on the one hand, and the day of his advent [the Second Coming], on the other (2:394).

This is the position taken by Kik in his exposition of Matthew 24. But unlike Murray, Kik does not argue that verses 3-14 refer to the entire "inter-adventual period" between the two physical comings of Jesus. Kik writes:

> The first 35 verses of Matthew 24 relate to the destruction of Jerusalem and the events preceding that destruction. With 36 a new subject is introduced, namely, the second coming of Christ and the attendant final judgment. This forms the content of Matthew 24:36-25:46.

For Kik, everything prior to Matthew 24:35 was fulfilled during that generation. Amillennialist Sam Storms adopts a position similar to Kik's,

---

26. See chapter 20 for a discussion of the transition text issue.

but unlike Murray and Waldron, he does not flip-flop between the events of AD 70, the interadventual period, and the Second Coming. Everything Jesus describes through verse 34 refers to events that were fulfilled in that generation.[27] What the Bible means by "heaven and earth" passing away is developed in greater detail in chapter 15 of my book *Last Days Madness* and chapter 10 of *Identifying the Real Last Days Scoffers*.

One thing to consider is the order of events in Matthew 24 and Luke 17:20-37. There's an interesting mix of events that is not often discussed by prophecy writers. Let's compare the order of events in Matthew 24 to the order of some of the same events in Luke 17: Jesus places the Noah's ark analogy (Matt. 24:37-39) before the events of Matthew 24:17-18 ("let him who is on the housetop not go down"), verse 27 ("for just as the lightning comes from the east"), and verse 28 ("wherever the corpse is, there the vultures will gather"). If the five prophetic events of Matthew 24 that are found in Luke 17:22-37 are numbered 1-2-3-4-5, Luke's numbering of the same events would be 2-4-1-5-3, with Matthew 24:35-36 in the middle.

The chart on page 307 shows that the order of prophetic events in both accounts falls on either side of the so-called transition text in Matthew 24:35. While Jesus identified that present generation as the one that would encounter the signs leading up to the destruction of Jerusalem, the day and the hour would not be known.[28] That's why Jesus told His disciples, "Therefore when you see the ABOMINATION OF DESOLATION which was spoken of through Daniel the prophet, standing in the holy place (let the reader understand), then those who are in Judea must flee to the mountains" (Matt. 24:15-16; Luke 21:20).

This means that the passing away of heaven and earth is most likely a reference to the passing away of the old covenant order represented by heavenly bodies. Crispin H.T. Fletcher-Louis offers a compelling case:

> That the principal reference of 'heaven and earth' is the temple-centered cosmology of second-temple Judaism which included

---

27. Sam Storms, *Kingdom Come: The Amillennial* Alternative (Ross-Shire, Scotland: Mentor, 2013), 237.

28. Curiously, dispensational author, Max Lucado pinpoints the date: "This gloomy prophecy was fulfilled on August 6, AD 70. Titus of Rome destroyed Jerusalem, killed a million Jews, and tore the temple apart stone by stone." *What Happens Next: A Traveler's Guide Through the End of the Age* (Nashville: Thomas Nelson, 2024), 43.

the belief that the temple is heaven and earth in microcosm.[29] Mark 13 and Matthew 5:18 refer, then, to the destruction of the temple as a passing away of an old cosmology and also, in the latter case, to the establishment of during Jesus' ministry and at His death and resurrection of a new temple cosmology—a new heaven and earth.... By 'heaven and earth' is meant the Jerusalem temple and the Torah constitution at the centre of which the former stands. Neither saying envisages the collapse of the space-time universe (as has been understood by modern interpretation). Both refer to the imminent end to the social, religious and economic structure of Israel's covenant relationship with God with the attendant destruction of the temple.... [W]e should consider favourably the minority interpretation which has explored the possibility that the passing away of heaven and earth refers figuratively to events within history.[30]

The sun and moon going dim and the stars falling represent Israel under judgment (Matt. 24:29; cf. Gen. 37:9; Rev. 12:1), a common way the Old Testament depicts national judgment (Isa. 13:10; 24:23; 34; Ezek. 32:7-8; Joel 2:10, 31; 3:15-16; Amos 5:20; 8:9; Zeph. 1:15; Acts 2:19-20; Rev. 6:12-17; 8:12). Jesus' disciples would not have considered that Jesus was referring to the end of the physical cosmos. They were well aware of this type of language. The Old Testament was full of it. Why would cosmic language mean something different when Jesus quoted directly from sections of Scripture that referenced national judgment (Isa. 13:9-11; 34:1-5), including Israel (Zeph. 1:1-4)? With the coming of Jesus, the old has passed away to make way for the new:

The expression "new heavens and new earth," while it can refer to a transfigured cosmos, can also refer to a new order on the earth:

---

29. According to Josephus in his *Antiquities of the Jews*, the temple itself represented the world: "The tabernacle proved to be an imitation of the system of the world; for that third part thereof which was within the four pillars, to which the priests were not admitted, is, as it were, a heaven peculiar to God. But the space of the twenty cubits is, as it were, sea and land, on which men live, and so this part is peculiar to the priests only." (Josephus, *Antiquities of the Jews*, Book 3, Ch. 6, Paragraph 4, section 123.)

30. Crispin H. T. Fletcher-Louis, "The Destruction of the Temple and the Relativization of the Old Covenant: Mark 13:31 and Matthew 5:18," *Eschatology in Bible & Theology*, 145, 146, 149.

new rulers and new people. At the Cross and Resurrection of our Lord, the old Adamic heavens and earth were shaken down, and a new heavens and earth were set up, with the God-man seated on the heavenly throne. Thus, in a judicial sense, the New Heavens and Earth began at that time.... But, each time God brought judgment on His people during the Old Covenant, there was a sense in which an old heavens and earth was replaced with a new one: New rulers were set up, a new symbolic world model was built (Tabernacle, Temple), and so forth.[31]

Consider these words by C.H. Spurgeon who believed that "new heaven and new earth" language was indicative of a new covenant, of which there were many inaugurations in Scripture:

Did you ever regret the absence of the burnt-offering, or the red heifer, of any one of the sacrifices and rites of the Jews? Did you ever pine for the feast of tabernacle, or the dedication? No, because, though these were like the old heavens and earth to the Jewish believers, they have passed away, and we now live under a new heavens and a new earth, so far as the dispensation of divine teaching is concerned. The Substance is come, and the shadow has gone—and we do not remember it.[32]

Commentator John Brown (1784-1858), in his three-volume work *Discourses and Sayings of Our Lord Jesus Christ*, writes:

"Heaven and earth passing," understood literally, and the period when that is to take place, is called the "end of the world." But a person at all familiar with the phraseology of the Old Testament Scriptures knows that the dissolution of the Mosaic economy, and the establishment of the Christian,

---

31. James Jordan, *Through New Eyes: Developing a Biblical View of the World* (Brentwood, TN: Wolgemuth & Hyatt, 198), 67, 167

32. C.H. Spurgeon, "God Rejoicing in the New Creation" (no. 2211), *Metropolitan Tabernacle Pulpit* (July 5, 1891), 37:354. "There is to be a literal new creation, but that new creation has commenced already; and I think, therefore, that even now we ought to manifest a part of the joy. If we are called upon to be glad and rejoice in the completion of the work, let us rejoice even in the commencement of it.... He has commenced it thus—by putting new hearts into as many as he has called by his Spirit, regenerating them, and making them to become new creatures in Christ Jesus. These the apostle tells us are a kind of first fruits of this now creation" (443).

is often spoken of as the removing of the old earth and heavens, and the creation of a new earth and new heavens.... The period of the close of one dispensation, and the commencement of the other, is spoken of as "the last days," and "the end of the world;" and is described as a shaking of the earth and heavens, as should lead to the removal of the things which were shaken [Hag. 2:6; Heb. 12:26-27].[33]

This type of prophetic language fills the Old Testament and goes a long way to help explain what Jesus is describing in the Olivet Discourse that would take place before that generation passed away.

## THE SIGN OF THE SON OF MAN IN HEAVEN

Once again, the way Murray understands the meaning of "the end of the age" affects his interpretation of Matthew 24:30 and "the sign of the Son of Man in heaven." He sees this, as does Waldron, as a reference to "the advent and of the consummation of the age" (2:390), a yet physical coming of Jesus. He makes similar statements about "the coming of the Son of Man," "coming on the clouds of heaven," and the use of "trumpet" (Matt. 24:30-31).

Note that all these descriptive predictive events were to take place before Jesus' statement in verse 34: "this generation will not pass away until **all these things take place**." But how is it possible that these events could have been fulfilled during the time of Israel's judgment and the temple's destruction in AD 70? We are left with no other choice. Jesus said they would be fulfilled. We must take Him at His Word.

Most other prophecy writers agree that Jesus is quoting directly from Daniel 7:13.[34]

I kept looking in the night visions,
And behold, with the clouds of heaven
One like a Son of Man was coming,

33. John Brown, *Discourses and the Sayings of the Lord, Illustrated in a Series of Expositions*, 2 vols. in one (New York: Robert Carter & Brothers, 1875), 1:157. See Roderick Campbell, *Israel and the New Covenant* (Philadelphia: Presbyterian and Reformed, 1954), chap. 13.

34. For example, Tim LaHaye, gen. ed., *Prophecy Study Bible* (Chattanooga, TN: AMG Press, 2000), 1040, note on Matthew 24:29-31.

And He came up to the Ancient of Days
And was presented before Him.

While LaHaye writes that Daniel 7:13 reveals "that Christ will come from heaven to the earth," this is not what the text says. The Ancient of Days is enthroned in heaven, not on earth or in the "sky" (Dan. 7:9). Daniel 7:13 is quoted again, along with a portion of Psalm 110:1, when Caiaphas the high priest asks Jesus if He is "the Christ, the Son of God" (Matt. 26:63). Jesus says to him, "You have said it yourself; nevertheless I tell you, hereafter[35] you [plural] shall see the Son of Man sitting at the right hand of power, and coming on the clouds of heaven" (Matt. 26:64; see Heb. 8:1-2). Nothing is mentioned, as LaHaye insists, about Jesus returning to earth "with the 'clouds of heaven' to be worshiped."[36] LaHaye claims to interpret the Bible literally. How can his interpretation be accurate if he completely misses what Daniel 7:13 actually states? R.T. France makes the following relevant points in his exposition of Matthew 26:64 and the similar language used in 24:30:

> *Coming on the clouds of heaven* (together with the phrase 'the Son of man') is a clear allusion to Daniel 7:13, already similarly alluded to in 24:30.... We have seen that its natural application in terms of its Old Testament source is to the vindication and enthronement of the Son of man in heaven, not to a descent to earth. It is therefore in this verse a parallel expression to 'seated at the right hand of Power'; the two phrases refer to the same exalted state, not to two successive situations or events. In this verse the appropriateness of this interpretation is underlined by the fact that this is to be true 'from now on' (*hereafter* is a quite misleading rendering of the more specific phrase *ap' arti*, which, as in 23:39 and 26:29, denotes a new period beginning *from now*). Indeed it is something which Jesus' inquisitors themselves *will see* (an echo of Zc. 12:10, as in 24:30?), for it will quickly become apparent in the events of even the next few weeks (not to mention the subsequent growth of the

---

35. "Hereafter" does not mean "at the Final Judgment" when everybody will see Jesus, when at the name of Jesus every knee will bow and every tongue will confess "that Jesus Christ is Lord, to the glory of God the Father" (Phil. 2:11).

36. LaHaye and Jenkins, *Are We Living in the End Times?*, 225.

church) that the 'blasphemer' they thought they had disposed of is in fact now in the position of supreme authority.[37]

N.T Wright offers a similar interpretation of Matthew 26:64 that also quotes Daniel 7:13: "The Daniel text ... has nothing to do with a figure 'coming' *from* heaven *to* earth. Despite the widespread opinion that this is what it 'must' mean in the gospels, there is no reason to suppose that on the lips of Jesus, or in the understanding of the earliest traditions, it meant anything other than vindication. It speaks of exaltation: of one who, representing 'the people of the saints of the most high', is raised up from suffering at the hands of the beasts and given a throne to sit on, exercising royal power.... Jesus is not ... suggesting that Caiaphas will witness the end of the space-time order. Nor will he look out of the window one day and observe a human figure flying downwards on a cloud. It is absurd to imagine either Jesus, or Mark, or anyone in between, supposing the words to mean that."[38]

It seems obvious that Jesus was speaking of His enthronement that took place at His ascension when "He was received up into heaven and sat down at the right hand of God" (Mark 16:19; see Ps. 110:1; Acts 2:3-6). Soon after that event Jesus' disciples understood His redemptive mission. This is made evident when Stephen, "being full of the Holy Spirit, ... gazed intently into heaven and saw the glory of God, and Jesus standing at the right hand of God; and he said, 'Behold, I see the heavens opened up and the Son of Man standing at the right hand of God'" (Acts 7:55-56). How did Jesus get there? He ascended on the clouds of heaven to the Ancient of Days. Daniel 7:13 and Psalm 110:1 were fulfilled in the first century at Jesus' ascension (Acts 1:9-11).

Many assume that Jesus was saying that everyone on earth would see Him physically appear in the sky. Part of this assumption stems from a poor translation. First, the text does not speak of *Jesus* appearing in the *sky*. Rather, a word-for-word translation of the Greek reads, "Then will appear the *sign* of the Son of Man *in heaven*."[39] (The Greek word for

---

37. R. T. France, *Matthew: Tyndale New Testament Commentaries* (Grand Rapids, MI: Eerdmans, 1985), 381.

38. N. T. Wright, *Jesus and the Victory of God* (Minneapolis: Fortress Press, 1996), 524-525.

39. The use of the singular "heaven" is not an indication that "sky" is the better translation. Matthew uses the singular "heaven" for God's dwelling place in several places (e.g., Matt. 5:34; 6:10, 20; 11:25; 14:19; 16:1; 18:18; 21:25; 22:30; 23:22; 28:2).

"sky" and "heaven" is the same: *ouranos*.) The *"sign* of the Son of Man" is that Jesus is in heaven (cf. Rev. 12:1).[40] Jesus was telling His disciples to look for the sign of His enthronement in heaven. That turned out to be His ascension, a direct reference to Daniel 7:13 and Psalm 110:1. All Christians now look to "the Jerusalem above" (Gal. 4:26; also see John 4:21-24). That is why Paul could write, "If you have been raised up with Christ, keep seeking the things above, where Christ is, seated at the right hand of God" (Col. 3:1). When God raised Jesus from the dead, He "seated Him at His right hand in the heavenly places, far above all rule and authority and power and dominion, and every name that is named, not only in this age, but also in the one to come" (Eph. 1:20-21).

A generation would pass before the nation as a whole would understand that the earthly temple was no longer the dwelling place of God (it never really was). The destruction of the city of Jerusalem and the desolation of the temple pointed all eyes to focus on the New Jerusalem above. But when did *"they* see the Son of Man coming on the clouds of heaven with power and great glory"? (Matt. 24:30) Obviously before that first-century generation passed away. The language is similar to what Jesus told Nathanael: "And [Jesus] said to [Nathanael], 'Truly, truly, I say to you, you shall see the heavens opened, and the angels of God ascending and descending upon the Son of Man'" (John 1:51). The Greek word for "see" in John 1:51 is the same word used in Matthew 24:30: *horaō*. "Although Jesus is addressing Nathanael, the 'you' to whom he promises the vision of v. 51 is plural: the vision is probably for all the disciples, and by extension, for those also who would follow them."[41]

When did Nathanael and those with him "see" what Jesus said they would see? It's possible they actually did see what Jesus described but the event is not recorded in Scripture. Matthew Henry, in his comments on this passage, states the following: "There were many things which Christ did, and those in the presence of his disciples, which were not written (John 20:30), and why not this?" Therefore it's possible that at the time of Jerusalem's judgment and the temple's destruction, the Jews saw Jesus coming on the clouds of heaven, that is, the heavens opened and Jesus enthroned in heaven similar to what Stephen saw. Since

---

40. R. T. France, *The Gospel of Matthew: The New International Commentary on the New Testament* (Grand Rapids, MI: Eerdmans, 2007), 925-926.

41. D. A. Carson, *The Gospel According to John* (Grand Rapids, MI: Eerdmans, 1991), 163.

none of the New Testament books were written after the destruction of Jerusalem in AD 70,[42] there is no biblical record of it. What we do have, however, is the promise by Jesus that they would see it before their generation passed away.

The second confusion in the translation of Matthew 24:30 is the phrase "all the tribes of the earth will mourn," which is more accurately translated "all the tribes of the *land* will mourn." The Greek word for "earth" (*gēs*) is best translated as "land" as it is in Luke 21:23: "Woe to those who are pregnant and to those who are nursing babies in those days; for there will be great distress upon the land and wrath to this people," that is, the Jews of that generation. Jesus was warning His audience to flee Judea when they saw "Jerusalem surrounded by armies" (Luke 21:20). Only those near enough to the temple would be able to see the abomination of desolation ... standing in the holy place" (Matt. 24:15). The Olivet Discourse was clearly not a message to the world, but a warning to the tribes of Israel of the first century. Jesus told the "daughters of Jerusalem" to "weep for yourselves and for your children" (Luke 23:28-30). France writes:

> The witness of the "Son of Man coming on the clouds of heaven" will be "all the tribes of the land," who will greet his vindication not with acclamation but with mourning. The allusion is to Zech 12:10-14: "They will look on the one they have pierced, and they will mourn for him." There the mourners are identified as "the house of David and the inhabitants of Jerusalem" (v. 10), who are then listed by families (the families of David, Nathan, Levi, Shimei, and others, vv. 12-14). That is why the phrase [all the tribes

---

42. "Indeed, it is becoming an increasingly persuasive argument that all the New Testament books were written before 70 AD—within a single generation of the death of Christ." (John Ankerberg and John Weldon, *Ready With An Answer: For the Tough Questions About God* [Eugene, OR: Harvest House Publishers, 1997], 364-365). Reprinted as *Handbook of Biblical Evidences* (2008). "Most liberal scholars are being forced to consider earlier dates for the New Testament. Dr. John A.T. Robinson, no conservative himself, comes to some startling conclusions in his ground-breaking book *Redating the New Testament*. His research has led to his conviction that the whole of the New Testament was written before the fall of Jerusalem in AD 70 (Robinson, RNT)." Josh McDowell, *Evidence for Christianity: Historical Evidences for the Christian Faith* (Nashville, TN: Thomas Nelson, 2006), 80. Also see Norman L. Geisler and Frank Turek, *I Don't Have Enough Faith to Be an Atheist* (Wheaton, IL: Crossway, 204), 237-239 and Kenneth L. Gentry, Jr., *Before Jerusalem Fell: Dating the Book of Revelation*, 2nd ed. (Powder Springs, GA: American Vision, 1998).

of the land will mourn] must refer to all the tribes of the land (i.e., as in Zech 12, a specifically Jewish mourning), not "of the earth." This is also required by the use of *phylē* [tribes], which in the NT (as normally in the LXX) is used specifically of the OT tribes (Matt 19:28; Luke 2:36; Acts 13:21; Rom. 11:1; Heb. 7:13-14; etc.).[43]

Barry Horner takes a similar position of the translation of the Greek word *gēs*, although he applies its fulfillment to a yet future time. "In the phrase *hai phulai tēs gēs*, 'the tribes of the earth,' if *tēs gēs* is uniformly translated in the NT as 'the earth,' then the absence of any mention of the land of Israel there is virtually guaranteed. But the context suggests that Zech. 12:10, 14 is inferred by Matthew in this instance, in which case 'the tribes of the Land [of Israel]' is a more appropriate translation."[44]

The tribes of Israel mourned because they understood that judgment was a reality for them in their day as they saw their city and temple set ablaze by the invading Roman armies. They were warned to embrace Jesus as their promised Messiah, flee the city, or perish in the impending conflagration. The Jews who rejected Jesus because He was not their idea of a political savior died at the spear-point of Roman soldiers. Their Savior had come, and they had crucified Him.

## GATHERING THE ELECT

At least one commentator interprets this verse to mean a future physical ingathering of elect Jews by angels at the end of dispensationalism's version of the Great Tribulation. According to his interpretation, angels will literally search the globe and pluck Jews from where they live and carry them to Israel.[45] This is highly unlikely since the imagery of gathering is used throughout the Old Testament to describe God calling His people to forsake their wicked ways and worship Him (e.g., Isa. 11:12;[46] 27:12-13).

---

43. France, *The Gospel of Matthew*, 925.

44. Barry Horner, *Future Israel: Why Christian Anti-Judaism Must be Challenged* (Nashville: Broadman & Holman, 2007), 229.

45. This view is held by Thomas Ice as reported to me by Kenneth L. Gentry, Jr., who heard him state this interpretation.

46. The reference to "second time" in Isaiah 11:11 requires a first time. In 11:16 we read that the first time was when Israel "came up out of the land of Egypt." The second time was

No longer is the gospel only for the "lost sheep of the house of Israel" (Matt. 10:6; 15:24) but "that He might also **gather** together into one the children of God who are scattered abroad" (John 11:52), an event prophesied by Isaiah: "The Lord God, who gathers the dispersed of Israel, declares, 'Yet others I will gather to them, to those already gathered'" (Isa. 56:8). Jesus may have had in mind the Jews "in the dispersion [διασπορά]" (James 1:1) as well as Gentiles (Rom. 9:24-26).

In context, Matthew 24:31 could describe the spread of the gospel to the nations and their eventual discipleship (28:18-20). This helps explain why the Greek word *angelos* can be translated "messenger" and refer to human messengers and not supernatural beings. For example, John the Baptist was God's "messenger" who prepared the way for Jesus (Matt. 11:10; Mark 1:2). The disciples of John are called "messengers" (Luke 7:24, 27). Jesus "sent messengers on ahead of Him" (Luke 9:52).

Rahab "received the messengers and sent them out by another way" (James 2:25). In each of these examples, the Greek word *angelos* is used. Dispensational prophecy writer Ed Hindson recognizes this use of *angelos*: "The term *angel* (Greek, *angelos*) means 'messenger.' God's angels are His divine messengers (Heb. 1:14; Rev. 1:1), and His true prophets and preachers are called angels of the churches (Rev. 2:1, 8, 12, 18; 3:1, 7, 14)."[47]

R. T. France, while acknowledging that *angelos* can be translated as "messenger," takes the more traditional view that it refers to supernatural beings during the period leading up to and including the destruction of Jerusalem in AD 70. His following comments are based on the parallel passage in Mark 13:27:

> I once argued that, since the basic meaning of [*angelos*] is "messenger" (even though its NT uses are predominately in the secondary sense of "angel"), here "the context favours strongly the primary meaning."[48] In that case v. 27 [of Mark 13] would be describing the work of Christian missionaries, sent out by

when they returned from their post-exile captivity. See chapter 13 of this book.

47. Ed Hindson, "False Christ's, False Prophets, Great Deception," *Foreshadows of Wrath and Redemption*, William T. James, ed. (Eugene, OR: Harvest House, 1999), 33.

48. France, *Jesus and the Old Testament*, 238, "with references to others such as R. A. Knox and P. Carrington who have adopted the same interpretation" (France, *The Gospel of Mark*, 536, note 24).

the enthroned Son of Man in 8:38, and in the absence of any clear indication that the normal NT meaning of [*angelos*] is inappropriate here, I now think it more likely that angels are here credited with a "missionary" role in the ingathering of God's people; cf. the description of angels in Heb. 1:14 as [*"Are they not all ministering spirits, sent out to render service for the sake of those who will inherit salvation?"*].[49]

In either case, whether gospel missionaries or angels, this event took place during the time of that first-century generation.

The phrase "from the four winds" is a reference to the geographical completeness of the land of Israel—from horizon to horizon as Mark describes it: "from the farthest end of the land, to the farthest end of heaven" (Mark 13:27). The "four winds" is used by Jeremiah (Jer. 49:36). The phrase "the four corners of the land" is sometimes interpreted as the four points of the compass. A similar idea is found in Isaiah 11:11-12 on which Edward J. Young comments:

> Isaiah does not intend us to understand that the earth actually has four corners. He is merely employing a manner of speaking taken from the idea of referring to the four corners of a garment as indicating the entirety of the garment. Our Lord was reflecting upon this passage when He said, "And he shall send his angels with a great sound of a trumpet, and they shall gather together his elect from the four winds, from one end of heaven to the other" (Matt. 24:31).[50]

Notice that Jesus does not say that His gathered elect will be brought back to the land. We know from the Olivet Discourse that the elect are already in the land!

The trumpet describes, in a symbolic way, the call of the gospel. When Israel was in captivity, we are told that "a great trumpet" was blown and those "who were perishing in the land of Assyria and who were scattered in the land of Egypt will come and worship the LORD in the holy mountain at Jerusalem" (Isa. 27:13). It's doubtful that exiled Jews in these faraway places actually heard a trumpet blow as they

49. R. T. France, *The Gospel of Mark* (NIGTC) (Grand Rapids, MI: Eerdmans, 2002), 536-537.

50. Edward J. Young, *The Book of Isaiah*, 3 vols. (Grand Rapids, MI: Eerdmans, 1965), 1:396-397.

made their way back to Israel. Rather, they heard God's inner and prophetic call to return. In a similar way, God's messengers proclaimed the gospel "to gather together His elect from the four winds, from one end of heaven to the other" (Isa. 58:1; Jer. 6:17; Ezek. 33:3-6; Rom. 10:18), the four points of the compass: "you will receive power when the Holy Spirit has come upon you; and you shall be My witnesses both in Jerusalem, and in all Judea and Samaria, and even to the remotest part of the earth" (Acts 1:8).

Matthew 24:31 draws upon Old Testament imagery to symbolize the evangelistic work about to commence, the great gathering of God's elect from around the land of Israel and beyond in what James and Peter describe in their letters the regathering of Israel (James 1:1; 1 Pet. 1:1) as well as those who were outside the covenant.

Those who were once "separate from Christ," "excluded from the commonwealth of Israel, and strangers to the covenants of promise," and "who formerly were far off have been brought near by the blood of Christ" (Eph. 2:12-13). The word for "gather" (Matt. 24:31) is the Greek word *synagogē* which refers to a gathered assembly of believers. Many in Judea rejected Christ and became a "synagogue of Satan" (Rev. 2:9). The true synagogue of God is made up of believing Jews and Gentiles from around the world, "from every nation and all tribes and peoples and tongues" (Rev. 7:9; cf. 5:9; Acts 2:5). The land of Israel was no longer the center. Churches were planted throughout the Roman Empire.

This ingathering is described by Paul as he quotes Isaiah's prophecy on how the rejection of the gospel by the Jews would broaden the gospel to the nations (Acts 28:24-28; cf. Rom. 11:12-15): "Therefore let it be known to you that the salvation of God has been sent to the Gentiles; they will also listen" (Acts 28:28). The word translated "Gentiles" is from the Greek word ἔθνεσιν from which we get the word "nations."

James Jordan offers a different interpretation that also applies to the events of that Apostolic generation:

> This language might be taken as a general reference to the whole earthly world, except for the fact that it fits so very well with what we find, again, in Revelation. The dead saints "under the altar" are in "paradise" or "Abraham's bosom," a location symbolically equivalent to the firmament heavens that are right below the throne-heavens (Rev. 6:9-11). It is these elect, and their newly-

massacred brethren who come out of the Great Tribulation, who are gathered before the Throne in Revelation 15.

*****

And since Jesus died to gather together all those, Jew and Gentile, who were scattered abroad (John 11:52), it is possibly the re-formation of the Church after the Great Tribulation that is in view in Matthew 24:30. Given the parallels with Revelation, however, and remembering that Revelation is the Johannine version of Jesus' eschatological discourse, I am strongly inclined to believe that it is the gathering of the saints in heaven that is here spoken of. The trumpet would be the last or seventh trumpet, which is sounded by one of the twenty-four archangel-elders in Revelation 11:15-18. This event happens right after the Great Tribulation, which in Revelation 11 is pictured as the martyrdom of the two witnesses.[51]

## Conclusion

Murray and Waldron make a valiant attempt to find a solution to understanding the Olivet Discourse. Unfortunately, they get off track by not paying close attention to the text. By letting Scripture interpret Scripture, the only conclusion we can come to is that Jesus had His present generation in view as He outlined the event leading up to and including the destruction of Jerusalem that took place in AD 70.

---

51. James Jordan, *Matthew 23-25: A Literary, Historical, and Theological Commentary* (Powder Springs, GA: American Vision, 2022), 180-181

# CHAPTER 5

# Flavius Josephus and Preterism

James Hamilton, representing a hybrid view of historical pre-millennialism, said that if preterists didn't have Josephus, they wouldn't be preterists. I heard from a reliable source that he has made similar claims in his classes at Southern Baptist Theological Seminary where he is professor of biblical theology: "Without Josephus preterism wouldn't have a leg to stand on," as one student of his put it in an e-mail to me. The curious thing about Hamilton's claim is that other than one Josephus reference during the Symposium, my entire presentation came from the Bible, beginning with Revelation 22:10, 1:1 and 1:3 and moving on to Matthew 21-24, spending almost all my time going through the Olivet Discourse comparing Scripture with Scripture, not Josephus.[1]

My only Josephus reference was about the woman who killed, cooked, and ate her own child during the siege of Jerusalem (cf. Jer. 19:9; Lam. 2:20; 4:10; Ezek. 5:10). Adam Clarke offers the following reference to Josephus in his commentary on Leviticus 26:29:

> *Ye shall eat the flesh of your sons, etc.*—This was literally fulfilled at the siege of Jerusalem. Josephus, *Wars of the Jews* [Book 6, Chap. 3, sec. 4], gives us a particular instance in dreadful detail of a woman named Mary, who, in the extremity of the famine during the siege, killed her sucking child, roasted, and had eaten part of it when discovered by the soldiers!

The works of Josephus have been used for centuries, and not just by preterists. In fact, Hamilton uses Josephus to support the canonicity of the Old Testament. In his article "Scripture: The Evangelical View,"

---

1. John Bray references Josephus in his commentary *Matthew 24 Fulfilled*, 5th ed. (Powder Springs, GA: American Vision, [1996] 2008). David Chilton includes the appendix "Josephus on the Fall of Jerusalem" in his book *Paradise Restored: A Biblical Theology of Dominion* (Dallas, GA: Dominion Press, [1985], 2023). Both are available at AmericanVision.org

he includes the following subheading: "Other Jewish Writings and the OT Canon." He introduces the section, "The evidence drawn from both ancient testimony and the surviving manuscripts supports the evangelical understanding of the Old Testament canon." An example of "ancient testimonies" is the works of Flavius Josephus (37-100 AD). "Josephus's statement in *Against Apion*," Hamilton writes, "also provides strong evidence on the Old Testament canon." The following is a quotation from Josephus (the footnote references are Hamilton's):

> Seeing that with us it is not open to everybody to write the records, and that there is no discrepancy in what is written;[2] seeing that, on the contrary, the prophets alone had this privilege, obtaining their knowledge of the most remote and ancient history through the inspiration which they owed to God,[3] and committing to writing a clear account of the events of their own time just as they occurred[4]—it follows, I say, that we do not possess myriads of inconsistent books, conflicting with each other. Our books, those which are justly accredited, are but two and twenty, and contain the record of all time. Of these, five are the books of Moses, comprising the laws and the traditional history from the birth of man down to the death of the lawgiver. This period falls only a little short of three thousand years. Form the death of Moses until Artaxerxes, who succeeded Xerxes as king of Persian,[5] the prophets subsequent to Moses wrote the history of the events of their own times in thirteen books.[6] The remaining four books[7] contain hymns to God and precepts for the conduct

---

2. ["Josephus clearly thinks that the writings of the Old Testament do not contradict each other."]

3. ["Josephus manifestly states that only the writings of prophets who were inspired by God were recognized as Scripture."]

4. ["Josephus states that the writings of the inspired prophets are perspicuous—clear account—and *historically accurate*—'just as they occurred.'"]

5. ["From this statement and the reference to Artaxerxes that follows a few phrases later, we see that Josephus regards the whole of the Old Testament to have been completed by around 465 BC."]

6. ["Probably (1) Joshua, (2) Judges and Ruth, (3) Samuel, (4) Kings, (5) Chronicles, (6) Ezra and miah, (7) Esther, (8) Job, (9) Isaiah, (10) Jeremiah, (11) Ezekiel, (12) Minor Prophets, (13) Daniel."]

7. ["Probably (1) Psalms, (2) Song of Songs, (3) Proverbs, (4) Ecclesiastes."]

of life. From Artaxerxes to our own time the complete history has been written, but has not been deemed worthy of equal credit with the earlier records, because of the failure of the exact succession of the prophets.[8] We have given practical proof of our reverence for our own Scriptures. For, although such long ages have now passed, no one has ventured either to add, or to remove, or to alter a syllable;[9] and it is an instinct with every Jew, from the day of his birth, to regard them as the decrees of God,[10] to abide by them, and, if need be, cheerfully to die for them.[11]

Earlier in his article, Hamilton points out that the "extra-canonical literature also testifies to" the reality that "the sixty six books of the protestant canon have been recognized as inspired."

Does this mean that without the testimony of Josephus and other ancient non-biblical writers that the books that make up the Old Testament canon would be unsupportable? Hamilton would never argue this way. So why is it appropriate for him to use extra-canonical sources to support his argument for the full inclusion of the books of the Old Testament into the biblical canon, but it's inappropriate for preterists to appeal to Josephus (an eyewitness) to corroborate what

---

8. ["Josephus draws a firm line between the Old Testament and the Apocrypha, and his basis for drawing that line is the fact that the Apocrypha were not written by inspired prophets."]

9. ["It is not difficult to harmonize the evidence that some things in the OT were updated with what Josephus says here about nothing being altered. From his statements that—it is not open to everybody to write the records—and from his assertion that only inspired prophets had the privilege, we can also say the following: while anyone might undertake an effort to edit or alter a text previously recognized as sacred Scripture, from what Josephus says we have evidence that the community would only accept alterations or updates done by those recognized as inspired by the Holy Spirit. Therefore, the evidence would seem to allow for someone like Ezra, who was recognized as an inspired author of Scripture, to update place names and perhaps arrange the final form of the Psalter. See further Michael A. Grisanti, 'Inspiration, Inerrancy, and the OT Canon: The Place of Textual Updating in an Inerrant View of Scripture,' *JETS* 44 (2001), 577-98."]

10. ["Josephus indicates that all Jews regard these twenty two books, which can be identified as the thirty nine books of the Protestant Old Testament, as the unalterable, error free, authoritative, inspired word of God. On the reference to the twenty two books of the Old Testament, see Beckwith, *The Old Testament Canon of the New Testament Church*, 235-40, 263-64."]

11. [Josephus, *Against Apion*, trans. J. St. J. Thackeray, LCL (Cambridge: Harvard University Press, 1926), 1.37-42 (LCL 186:177-81).]

Jesus predicted about the destruction of Jerusalem found in the Olivet Discourse?

Why is it OK to use Josephus as a supporting testimony in one case but not the other? Hamilton commits what has become known as the "Taxicab Fallacy," someone who pursues a line of reasoning to defend his worldview but then jumps out of the system when the same line of reasoning is used against it. It's OK to ride in the Josephus taxi on some topics but not when it comes to supporting a preterist view of eschatology.

Like Hamilton, who first appeals to the Bible in "The Witness of the OT to Its Own Canonicity" and only secondarily to non-biblical sources, preterists begin with the "witness" of Jesus to His own testimony and only secondarily to non-biblical historical sources like Josephus, Suetonius, and Tacitus. Preterists agree with Hamilton when he writes, "The Old Testament bears witness to its own canonicity by evidencing a recognition of certain writings as those in which God has spoken."

Preterists argue in the same way when they contend that the Olivet Discourse is a prophetic description of events leading up to and including the destruction of the temple and the divine judgment on Jerusalem that took place in AD 70. Jesus' words as recorded by the three gospel writers bear witness to the argument that the first-century destruction of Jerusalem in AD 70 is in view based on a number of contextual factors like audience reference (second person plural "you"), the way "this generation" is used repeatedly in the gospels to mark out that present generation as the affected generation, and actual references to fulfilled events (e.g., earthquakes, false prophets, famines, persecution, tribulation, etc.).

Taking Hamilton's opening sentence introducing his use of biblical sources in support of the canonicity question, I've reformulated it and applied it to the preterist understanding of Jesus' pronouncement about the destruction of Jerusalem that would take place within a generation and would mark the end of the old covenant age (Matt. 24:3; 1 Cor. 10:11; Heb. 1:1-2; 9:26; 1 Peter 4:7): The New Testament bears witness to its own revelatory character by appealing to "certain writings as those in which God has spoken," namely, Jesus' own words in the Olivet Discourse found in Matthew 24, Mark 13, and Luke 21.

## Historical Validation

While the Bible is the best interpreter of itself, it helps to have non-biblical historical sources from the same time period to help flesh out details not found in Scripture and to support what is found in the biblical text. The writings of Josephus are some of those historical works. We would be foolish to ignore them.

Entire fields of study are based on digging up the past looking for collateral historical information to shed light on the biblical record. As we saw, Hamilton follows this approach for canonicity. Others in the evangelical community follow a similar methodology. A good example is Edwin Yamauchi's *The Stones and the Scriptures: An Evangelical Perspective* (1972). Biblical archeology is a growing field of study that adds to our understanding of the background of Scripture.[12]

Josephus offers eye-witness testimony of the siege and destruction of Jerusalem. Biblical scholars dream of having such material to compare to the testimony of Scripture. F. J. Foakes Jackson writes:

> No one interested in the study of the methods of ancient historians, or even of the sources of the record of facts of Scripture, can dispense with Josephus. In the New Testament, especially, scholars recognise a variety of sources for the Gospels and Acts. As their predecessors had done in regard to the Old Testament, they have realised that earlier documents were employed to produce the Hebrew and Christian books as we now have them.
>
> ******
>
> For the Jewish war and its terrific consequences Josephus is our only contemporary authority, most of Tacitus' account being hopelessly lost; and there is no orderly record from any other Jewish source in existence.[13]

---

12. James K. Hoffmeier, *The Archeology of the Bible* (Oxford, England: Lion Hudson, 2008).

13. F. J. Foakes Jackson, *Josephus and the Jews: The Religion and History of the Jews Explained by Flavius Josephus* (Grand Rapids, MI: Baker Book House, [1930] 1977), xiii, 181. For a more recent study, see Karen M. Kletter, "The Christian Reception of Josephus in Late Antiquity and the Middle Ages," *A Companion to Josephus,* Honora Howell Chapman and Zuleika Rodgers, eds. (Hoboken, NJ: Wiley-Blackwell, 2016).

In the short time I had at the Symposium to respond directly to Hamilton's absurd charge about Josephus, I pointed out that Jesus' words are alone sufficient that the Olivet Discourse is about the judgment of Jerusalem and the destruction of the temple that took place within a generation as Jesus predicted in the synoptic gospels. If Josephus' history had never existed, we would still believe Jesus when He said, "not one stone here will be left upon another, which will not be torn down" (24:2), and "this generation will not pass away until all these things take place" (24:34).

Jesus referred to the temple the disciples saw and pointed out to Him (24:2), the temple that Jesus said would be left to "this generation" (23:36)—their own generation—"desolate" (23:38). Coupled with the meaning of "this generation" (24:34) and how it always refers to the generation to whom Jesus was speaking, there is no need for extra-biblical historical information to verify what Jesus predicted. The thing of it is, we do have eyewitness testimony to what Jesus predicted and for that we should be thankful.

The fact that we do have the works of Josephus to corroborate the testimony of Scripture is looked upon by nearly all Christian scholars as a providential gift.

> Joseph son of Matthias, better known as Flavius Josephus—surnamed after his patron, the Roman Emperor Titus Flavius—was the greatest Jewish historian of antiquity. Without his work, much of the contemporaneous history of Israel would be floating in a vacuum. Josephus's vignettes concerning Jesus, John the Baptist and Jesus's brother, James, are the only pieces of outside evidence relating to first-century New Testament figures.
>
> ******
>
> The survival of Josephus's writings is due largely to the respect with which they were held by Christians because of the references to New Testament characters in the Antiquities. He almost enjoyed the dignity of a fifth evangelist and had a statue in Rome in the fourth century.[14]

---

14. Geza Vermes, "Jesus in the Eyes of Josephus," Standpoint (January/February 2010): http://standpointmag.co.uk/node/2507/full

A study of Church history shows that the works of Josephus were consulted by Christians very early. Heinz Schreckenberg and Kurt Schubert trace the use of the works of Josephus to the earliest of the ante-Nicene fathers beginning, possibly, with Clement of Rome (died *c.* 101), Melito of Sardis (died *c.* 190), Irenaeus (died *c.* 202), Tertullian (*c.* 160-*c.* 225), Hippolytus (170-235), and others. While the New Testament canon "was not compiled until the end of the second century, ... the reception of Josephus by early Christianity" had already begun "in this period."[15]

Schreckenberg and Schubert see a number of parallels between the Olivet Discourse, especially Luke's version, and Josephus' *Wars of the Jews*:

> For example, Luke 21:24 ('they will be carried captive into all countries') fits hand in glove with War 3:540; 6:384, 414-418 (the sale of captured Jews into slavery), a possibility already realized with much generalization and exaggeration by Eusebius, when he has 'the entire Jewish people' ... being sent into Roman slavery (GCS [*Die Griechischen Christlichen Schriftsteller*] 23:349, 17-20). Other Christian theologians referred Luke 21:23 to the shocking *teknophagia*[16] by Maria (War 6:301-213) [who because of hunger cooks and eats her own child]. Once Christian eyes had been opened to these possibilities, they divined that fall of Jerusalem already from the Old Testament (e.g., Dan. 9:26); just as in general since early Christian days or at the latest by the Middle Ages, New Testament words of doom and judgement of the most various kinds were seen as fulfilled in the events of [AD] 70 (e.g., Matt. 21:19-20, 33-46; 22:1-4).[17]

My presentation at the Symposium began with a full contextual study of the Olivet Discourse beginning with when Jesus "had approached Jerusalem and had come to Bethphage, at the Mount of Olives" (Matt. 21:1). I continued with chapters 22 and 23 and finally gave a quick verse-by-verse exposition of the 24th chapter with only one reference to Josephus, the same one mentioned above by

---

15. Heinz Schreckenberg and Kurt Schubert, *Jewish Historiography and Iconography in Early Medieval Christianity* (Minneapolis: Fortress Press, 1992), 41.

16. Eating of children.

17. Schreckenberg and Schubert, *Jewish Historiography and Iconography*, 132.

Schreckenberg and Schubert, the story of Mary who cooked and ate her own child.

Let's see how other Christian historians and scholars view the works of Josephus, beginning with the fourth-century historian Eusebius Pamphilius (*c.* 265-339) in his *Ecclesiastical History*:

> It is fitting to add to these accounts the true prediction of our Savior in which he foretold these very events. His words are as follows: "Woe unto them that are with child, and to them that give suck in those days! But pray ye that your flight be not in the winter, neither on the Sabbath day; For there shall be great tribulation, such as was not since the beginning of the world to this time, no, nor ever shall be" [Matt. 24:19-21]. The historian [Josephus], reckoning the whole number of the slain, says that eleven hundred thousand persons perished by famine and sword, and that the rest of the rioters and robbers, being betrayed by each other after the taking of the city, were slain. ... These things took place in this manner in the second year of the reign of Vespasian, in accordance with the prophecies of our Lord and Savior Jesus Christ, who by divine power saw them beforehand as if they were already present, and wept and mourned according to the statement of the holy evangelists, who give the very words which be uttered, when, as if addressing Jerusalem herself, he said: "If thou hadst known, even thou, in this day, the things which belong unto thy peace! But now they are hid from thine eyes. For the days shall come upon thee, that thine enemies shall cast a rampart about thee, and compass thee round, and keep thee in on every side, and shall lay thee and thy children even with the ground" [Luke 19:42]. And then, as if speaking concerning the people, he says, "For there shall be great distress in the land, and wrath upon this people. And they shall fall by the edge of the sword, and shall be led away captive into all nations. And Jerusalem shall be trodden down of the Gentiles, until the times of the Gentiles be fulfilled" [Luke 21:23-24]. And again: "When ye shall see Jerusalem compassed with armies, then know that the desolation thereof is nigh" [Luke 21:20]. If anyone compares the words of our Savior with the other accounts of

the historian [Josephus] concerning the whole war, how can one fail to wonder, and to admit that the foreknowledge and the prophecy of our Savior were truly divine and marvelously strange (Book III, Ch. VII).

Robert E. Van Voorst, *Jesus Outside the New Testament: An Introduction to the Ancient Evidence:*[18]

One of the reasons Christians copied Josephus's works was that they provided rich information on a few figures of the New Testament, especially John the Baptizer, James the leader of the early Jerusalem church, and Jesus.

Steve Mason, *Josephus and the New Testament:*

Every student of the Bible realizes that Josephus is extremely significant for New Testament study. He was born in AD 37, just a few years after Jesus' death and not much later than Paul's conversion to Christianity. He grew up in Jerusalem ... Thus Josephus' works offer us a potential gold mine for understanding the world of the New Testament as well as being a resource that is not even remotely paralleled in another ancient writer.[19]

Cleon L. Rogers, Jr., *The Topical Josephus:*

The importance of Josephus for the study of the New Testament cannot be stressed enough. It would not be an overstatement to say that, if it were possible to have only one work to use in a study of the New Testament, the writings of Joseph ben Mattias, better known as Flavius Josephus (or just Josephus) would be the correct choice.... His life as a Jewish priest, Pharisee, and Jewish army general in charge of Galilee, and his being an eyewitness of the Roman destruction of Jerusalem in AD 70 make him well qualified to give firsthand information about life in Palestine during the New Testament period.[20]

---

18. Robert E. Van Voorst, *Jesus Outside the New Testament* (Grand Rapids, MI: Eerdmans, 2000), 83.

19. Steve Mason, *Josephus and the New Testament* (Peabody, MA: Hendrickson Publishers, 1992), 2.

20. Cleon L. Rogers, Jr., The Topical Josephus: Historical Accounts that Shed Light on the Bible (Grand Rapids, MI: Zondervan, 1992), 11.

Darrell L. Bock and Gregory J. Herrick, eds., *Jesus in Context: Background Readings for Gospel Study*:

> When we think of the history of Judaism during the first century AD and about the first century in general, pride of place goes to the pro-Roman, Jewish general and historian Josephus (AD 37- c. 100). Without him, we would know far less about this period. His four works give an account ranging from the time of Genesis to Jerusalem's fall in AD 70 and the resulting political fallout.... At one time in the West's educational system, Josephus was the text read most after the Bible.[21]

During the Symposium, Hamilton said if the destruction of Jerusalem was the fulfillment of the Olivet Discourse, then why didn't the biblical writers comment about the subject after the event? The answer is quite simple: The New Testament books were written before AD 70. John A. T. Robinson, in his book *Redating the New Testament*,[22] developed the thesis that every New Testament book was written before the destruction of Jerusalem, including the book of Revelation. There are many events recorded in the Bible that are not found in non-biblical historical works. Consider everything from the announcement to Zechariah that his wife Elizabeth would give birth to John the Baptist and the ascension of Jesus into heaven and much of what is in between.

There aren't many historical works from the first century that touch on the period, so to find a source as complete as the works of Josephus of that period of history is a providential find of the first order.

Through a process of discovery, I found that a preterist interpretation of the Olivet Discourse was a common feature in commentaries and in various narrative-style books that describe the fall of Jerusalem in AD 70 as it is outlined in the Olivet Discourse of the synoptic gospels.

• Thomas Newton, *Dissertations on the Prophecies* (1754). Newton, like James Hamilton, was a premillennialist, but

21. Darrell L. Bock and Gregory J. Herrick, eds., *Jesus in Context: Background Readings for Gospel Study* (Grand Rapids, MI: Baker Academic, 2005), 19-20.
22. John A. T. Robinson, *Redating the New Testament* (London: SCM Press Ltd., 1976).

unlike Hamilton, Newton is a preterist when it comes to much of the Olivet Discourse.

- miah Nisbett, *The Prophecy of the Destruction of Jerusalem* (1787).[23]
- George Halford, *The Destruction of Jerusalem: An Absolute and Irresistible Proof of the Divine Origin of Christianity, etc* (1805).
- William Patton, *The Judgment of Jerusalem Predicted in Scripture, Fulfilled in History* (1876).
- Alfred J. Church, *The Story of the Last Days of Jerusalem* (1902).

There are also numerous editions of Alexander Keith's (1791-1880) *Evidence of the Truth of the Christian Religion Derived from the Literal Fulfillment of Prophecy, etc.*, first published in 1832, in which he includes a chapter on "The Destruction of Jerusalem." It went through numerous editions and many printings.

Keith's apologetic work on prophecy was designed to counter liberal claims that the Bible is merely the work of men. Bible prophecy, Keith maintained, demonstrated that this was an impossible claim that could not be defended in terms of many examples of fulfilled prophecy. Edward Giddings, in his book *American Christian Rulers*, "relates how Keith's book was instrumental in persuading Supreme Court chief justice John Marshall of the messianic claims of Jesus Christ in the days before his death on July 6, 1835."[24] The following is from Giddings:

[Marshall] believed in the truth of the Christian revelation, but not in the divinity of Christ; therefore he could not commune in the Episcopal Church. But, during the last months of his life, he read Keith on Prophecy, where our Saviour's divinity is incidentally treated, and was convinced by his work, and the fuller investigation to which it led, of the supreme divinity of the Saviour.[25]

---

23. Republished as *The Destruction of Jerusalem, the Mysterious Language of St. Paul's Description of the Man of Sin, and the Day of the Lord* (Powder Springs, GA: American Vision, 2023).

24. Eric Rauch, Publisher's Foreword, Alexander Keith, *Evidence of the Truth of the Christian Religion: Derived from the Literal Fulfillment of Prophecy* (White Hall, WV: Tolle Lege Press, [1834] 2011), v.

25. Edward Giddings, *American Christian Rulers, or Religion and Men of Government* (New York: Bromfield and Company, 1889), 332. *American Christian Rulers* was reprinted by

Keith used a number of extra-biblical sources, as do almost every Bible expositor, ancient and modern, to offer support for the biblical record regarding fulfilled prophecy. It was no different when he came to the Olivet Discourse as this citation from Philip Doddridge's (1702-1751) *Family Expositor*, first published in six volumes from 1739 through 1756, shows:

> The particular parts of the whole discourse have been admirably illustrated by many learned commentators. Christian writers have always, with great reason, represented *Josephus's History of the Jewish War*, as the best *commentary on this chapter*, (Matt. xxiv.) and many have justly remarked it, as a wonderful instance of the care of Providence for the *Christian church*, that *he*, an eye witness, and in these things of so great credit, should (especially in such an extraordinary manner) be *preserved*, to transmit to us a collection of important facts, which so exactly illustrate this noble prophecy in almost every circumstance.[26]

In the Preface to the 1785 Maynard Edition of *The Whole Genuine and Complete Works of Flavius Josephus*, the following comment is made by the translator George Henry Maynard:

> The Works of Josephus have ever been held by the pious and learned of all ages in the highest veneration, from their acknowledged tendency to elucidate the sacred records in particular, and promote the acquisition of History in general.[27]

The works of Josephus find a key place among Bible commentators and Christian historians. William Wotton (1666-1727) says of Josephus,

> He is certainly an author very justly to be valued, notwithstanding all his faults. His history of the Jewish war is a noble demonstration of the truth of the Christian religion: by showing, in the most lively manner, how the prophecies of our

American Vision Press, Powder Springs, Georgia, in 2011. The corresponding page number in the new edition is 348.

26. Philip Doddridge, *The Family Expositor; or, A Paraphrase and Version of the New Testament; with Critical Notes and A Practical Improvement on each Section*, 6 vols. 8th ed. (Charlestown, MA: Etheridge and Co., 1807), 2:360, note e.

27. London: Printed for J. Cooke, 1785.

blessed Lord, concerning the destruction of Jerusalem, were literally fulfilled in their fullest extent.[28]

Archbishop John Tillotson (1630-1694) delivered several sermons under the title "The Evidences of the Truth of the Christian Religion" in which he expounded on the remarkable fulfillment of Jesus' prophecy about the destruction of Jerusalem based on the Olivet Discourse.

After devoting a considerable amount of space to the biblical material found in the three gospel accounts of the Olivet Discourse, Tillotson adds to the biblical evidence by referencing Josephus:

Not only those who lived in that Age were capable of Satisfaction concerning the Accomplishment of this Prediction of our Saviour; but that we also might receive full Satisfaction concerning this, the Providence of God hath so order'd it, as to preserve to us a more punctual credible History of the Destruction of *Jerusalem*, than there is of any mother Matter whatsoever so long since done.

And this is more considerable, than possible at first we may imagine, For, We have this Matter related, not by a Christian, (who might be suspected of Partiality and a Design to have parallel'd the Event with our Saviour's prediction,) but by a *Jew*, both by Nation and Religion, who seems designedly to have avoided, as much as possibly he could, the very mention of the Christian Name, and all particulars relating to our Saviour, though no Historian was ever more punctual in other things.

We have this Matter related by one that was an Eye-witness of all those sad Calamities that befell the Nation of the *Jews,* and during the War in *Galilee* against *Vespasian,* was one of their Chief Commanders, and being taken by the Romans, was in their Camp all the time that *Jerusalem* was besieged.

As he was an Eye-witness, and so able to give the truest Account of those Matters, so hath he always had the Repute of a most faithful Historian....

---

28. William Wotton, Preface, *Miscellaneous Discourses Relating to the Traditions and Usages of the Scribes and Pharisees in our Blessed Saviour Jesus Christ's Time* (London: Printed by W. Bowyer for Tim. Goodwin, 1718), 49.

There is no ancient History extant, that relates any Matter with so much particularity of circumstances, as *Josephus* does this of the *Jewish* Wars, especially the Siege and Destruction of *Jerusalem*.

That the Providence of God may appear the more remarkable in this History, which is the only punctual one that hath been preserved down to us of this great Action, it will be worth our Observation to consider, how remarkably this Person was preserved for the writing of this History.[29]

Similar to this is the testimony of M. Tillemont (1637-1698) who had "a reputation for accuracy, detail and conscientiousness."

God has been pleased to choose for our information in this history, not an apostle, nor any of the chief men of the church, but an obstinate Jew, whom neither the view of the virtue and miracles of the Christians, nor the knowledge of the law, nor the ruin of his religion and country, could induce to believe in and love the Messiah, who was all the expectation of the nation. God has permitted it so to be, that the testimony which this historian gave to an event, of which he did not comprehend the mystery, might not be rejected either by Jews or Heathens: and that none might be able to say, that he had altered the truth of things to favour Jesus Christ and his disciples.[30]

Even earlier (fifth century) we find the comments of Isidore of Pelusium:

If you have a mind to know what punishment the wicked Jews underwent, who ill-treated the Christ, read the history of their destruction, writ by Josephus, a Jew indeed, but a lover or truth, that you may see the wonderful story, such as no time ever saw before since the beginning of the world, nor ever shall be. For that none might refuse to give credit to the history of their incredible and unparalleled sufferings, truth found out not a

---

29. John Tillotson, "The Evidences of the Truth of the Christian Religion," *The Works of the Most Reverend Dr. John Tillotson*, 2 vols., 3rd ed. (London: Printed for Benjamin and Samuel Tooke, *et al.*, 1732), 2:563-564. Sermon 186.

30. Sébastien LeNain de Tillemont, *Qui comprend la ruine des Juifs* [*Which includes the Destruction of the Jews*] (1692), *Art, I.* p. 722.

stranger, but a native, and a man fond of their institutions, to relate them in a doleful strain.[31]

Joseph Sievers, writing for the Pontifical Biblical Institute in Rome, Italy, states the following:

During the Middle Ages, Josephus was the most widely read ancient author in Europe. Schreckenberg, here following Eisler, states that Josephus' literary influence had no equals, with the sole exception of the Bible. Over 130 Greek and about 230 Latin [manuscripts], and innumerable citations in later authors are telling signs of a broad interest in his works. There is also a large number of early prints of Josephus' works. Between 1470 and 1535 there were over twenty printings of Latin translations of Josephus.[32]

Here are some of conclusions by Karen M. Kletter:

The influence and role of Josephus in Christian tradition are so vast and primordial and intersect with so many strands of interpretation and historical *topoi* that they remain difficult to characterize.... I've only touched the surface on this topic being limited by time and access to a seminary library.... Josephan material was pervasive in Christian exegetical and historical tradition, in a variety of contexts that crossed generic lines. Josephus offered a link to Christianity's Jewish and Roman past, for example, in certain readings of the Hebrew Bible, or in Jewish War's convincing narrative for the displacement of the Jews by the Christians as God's chosen in its dramatic account of the Roman destruction of Jewish Jerusalem. The past that was encountered by Christians using Josephus's works was unencumbered by associations with the Jewish present or with the ancient world's pagan sensibilities.... Christian authors interested in history recognized that the works of Josephus

---

31. Samuel Burder, Editor's Preface (1811), *The Genuine Works of Flavius* Josephus, 4 vols. (New York: William Borradaile, 1823), 1:vii. Also see H. Schreckenberg and K. Schubert, *Jewish Traditions in Early Christian Literature* (Leiden and Boston: Brill Academic Pub (1992), 79-80.

32. Joseph Sievers, "New Resources for the Study of Josephus" (2000).

were capable of linking and aiding in the interpretation of events across historical, geographical, and cultural divides.[33]

James Hamilton's claim that preterism would not exist if preterists did not have the works of Josephus is an opinion with no historical substance. Preterist interpretations of the Olivet Discourse begin with the text of Scripture as I demonstrated in my Symposium presentation and all my books and articles dealing with eschatology. Josephus is a helpful secondary, although not inspired, historical source. Even so, the history of the church shows that the works of Josephus were consulted regularly and not just by preterists. As in this chapter, even James Hamilton appealed to Josephus as a reliable historical source.

---

33. Kletter, "The Christian Reception of Josephus in Late Antiquity and the Middle Ages," 379-380.

# CHAPTER 6

# Isaiah 17 Fulfilled

B ecause of the latest developments in Syria and the Middle East generally, prophecy prognosticators are coming out of the woodwork ... again. The same thing happened in 2011 when prophecy hobbyists claimed Isaiah 17 was being fulfilled right before our eyes. Here's an example from a video that was uploaded on July 21, 2011:

> Damascus in Isaiah 17 is going to be destroyed in 1 day. **This is about to occur in our lifetime in just a matter of months**. It's in the news and everywhere you look! This is going to fulfill one of the biggest biblical prophecies of all time! Be ready for Christ's Return after this occurs! I hope this gives you hope of His coming!

Notice the time reference: "in just a matter of months" from July 2011. This makes it a false prophecy about a true prophecy that was fulfilled nearly 2,700 years ago. Never learning and people forgetting, the claim is being made again that the events prophesied in Isaiah 17 about Damascus were never fully fulfilled in history, and like clockwork, naïve Christians are getting sucked in.

The topic has even gotten attention from the mainstream media. *TIME* magazine picked up on the story. So did the *Huffington Post, Mother Jones*, and *USA Today* among other media outlets. Glenn Beck's *The Blaze* ran an extended article on the topic: "Why Some Believe These 'End Times' Bible Verses Could Hold the Key to the Syrian Crisis."

Not all end-time prognosticators teach that the Damascus prophecy is being fulfilled in our day. Surprisingly, Dr. Charles Dyer, who is a professor at the Moody Bible Institute in Chicago, argues that Damascus "was destroyed in the 7th and 8th centuries" BC. I say surprisingly since in 1991 he wrote *The Rise of Babylon: Sign of the End Times* in which he claimed that present-day Iraq under Saddam Hussein was the Babylon of Isaiah 13 and Revelation (16:19; 17:5; 18:2, 10, 21). He maintained that Saddam Hussein's building program was proof that Babylon would rise from the desert sands in fulfillment of Bible prophecy.

Dyer's book even had Saddam in a Nebuchadnezzar look-a-like pose with the following caption:

SADDAM HUSSEIN and the ancient world conqueror Nebuchadnezzar. Not only do they look alike, but their mission is the same—to control the world. And the symbol of this world domination is an ancient city [Babylon].....

It's obvious that Dyer took a different approach when it came to the Damascus prophecy:

Isaiah 17 predicted the destruction of the city, along with the destruction of the northern kingdom of Israel.... Damascus was captured by Assyrians in 732 BC and the northern kingdom of Israel fell when the capital city of Samaria was captured by the Assyrians in 722 BC.

And 100 years later, the prophet Jeremiah also predicted the fall of Damascus, which had been rebuilt, he added. "His message was fulfilled when the city was captured by Nebuchadnezzar of Babylon."

In addition to Dyer, dispensational author Mark Hitchcock, who sees prophetic fulfillment in everything that's going on today, makes the case that the Damascus prophecy has been fulfilled. After offering a helpful critique of some speculative interpretations of the Isaiah 17 prophecy, Hitchcock offers this cogent commentary:

I believe it makes more sense to hold that Isaiah 17 was fulfilled in the eighth century BC when both Damascus, the capital of Syria, and Samaria, the capital of Israel, were hammered by the Assyrians. In that conquest, both Damascus and Samaria were destroyed, just as Isaiah 17 predicts. According to history, Tiglath-pileser III (745-727 BC) pushed vigorously to the west, and in 734 the Assyrians advanced and laid siege to Damascus, which fell two years later in 732.[1]

It's unfortunate that Hitchcock couldn't leave well enough alone. At the end of the chapter he writes, "Having said that, I do believe that events today in Syria point toward the fulfillment of biblical prophecies that

---

1. Mark Hitchcock, *Middle East Burning: Is the Spreading Unrest as Sign of the End Times?* (Eugene, OR: Harvest House Publishers, 2012), 176.

have not yet come to pass." He claims that "the stage is being set for a Middle East peace treaty prophesied in Daniel 9:27."[2] There is no mention of a Middle East peace treaty in Daniel 9:27, an antichrist, a gap of nearly 2,000 years, a rebuilt temple, a covenant with the Jews, etc.[3]

Even Tim LaHaye's *Prophecy Study Bible* concludes that the Isaiah 17 prophecy was fulfilled when "God used Tiglath-pileser of Syria to destroy Damascus in 732 BC"[4] Notice the word "destroy." The same is true of the comment on the passage found in *The Apologetics Study Bible*:

> Damascus continued to be a city in the OT era (Ezk 27:18), the NT (Ac 9:19-27), and today. This does not negate Isaiah's prophecy, which referred to the destruction of Damascus as the powerful capital of Syria during the Syro-Ephraimite War. His words were consistent with his prophecy about the fall of Damascus in 7:7-8 and 8:4, and his announcement that Assyria defeated Damascus and exiled its inhabitants to Kir (2 Kg 16:9). After many years in ruin, it later became a small city in the Assyrian province of Hamath. Isaiah was not claiming that it would remain a ruin for all time.[5]

I've written articles about how modern-day prophecy writers twist and distort prophetic texts that end up being used by skeptics to call the authority of the Bible into question. Biblical skeptic Tim Callahan follows the arguments of today's prophecy watchers and concludes along with them that the prophecy has not been fulfilled, thus, making it a false prophecy. He writes, Damascus "has been sacked numerous times, to be sure. But the prophecy explicitly states that it would cease to be a city forever, and the prophecy is explicitly wrong. Curiously, neither Gleason Archer[6] nor Josh McDowell[7] mentions this failed

---

2. Hitchcock, *Middle East Burning*, 178.

3. See Gary DeMar, *Last Days Madness: Obsession of the Modern Church*, 4th ed. (Powder Springs, GA: American Vision, 1999), chap. 25.

4. Tim LaHaye, gen. ed., *Tim LaHaye Prophecy Study Bible* (Chattanooga: AMG Publishers, 2000), 707, note on 17:1-14.

5. Gary Smith, "Isaiah," *The Apologetics Study Bible*, gen. ed. Ted Cabal (Nashville: Holman Bible Publishers, 2007), 1015, note on 17:1.

6. Gleason L. Archer, *Encyclopedia of Bible Difficulties* (Grand Rapids, MI: Zondervan, 1982).

7. Josh McDowell, *Evidence that Demands a Verdict* (San Bernardino, CA: Here's Life Publishers, 1979).

prophecy."[8] The reason is clear as to why they don't. The Hebrew text does not include the word "forever" in 17:2. More about this below.

Here are five contemporary examples from evangelical, Bible-believing prophecy writers who claim—like the skeptic Callahan—that the Damascus prophecy found in Isaiah 17 (and Jer. 49:23-27) has not been fulfilled:

- **Joel C. Rosenberg**: "These prophecies have not yet been fulfilled. Damascus is one of the oldest continuously inhabited cities on earth. It has been attacked, besieged, and conquered. But Damascus has never been completely destroyed and left uninhabited. Yet that is exactly what the Bible says will happen."

- **Jan Markell**, founder and director of Minnesota-based Olive Tree Ministries, says "the Syrians' use of chemical weapons makes her think about Isaiah 17, which foretells the complete destruction of Damascus, which hasn't happened in thousands of years."

- **Harry Bultema**: "The judgment that will strike Damascus is that it will be no longer a city but a *ruinous heap*. This prediction has yet to be completely fulfilled, for in Jeremiah's day it was a flourishing city, and even today is said to be the oldest city in the world (cf. Genesis 15:2 where Damascus is already mentioned). According to II Kings 16:9 Tiglath-pileser captured it and killed its king Rezin; but he did not make it *a heap*."[9]

- **Thomas Ice**: "Most commentators contend that Isaiah 17:1-3 was fulfilled in 732 BC at the conquest of Tiglath-pileser.[10] However, Tiglath-pileser did not totally destroy the city, but merely captured it, as has happened numerous times throughout its history."

- **Britt Gillette**: "In the very near future, Damascus will once again play a major role in human events. The prophet Isaiah

---

8. Tim Callahan, *Bible Prophecy: Failure or Fulfillment?* (Altadena, CA: Millennium Press, 1997), 60-61.

9. Harry Bultema, *Commentary on Isaiah* (Grand Rapids: Kregel Publishers, 1981), 184.

10. For example, Peter A. Steveson, *A Commentary on Isaiah* (Greenville, SC: BJU Press, 2003), 142. See also, John D. W. Watts, *Word Biblical Commentary: Isaiah 1-33*, rev. ed. (Nashville: Thomas Nelson, 2005), 293.

provides us with God's commentary on a future conflict between Damascus and Israel, and in so doing, he reveals certain prophecies which have been partially fulfilled in the past. However, the ultimate fulfillment of Isaiah 17 remains in the future."

You get the picture. According to the above comments, the belief among futurists is that Isaiah 17, and its counterpart in Jeremiah 49:23-27, have not been completely fulfilled because Damascus is still in existence. How can a prediction about cities that would become a "heap of ruins" still be in existence today?

## Forever and Ever?

The first item that needs to be discussed is the addition of "forever" to Isaiah 17:2 that is not found in the majority of Bible translations. The *TIME* magazine article offers this translation of Isaiah 17:1-2: "See, Damascus will cease to be a city and will become a heap of ruins. Her towns will be deserted forever." I've checked numerous translations, and only a few include the word "forever." The Revised Standard Version reads "her cities will be deserted forever," while the New American Standard version includes a marginal note that includes the phrase "forever."

The use of "forever" is based on the Septuagint (LXX) Greek translation of Isaiah 17:1-2 that reads as follows:

See, Damascus will be removed from among cities
and will become a ruin, abandoned forever,
to be a fold and resting place for flocks,
and there will be no one to drive them away

The translations that do not include the word "forever" follow the Hebrew text. The LXX uses the phrase εἰς τὸν αἰῶνα (*eis ton aiōna* = "into the ages") to translate a disputed Hebrew word. The "forever" translation is based on the Hebrew word "Aroer" which in other contexts is the name of a city.

The *Hebrew and English Lexicon of the Old Testament* considers the word עֲרֹעֵר to be a proper noun, a place, a particular city named "Aroer"—"a Biblical town on the north bank of the River Arnon to the east of the Dead Sea, in present-day Jordan." There are three cities in the Bible named Aroer, "one in the territory of Judah (1 Sam. xxx. 28), one at the southern extremity of the land of Israel east of Jordan (Jos. xii. 2, xii, 6), a third farther north and near to Rabbah (Jos. xiii. 25, Num xxxii. 24)."[11]

I checked numerous commentaries and found several[12] that follow the LXX translation and others[13] that mention the LXX variation but do not follow it. So why the difference in translation? How does the city "Aroer" become the phrase "abandoned forever" in Greek? A little knowledge of the Hebrew alphabet is necessary in order to understand why the LXX translators came up with εἰς τὸν αἰῶνα ("into the ages") in Isaiah 17:2. The Hebrew letters r (ר) and d (ד) are similar in shape and form. The resh (ר) is rounded while the daleth (ד) is squared on their right corners. So arõ 'er (עֲרֹעֵר = Aroer) becomes 'adê ad (עַד־עַד) for the LXX translators. The double use of the Hebrew עַד is translated as "forever and ever" elsewhere in Isaiah (e.g., Isa. 30:8; 32:14, 17; 34:17; 59:21).

Other than the LXX, there does not seem to be any reason to adopt changing the Hebrew letters. These comments from the *Pulpit Commentary* are interesting and might shed light on the historicity of the city of Aroer as it relates to the Damascus prophecy:

> Sargon's annals tell us of a "Gal'gar," a name well expressing the Hebrew רערע, which was united in a league with Damascus, Samaria, Arpad, and Simyra, in the second year of Sargon, and was the scene of a great battle and a great destruction. Sargon besieged it, took it, and reduced it to ashes ('Records of the Past,' 50. s.e.). There is every reason to recognize the "Aroer" of this verse in the "Gargar" of Sargon's inscriptions. **They shall be for flocks** (comp. Isaiah 5:17; 7:25). It marked the very extreme of desolation, that cattle should be pastured on the sites of cities. **None shall make them afraid**; i.e. "there shall be no inhabitants to make any objection."

John N. Oswalt notes that the Hebrew construction "the cities of Aroer" constitutes "a very special wordplay"[14] that 'adê ad (עַד־עַד) does

---

11. J. A. Alexander, *Commentary on the Prophecies of Isaiah*, 2 vols. in 1 (Grand Rapids, MI: Zondervan [1875] 1953), 1:333.

12. See George Buchanan Gray, *A Critical and Exegetical Commentary on the Book of Isaiah, I-XXXIX* (New York: Charles Scribner's Sons, 1912), 298.

13. See John A. Martin, "Isaiah," *The Bible Knowledge Commentary: Old Testament*, eds. John F. Walvoord and Roy B. Zuck (Victor Books/Scripture Press, 1985), 1064.

14. John N. Oswalt, *The Book of Isaiah: Chapters 1-39*, NICOT (Grand Rapids, MI:

not give. So it's most probable that the Hebrew is correct and the LXX's reworking of the Hebrew is based more on an interpretive hunch than actual manuscript evidence.

Contextually, Isaiah does not use עַד in places that describe the ultimate destinies of cities. This means that its use in Isaiah 17:2 would seem to be out of character with how עַד is used elsewhere in Isaiah and translated as "forever" (Isa. 9:6; 26:4; 30:8; 45:17; 57:15; 64:9; 65:18). Isaiah prefers to use the Hebrew word *olam* when he's describing the destruction of an enemy or city (14:20; 25:2; 32:14; 34:10).

Compare Isaiah 25:2 with 17:2 and notice that the Hebrew word *olam* is used for the word "forever" for an unnamed city:

> For You have made a city into a heap,
> A fortified city into a ruin;
> A palace of strangers
> is a city no more forever [*olam*],
> It will never be rebuilt.

We know from the history of the period that a number of cities were destroyed never to be rebuilt, for example, Babylon:

> And Babylon, the beauty of kingdoms,
> the glory of the Chaldeans' pride,
> Will be as when God overthrew Sodom and Gomorrah.
> It will never be inhabited or lived in
> from generation to generation;
> Nor will the Arab pitch his tent there,
> Nor will shepherds make their flocks lie down there
> (Isa. 13:19-20).

The use of *olam* in a context that is very similar to what's found in Isaiah 17:2 may be one of the reasons that the majority of translations stay with the Masoretic Hebrew text *arō 'ēr* (עֲרֹעֵר) instead of the LXX variation עַד־עַד since עוֹלָם (*olam*) is the preferred word used by Isaiah when the destruction of cities and nations are in view. So if the Hebrew is followed, there is nothing in Isaiah 17 that indicates that Damascus and its surrounding cities would be destroyed "forever."

---

Eerdmans, 1986), 348, note 3.

## Timing

"When" a prophet says a prophecy is to be fulfilled it's important to determine what events fulfilled the prophecy. Time indicators can tell us if the prophecy is going to be fulfilled in the distant future or in the near future. Sometimes a prophecy's fulfillment is open ended. The New American Standard has "Damascus is **about to be removed** from being a city" (Isa. 17:1). According to Oswalt in his commentary on Isaiah, the Hebrew construction "*hinnēh … mûsār* is a participial construction indicating imminent action, 'Behold, Damascus is on the point of being removed.'"[15]

Joel Rosenberg, who believes Isaiah 17 is a prophecy that has not been fulfilled, appeals to other chapters in Isaiah in an attempt to make his case that the Damascus prophecy is like Babylon, never really fulfilled:

In Isaiah 13, we read about the coming judgment/destruction of Babylon. But the context makes it clear that the prophecies will happen deep in the End Times, just prior to the Second Coming of Christ. In Isaiah 13:6, for example, we read, "Wail, for the Day of the Lord is near!" In Isaiah 13:9, we read, "Behold, the Day of the Lord is coming." Both of these references indicate that the prophecies concerning the destruction of Babylon will occur in the last days leading up to the "Day of the Lord," an eschatological biblical term that refers to the actual, literal, physical return of Christ to earth at the end of the Tribulation.

How can a prophecy state that "the Day of the Lord is near" (Isa. 13:6) when, according to Rosenberg, the prophecy hasn't been fulfilled yet? John Walvoord, who Rosenberg quotes approvingly, makes a valuable comment about the multi-faceted character and application of the meaning of the Bible's use of "the day of the Lord": "The 'Day of the Lord' is an expression frequently used in both the Old and New Testaments to describe any period of time during which God exercises direct judgment on human sin. The Old Testament records a number of times when Israel endured a day of the Lord, lasting a few days or, in some cases, several years."[16]

---

15. Oswalt, *The Book of Isaiah: Chapters 1-39*, 348, note 1.

16. John F. Walvoord, *Prophecy: 14 Essential Keys to Understanding the Final Drama* (Nashville, TN: Thomas Nelson, 1993), 114-15.

"Day of the Lord" is not code for "deep in the End Times, just prior to the Second Coming of Christ." Consider these extended remarks by dispensational prophecy writer Ronald Showers on the meaning of "day of the Lord":

> The Day of the Lord refers to God's special interventions into the course of world events to judge His enemies, accomplish His purpose for history, and thereby demonstrate who He is—the sovereign God of the universe (Isa. 2:1-2; Ezek. 13:5, 9, 14, 22-23; 30:3, 8, 19, 25-26).
>
> Evidence for this significance of the Day of the Lord is found in references in the Scriptures to past Days of the Lord. The Bible indicates that there have been several past Days of the Lord in which God exercised and demonstrated His sovereign judgment on other nations. He raised up Assyria to judge the northern kingdom of Israel during the 700s BC (Amos 5:18, 20), Babylon to judge the southern kingdom of Judah during the 600s and 500s BC (Lam. 1:12; 2:1, 21-22; Ezek. 7:19; 13:5; Zeph. 1:7-13; 2:2-3), Babylon to judge Egypt and its allies during the 500s BC (Jer. 46:10; Ezek. 30:3), and Medo-Persia to judge Babylon during the 500s BC (Isa. 13:6, 9).[17]

Notice his statement about the judgment of Babylon in Isaiah 13, thus, contradicting Rosenberg's claim that the Babylonian judgment is yet in our future. Isaiah 13 is a description of a localized judgment of a world power that existed long ago. Who did God raise up to judge Babylon? "Behold, I am going to stir up the Medes against them" (13:17a). There are no Medes today. We know from Daniel that Darius the Mede conquered Babylon (Dan. 5:30-31).

To claim that after 2,700 years the Damascus prophecy has not been completely fulfilled is to question the integrity of the Bible as skeptic Tim Callahan has done. "Being removed" does not necessarily mean "being removed forever."

## A Heap of Ruins
If the Hebrew text is followed, the cities, including Damascus, are not said to be a "heap of ruins" forever, only that they would be destroyed

---

17. Ronald Showers, "The Biblical Concept of the Day of the Lord," *Israel My* Glory (April/May 1992), 30.

and become a "heap of ruins." Consider language about the judgment of Jerusalem by the Babylonians:

> "Thus says the Lord GOD, 'This is Jerusalem; I have set her at the center of the nations, with lands around her. But she has rebelled against My ordinances more wickedly than the nations and against My statutes more than the lands which surround her; for they have rejected My ordinances and have not walked in My statutes.' Therefore, thus says the Lord GOD, 'Because you have more turmoil than the nations which surround you and have not walked in My statutes, nor observed My ordinances, nor observed the ordinances of the nations which surround you,' therefore, thus says the Lord GOD, 'Behold, I, even I, am against you, and I will execute judgments among you in the sight of the nations. **And because of all your abominations, I will do among you what I have not done, and the like of which I will never do again**'" (Ezek. 5:7-9).

As compared to every other nation, Israel's judgment would be worse ("I will do among you what I have not done"), and that would have to include the judgment on Damascus and her surrounding cities. And yet, we know that after 70 years of captivity (2 Chron. 36:20-21; Ezra 1:1; Jer. 25:11-12; 29:10; Dan. 9:1-2; Zech. 7:5) God restored the people of Israel to their land and Jerusalem as a city (Ezra 4:24; 6:1-15; Neh. 2:1-8; 3:1). The German cities of Dresden and Berlin became a "heap" after incessant firebombing as did Hiroshima and Nagasaki after atomic bombs were dropped on them. They did not remain "heaps" forever. Becoming a heap does not mean total annihilation forever.

A study of the historical record indicates that Damascus became a heap as Isaiah predicted. Consider these examples:

- *The Encyclopedia Britannica* **(11th ed)**: "Tiglath-Pilesar invaded Syria, and in 732 succeed in reducing Damascus ... Except for the abortive uprising under Sargon in 720, **we hear nothing more of Damascus for a long period**."
- *International Standard Bible Encyclopedia*: "Damascus had now lost its political importance, and for more than two centuries we have only one or two inconsiderable references to it. It is mentioned in an inscription of Sargon (722-705 BC) as having taken part in an

unsuccessful insurrection along with Hamath and Arpad. There are incidental references to it in Jer 49:23 ff and Ezek 27:18; 47:16 ff."

- **Baker Encyclopedia of the Bible**: "[T]he city's doom was predicted by Isaiah (8:4; 17:1), Amos (1:3-5), and Jeremiah (49:23-27). Rejecting God, Ahaz of Judah turned for protection to an alliance with the Assyrians, whom he bribed with the temple treasure. The Assyrian king Tiglath-pileser III ('Pul') agreed and marched against the Syro-Israelite confederation. After defeating Israel he attacked Damascus, **plundered the city**, deported the population, and replaced them with foreigners from other captured lands. Damascus was no longer an independent city-state."
- **William Smith's Dictionary of the Bible**: "Under Ahaz it was taken by Tiglath-pileser, (2 Kings 16:7, 8, 9) **the kingdom of Damascus brought to an end, and the city itself destroyed**, the inhabitants being carried captive into Assyria. (2 Kings 16:9) comp[are] Isaiah 7:8 and Amos 1:5. Afterwards it passed successively under the dominion of the Assyrians, Babylonians, Persians, Macedonians, Romans and Saracens, and was at last captured by the Turks in 1516 AD The conquest of Damascus by Tiglath-Pileser III (733-732 BC) is the final result of the Assyrian intervention against the anti-Assyrian coalition of Rezin of Damascus and Pekah of Israel against Ahaz of Judah. Rezin and Pekah tried to capture Jerusalem, capital city of the kingdom of Judah, but they failed (about 735-734 BC). Tiglath-Pileser III came to the aid of Ahaz of Judah, who promptly asked for the help of the Assyrian king. **He finally destroyed the power of Damascus, by besieging the city**, forcing king Rezin to surrender, as well as by conquering the whole region once under the control of Damascus. Rezin of Damascus died during the siege, according to the Bible (II Kings 16:9). After the conquest by Tiglath-Pileser III, Damascus was no longer the capital of the independent and rich kingdom of Aram."[18]

---

18. Davide Nadali, "Sieges and Similes of Sieges in the Royal Annals: The Conquest of Damascus by Tiglath-Pilester III," KASKAL *Rivista di storia, ambienti e culture del Vicino Oriente Antico*, vol. 6 (2009), 138.

Contemporaneous with what happened to Damascus, "in that day the glory of Jacob will fade" [lit. "be made thin"] and the fatness [Isa. 10:16] of his flesh will become lean" (Isa. 17:4). This most likely refers to the famine that followed the siege and deportation of the northern tribes (2 Kings 16:9). Damascus was utterly destroyed in fulfillment of what was predicted in Isaiah 17. The destroyer himself —Tiglath-pileser—said so in his *Annals*:

> "I took 800 people together with their property, their cattle (and) their sheep as spoil. I took 750 captives of the cities of Kurussa (and) Sama (as well as) 550 captives from the city of Metuna as spoil. **I destroyed 591 cities from the 16 districts of Damascus like ruins from the Flood.**"[19]

Tiglath-pileser "destroyed" Damascus—made it a "heap"—just like Isaiah predicted. The Bible is true, and all modern-day prophecy writers who claim that the Isaiah 17 passage has not been fulfilled have unwittingly aligned themselves with skeptics and promoters of war because—according to their repeated claims—prophecy demands it.

## Conclusion

Bill Salus, author of *Revelation Road: Hope Beyond the Horizon,* "postulates that Isaiah 17:14 predicts Damascus disappears into dust overnight, probably resulting from a nuclear attack." Here's how an article on the Rapture Ready web site positions the argument:

> The ultimate fulfillment of Isaiah 17 remains in the future. The current existence of Damascus, which will one day cease to be a city, as well as the historical absence of the coalition of nations prophesied to attack Israel and be destroyed by God, is proof that Isaiah 17 prophesies events yet future.

So how could a city that was prophesied to be completely destroyed still be in existence hundreds of years after a prophecy was given about a complete and permanent destruction?

------

19. Brent A. Strawn, Sarah C. Melville, Kyle Greenwood, and Scott Noegelm "Neo-Assyrian and Syro-Palestinian Texts II," *Ancient Near East: Historical Sources in Translation* (Blackwell Sourcebooks in Ancient History), ed. Mark W. Chavalas (Wiley-Blackwell, 2005), 333.

The Rapture Ready author argues that Psalm 83 is referring to the same series of events. He backs up his claim by quoting the following from the *New Living Translation*: "This is the just reward of those who plunder and destroy the people of God" (Isa. 17:14).

Futurists would argue from Isaiah 17:14 that any nation that attacked God's chosen nation of Israel will be "no more" (17:14a). Nazi Germany attacked the Jews without mercy. More than 6 million Jews were slaughtered. If we follow the logic of futurists who argue that an attack on Israel is a certain forever-destruction, then why is Germany a thriving nation today? The comments made about Damascus in Isaiah 17 are not to be read as a prophecy about perpetual desolation. The prophecy is dealing with Damascus at that point in time. Henry Cowles writes the following in his commentary on Isaiah 17: "Damascus ceases to be a *royal city* the capital of an empire, though it was afterward rebuilt and still stands."[20] Similar complete seemingly worldwide destruction language is found in Zephaniah:

I will completely remove all *things*
From the face of the earth," declares the LORD.
I will remove man and beast;
I will remove the birds of the sky
And the fish of the sea,
And the ruins along with the wicked;
And I will cut off man from the face of the earth," declares the
LORD (Zeph. 1:2-3).

Zephaniah is not describing events related to the end of the world. It's a prophecy "against Judah and against all the inhabitants of Jerusalem" (1:4) in the time of Zephaniah. When were these things going to happen?: "For the day of the Lord is **near**" (1:7). Near for them, not near for us. This was a local judgment against God's own people that if interpreted like futurists interpret Isaiah 17 would mean not only the end of God's people but the end of everything! But everything was not completely removed from the earth. We're still here.

--------

20. Henry Cowles, *Isaiah; With Notes, Critical, Explanatory and Practical, Designed for Both Pastors and People* (New York: D. Appleton and Co., 1880), 133.

The Bible is the best interpreter of the Bible. Be cautious of peddlers of prophetic prognostication. They may end up leading us into war, not based on the Bible, but on their misreading of it.

# CHAPTER 7

# Blood Moons, Eclipses, and the Integrity of the Bible

F or centuries prophecy writers have been predicting prophetic events based on supposed end-time indicators, from wars and rumors of wars to earthquakes and stellar phenomena like comets and storms. The latest prophetic speculation centers around four "blood moons" called a "tetrad," four moons that appear over a two-year period (e.g., 2014 and 2015). Some prophecy theorists maintain that the blood moons are related to the "rapture" and other last day events like Israel bombing Iran and Russia invading Israel and so much more of which the Bible doesn't say anything.

Not long ago Christians were told by prophecy speculator Hal Lindsey that the decade of the 1980s was the "countdown to Armageddon"[1] and the "rapture of the church." When Israel became a nation again in 1948, prophecy writers argued that the final generation before the "rapture" of the church had been born and that within 40 years of that date the church would be caught up and taken off the earth so Christians would not have to endure the horrors of the Great Tribulation.

Hal Lindsey popularized this view in his 1970 bestselling book *The Late Great Planet Earth*.

> The most important sign in Matthew has to be the restoration of the Jews to the land in the rebirth of Israel. Even the figure of speech "fig tree" has been a historic symbol of national Israel. When the Jewish people, after nearly 2,000 years of exile, under relentless persecution, became a nation again on 14 May 1948 the "fig tree" put forth its first leaves. "Jesus said that this would

---

1. Hal Lindsey, *The 1980's: Countdown to Armageddon* (King of Prussia, PA: Westgate Press, 1980).

indicate that He was "at the door," ready to return. Then He said, "Truly I say to you, *this generation* will not pass away until all these things take place" (Matthew 24:34, NASB).

What generation? Obviously, in context, the generation that would see the signs—chief among them the rebirth of Israel. A generation in the Bible is something like forty years. If this is a correct deduction, then within forty years or so of 1948, all these things could take place. Many scholars who have studied Bible prophecy all their lives believe that this is so.[2]

In an interview published in *Christianity Today* in April 1977, Ward Gasque asked Lindsey, "But what if you're wrong?" Lindsey replied: "Well, there's just a split second's difference between a hero and a bum. I didn't ask to be a hero, but I guess I have become one in the Christian community. So I accept it. But if I'm wrong about this, I guess I'll become a bum."[3]

In the same interview, Lindsey said he did not "know how long a Biblical generation is. Perhaps somewhere between sixty and eighty years."[4] Sixty years came and went in 2008 and 70 years in 2018. When eighty years comes and goes, I suspect that either a generation will become longer or the start date will change or probably both.

In an article titled "The Eschatology of Hal Lindsey," published in 1975, Dale Moody wrote: "If the 'Great Snatch,' as Lindsey repeatedly calls the Rapture, does take place before the Tribulation and by 1981, I will beg forgiveness from Lindsey for doubting his infallibility as we meet in the air."[5]

The late Chuck Smith (1927-2013) wrote in his 1976 book *The Soon to be Revealed Antichrist* that "we are living in the last generation which began with the rebirth of Israel in 1948 (*see* Matt. 24:32-34)." He repeated the claim in his 1978 book *End Times*:

> If I understand Scripture correctly, Jesus taught us that the generation which sees the "budding of the fig tree," the

---

2. Hal Lindsey, *The Late Great Planet Earth* (Grand Rapids, MI: Zondervan, 1970), 53-54.

3. W. Ward Gasque, "Future Fact? Future Fiction?," *Christianity Today* (April 15, 1977), 40.

4. Gasque, "Future Fact? Future Fiction?," 40.

5. Dale Moody, "The Eschatology of Hal Lindsey," *Review and Expositor*, 72 (Summer 1975), 278.

birth of the nation of Israel, will be the generation that sees the Lord's return. I believe that the generation of 1948 is the last generation. Since a generation of judgment is forty years and the Tribulation period lasts seven years, I believe the Lord could come back for His Church any time before the Tribulation starts, which would mean any time before 1981. (1948+40-7 = 1981).[6]

Prophecy writer, religious cult critic, and New Age foe Dave Hunt (1926-2013), who also believed that Israel's national reestablishment was *the* time indicator and sign for future prophetic events,[7] lamented that Lindsey's prophetic recklessness had a negative effect on many Christians:

> Needless to say, January 1, 1982, saw the defection of large numbers from the pretrib[ulational rapture] position.... Many who were once excited about the prospects of being caught up to heaven at any moment have become confused and disillusioned by the apparent failure of a generally accepted biblical interpretation they once relied upon.[8]

## Halley's Comet and the Jupiter Effect

On December 31, 1979, Chuck Smith told those who had gathered for the end of the year service that the "rapture" would take place before the end of 1981, seven years before the 1988 endpoint of the 40 year generation that began when Israel was reconstituted as a nation in 1948.

Smith claimed that because of ozone depletion the image depicting a scorching sun in Revelation 16:8 would be fulfilled during the post "rapture" tribulation period: "And the fourth angel poured out his bowl upon the sun; and it was given to it to scorch men with fire."

In addition, Halley's Comet would pass near earth in 1986 and would wreak havoc on those left behind as debris from its million-mile-long tail pummeled the planet. Here's how Smith explained the prophetic scenario in his book *Future Survival* which is nearly identical to what appears on the taped message:

---

6. Chuck Smith, *End Times* (Costa Mesa, CA: The Word for Today, 1978), 35.
7. Dave Hunt, *Whatever Happened to Heaven?* (Eugene, OR: Harvest House, 1988), 64.
8. Hunt, *Whatever Happened to Heaven?*, 68.

The Lord said that towards the end of the Tribulation period the sun would scorch men who dwell upon the face of the earth (Rev. 16). The year 1986 would fit just about right! We're getting *close* to the Tribulation and the return of Christ in glory. All the pieces of the puzzle are coming together.[9]

Nothing prophetically or terrestrially significant happened in 1986 related to Halley's Comet, and there is no reason why it should have since it's been a predictable phenomenon for more than two millennia as it makes its way around the sun every 75 to 76 years.

There was another astronomical event that caught the attention of scientists, prophecy writers, and even atheist polymath Isaac Asimov who wrote the foreword to the 1974 book *The Jupiter Effect: The Planets as Triggers of Devastating Earthquakes*. The following is from a 1997 lecture by Damian Thompson, author *of* The End of Time: Faith and Fear in the Shadow of the Millennium:

Back in 1982, there was terrific excitement in New Age circles at the approach of something called the 'Jupiter Effect,' an alignment of the planets which a couple of maverick scientists predicted would slow down the earth's rotation, leading to an earthquake which would destroy Los Angeles. Leading fundamentalists might be expected to scoff at this; instead, they jumped straight on the bandwagon. Hal Lindsey, author of *The Late, Great Planet Earth*,[10] wrote that "what we can expect in 1982 is the largest outbreak of killer quakes ever seen in the history of planet earth along with radical changes in climate." Not to be outdone, Pat Robertson suggested that the chaos caused by the Jupiter Effect might prove the perfect cover for a Soviet strike against the US. But this prospect did not worry the Southwestern Radio Church: it suggested that the Rapture might occur just before the planetary alignment, that the earth would be righted on its axis, and that pre-Flood conditions would be restored.[11]

---

9. Chuck Smith, *Future Survival* (Costa Mesa, CA: The Word for Today, [1978] 1980), 21.

10. Also see Lindsey, *The 1980's: Countdown to Armageddon*, 30-31.

11. Quoted in Charles Cameron, "Overdetermined and Underestimated," *The Arlington Institute: Project Y2K* (July 5, 1999).

As we now know (and should have known then) there was no Jupiter Effect on March 10, 1982 and no Mars Effect when Mars and the Earth aligned with the sun in a cosmic event called "opposition" on April 8, 2014. It happens every 26 months. Astrophysicist John R. Gribbin, one of the authors of the best-selling book *The Jupiter Effect,* admitted in his 1999 book *The Little Book of Science* that "there is no Jupiter effect" and "I'm sorry I ever had anything to do with it."[12]

But the people who get caught up in the latest end-time speculative prophecy story either have short memories of past predictions or no knowledge at all. Without having all the facts or a worksheet of past failed prophetic claims, it's not hard to convince the uninformed, who are easily persuaded by some silver-tongued orator who claims to have some clear eye into the future based on special knowledge, that something in the heavens is a clear sign from God that the end is near.

If you talk to many Christians about Bible prophecy, most likely you will hear them claim that all the signs for some impending prophetic event are unfolding right before our eyes. When popular prophecy writers bring up anything that might appear in the heavens, people pay attention. You don't have to spend a lot of time watching the History Channel and a show like "7 Signs of the Apocalypse" to be sensitive to events like an asteroid strike, a pole shift like the one depicted in the film *2012*, and the Yellowstone National Park super volcano that some scientists claim has the potential to erupt with a force 2,000 times greater than the volcanic eruption of Mount St. Helens that occurred on May 18, 1980.

## What Are 'Blood Moons'?

The appearance of the reddish color of the moon takes place during a lunar eclipse when the earth aligns between the sun and the moon at the proper angle and the earth's shadow falls on the moon. Of course, the moon does not turn red, and it certainly does not turn to blood. A real prophetic sign would be if the moon actually turned to blood like God turned the Nile River into blood. Now that would be a sign of things to come!

---

12. John Gribbin, *The Little Book of Science* (New York: Barnes & Noble, 1999), 39. If only Christian prophecy prognosticators would admit their mistakes as candidly as Dr. Gribbin did.

During a lunar eclipse, the Moon passes behind the Earth's shadow, which darkens it. If you could take a look at the Earth from inside its shadow, you would see that the atmosphere around the edge of the entire planet glows red. Once again, this is because large amounts of atmosphere will scatter away the blue/green light and let the red light go straight through. During a lunar eclipse, the Moon passes fully into the shadow of the Earth and it's no longer being illuminated by the Sun; however, this red light passing through the Earth's atmosphere does reach the Moon, and shines on it.

So-called blood moons are not unusual. There have been many of them. There have even been tetrads. The question is, are these total lunar eclipses prophetically significant? Those who point to "signs in the heavens" as prophetic indicators are often very selective. They only see significance when they can find events they claim are prophetically noteworthy and ignore those that aren't. For a sign to be a sign it must be unusual, and people have to have some idea why it's a sign at the time it appears.

One of the first people to find prophetic significance with the blood moon tetrad is Mark Blitz:

> Mark [Biltz of El Shaddai Ministries in Puyallup, Washington] found that we have had blood-red moons on the first day of Passover and the first day of Sukkot on back-to-back years seven times since 1 AD. Three of these occurrences were connected to 1492 (the final year of the Spanish Inquisition), 1948 (statehood for Israel and the War of Independence), and 1967 (the Six-Day War)—some of the most significant days in Jewish history.
>
> "The others were in 162/163 AD, 795/796 AD, 842/843 AD and 860/861 AD We don't have any historical connections for these years at this time, but we do know of significant Jewish persecution during the eighth and ninth centuries."

The two full lunar eclipses occurred in 1493/1494 and 1949/1950, not in 1492 and 1948. Why did the lunar eclipses appear *after* these events if blood moons are *prophetic* signs? In biblical terms, a sign takes place *at the time of* or *before* a prophetic event, not after. Mark Hitchcock makes a good point about the 1493/1494 blood moons in his book *Blood Moons Rising*:

> [I]n a day when communication was severely limited, how many people in the world were even aware of the Edict of Expulsion in Spain in 1492? Most people in the world knew nothing about the Great Expulsion of the Jews or the discovery of the New World. And, as noted previously, lunar eclipses are not global events. So, it's worth asking—how can the blood moon tetrad of 1493-1494 be a sign of an event in 1492 that most of the world at the time never saw and never knew occurred?[13]

It's not as if eclipses and moons that look red were foreign to the astronomers of that time. Christopher Columbus was able to intimidate the natives of Jamaica to supply food for his crew by precisely predicting a lunar eclipse for February 29, 1504. He carried an almanac produced by Abraham Zacuto (1452-1515) that contained astronomical tables that covered the years 1475-1506. The lunar eclipse and the red moon appeared as Columbus had predicted.

Notice the years of the early tetrads (AD 162/163, 795/796, 842/843 and 860/861) and this comment: "We don't have any historical connections for these years at this time." Why not? If blood moons are so prophetically significant, there should have been major prophetic events related to Israel over Israel! And if the four blood moons in 2014 and 2015 are so significant for Israel, then why is it that "Data published by NASA reveals that all but the last of the four eclipses will not be visible from the Middle East, and even the fourth will only be partially visible." This makes no sense if the blood moons are for and about Israel.

The 2014-2015 blood moons aren't even the first tetrads of this century, and they won't be the last as this chart shows:

1. Tetrad: 2003-2004
2. Tetrad: 2014-2015
3. Tetrad: 2032-2033
4. Tetrad: 2043-2044

---

13. Mark Hitchcock, *Blood Moons Rising: Bible Prophecy, Israel, and the Four Blood Moons* (Carol Stream, IL: Tyndale House Publishers, 2014), 133.

5. Tetrad: 2050-2051
6. Tetrad: 2061-2062
7. Tetrad: 2072-2073
8. Tetrad: 2090-2091

If blood moons are prophetically significant for Israel, then why weren't there any blood moons before or during Israel's two most bloody periods in history, the destruction of Jerusalem that took place in AD 70 and the holocaust?

What about these blood moons coinciding with Passover (April 15, 2014 and April 4, 2015) and Sukkot or the Feast of the Tabernacles (October 8, 2014 September 28, 2015)? James Vincent makes an important point:

> This is certainly unusual but hardly surprising given that the Jewish calendar is based partly on lunar cycles: Passover is always marked by a full moon and a lunar eclipse cannot—by definition—happen at any other time apart from a full moon.

Consider what the Apostle Paul wrote:

> Therefore no one is to act as your judge in regard to food or drink or in respect to a festival or a new moon or a Sabbath day—things which are a mere shadow of what is to come; but the substance belongs to Christ (Col. 2:16-17).

The Jewish feast days and festivals no longer have any relevance since Jesus has come and fulfilled them, as He did with all the Old Covenant types and shadows (Luke 21:22; 24:27, 44). This is carried over into the New Testament. James B. Jordan offers some helpful commentary on this type of language:

> Anyone familiar with the Hebrew Scriptures would recognize immediately that what Jesus says about the sun, moon, and stars [in Matt. 24:29] is not to be taken to refer to the physical cosmos but to the political cosmos.... The prophets often see the "sun, moon, and stars" falling to the earth. One of the most frequently encountered mistakes in the interpretation of Biblical prophecy today is the notion that this always refers to the end of the world at the Second Coming of Jesus Christ.

Actually, though, this expression always refers to the collapse of some particular nation.

For example, there's the description of a male goat in Daniel 8:10 that causes "stars to fall to the earth," an action in itself that would destroy the earth. These fallen stars are then "trampled" by the goat. Most likely the goat refers to a civil ruler, and the stars are civil powers under the ruler's dominion. How should we understand Judges 5:20 when it states that "the stars fought from heaven, from their courses they fought against Sisera"?[14]

In Genesis 37 and Revelation 12 the sun, moon, and stars represent Israel in its civil and religious capacity as they often do for other nations. For example, Babylon's destruction more than 2,500 years ago is represented by something that was said to happen to the sun, moon, and stars:

> Behold, the day of the Lord is coming,
>     Cruel, with fury and burning anger,
> To make the land a desolation;
>     And He will exterminate its sinners from it.
> For the stars of heaven and their constellations
>     Will not flash forth their light;
> The sun will be dark when it rises
>     And the moon will not shed its light.
> (Isa 13:9-11; also see 24:23; 50:3; Ezek 32:7)

We know this prophetic description is about Old Testament Babylon because we're told that God's is going to "stir up the Medes against them" (Isa. 13:17). We read about the fulfillment in Daniel 5.

John A. Martin, writing in the *Bible Knowledge Commentary*, argues that "the statements in [Isaiah] 13:10 about the heavenly bodies (**stars ... sun ... moon**) no longer functioning may figuratively describe the total turnaround of the political structure of the Near East. The same would be true of **the heavens** trembling **and the earth** shaking (v. 13), figures of speech suggesting all-encompassing destruction."[15]

---

14. *Matthew 23-25: A Literary, Historical, and Theological Commentary* (Powder Springs, GA: American Vision, 2022), 164, 168

15. John A. Martin, "Isaiah," *The Bible Knowledge Commentary: Old Testament*, eds. John F. Walvoord and Roy B. Zuck (Wheaton, IL: Victor Books, 1983), 1059.

Charles L. Feinberg, writing in the *Liberty Bible Commentary*, states, "The **sun, moon,** and **stars** indicate a complete system of government and remind the reader of Genesis 37:9."[16] Notice that Feinberg argues that sun, moon, and stars relate to "a complete system of government" and not literal stellar phenomena. He also references Genesis 37:9 where sun, moon, and stars are used as symbols for Israel. Other commentators follow a similar pattern of interpretation. In none of these examples does anything actually happen to the sun, moon, and stars. They represent a symbolic de-creation, a time of judgment on a national scale.

When the sun, moon, and stars are high in the heavens giving off their light, God is pleased with the nations. When the sun and moon go dark and the stars fall, this is a sign of God's displeasure and judgment. So-called blood moons are not in the picture in any of these predictive events. We see a similar motif in the New Testament. God describes Israel's coming calamity in AD 70 when the Roman army razed the temple (Matt. 24:2) and destroyed the city using examples of national judgment borrowed from the Old Testament that Jesus applied to first-century Israel:

"But immediately after the tribulation of those days THE SUN WILL BE DARKENED, AND THE MOON WILL NOT GIVE ITS LIGHT, AND THE STARS WILL FALL [Isa. 13:10; Amos 5:20; 8:9; Zeph. 1:15] from heaven, and the powers of the heavens will be shaken" (Matt. 24:29; also see Heb. 12:25-29).

Again, nothing physical takes place with the sun, moon, and stars. There were no blood moons in AD 70, just like there were no blood moons when Israel was taken into captivity in 586 BC by the Babylonians (Dan. 1:1). All the action and change takes place on earth to nations.

With this brief background, we can make some sense of the blood moon language quoted by Peter at Pentecost. Note that the words in SMALL CAPS are direct quotations from the Old Testament:

"'AND IT SHALL BE IN THE LAST DAYS,' GOD SAYS, 'THAT I WILL POUR FORTH OF MY SPIRIT ON ALL MANKIND; AND YOUR SONS AND YOUR DAUGHTERS SHALL PROPHESY, AND YOUR YOUNG

16. Charles L. Feinberg, "Revelation," *Liberty Bible Commentary: New Testament*, eds. Jerry Falwell and Edward E. Hindson (Lynchburg, VA: Old-Time Gospel Hour, 1982), 820.

MEN SHALL SEE VISIONS, AND YOUR OLD MEN SHALL DREAM DREAMS; EVEN ON MY BONDSLAVES, BOTH MEN AND WOMEN, I WILL IN THOSE DAYS POUR FORTH OF MY SPIRIT AND THEY SHALL PROPHESY. 'AND I WILL GRANT WONDERS IN THE HEAVENS ABOVE AND SIGNS ON THE EARTH BELOW, BLOOD, AND FIRE, AND VAPOR OF SMOKE. **THE SUN WILL BE TURNED INTO DARKNESS AND THE MOON INTO BLOOD,** BEFORE THE GREAT AND GLORIOUS DAY OF THE LORD SHALL COME. AND IT SHALL BE THAT EVERYONE WHO CALLS ON THE NAME OF THE LORD WILL BE SAVED'" (Acts 2:17-21).

Peter makes it clear that these events were taking place among the Jews of his day. Prophecy was being fulfilled right there and then. If you recall, at Pentecost "there were Jews living in Jerusalem, devout men from every nation under heaven" (Acts 2:5). (The "under heaven" language may be significant to this entire discussion recalling the promise made to Abraham: Gen. 15:5; Deut. 1:10). They witnessed extraordinary events, hearing the gospel being spoken in their own language: "This is what was spoken through the prophet Joel" (2:16, 28-32). What's the "this" he was referring to? The events of Pentecost, not events in the distant future. The "last days" were the last days of the Old Covenant that was passing away (Heb. 1:1-2; 1 Cor. 10:11; Heb. 9:26).

Notice that Joel does not prophesy that the moon will be "like" or "as blood," as Revelation 6:12 states, but that it will actually be "turned ... into blood." Even John Hagee, who argues for a literal interpretation of the Bible for other prophecies, notes that "the moon does not actually turn to blood, but it does appear blood-red."[17] Neither Joel nor Peter says that the moon will "appear blood-red." They say it would turn into blood. A blood moon is not in view. There's something else going on that is often missed by prophecy writers.

As has been noted, the blood moon prophecy of Joel doesn't say that the moon will look blood red; it states that it will turn into blood:

I will display wonders in the sky and on the earth,
    Blood, fire and columns of smoke.
The sun will be turned into darkness
    And the moon into blood

---

17. John Hagee, *Four Blood Moons* (Franklin, TN: Worthy Publishing, 2013), 19.

Before the great and awesome day of the Lord comes
(Joel 2:30-31; Acts 2:19-21).

Why doesn't anyone mention anything about the sun turning into darkness and stars falling (Rev. 6:12-14) in today's discussion about blood-red moons? It's a package deal. If we are to interpret Joel's prophecy and similar prophetic passages correctly, we must understand how this type of language is used elsewhere in Scripture. See passages like Isaiah 13:13, 34:4, 51:6, Ezekiel 32:7-8, and many more. As a reminder, it is important to note that Israel is symbolized as sun, moon, and stars (Gen. 37:9-10; Matt. 24:29; Rev. 6:12-14; 12:1-2).

So what did Joel and Peter mean? Remember that what they wrote is a revelation from God; it's God-breathed language (2 Tim. 3:16). If we are to interpret the passage correctly, we must understand how this type of language is used elsewhere in Scripture. James Jordan gets to the heart of the passage's meaning:

> The turning of the moon to "blood" points, I believe, to something particularly Jewish: the sacrificial system. If they will not accept the blood of Jesus Christ, the final Sacrifice, then they themselves will be turned into blood. They will become the sacrifices. That is what the prophesied war is all about. That is what the destruction of Jerusalem in AD 70 was all about.
>
> But Joel is issuing a warning. Those who listen can escape. "And it will come about that whoever calls on the name of Yahweh will be delivered; for 'on Mount Zion and in Jerusalem there will be those who escape,' as Yahweh has said, even among the survivors whom Yahweh calls" (Joel 2:32). Just as Isaac escaped death on Mount Zion because of the substitute ram that God provided (Genesis 22:14), so those who trust in the Lamb of God will escape the destruction of Jerusalem in AD 70. Such is Joel's warning, reiterated by Peter on the day of Pentecost.
>
> And also reiterated by John. Prophesying this same event, the destruction of Jerusalem, John writes, "And I looked when He broke the sixth seal, and there was a great earthquake; and the sun became black as sackcloth made of hair, and the whole moon became like blood; and the stars of the sky fell to the earth,

as a fig tree casts its unripe figs when shaken by a great wind" (Revelation 6:12-13). The fig tree is a standard symbol for Israel, especially in this context (Matthew 21:19; 24:32-34; Luke 21:29-32). Both sackcloth and blood remind us of the Levitical system, the blood for sacrifices, and the sackcloth for the mourning associated with affliction ("leprosy") and uncleanness.

In this way, the astral symbols are given peculiar coloring depending on context. The Babylonians worshipped the stars, and so they are extinguished. The Egyptians worshipped the sun, so God darkens it. The Jews continued to maintain the sacrifices, so the moon is turned to blood.

To round out this discussion, we need only look at one more passage. After promising the coming of the Spirit and the judgment upon apostate Israel in Joel 2, God goes on to say in chapter 3 that He will shake down all the nations of the world, and bring them to their knees. Speaking of the nations, He says that "the sun and moon grow dark, and the stars lose their brightness" (Joel 3:15).

In conclusion, the symbolism of universal collapse, the extinction of sun, moon, and stars, has reference to the fall of nations and empires. In Hebrew Scriptures it was used for Babylon, for Egypt, for Israel, and for the nations in general. At the destruction of Jerusalem, the Jewish sun went into black eclipse, mourning in sackcloth, and the Jewish moon went into red eclipse, the blood-red of sacrifice.[18]

From what we've seen of how the Bible uses sun, moon, and stars to represent nations—either good (blessing) or bad (judgment)—nothing physically happens to the sun, moon, and stars. All that happens takes place on earth and the sun, moon, and stars retain their place in the heavens.

If Christians persist in claiming this sign or that sign is an indication of "imminent" prophetic events related to the "last days" and the supposed "rapture" of the church, they will only do damage to the integrity of the Bible and the reliable witness of the Christian witness to world in need of the gospel of Jesus Christ. How many more failed predictions do we have to endure before Christians say "enough"?

---

18. Jordan, *Matthew 23-25*, 173-174.

## Eclipses

It's been embarrassing reading and listening to Christians who pushed the belief that the April 8, 2024, solar eclipse was an end-time event sign. Why do so many Christians fall for these types of end-time hoaxes? I first saw it in 1973 with Hal Lindsey's mega-bestseller *The Late Great Planet Earth*. Long before Lindsey, prophetic speculation was rampant, and it's no less true today.

It's all over Facebook. Someone puts up what the Bible says on the subject, and hundreds (sometimes thousands) of people voice their approval. It even comes from Christians who are not sensationalists. The question of the "delay of the Parousia" came up. Here are some of his responses. First, he listed Matthew 24:14. It's obvious that what Jesus said here was fulfilled before that generation passed away (24:34) based on what we find in Romans 1:8; 16:26; Colossians 1:6, 23, and other passages like 1 Thessalonians 8 and 1 Timothy 3:16. The Greek word often translated as "world" in Matthew 24:14 is *oikoumenē* not *kosmos*. It has the same meaning in Luke 2:1 and Acts 11:28. He also appeals to 2 Thessalonians 2:1-12 because he claims it "contains Paul's explicit teaching that the signs of the apostasy and the man of lawlessness must occur 'first,' and it connects these events with a period just prior to Christ's second coming." The temple was still standing when Paul wrote to the Thessalonians and the "man of lawlessness" was restrained the: "you know what restrains him **now**" (v. 6). There was an apostasy in that Apostolic generation. I cover all of this in two chapters on 2 Thessalonians 2 in my book *Last Days Madness*.

Then I saw Keith Tankersley reference Isaiah 13:6-13 accompanied by an image of the Sun in eclipse with the following: "One day, the world will standstill to see Jesus in the sky!" I responded: "For Babylon in the Old Testament. Context matters." Isaiah 13:1 begins with "The oracle concerning **Babylon** which Isaiah the son of Amoz saw." Verse 6 states, "Wail, for the day of the Lord is **near**." Near for whom? Old Testament Babylon! Reading further, we find:

> For the stars of heaven and their constellations
> will not give their light.
> The rising sun will be darkened,
> and the moon will not give its light (v. 10).

And this:

> Therefore I will make the heavens tremble,
> and the earth will be shaken from its place
> at the wrath of the LORD of Hosts
> on the day of His burning anger (v. 13).

Let's not forget this:

> Behold, I will stir up against them the Medes,
> who have no regard for silver
> and no desire for gold.
> Their bows will dash young men to pieces;
> they will have no mercy on the fruit of the womb;
> they will not look with pity on the children.
> And **Babylon**, the jewel of the kingdoms,
> the glory of the pride of the Chaldeans,
> will be overthrown by God
> like Sodom and Gomorrah (vv. 17-19).

Tankersley responded to my "For Babylon in the Old Testament. Context matters" with the following:

> For the second coming of Christ in the New Testament too! When He comes to judge the world in righteousness, Acts 17:31. Yeah context matters! Clearly eschatology does too! Perhaps I should have used this one in the caption instead: "Then the kings of the earth and the great ones and the generals and the rich and the powerful, and everyone, slave and free, hid themselves in the caves and among the rocks of the mountains, calling to the mountains and rocks, "Fall on us and hide us from the face of him who is seated on the throne, and from the wrath of the Lamb, for the great day of their wrath has come, and who can stand?" (Revelation 6:16-17)

Question: Did the Sun and Moon physically go dark in Isaiah's day? Not obscured with clouds. Did the heavens physically tremble? Was the earth physically shaken from its place? Did this happen when the **Medes** (the original context) vanquished Babylon in a single night (Dan. 5:30), because that was the nation that in earthly terms brought it about (Isa. 13:17). The language is metaphorical, something that even dispensationalists admit. For example: "The statements in 13:10 about the heavenly bodies (**stars ... sun ... moon**) no longer functioning may figuratively describe the total turnaround of the political structure of the Near East. The same would be true of **the heavens** trembling **and the earth** shaking (v. 13), figures of speech suggesting all-encompassing destruction."[19]

Jesus quotes the Isaiah passage in Matthew 24:29 and applies it to the judgment on that Apostolic generation (24:33-34). This means that nothing physical happened to the sun, moon, or stars (Isa. 34:4). If these passages did not refer to physical changes in the cosmos when the Medes conquered Babylon and when Jerusalem fell in AD 70, are futurists claiming that at Jesus' Second Coming the actual Sun and Moon will go dark and literal stars will fall to the earth like we see in Revelation 6?

> And I looked when He broke the sixth seal, and there was a great earthquake; and the sun became as black as sackcloth made of hair, and the whole moon became like blood; and the stars of the sky fell to the earth, as a fig tree drops its unripe figs when shaken by a great wind. The sky was split apart like a scroll when it is rolled up, and every mountain and island was removed from its place (vv. 12-14).

If the description of these events take place in the sixth chapter of Revelation, there is no way the events described in chapters 7-22 could happen.

Let's look at Tankersley's New Testament references. First, is Acts 17:31 describing the end of the world as we know it?

> He has set a day on which He is **about to** [μέλλει] judge the world [οἰκουμένην] in righteousness through a Man whom He has appointed, having furnished proof to all people by raising Him from the dead.

Paul is not describing some end of the world event. He was warning the Athenians that they would not escape God's judgment. If the nation of Israel did not escape judgment, and Babylon, and the Medes and the Persians, and their own ancestors did not escape God's judgment, the Athenians would not escape it either. If the threat Paul made to the

---

19. John A. Martin, "Isaiah," *The Bible Knowledge Commentary*, 1:1059.

Athenians is yet to happen, they could have reasoned, "This doesn't affect us. This event is far in the future. 'Eat, drink, and be merry for tomorrow we die'" (Isa. 22:13; Eccl. 8:15; 1 Cor. 15:32; and Luke 12:19) because the judgment is for people far distant from us." C.K. Barrett made the following observation in his commentary on Acts 17:31: "It is implied that the day is near, otherwise the warning would carry little force."[20]

Peter establishes the nearness of this judgment: "but they will give an account to Him who is **ready**[21] to judge the living and the dead…. The end of all things is **near**…. For it is time for judgment to begin with the household of God; and if **it begins with us first**, what will be the outcome for those who do not obey the gospel of God?" (1 Peter 4:5, 7, 17). Judgment is not a one-time end-time event, and in all the examples so far not one of them was cosmic.

I'm not sure if Tankersley has thought through his appeal to Revelation 6:15-17 in defense of his end-time view. Why did he skip verses 12-14 that describe Isaiah 13-like language but then adds "the stars of the sky/heavens fell to the earth, as a fig tree casts its unripe figs when shaken by a great wind" (v. 13). If **physical** stars fall to Earth, then Earth will be **physically** destroyed. In Revelation 12, we find this:

> Then another sign appeared in heaven: and behold, a great red dragon having seven heads and ten horns, and on his heads were seven crowns. And his tail **swept away a third of the stars of heaven and hurled them to the earth**. And the dragon stood before the woman who was about to give birth, so that when she gave birth, he might devour her Child.

Given the physicalist interpretation, Earth was destroyed in Revelation 6 because of falling stars and destroyed again when another star "had fallen to the earth" (or land) in 9:1, and for a third time when the dragon's tail "swept away a third of the stars of heaven and hurled them to the earth." After these three stellar events in Revelation, Earth is still intact, so much so, given fanciful futurist arguments, to set up electronic surveillance on the world's population!

---

20. C. K. Barrett, Acts, *International Critical Commentary*, 2 vols. (T.&T Clark, 2004).

21. "*Eggízō* expresses 'extreme closeness, immediate imminence—even a presence ('It is here') because the moment of this coming happened (i.e., at the beginning of Jesus' ministry)' (J. Schlosser)."

Yes, Mr. Tankersley, it does look like the Isaiah passage, and because it does, it most likely applied in a similar way—a description of the judgment of a nation, not the whole wide world. Was Israel judged in a way like Babylon? Yes, it was. Jesus said it would be (Matt. 24:29) before their generation passed away (24:34). The description is hyperbolic metaphorical language, otherwise stars falling to Earth by a dragon's tail does not make any sense.

Then there's the timing factor (see Rev. 1:1, 3, 9; 22:6, 10, 12, 20). Note this from Revelation 6:16: "Fall on us and hide us from the face of Him who is seated on the throne, and from the wrath of the Lamb, for **the great day of their wrath has come**, and who can stand?" Where is this found in Scripture?

> And following Him was a large crowd of the people, and of women who were mourning and lamenting Him. But Jesus turning to them said, "Daughters of Jerusalem, stop weeping for Me, but w**eep for yourselves and for your children**. "For behold, **the days are coming** when they will say, 'Blessed are the barren, and the wombs that never bore, and the breasts that never nursed.' "Then they will begin TO SAY TO THE MOUNTAINS, 'FALL ON US,' AND TO THE HILLS, 'COVER US.' "For if they do these things when the tree is green, what will happen when it is dry?" (Luke 23:17-31)

Jesus described the people of His own day. James Hamilton, a pre-millennialist, writes in his commentary on Revelation that "the opening of the seals in chapter 6 corresponds to what Jesus describes in the Olivet Discourse in the Synoptic Gospels."[22] I agree because both descriptions portray events in the lead up to the destruction of the temple and the judgment on NT Israel in AD 70.[23] See Hamilton's comparison chart on page 119.

---

22. James M. Hamilton, Jr., *Revelation: The Spirit Speaks to the Churches* (Wheaton, IL: Crossway, 2012), 166-167. Also, Louis A. Vos, *The Synoptic Traditions in the Apocalypse* (Kampen, Netherlands: J. H. Kok N. V., 1965), 181-188.

23. See my books *Is Jesus Coming Soon?*, *Last Days Madness*, and *Wars and Rumors of Wars*, and John Bray's *Matthew 24 Fulfilled*, miah Nisbett's *The Destruction of Jerusalem*, James Jordan's *Matthew 23-25*, and David Chilton's *The Great Tribulation, Paradise Restored*, and *The Days of Vengeance: An Exposition of the Book of Revelation*. Also refer to the two-volume commentaries by Peter J. Leithart and Kenneth L. Gentry.

| | | |
|---|---|---|
| **Dan. 9:26**—And the people of the prince who is to come shall destroy the city and the sanctuary [cf. Rev. 11:2]. Its end shall come with a flood, and *to the end there shall be war.* Desolations are decreed | **Matt. 24:4-5 (Mark 13:5, 6; Luke 21:8)**—warning not to be lead astray by impostors who come in Jesus' name saying "I am the Christ." | **Rev. 6:1, 2**—at the opening of the first seal, a rider on a white horse goes out conquering and to conquer, similar to the way that Jesus comes in Revelation 19. |
| | **Matt 24:6 (Mark 13:7; Luke 21:9)**—wars and rumors of wars, "for this must take place, *but the end is not yet*" (cf. Rev. 4:1) | **Rev. 6:3, 4**—at the opening of the second seal, a rider on a red horse goes out to take peace from the earth, being given a great sword. |
| | **Matt 24:7 (Mark 13:8; Luke 21:11)**—famine, "*the beginning of the birth pains*" | **Rev. 6:5, 6**—At the opening of the third seal, a rider on a black horse goes out with scales, and the price of wheat and barley is greatly inflated. |
| | **Matt. 24:7, 9-12**—famine, tribulation, believers put to death, hated, falling away, betrayal, false prophets, lawlessness. | **Rev. 6:7, 8**—at the opening of the fourth seal, a rider named Death rides on a pale horse, and Hades follows, and they kill with sword, famine, pestilence, and wild beasts. |
| | **Matt. 24:14**—the Gospel of the kingdom is proclaimed to whole world, "then the end will come." | **Rev. 6:9-11**—at the opening of the fifth seal, John sees martyrs under the altar, and they are told that the number of martyrs must be completed before the end comes. |
| **Dan. 9:27**—"And he shall make a strong covenant with many *for one week, and for half of the week* he shall put an end to sacrifice and offering. And on the wing of abominations shall come one who makes desolate, until the decreed end is poured out on the desolator." | **Matt. 24:15** (Mark 13:14)—"the abomination of desolation." | **Rev. 11:2**—the courts of the temple trampled for forty-two months; **Rev. 13:14, 15**—the image of the beast speaks and is worshiped. |
| | **Matt. 24:29** (Mark 31:24-25; Luke 21:25)—"the sun will be darkened, and the moon will not give its light, and the stars will fall from heaven." | **Rev. 11:2-13**—at the opening of the sixth seal, there is an earthquake (cf. Matt 24:7), and "the sun became black as sackcloth, the full moon became like blood, and the stars of the sky fell to the earth" (cf Rev. 8:12; 9:2). |
| | **Matt. 24:32-33** (Mark 13:28-29; Luke 21:29-31)—the parable of *the fig tree*: summer is near when its leaves appear, and these signs mean the end is near | **Rev. 6:13**—"*the fig tree* sheds its winter fruit when shaken by a gale." |
| | **Matt. 24:30 (Mark 13:26; Luke 21:27)**—"Then will appear in heaven the sign of the Son of Man, and then all the tribes of the earth will mourn, and *they will see the Son of Man* coming on the clouds of heaven with power and great glory." | **Rev. 6:15-17**—kings, great ones, generals, the rich, the powerful, everyone seeks to hide "from the face of him who is seated on the throne, and *from the wrath of the Lamb*, for the great day of their wrath has come, and who con stand?" |
| | **Matt. 24:13-14, 22, 24, 31**—*the elect* will persevere until the end, the gospel will go to all the elect, the days will be cut short for the elect, the elect will not be led astray, and they will be gathered. | **Rev. 7:1-17**—*the elect* are sealed. |
| | **Matt. 24:21**—"great tribulation." | **Rev. 7:14**—"the great tribulation." |
| | **Matt. 24:31**—"he will send out his angels with a loud trumpet call." | **Rev. 8:1-5**—at the opening of the seventh seal, John sees seven angels with seven trumpets (does Matthew's single trumpet become seven trumpets the way that Jeremiah's seventy years become seventy sevens of years in Daniel?). |
| | **Matt. 24:31**—the angels will gather the elect from the four winds, from one end of heaven to the other." | **Rev. 14:14-16**—the angels and the one like a son of man harvest the earth. |

Jesus mentioned in Luke's Gospel, "Woe to those who are pregnant and to those who are nursing babies in those days; for there will be great distress upon the land and wrath to this people" (21:23). The barren at that time would die childless, and those who were pregnant will be in great distress because they most likely would not be able to care for their children. Josephus, an eyewitness of the horrors of the Roman siege, described a particular event:

> There was one Mary, the daughter of Eleazar, illustrious for her family and riches. She having been stripped and plundered of all her substance and provisions by the soldiers, out of necessity and fury killed her own sucking child, and having boiled him, devoured half of him, and covering up the rest preserved it for another time. The soldiers soon came, allured by the smell of victuals, and threatened to kill her immediately, if she would not produce what she had dressed. But she replied that she had reserved a good part for them, and uncovered the relics of her son. Dread and astonishment seized them, and they stood stupefied at the sight.[24]

By following the lead of Scripture, "searching the Scriptures daily to see whether these things are so," we will not be led astray by prophetic speculators who can't seem to get it through their heads that stellar phenomena language is about local judgments on nations. Nothing physically happened to the Sun, Moon, and stars. The heavens did not physically "role up like a scroll" or "vanish like smoke" (Isa. 34:4; 51:6; Heb. 11:11-12).

Does any of this mean God does not judge nations anymore? Not at all. But it's important that we do not apply fulfilled prophecy to future events. Historical context is necessary to interpret the Bible accurately. How did the first readers understand what was being described in terms of the literary devices used in their day?

---

24. Thomas Newton, *Dissertations on the Prophecies, Which Have Remarkably Been Fulfilled, and at this Time are Fulfilling in the World* (London: J. F. Dove, 1754), 345-346.

## CHAPTER 8

# Does Isaiah 66:8 Predict the 1948 Modern State of Israel?

Who has heard such a thing? Who has seen such things? Can a land be brought forth through labor pains in one day? Can a nation be born all at once? As soon as Zion was in labor pains, she also gave birth to her sons (Isa. 66:8).

I received an email from a pastor who stated the following: "I keep hearing … that Isaiah 66:8 is fulfilled in modern-day Israel. I have looked at these verses in every way and cannot get that reading even with a dispensational hermeneutic…. Can you tell me how they might see this verse to use it in this way and can you give me some help with what Isaiah is actually saying?" I would first note that the New Testament is the best interpreter of the Old Testament, and the New Testament does not say one word about Israel becoming a nation again or the need for it to happen. If the reestablishment of the state of Israel is a fundamental doctrine, it seems to me that Jesus and the New Testament writers would have said something about it. In fact, Israel was a nation in the first century. "The subject of the land is conspicuous by its absence in the letters of Paul. He seems to show no interest in the land in the purposes of God."[1]

Jesus is the focus of the New Testament as He was of the Old Testament. The Apostle Paul could have saved himself a lot of trouble with his fellow countrymen if he had said that one day God will restore the temple and land to Israel making the state of Israel the center of the world. "If Luke and the early Christian church thought in terms of conquest [see the book of Joshua 11:23; 14:15; 21:44; 23:1], they were

---

1. Colin Chapman, *Whose Promised Land?: The Continuing Crisis Over Israel and Palestine* (Grand Rapids, MI: Baker Books, 2002), 164.

thinking of the conquest not of the land but of the whole world [Rom. 4:13]. The only sword that would be used for this conquest was the sword of the word of God which would enable those who believed it to possess the inheritance that God had promised them."[2]

It's one thing to ask a question and study the topic. It's another thing to say something like this popular pastor told his congregation to do: "In your Bible, right next to Isaiah 66:8, you can write down May 14, 1948." No, you can't! Take heed how the book of Revelation ends (22:18-19). The video that this statement is taken from has tens of thousands of views. Every wind of bad doctrine is blowing today when it comes to eschatology. Is modern-day Israel the topic of Isaiah 66 or is the final chapter in this rich redemptive book describing events surrounding the return from exile and extending to the New Testament work of Jesus and the outpouring of the Holy Spirit in creating a new redemptive nation made up of Jews and Gentiles?

The book of Isaiah was written in the 8th century BC. The return from exile **back to the land** happened in the 6th century BC. The temple was rebuilt around 516 BC (Ezra 6:15). A second return took place around 458 BC led by Ezra (Ezra 7-8; see Isa. 11:11). miah rebuilt the walls around Jerusalem in 445 BC (Neh. 1:1-7:73). The following is from Robert Cruickshank, Jr.

> As one can see, all of the critical predictions and fulfillments, regarding the return to the land and the rebuilding of the temple, have been historically fulfilled. The only Old Testament prophet in the lineup after these events was Malachi, and one will search Malachi in vain for any mention of a return or a rebuilding. Why? Because these prophecies had been fulfilled by the time Malachi wrote. As William Cox noted, "When a vessel has been filled full (the literal meaning of fulfill) it is impossible to add more in that vessel."[3]

It always amazes me that prophecy pundits skip over so much of biblical history to get to 1948 claiming modern-day Israel is the fulfillment of so many OT texts when the time line from Isaiah to Malachi is the history

---

2. Chapman, *Whose Promised Land?*, 163.

3. William Cox, *Biblical Studies in Final Things* (Phillipsburg, NJ: Presbyterian and Reformed, 1966), 63.

we should focus on because of its proximity to the promises made. "The great majority of books on eschatology are written from the side of Christian fundamentalism…. Coming to grips with the historical background of the biblical texts is the part of that challenge most often ignored by eschatology books."[4] Here's an example by someone named Chadwick Harvey who ignores the biblical time line:

> The prophecy of Isaiah 66 gives us great wisdom, knowledge, and understanding of specific events that will occur before Messiah's Second Coming. This incredible prophecy is not only the foundation of all of the end of the age prophecies, but it also proclaims in summary, God's prophetic timeline. Here is the order of events in Isaiah 66.
>
> 1. Messiah's birth (Isaiah 66:7)
> 2. Israel becoming a nation again (Isaiah 66:8)
> 3. The children of Israel recapturing Jerusalem as their capital (Isaiah 66:8-9)
> 4. Messiah's Second Coming (Isaiah 66:14-16)
> 5. Messiah's Millennial Reign on Earth—1,000 years (Isaiah 66:18-21)
> 6. The New Jerusalem—Eternity (Isaiah 66:22-24)

What's missing from this time line? Everything related to Israel returning from the exile, the fulfillment after the return from exile (see Ezra, miah, Esther), the redemptive work of Jesus' earthly ministry outlined in four gospels, and the inauguration and growth of the NT *ekklēsia* (Acts 5:11; 8:1-4) described in the book of Acts and the epistles. Harvey jumps from the incarnation, ignoring around 700 years of OT history, and lands in Israel in 1948. Absurd. Even the *Scofield Reference Bible*, from the 1909 to 1945 editions, does not apply Isaiah 66:8 to the return of Israel in the future. The *Apologetic's Study Bible* does not have a note on 66:8, but it does have the following note on 66:21 to "gather all nations and languages."

> These people could be understood as faithful Israelites who had lived dispersed among the nations for many years (see Acts 2:5-11). More likely, Isaiah saw God giving the non-

---

4. Quoting Craig C. Hill's *In God's Time: The Bible and the Future* (2002), 10. George Mitrov, "Isaiah 65-66. New Heavens & New Earth," gmitrov.wixsite.com/website (Winter 2022), 1 note 1.

Israelites in His kingdom equality with Israelite believers. That is certainly what the apostles believed and taught in the NT; Paul celebrated how Christ has broken down the division between Jew and non-Jew (Eph 2:13-16), who together make up the new temple of the Lord (Eph. 2:19-21).

William Edward Biederwolf's *The Millennium Bible* does not include a note on Isaiah 66:8 (1924). There is no note on Isaiah 66:8 by premillennialist J. Barton Payne in his comprehensive *Encyclopedia of Biblical Prophecy* (1973). You won't find a comment in John F. Walvoord's *The Prophecy Knowledge Handbook: All the Prophecies of Scripture Explained in One Volume* (1990). In his 1991 book *Major Bible Prophecies: 37 Crucial Prophecies that Affect You Today* there is no mention of the 1948 reestablishment of Israel in 66:7-8. Walvoord was a dispensationalist.

There is no mention about Israel and 1948 in the *Prophecy Study Bible* (2000). Contrary to these and other works, *The Popular Bible Prophecy Commentary* edited by Tim LaHaye and Ed Hindson does apply Isaiah 66 to "The Rebirth of Israel" (148-150) as does the dispensational *Bible Knowledge Commentary* (1985) skipping the return of the Jews to their land after the Babylonian exile. It would be interesting to check all the published commentaries on Isaiah to see how many of them mention 1948.

Dispensationalists have a problem on their hands claiming that Israel becoming a nation again at any time prior to the "rapture of the church" is a fulfillment of Bible prophecy. Dispensationalism teaches that there are no signs before the "rapture." If there are signs, then the "rapture" is not an any-moment event. You can't believe in a pre-trib rapture and believe that Israel becoming a nation again in 1948 is "the" prophetic sign.[5] The late John R. Rice (1895-1980), a Baptist pastor and founder of the bi-weekly publication *The Sword of the Lord*, had this to say about Israel's national status: "Thus the trouble in Jerusalem, and the dispersion of Jews among all the nations of Jerusalem throughout this whole age, is simply a continuation of the punishment of God upon the whole race of Jews."[6] He went on to write the following:

---

5. See my book *Ten Popular Prophecy Myths Exposed and Answered*, 2nd ed. (Powder Springs, GA: American Vision, [2010] 2024), chap. 2 and Appendix B.

6. John R. Rice, *The King of the Jews: A Commentary on the Gospel According to Matthew* (Murfreesboro, TN: Sword of the Lord Publishers, 1955), 369.

Some Christian writers regard the atomic bomb, the rise of Russia, the founding of the new Israel state, the last world war (as they regarded the first world war), as evidence that we are in the very last days before Jesus comes."[7]

See my book *10 Popular Prophecy Myths Exposed and Answered* for more details on the any moment "rapture" premise and how it does not fit with any of the "signs" prophecy pundits claim as proof that the rapture, or as David Jeremiah calls it, "The Great Disappearance." This means that anything happening today cannot be tied to Bible prophecy. But to say this out loud would mean that prophecy book sales would plummet.

If "born in a day" is taken literally, then the prophecy wasn't fulfilled May 14, 1948. The process of establishing a national homeland for the Jews goes back to Theodor Herzl who was the founder of the Modern Zionist movement. In his 1896 pamphlet *Der Judenstaat* (*The Jewish State*), he envisioned the founding of a future independent Jewish state. Then there is the 1917 Balfour Declaration. Here's the original letter from Arthur Balfour to Walter Rothschild November 2, 1917:

His Majesty's Government view with favour the establishment in Palestine of a national home for the Jewish people, and will use their best endeavours to facilitate the achievement of this object, it being clearly understood that nothing shall be done which may prejudice the civil and religious rights of existing non-Jewish communities in Palestine, or the rights and political status enjoyed by Jews in any other country.

Statehood was a long process. Furthermore, there is nothing in the context of Isaiah 66 that gives any indication that what is described refers to events 2,600 years in the future from the time the prophecy was revealed to Isaiah. There are more immediate events that fit the context. For example:

7. The next eight verses [7-12] use birth and child imagery to describe the emergence of the new city. The suddenness of the events is portrayed in this verse: *Before ... labor, she gives birth.* Jerusalem's destruction in 587 BC had left marks on the city

---

7. John R. Rice, *We Can Have Revival Now* (Wheaton, IL: Sword of the Lord Publishers, 1950), 41. See Gary DeMar, *Ten Popular Prophecy Myths Exposed and Answered* (Powder Springs, GA: American Vision, 2024) Appendix B.

which were not removed until  miah rebuilt the walls in 437 BC (see Bright, *HI*,[8] 381). After that long wait of well over a century, it took only two years for  miah to complete the wall. It was an unbelievable feat. The metaphor picks up imagery from 49:20-21 (See Rev. 12:5).

8. *Who ever heard of such a thing? ... Zion has gone into labor and birthed her children.* The achievements of Ezra and miah were memorable. They accomplished more in a short period than anyone else in the century before and century after them. *The children of Zion* are at the new covenant community of faithful servants of Yahweh. This passage develops the theme of 65:8-10, 13:25; Deut 8:5; Jer. 31:20; Hos 11:1. The reference to children could also be to the new inhabitants (see Neh 11).[9]

Zionism is secular. Compare the return of Jews in 1948 to what is now called "Palestine," where many Jews were living when Jews migrated before and after 1948, to the return of the Jews from the Babylonian captivity:

> Then  miah, who was the governor, and Ezra the priest *and* scribe, and the Levites who taught the people said to all the people, "**This day is holy** to the LORD your God; do not mourn or weep." For all the people were weeping when they heard the words of the law. Then he said to them, "Go, eat of the fat, drink of the sweet, and send portions to him who has nothing prepared; for **this day is holy** to our Lord. Do not be grieved, for the joy of the LORD is your strength." So the Levites calmed all the people, saying, "Be still, for **the day is holy**; do not be grieved." All the people went away to eat, to drink, to send portions and to celebrate a great festival, because they understood the words which had been made known to them (Neh. 8:9-12).

There is a stark difference between the two returns. They remain stark today. Modern-day Israel did not come into existence in a way as described in  miah and that the NT requires. Compare it to the events surrounding Pentecost. Hal Lindsey wrote, "This dispersion began to draw to a close in May of 1948 when, against all odds, Israel

---

8. John Bright, *A History of Israel*, 3rd ed. (Philadelphia: Westminster, 1981).

9. John D. W. Watts, *Isaiah 34-66*, Word Biblical Commentary (Waco, TX: Word Books, 1987), 25:363.

was **reborn** as a nation."[10] As a secular nation, yes, but not in terms of what Jesus said to Nicodemus: "Jesus answered and said to him, 'Truly, truly, I say to you, unless one is born again he cannot see the kingdom of God'" (John 3:3). In terms of what the Bible requires, the Jews are no different from the Muslims when it comes to who Jesus is. What counts is "a new creation" (Gal. 6:15; see 2 Cor. 5:17).

Isaiah was written before the events of the Babylonian exile and return. The natural or "literal" interpretation would apply the prophecy to events of those living under the Old Covenant. If not then, the NT is the next option rather than the modern-day Zionist movement to Israel. Matthew Poole explains Isaiah 66:7-8 as applying to the New Covenant:

> The prophecy ... seems rather to refer to the coming of Christ, and the sudden propagation of the gospel. The popish interpreters applying it to the Virgin Mary bringing forth Christ, is like other of their fond dreams.
>
> As soon as Zion travailed, she brought forth children; as soon as the church of the Jews began to move out of the captivity of Babylon, God put it into the hearts of multitudes to go up, Exodus 1:5 Isaiah 2:1, 2, &c. Or, as soon as the voice of the gospel put the church of the Jews into her travail, in John the Baptist's, Christ's, and the apostles' times, it presently brought forth. In John Baptist's time, *the kingdom of heaven suffered violence, and the violent took it by force*, Matthew 11:12; and it continued so, as three thousand were converted at Peter's sermon, Ac 2. The Gentiles were the children of Zion, being planted into their stock, the law of the gospel first going out of Zion.

The NT is filled with examples of a new nation being established. Listen to what Jesus said to the unbelieving religious leaders who wanted to destroy Him:

> "Therefore I say to you [those in Jesus' audience], **the kingdom of God will be taken away from you and given to a nation** [ἔθνει/*ethnei*], **producing the fruit of it**. And he who falls on this stone will be broken to pieces; but on whomever it falls, it will scatter him like dust." When the **chief priests and the**

---

10. Hal Lindsey, "Who Owns the Holy Land?," WND (May 1, 2002): https://bit.ly/3Ypdr0Y

**Pharisees** heard His parables, they understood that **He was speaking about them**. When they sought to seize Him, they feared the people, because they considered Him to be a prophet (Matt. 21:43-44).

E.W. Bullinger's *The Companion Bible* (1909) has this note on Isaiah 66:8: "nation: i.e. the righteous nation of [Isa.] 26.2 ['Open the gates, that the righteous nation may enter/The one that remains faithful.'] referred to in *v.* 7 [of Isa. 26: 'The way of the righteous is smooth; O Upright One, make the path of the righteous level']. **Matt. 21.43**." In terms of biblical theology, especially when evaluated by Deuteronomy 26-28 and the NT, modern-day Israel is not a righteous nation.

Take note of the Parable of the Landowner (Matt. 21:33-41). There is no indication in these and other passages that the modern state of Israel is a fulfillment of any prophecy, OT or NT.

It's important to read Matthew 21-25 to get the entire context, especially Jesus cursing the fig tree (Israel) and the mountain (where the temple stood) cast into the sea (21:18-22), the burning of the city (Jerusalem) (22:7), their "house [the temple] left to [them] desolate" (23:38), and the prophecy of the temple's destruction before that Apostolic generation passed away (24:1-3, 34).[11] These physical outward types of the coming kingdom referred to Old Covenant Israel that was remade in Christ. A drastic change took place. Physical Jerusalem (Gal. 4:21-31) and Zion were of no redemptive consequence in the NT (Heb. 12:18-24).

- For it is written that Abraham had two sons, one by the slave woman and one by the free woman. But the son by the slave woman was born according to the flesh, and the son by the free woman through the promise. This is speaking allegorically, for **these women are two covenants**: one coming from Mount Sinai giving birth to children who are to be slaves; she is Hagar. Now this Hagar is Mount Sinai in Arabia and corresponds to the present Jerusalem, for she is enslaved with her children. But the Jerusalem above is free; she is our mother (Gal. 4:22-26).

- But **you have come to Mount Zion** and to the city of the living God, **the heavenly Jerusalem**, and to myriads of angels, to the

---

11. See DeMar, *Wars and Rumors of Wars*, *Last Days Madness*, *Matthew 24 Fulfilled*, and *Matthew 23-25* for a discussion of these prophetic texts.

general assembly and church of the firstborn who are enrolled in heaven, and to God, the Judge of all, and to the spirits of the righteous made perfect, and to Jesus, the mediator of a new covenant, and to the sprinkled blood, which speaks better than the blood of Abel (Heb. 12:22-24).

This "nation producing the fruit of it" was not a new geographical physical land nation any more than when Paul told the Corinthains, "we are the temple of the living God" (2 Cor. 6:16) was a new physical temple.

If Isaiah 66:7-14 refers to the NT era, Jesus' prophecy of a "nation producing the fruit of it" being established in one day can be found in Acts 2 when there were "Jews living in Jerusalem from every nation under heaven" (v. 5). In this case, the NT *ekklēsia* (a word used to describe Israel in the OT: Acts 7:38, Heb. 2:12) was born in a day! Now read Isaiah 66:8 within the context of the above passages:

Who has heard such a thing? Who has seen such things?
Can a land be born in one day?
Can a nation be brought forth all at once?
As soon as Zion travailed, she also brought forth her sons.

Homer Hailey shows that the prophecy has a Messianic goal. It's about Jesus and the redemptive fruit of His work:

The present passage gives prominence to the sudden birth of the *man-child*, the new *nation* and *land*, and *her children*. The *man-child* seems to be none other than the long-expected Servant, the Messiah born of the spiritual Zion (see the comments on 49:1; cf. Mic. 4:10; 5:2-3; Rev. 12:1-5),[12] who will "suddenly come to his temple" (Mal. 3:1). *Who hath heard such a thing?* Here is something unparalleled in history; for immediately following the birth of the Man-Child, a nation, its land, and Zion's children are brough forth. On the entrance of Christ into the world and the events of Pentecost can be in view here; the

---

12. See Homer Hailey, *Revelation: An Introduction and Commentary* (Grand Rapids, MI: Baker Books, 1979), 267-272.

Son was exalted, the new nation was established, and Zion's children began to multiply (Acts 2; 4:4).[13]

These "sons" were believing Jews—thousands of them (Acts 2:41 [~3000]; 4:4 [~5000]; 21:20 ["many thousands": μυριάς/*myriads*]). When the persecution started, notice what these believing Jews living in Jerusalem did.

> Saul was in hearty agreement with putting him to death. And on that day a great persecution began against the church in Jerusalem, and **they were all scattered throughout the regions of Judea and Samaria, except the apostles.** Some devout men buried Stephen, and made loud lamentation over him. But Saul began ravaging the church, entering house after house, and dragging off men and women, he would put them in prison. Therefore, those who had been scattered went about preaching the word. **Philip went down to the city of Samaria** and began proclaiming Christ to them (Acts 8:1-4).

Remember what Jesus told His disciples prior to His ascension:

> So when they had come together, they were asking Him, saying, "Lord, is it at this time You are restoring the kingdom to Israel?" He said to them, "It is not for you to know times or epochs which the Father has fixed by His own authority; but you will receive power when the Holy Spirit has come upon you; and **you shall be My witnesses both in Jerusalem, and in all Judea and Samaria, and even to the remotest part of the earth**" (1:6-8).

Jesus answered their question with a statement about the worldwide proclamation of the gospel not a reinstitution of the Old Covenant Jerusalem-centered kingdom. The kingdom was international. The church grew and advanced.

- The word of God kept on spreading; and the number of the disciples continued to increase greatly in Jerusalem, and a great many of the priests were becoming obedient to the faith (6:7).

---

13. Homer Hailey, *A Commentary on Isaiah with Emphasis on the Messianic Hope* (Grand Rapids, MI: Baker Books, 1985), 524.

- So the church throughout all Judea and Galilee and Samaria enjoyed peace, being built up; and going on in the fear of the Lord and in the comfort of the Holy Spirit, it continued to increase (9:31).
- But the word of the Lord continued to grow and to be multiplied (12:24).
- And the word of the Lord was being spread through the whole region. But the Jews incited the devout women of prominence and the leading men of the city, and instigated a persecution against Paul and Barnabas, and drove them out of their district. But they shook off the dust of their feet *in protest* against them and went to Iconium (13:49-51; also 19:20).

This would have been the perfect time for Paul and Barnabas to tell their countrymen that the rapture of the church could happen at any moment and God would again restore Israel to her unique status. Instead, they "shook off the dust of their feet." The book of Acts ends with Paul "proclaiming the kingdom of God" (28:31). He does not say anything about the restoration of the Old Covenant order or the land. Israel (to the Jew first) served God's purpose to take the gospel to the world: "For so the Lord has commanded us, 'I HAVE PLACED YOU AS A LIGHT FOR THE GENTILES, THAT YOU SHOULD BRING SALVATION TO THE END OF THE EARTH'" (13:47; also, Luke 2:32; Isa. 49:6). The kingdom is Jesus-centered, not physical Israel-centered.

Peter wrote to believers in his day, "But you are a CHOSEN RACE, A ROYAL PRIESTHOOD, **A HOLY NATION** [Ex. 19:6], A PEOPLE FOR God's OWN POSSESSION, that you may proclaim the excellencies of Him who has called you out of darkness into His marvelous light; or you once were NOT A PEOPLE, but **now** you are THE PEOPLE OF GOD; you had NOT RECEIVED MERCY, but **now** you have RECEIVED MERCY" (1 Peter 2:9-10). Notice how Peter quotes OT passages that referred to Israel but were applied to the NT *ekklēsia* (Acts 5:11; 8:1-4) that included believing Jews and Gentiles. Peter was not describing a distant reestablishment of Israel in 1948 but what was taking place in his day—the "now" of their day.

How is it possible to skip over events in the OT and NT to interpret Isaiah 66:8 when all the elements are found in both Testaments? John N. Oswalt writes:

The significance of *zākār*, "male," here [66:7] is unclear. The Targ[um Jonathan] paraphrases "her king will be revealed," which is plainly a messianic reference. Rev. 12:5 uses similar terminology in what is apparently a messianic setting. Without further indications in the immediate context, however, it is impossible to make definitive judgment. It may be that the term is used because a male was understood to be the progenitor of a nation. On the apparent influence of this verse (and all of ch. 66) on the NT, see R. Aus, "The relevance of Isaiah 66:6 to Revelation 12 and 2 Thessalonians 1."[14]

Note that Oswalt does not interpret 66:7-8 as the 1948 "rebirth" of Israel. He does not apply these verses to "a single historical event" but "applies," according to John Calvin (1509-1564), "to a number of events in redemption history" beginning with "the release from captivity, which suddenly became a reality with Cyrus's conquest of Babylon" and including the Reformation. Oswalt concludes that "in a single moment Zion will give birth to a brand-new people, a people forever set free from the curse of sin."[15]

J. Alec Motyer writes about Isaiah 66:21 that "Jerusalem is not the literal city but the city of Galatians 4:25-26; Hebrews 12:22; Revelation 21."[16]

James Jordan offers a compelling summary of the prophets and what they were prophesying at the direction of the Holy Spirit:

> Ezekiel 34 states that God will act as Good Shepherd to Israel, and will bring them back into the land. He continues this theme in Ezekiel 36, saying that God will make a new covenant with Israel. The inauguration of this new covenant, which we can call the Restoration Covenant, is described in Zechariah 3, where God removes the filth from Joshua the High Priest and restores the Temple and priesthood. Of course, Ezekiel's language in Ezekiel 36:25-27 is picked up in the New Testament and applied

---

14. John N. Oswalt, *The Book of Isaiah: Chapters 44-66* (Grand Rapids, MI: Eerdmans, 1998), 2:674, note 674.

15. Oswalt, *The Book of Isaiah*, 2:675.

16. J. Alec Motyer, *The Prophecy of Isaiah: An Introduction and Commentary* (Downers Grove, IL: InterVarsity Press, 1993), 540.

to the New Covenant, but we need to understand that the first fulfillment of his words was in the Restoration Covenant, which was of course a type of the New Covenant.

Ezekiel continues in Ezekiel 37 with the vision of the valley of dry bones. The Spirit of God would be given in greater measure than ever before (though of course not as great as at Pentecost in Acts 2), and the result would be a restoration of the people. No longer would there be a cultural division between Judah and Ephraim, but all would be together as a new people. (Their new name as a whole would be "Judahite, Jew.")[17]

## What Do Commentators Say?

You don't have to take my word for my view on this. As always, I check my work with other sources. In the cases below, with commentators who do not have an eschatological ax to grind. Most of today's popular prophecy pundits work within the bubble of an existing system that has little biblical support when examined by comparing Scripture with Scripture without adding elements to passages that are not present but needed.

### John D. W. Watts

Ver. 7 The next eight verses use birth and child imagery to describe the emergence of the new city. The suddenness of the events is portrayed in this verse" *Before ... labor, she gives birth.* Jerusalem's destruction in 587 BC had left marks on the city which were not removed until  miah rebuilt the walls in 437 BC (see Bright, *HI*, 381). After that long wait of well over a century, it took only two years for  miah to complete the wall. It was an unbelievable feat. The metaphor picks up imagery from 49:20-21 (See Rev. 12:5).

Ver. 8 *Who ever heard of such a thing? ... Zion has done into labor and birthed her children.* The achievements of Ezra and  miah were memorable. They accomplished more in a short period than anyone else in the century before and century after them. *The children of Zion are at the new covenant community of faithful servants of Yahweh.*

17. *Esther in the Midst of Covenant History* (Niceville, FL: Biblical Horizons, 2001), 5-6. Unpublished manuscript.

This passage develops the theme of 65:8-10, 13:25; Deut 8:5; Jer. 31:20; Hos 11:1. The reference to children could also be to the new inhabitants (see Neh 11).[18]

## *A Critical Commentary and Paraphrase on the Old Testament and the Apocrypha*

Ver. 7. *Before she travailed, she brought forth.*] Here begins a new paragraph, containing a description of the sudden increase of the Christian church, upon God's rejecting the Jews, and destroying their temple and worship. The very destruction of the Jewish polity making way for the growth of the gospel, inasmuch as it abated that opposition which the Jewish zealots all along gave to the spreading of it; and the abolishing the Jewish worship contributed very much to the abrogating the law of Moses, and burying it with silence and decency. (See Rom. xi.11.) The church is described here as a travailing woman, the mother of all true believers. (See liv.1. Gal. iv.26.)

*Before her pain came, she was delivered of a man-child.*] The expressions import how suddenly and quickly Christianity was spread and propagated over the world. And this latter sentence alludes to the Hebrew women being delivered of their male children, before the midwives could come to them, (Exod. i.19.) The propagating the kingdom of Christ, is, in like manner, described by a woman's travailing, and bringing forth a man-child, Rev. xii.1, 2, 5. which place plainly alludes to the words here.

Ver. 8. *Shall the earth be made to bring forth in one day? or shall a nation be born at once?*] The suddenness of this event is as surprising, as if the fruits of the earth, which are brought to perfection by slow degrees, should blossom and ripen all in one day. And the fruitfulness of this spiritual increase is as wonderful, as if a whole nation were born at once, or by one woman. We may understand the former part of this sentence of the speedy propagation of the gospel through the world, and the latter part of it of the sudden conversion of the Jews, and their union with the Gentiles into one church, when God will remove the iniquity of the land in one day, as it is foretold, Zech. iii. 9. (Compare

---

18. John D. W. Watts, *Isaiah 34-66*, Word Biblical Commentary (Waco, TX: Word Books, 1987), 25:363.

Micah v. 3.) These two events, though distant in time [to Isaiah's day], yet will agree very much in the swiftness of their progress.[19]

### An Old Testament Commentary for English Readers
(7) Before she travailed... — Tho mother, as the next verse shows, is Zion ; the man-child, born at last without the travail-pangs of sorrow, is the new Israel, the true Israel of God. The same figure has met us in chaps. xlix.17-21, liv.1, and is implied in Matt. xxiv. 8. Its antithesis is found in chap, xxxvii. 3.
(8) Shall the earth be made... —Better, *Shall a land be made to travail.* The usually slow processes of national development are contrasted with the supernatural rapidity of the birth and growth of the new Israel.[20]

### The Nelson Study Bible
66:7, 8 **Before she ... gave birth** represents the birth of the community from the cast-out worshipers as coming so quickly that it will be without pain. At times, Zion is pictured as the daughter of the Lord (1:8); here she is the mother of His people. The **male child** and **her children** may refer to Christ and His Church.

### New Self-Interpreting Bible Library
Ver. 7. When Christ, as 'a child born, a son given, came in the flesh, a remnant were doubtless expecting and praying for his appearing; but as a nation and church, the Jews neither expected nor desired such a Redeemer.

V. 8. *For as soon as Zion prevailed.* 'But as soon as Zion travailed,' &c. of which see the wonderful conversions produced by a single apostolic address, Ac. 2.41; ["So then, those who had received his word were baptized; and that day there were added about three thousand souls."] 4:4 ["But many of those who had heard the message believed; and the number of the men came to be about five thousand."]. And surely what God has effected once he is able to accomplish again.[21]

---

19. Patrick, Lowth, Arnald, Whitby, and Lowman, *A Critical Commentary and Paraphrase on the Old Testament and the Apocrypha*, new ed. (London: 1822), 3:587.

20. Charles John Ellicott, ed., *An Old Testament Commentary for English Readers*, 4 vols. (London: Cassell and Company, Limited, 1884), 4:575.

21. *New Self-Interpreting Bible Library* (St. Louis: The Bible Educational Society, 1916),

### *John Addison Alexander*

Before she travailed she brought forth before her pain came she was delivered of a male. All interpreters agree that the mother here described is Zion that the figure is essentially the same as in ch. 49:21 and that in both cases an increase of numbers is represented as a birth while in that before us the additional idea of suddenness is expressed by the figure of an unexpected birth.... This verse [66:7] ... represents the event previously mentioned. The terms of the sentence are exceedingly appropriate both to the return from Babylon and the future restoration of the Jews [after the exile] but admit at the same time of a wider application to the change of dispensations as the birth of the church of the New Testament.[22]

### *Pulpit Commentary* on Isaiah

Verses 7, 8.—Before she travailed, etc. Without any long delay, without any labour pains, Zion will bring forth a man-child—a whole nation, which wilt be born at once, and not grow up by slow degrees. The occupation of Jerusalem by the great body of the returned exiles (Ezra 2:1; 3:1) is intended. Such a second birth of a nation was strange, and without precedent (comp. Isaiah 42:9; 43:19). Shall the earth [*eretz*] be made to bring forth in one day? rather, can *a land be brought forth in one day*? It is not only a people, but a country, that is born anew; not only the Jews, but Judaea.

Verse 22.—As the new heavens and the new earth, which I will make, shall remain. The "new heavens and the new earth," once created, continue forever (comp. Rev. 21:1-27; 22:1-5). So shall your seed and your name remain. This statement is usually taken to be a promise of some special pre-eminence to the Jew over the Gentile in the final kingdom of the redeemed. But St. Paul speaks of all such privileges as already abolished in his day (Col. 3:11); and, if the priesthood is to be common to both Gentile and Jew, the principle of equality would seem to be conceded. Perhaps no more is here meant than that, as the "new heaven and new earth" will always remain, so there will always remain a seed of true believers to worship God in them.

---

3:1227.

22. Joseph Addison Alexander, *Commentary on the Prophecies of Isaiah*, one-volume ed. (Grand Rapids, MI: Zondervan, [1865] 1953), 2:455-456.

## Albert Barnes' *Notes on the Bible*

Before she travailed, she brought forth — That is, Zion. The idea here is, that there would be a great and sudden increase of her numbers. Zion is here represented, as it often is, as a female (see Isa. 1:8), and as the mother of spiritual children (compare Isa.54:1; 49:20-21). The particular idea here is, that the increase would be sudden—as if a child were born without the usual delay and pain of parturition. If the interpretation given of Isaiah 66:6 be correct, then this refers probably to the sudden increase of the church when the Messiah came, and to the great revivals of religion which attended the first preaching of the gospel. Three thousand were converted on a single day (Acts 2), and the gospel was speedily propagated almost all over the known world. Vitringa supposes that it refers to the sudden conversion of the Gentiles, and their accession to the church.

## "Isaiah 40-66" by Marvin A. Sweeney[23]

It is noteworthy, therefore, that 66:2, 5 employ the Hebrew term hārēdîm, "those who tremble" at YHWH's word (i.e., those who stand in awe of YHWH and will do what YHWH expects), insofar as it is the same term employed for the self-designation of the community under Ezra (Ezra 9:3; 10:4…). Convincing the people to support such an enterprise, particularly in the aftermath of the Babylonian exile and the rebuilding of the temple, was a key challenge for a people that continued to live in economic hardship and under threat by the various brigands and marauders of western Asia during the Persian period. Consequently, the differentiation between the wicked and the righteous served a rhetorical end to convince the people that they would not want to be accounted among the wicked who ignored YHWH and the temple, but instead among those who supported YHWH, the creator of the universe and the redeemer of Israel, in YHWH's efforts to restore the temple to its proper role as the holy center of the Jewish people in Jerusalem and as the holy center of creation at large.

In short, chs. 65-66 were written … in an effort to support the temple reforms of miah and Ezra.

---

23. Rolf P. Knierim, Gene M. Tucker, and Marvin A. Sweeney, eds., *The Forms of the Old Testament Literature* (Grand Rapids, MI: Eerdmans, 2016).

*****

Isaiah 65-66 functions as the conclusion to the book of Isaiah as a whole by pointing to the anticipated restoration of Jerusalem that will follow from the punishment and exile suffered by the city since the Assyrian period.

*****

Isaiah 66:20-21 "refers to YHWH's choosing priests and Levites from the exiled Israelites who are returned by the nations to Zion.

# CHAPTER 9

# Disputing Ray Comfort's "Ten Indisputable Signs"

Ray Comfort has produced a video that claims there are "ten prophecies that reveal the future of the world," signs that are "undeniable evidence that we are living in the last days." Where have we heard this before? He's not the first person to make predictions based on specific signs. Actually, it's quite common. In 1919, Lewis Sperry Chafer wrote *Seven Biblical Signs of the Times*.[1] He assured his readers of more than 100 years ago that the rapture "is imminent, and has been since the first promise regarding it was given."[2] In 1979 Colin Hoyle Deal wrote *Christ Returns by 1988: 101 Reasons Why*. In 1988 the World Bible Society sent out a fund-raising letter with the following appeal:

> I beg you, as brothers and sisters in the Lord, to take time to read the first ten reasons the Rapture is in 1988 and the first ten pages of *The Bible Dates of the 7th Week in Daniel, Armageddon and the Millennium*. If you are not totally convinced of the Bible dates, I've sounded the trumpet, and I rest my case. We, as Christian booksellers, are responsible to make known to the Body of Christ these upcoming events. The watchman is held responsible, and the blood is on his hands if he doesn't sound the alarm.

---

1. "[1] The Jew arises to national life; [2] Gentile governments turn to democracy; [3] Jerusalem is released from the overlordship of Gentiles; [4] Prophecy is unveiled; [5] Knowledge increases, and men run to and fro, and all creation is to be delivered from the bondage of corruption; [6] An apostasy must appear which retains the outward form of godliness, but denies the power thereof; [7] And treasure must be heaped together for the 'last days.' These are God's signs and they are being fulfilled at this moment. The rugged mountains appear; but our blessed haven in the presence of our Lord is even nearer. May this solemn truth lead us to be instant in season and out of season in the work which He has given us to do!" Lewis Sperry Chafer, *Seven Biblical Signs of the Times* (Chicago: Bible Institute Colportage Association, [1919] 1928).

2. Chafer, *Seven Biblical Signs of the Times*, 10.

Mirroring the seven-fold numbering of end-time signs, in 2003 Mark Hitchcock wrote a book with a similar title—*Seven Signs of the End Times*.[3] I have a library full of similar books that have made the same type of claims over the centuries.[4]

Ray Comfort has put himself on the front lines defending the Christian faith by confronting the spirit of the age and those who promote it, especially atheists and skeptics of the Bible's inerrancy. This is a good thing. But one of the recurring arguments used by atheists against the reliability of the Bible is the claim that it falsely predicts the return of Jesus within a generation of the time He delivered the prophecy known as the Olivet Discourse to a group of His disciples around the year AD 30: "This generation will not pass away until all these things take place" (Matt. 24:34). The "all these things" refer to earthquakes, wars and rumors of wars, famines, stellar phenomena, tribulation, apostasy, tribulation, and other seemingly end-time signs. This would also include "the Son of Man coming on the clouds of heaven with power and great glory" (24:30; also see Dan. 7:13; Matt. 26:64; Mark 13:26; 14:62; Luke 21:27; Rev. 1:7, 13; 14:14).[5]

There is a long history of skeptics turning to Bible prophecy and claiming Jesus was wrong about the timing of His coming and the signs associated with it. Bertrand Russell wrote the following in *Why I Am Not a Christian*, a lecture he delivered on March 6, 1927 to the National Secular Society:

> I am concerned with Christ as he appears in the Gospel narrative as it stands, and there one does find some things that do not seem to be very wise. For one thing, He certainly thought that His second coming would occur in clouds of glory before the death of all the people who were living at that time. There are a great many texts that prove that and there are a lot of places

3. Mark Hitchcock, *Seven Signs of the End Times* (Sisters, OR: Multnomah Publishers, 2003).

4. For a historical study of how prophetic passages have been misapplied for nearly 2,000 years, see Francis X. Gumerlock, *The Day and the Hour: Christianity's Perennial Fascination with Predicting the End of the World* (Powder Springs, GA: American Vision, 2000).

5. See Gary DeMar, *Is Jesus Coming Soon?* (Powder Springs, GA: American Vision, 2006), *Last Days Madness: Obsession of the Modern Church*, 4th ed. (Powder Springs, GA: American Vision, 1999), and *Wars and Rumors of Wars*, updated ed. (Powder Springs, GA: American Vision, [2017] 2023).

where it is quite clear that He believed that His coming would happen during the lifetime of many then living. That was the belief of His earlier followers, and it was the basis of a good deal of His moral teaching.[6]

There have been others.[7] Two recent ones come to mind. Bart Ehrman, author of numerous books critical of the New Testament, became skeptical of the authority of the New Testament because of eschatology. His best-selling book *Misquoting Jesus* describes how he struggled to reconcile what he believed to be errors in the Bible.[8] His pilgrimage from Moody Bible Institute to Princeton University changed him forever. His trek down the road to skepticism began with what he describes as "one of the most popular books on campus" at the time, Hal "Lindsay's [*sic*] apocalyptic blueprint for our future, *The Late Great Planet Earth.*" Ehrman writes that he "was particularly struck by the 'when'" of Lindsey's prophetic timetable in Matthew 24:34 where Jesus states, "this generation will not pass away until all these things take place."

The other one was the response that Douglas Wilson gave to atheist Christopher Hitchens in a debate they had that was later produced as the film *Collision* in 2009.[9] Like Jonathan the Skeptic and Bart Ehrman, Hitchens charged that Jesus was in error because He predicted His coming within a generation, and it did not come to pass. Here's how the exchange went:

**Christopher Hitchens**: [Jesus said that] He would reappear in the lifetime of His disciples.

**Douglas Wilson**: No.

**Hitchens**: Yes.

---

6. Bertrand Russell, *Why I Am Not a Christian* (New York: Simon and Schuster, 1957), 16.

7. Gerald A. Larue, "The Bible and the Prophets of Doom," *Skeptical Inquirer* (January/February 1999), 29; Michael Shermer, *How We Believe: The Search for God in an Age of Science* (New York: W.H. Freeman and Company, 2000), 1-7; Tim Callahan, *Bible Prophecy: Failure or Fulfillment?* (Altadena, CA: Millennium Press, 1997), 204-229.

8. Bart D. Ehrman, *Misquoting Jesus: The Story Behind Who Changed the Bible and Why* (New York: HarperCollins, 2005).

9. https://en.wikipedia.org/wiki/Collision_(2009_film)

**Wilson**: No, He said he was going to come back and destroy Jerusalem, which He did in 70 AD. Right on the money.

**Hitchens**: The Roman Empire didn't do this?

**Wilson**: No, He said "this generation will not pass away until all of these things are fulfilled."

**Hitchens**: Oh, God.

**Wilson**: The moon ... hang on a second. This is really important, actually.

**Hitchens**: I know it is, yeah.

**Wilson**: When Jesus says in Matthew 24, the moon, the sun is going to go out and the stars fall from the heavens, he is quoting from Isaiah 13, and Isaiah 34. There is de-creation language throughout the Old Testament. Every time it occurs in the Old Testament, it always refers to a military destruction of a nation or a city-state, always. In Isaiah 13, an oracle against the king of Babylon, and then you have the same de-creation language, and then Jesus says in Matthew 24, not one stone is going to be left on another. The disciples say when is it going to happen and Jesus quotes Isaiah, so Jesus is not talking about the end of the space-time universe. He simply isn't. It has nothing whatever to do with that. It has to do with the destruction of Jerusalem, which happened within one generation, just as Jesus said, authenticating him as a prophet.[10]

Wilson demonstrated, as I will show below, that Jesus was referring to a judgment coming that did take place before that generation passed away. It's the only way to read the Olivet Discourse, and the skeptics are reading it the right way. Unfortunately, too many Christians give the wrong answer to the question, "So, why didn't Jesus return before that generation passed away like He said He would?"

Ray Comfort's response was similar to an article he had written that appeared on the website of Christian Worldview Network on May 14, 2008.

---

10. From Joel McDurmon, *Collision: The Official Study Guide* (Powder Springs, GA: American Vision Press, 2010), 85-86.

The End of the Age? Don't let doomsday prophets fool you. Just because there's been another big earthquake, it doesn't signal the end of the world. It does, however, bring us closer to what the Bible calls the end of the age.' Do you want evidence that the Bible is the Word of God? Of course you don't, but here it is anyway: Look at the signs the Bible speaks of (combined from Matthew 24; Mark 13; Luke 21; 1 Timothy 4; and 2 Timothy 3), and relate that to contemporary life on earth. It says that at the end of the age there will be earthquakes in various places, famines, diseases, people becoming fearful of the future, nation rising against nation, wars, people would be deceived by religious leaders who said they were from God, a dead religious system, materialism, a forsaking of the Ten Commandments, money-hunger preachers who would have big followings and slur the name of Christ (see 2 Peter 2:1-3), a denial of the Noahic flood (how true is that one!), increase in violence (watch the news tonight), haters of God (listen to His name blasphemed daily), an increase in knowledge (think of the Internet/computer age), an increase in travel (air travel), false converts who would fall away from the Christian faith and get into the occult (see 1 Timothy 4:1-5). Scripture also says that mockers would say that these signs have always been around (did you just say that?). We are even told why they would mock such clear truth—because they love their lust (2 Peter 3:1-7). That cuts close to the bone. Imagine that—a 2,000 year-old Book predicts what you would say, and why you would say it. Here's the trump card. Jesus said to watch for when the Jews regained Jerusalem (see Luke 21:24). That happened in 1967, after 2,000 years of the Jews not having a homeland, they stepped into Jerusalem, bringing into culmination all the signs of the times. Don't test God's patience. You had better get right with Him today, before it's too late.

He repeats these unconvincing arguments in a 2009 blog post.[11] After these articles appeared, I wrote a response pointing out some of the

11. A Question from a Skeptic (June 26, 2009): Jonathan: "Could anyone of you believers tell me when the end times will happen, besides soon? It seems to me that the end times have been preached by man ever since the time they created their fictional deities."

**Ray Comfort:** "Here are some of the 'signs' of which the Bible speaks. Nation will rise

flaws in his argument. After reading my articles, Ray called me and left a voice message. I called him back, and we spoke about the articles. Near the end of our conversation, Ray said the following to me: "I'm never going to write on Bible prophecy again since it seems I don't know much about it."

Well, his video indicates that he's back to the topic of Bible prophecy. The following content is what I had written in response to Ray's earlier

against nation. Wars. Earthquakes in various places. Money-hungry preachers will deceive many and slur the name of Christianity. It predicts a forsaking of the institution of marriage, an increase in knowledge (think of the computer era) and an increase in travel (think of air flight, train, car, etc.). A belief in 'fables' (Santa Claus, etc.), and a general denial of the world-wide Noahic flood. There will be an increase in dietary concern, a forsaking of the Ten Commandments, and Israel (Jerusalem in particular) will become a huge unsolvable problem for the nations of the world. Life will become fearful for many, and men will have heart failure because of concern for the things that happen on the earth. The Scriptures speak of a cold hypocritical religious system with a mere 'form of godliness.'

'There will be skeptics of Christianity who will particularly mock the thought of the Second Coming. The Bible even perfectly predicts your philosophy and the reason why you mock the thought. It says you will say that these signs have always been around, and you will do this for two reasons: 1. because you don't realize that God is not subject to the dimension of time (a day to Him is as a thousand years to us), and 2. because of your love of lust. However, the big 'sign' to look for is the Jews re-possession of the city of Jerusalem. That happened in 1967. For the first time in 2,000 years without a homeland, they obtained Jerusalem, and they now occupy that holy city. Despite all this, Jesus said that the gospel must be preached to the ends of the earth, and we are trying to do that in the hope that people like you will come to your senses. There's a reason why we are so concerned for you. This is because the first time Jesus came, He came a harmless lamb to suffer for the sins of the world. The second time He will come in perfect Judgment, as the conquering King of Kings and Lord of Lords. The sky will part, there will be a great noise, lightning, and incredible power. The Bible warns that He will come in a holy wrath, to punish murderers, rapists, thieves, liars, fornicators, blasphemers, adulterers, and the disobedient. It will be so fearful, humanity will call for rocks to fall on them to hide them from His power. Here are some details of what will happen:

"... and to give you who are troubled rest with us when the Lord Jesus is revealed from heaven with His mighty angels, in flaming fire taking vengeance on those who do not know God, and on those who do not obey the gospel of our Lord Jesus Christ. These shall be punished with everlasting destruction from the presence of the Lord and from the glory of His power, when He comes, in that Day, to be glorified in His saints and to be admired among all those who believe, because our testimony among you was believed" (2 Thessalonians 1:7-10).

All these signs are deliberately hidden from the proud by what you are deceived into thinking is a fictional deity, in a Book you think is nothing but mythology. Your sin against God is way more serious than a heart attack. We are talking about where you will spend eternity: Heaven or Hell. If you are not sure what to do today, go to www.NeedGod.com

views about Bible prophecy. The **bold text comments** are Ray's. My comments follow in regular type:

> **Don't let doomsday prophets fool you. Just because there's been another big earthquake, it doesn't signal the end of the world. It does, however, bring us closer to what the Bible calls "the end of the age." Do you want evidence that the Bible is the Word of God? Of course you don't, but here it is anyway: Look at the signs the Bible speaks of (combined from Matthew 24; Mark 13; Luke 21; 1 Timothy 4; and 2 Timothy 3), and relate that to contemporary life on earth.**

I was hopeful when you began your article with "Don't let doomsday prophets fool you" and your admonition that another big earthquake does not "signal the end of the world" that you were not advocating that the "end of the age" was near and that we are moving to some climatic end-time event. Then you had to throw in "however" and appeal to Jesus' prophetic discourses (Matt. 24-25; Mark 13; Luke 17:22-37; 19:41-44; 21:1-36). The Olivet Discourse describes what would take place before "this generation," the Apostolic generation, passed away (Matt. 24:34), the generation two whom Jesus was speaking. Jesus always uses "this generation" to refer to His contemporaries (Matt. 11:16; 12:41, 42; 23:36; Mark 8:12; 13:30; Luke 7:31; 11:29, 30, 31, 32, 50, 51; 17:25; 21:32).

Jesus never uses "this generation" to refer to a future generation. For those who claim that "generation" (*genea*) really means "race," there are two problems. First, the Greek word *genea* cannot be made to mean "race," as in the "Jewish race." *Genea* means "generation" (e.g., Matt. 1:17; Luke 1:48; 9:41; Acts 14:16; 15:21; Eph. 3:5; Col. 1:26). The Greek word for "race" is *genos*.

Second, there is the logic of the verse. If *genea* is translated as "race," as in the "Jewish race, then Matthew 24:34 would read, "This Jewish race will not pass away until all these things take place." So when "all these things take place," the Jewish race will pass away. This doesn't make any sense since those who advocate for a yet future fulfillment of the passage focus on the Jews being reestablished as the people of God. How is that possible if the Jewish race passes away?

One additional argument needs to be dealt with. A popular way to interpret Matthew 24:34 is to have it read, "**The generation that sees these signs** will not pass away until all these things take place." I can get a verse to say almost anything if I remove some words and add others. Notice how "the" is substituted for "this."

Audience relevance is very important. It, along with time words, are keys that help us identify when a prophetic event is to take place We are told which generation will see "all these things": "so, YOU too, when YOU see all these things, recognize that He is near, right at the door" (Matt. 24:33). The "you" is a reference to Jesus' audience. Follow the use of "you" throughout the chapter and notice that the second person plural refers to Jesus' contemporaries (Matt. 24:2, 4, 6, 9, 15, etc.). If Jesus had a future generation in mind, He would have said "when *that* generation passes away" and "when *they* see." Jesus uses the near demonstrate "this" to indicate the generation that was present with Him. "This" is a near demonstrative in that it identifies items, places, and times that are near.

One last point needs to be considered. If Jesus was not referring to His present audience, then what words could He have used to make it clear that He was referring to His present audience that would "see all these things"? He couldn't have used "you" or "this generation" since those who hold to a yet future fulfillment of the passage maintain that these words refer to a future audience and time. The biblical approach is to take Jesus at His word. He said He would return before "this generation" (their generation) passed away, and He did.

> It says that at the end of the age there will be earthquakes in various places, famines, diseases, people becoming fearful of the future, nation rising against nation, wars, people would be deceived by religious leaders who said they were from God, a dead religious system, materialism, a forsaking of the Ten Commandments, money-hunger [*sic*] preachers who would have big followings and slur the name of Christ (see 2 Peter 2:1-3), a denial of the Noahic flood (how true is that one!), increase in violence (watch the news tonight), haters of God (listen to His name blasphemed daily), an increase in knowledge (think of the Internet/computer age), an increase in travel (air travel), false converts who would fall away from the Christian faith and get into the occult (see 1 Timothy 4:1-5).

Other than your references to modern technology, there is nothing in the above description that wasn't going on in the generation leading up to the destruction of Jerusalem in AD 70. There were earthquakes in various places. There's one mentioned in Acts 16:26. Historians of the day describe many more that occurred throughout the Roman Empire. A "great famine all over the world [lit., *inhabited earth*]" is mentioned in Acts 11:28 (also see Rom. 8:35) that took place during the reign of Claudius who was Roman emperor from AD 41 to 54.

While your unstated use of Daniel 12:4 to support the idea that the information age and air travel are "signs of the end times" may be popular, it is unfounded. Very few if any noted Bible scholars hold this view.

In the 19th century the locomotive was seen as the prophetic fulfillment of this passage. Even dispensational author Thomas Ice[12] recognizes that the interpretation you and many other popular prophecy writers have adopted have misread and misapplied Daniel 12:4. Daniel is referring to an increase in understanding of the prophecies concerning the coming Messiah which had been revealed to him and those of the first century in people like, Elizabeth, Zech. He is not referring to an increase in general information.

Peter doesn't say anything about "a denial of the Noahic flood" as an end-time sign. You're reading something into the passage that isn't there.

Interest in the occult was prevalent in the Old Testament period and early church (e.g., Acts 19:19, 23-41), as was homosexuality (Rom. 1:18-32; 1 Cor. 6:9; 1 Tim. 1:10). I suggest that you take a look at the first chapter of Romans to see how Paul described what was going on in his day:

> "And just as they did not see fit to acknowledge God any longer, God gave them over to a depraved mind, to do those things which are not proper, being filled with all unrighteousness, wickedness, greed, evil; full of envy, murder, strife, deceit, malice; they are gossips, slanderers, haters of God, insolent, arrogant, boastful, inventors of evil, disobedient to parents, without understanding, untrustworthy, unloving, unmerciful; and although they know the ordinance of God, that those who practice such things are worthy of death, they not only do the same, but also give hearty approval to those who practice them" (Rom. 1:28-32).

---

12. Thomas Ice, "Running to and Fro": http://goo.gl/EcQHfl

Similar wording is found in 2 Timothy 3:1-8. In this passage, Paul was explaining to Timothy how he should live in the midst of his corrupt culture. The use of "last days" in verse 1 is a reference to the last days of the old covenant (see Heb. 1:1-2; 1 Cor. 10:11; James 5:7-9).

There were Gnostics who taught that Jesus did not have a true human body, and Jews who denied the incarnation: "For many deceivers **have gone out** into the world who do not confess Jesus Christ as coming in the flesh. This is the deceiver and the antichrist" (2 John 7). Paul had to warn the Ephesian church of "savage wolves" who would come in among them, "not sparing the flock ... speaking perverse things to draw away disciples after themselves" (Acts 20:29-30). He warned the Corinthian church of "false apostles, deceitful workers" who transform "themselves into apostles of Christ" (1 Cor. 11:13). Paul instructed Timothy to stop false teachers (1 Tim. 1:3-4, 7, 19-20; 6:3-5, 20-21, 2 Tim. 2:16-18).

Peter wrote: "But there were also false prophets among the people, even as there will be false teachers **among you**, who will secretly bring in destructive heresies, even denying the Lord who bought them, and bring on themselves swift destruction. And many will follow their destructive ways, because of whom the way of truth will be blasphemed" (2 Pet. 2:1-2; cp. 2:1-22; 3:1-9). Notice Peter's use of "among you," his present audience. John writes: "Beloved, do not believe every spirit, but test the spirits to see whether they are from God, because many false prophets **have gone out into the world**" (1 John 4:1).

Again, John is describing what was happening in his day. There were those who had fallen away from the faith:

> Children, it is the last hour; and just as you heard that antichrist is coming, even now many antichrists have appeared; from this we know that it is the last hour. They went out from us, but they were not really of us; for if they had been of us, they would have remained with us; but they went out, so that it would be shown that they all are not of us" (1 John 2:18-19).

The use of "last days" and "end of the age" often leads interpreters to view these as references to a distant future time (1 Cor. 10:11; Heb. 1:1-2; 9:26; 1 Tim. 4; 2 Tim. 3). It's quite obvious, however, that the phrase refers to the end of the old covenant era. The writer of Hebrews makes this clear when he writes: "God, after He spoke long ago to the fathers in the prophets in many portions and in many ways, **in these last days** has spoken to us in His Son, whom He appointed heir of all things, through whom also He made the world [lit., ages]" (Heb. 1:1-2). The "ends of the ages" had come (1 Cor. 10:11), Paul informed the Corinthians. Jesus suffered at the "consummation of the ages" (Heb. 9:26).

Keep in mind that in the midst of all these corruptions, Paul left Timothy with this word of encouragement: "Just as Jannes and Jambres opposed Moses, so these men also oppose the truth, men of depraved mind, rejected in regard to the faith" (2 Tim. 3:8). There was no talk about the end of the world, the "rapture of the church," or an inevitable Middle-East conflagration. The world is in a mess today because Christians and the church have taken a back seat in the materialist's bus. A few dozen believers in Jesus' day changed the world. Think what could happen if today's millions of Christians caught Paul's optimistic vision of the future. We could change the world!

> Scripture also says that mockers would say that these signs have always been around (did you just say that?). We are even told why they would mock such clear truth—because they love their lust (2 Peter 3:1-7). That cuts close to the bone. Imagine that—a 2,000-year-old Book predicts what you would say, and why you would say it.

Jesus had made it clear that the events described in His prophetic discourses would take place before "this generation," their generation, passed away (Matt. 24:34), and the use of "this generation" in the gospels is always a reference to the generation to whom Jesus was speaking (see above). In addition, the New Testament describes prophetic events as being "near" (James 5:3, 7-9). Near to the close of that 40-year period—from the time the Olivet Discourse in Matthew 24 and Mark 13 were given and Peter wrote his epistle—critics were claiming that "all continues just as it was from the beginning of creation" (2 Pet. 3:4).

It's obvious that they were purposely misreading Scripture and history. History had not continued without any discontinuity. There had been many disruptions that God had brought about, including their nation's own judgments (e.g., Jer. 29; Dan. 1:1-2; 9:2).

Since the destruction of the temple had not taken place when Paul wrote his letter as Jesus had predicated such mocking was a manifestation of doubt and unbelief of the worst kind (Ps. 1:1-2). It showed that these scoffers were familiar with the prophecies but rejected them.

Soon after, however, their mocking turned to terror as the predicted great tribulation (Matt. 24:21) led to the destruction of the temple (24:2) and Jerusalem was "trampled underfoot by the Gentiles" (Luke 21:24; cp. Rev. 11:1-2) as Jesus had predicted. These scoffers were mocking in the Apostolic era: "But you, beloved, ought to remember the words that were spoken beforehand by the apostles of our Lord Jesus Christ, that they were saying to you, 'In the last time there will be mockers, following after their own ungodly lusts. These are the ones who cause divisions, worldly-minded, devoid of the Spirit'" (Jude 17-19).

Jude wasn't describing what will be in our day what but was happening in his day. These mockers were causing division in the church, and one of the divisions was the claim that the predicted fall of Jerusalem and the destruction of the temple would not come to pass as Jesus had stated. These scoffers were most likely Jews who had troubled the church throughout its early history. The reference to the "fathers" (2 Pet. 3:4) offers support for this view.

There isn't anything new about scoffers. A similar story is found in the Old Testament that is comparable to Jesus' description of the destruction of Jerusalem that He prophesied in the Olivet Discourse in the Synoptic Gospels and the description of the scoffers of their day mentioned by Peter and Jude:

[A]ll the officials of the priests and the people were very unfaithful following all the abominations of the nations; and they defiled the house of the Lord which He had sanctified in Jerusalem. The Lord, the God of their fathers, sent word to them again and again by His messengers, because He had compassion on His people and on His dwelling place; but they continually mocked the messengers of God, despised His words and scoffed at His prophets, until the wrath of the Lord arose against His people, until there was no remedy. Therefore, He brought up against them the king of the Chaldeans who slew their young men with the sword in the house of their sanctuary, and had no compassion on young man or virgin, old man or infirm; He gave them all into his hand. All the articles of the house of God, great and small, and the treasures of the house of the Lord, and the treasures of the king and of his officers, he brought them all to Babylon. Then they burned the house of God and broke down the wall of Jerusalem and burned all its fortified buildings with fire and destroyed all its valuable articles. Those who had escaped from the sword he carried away to Babylon; and they were servants to him and to his sons until the rule of the kingdom of Persia, to fulfill the word of the Lord by the mouth of Jeremiah, until the land had enjoyed its Sabbaths. All the days of its desolation it kept sabbath until seventy years were complete (2 Chron. 36:14-21).

The mockers had called into question the prophecies made by the prophets about the soon coming judgment on Judah. Their generation would see it come to pass, not some distant generation.

Peter and Jude didn't have a future worldwide Gentile audience in mind; they described "the blasphemy by those who say they are Jews and are not, but are a synagogue of Satan" (Rev. 2:9). Those of the "synagogue of Satan" are said to "lie" (3:9), so it is not conjecture to suppose that they might also be mockers of the truth (John 8:39-45). David Chilton offers a helpful summary of 2 Peter 3:

According to St. Peter's second epistle, Christ and the apostles had warned that apostasy would accelerate toward the end of the "last days" (2 Pet. 3:2-4; cf. Jude 17-19)—the forty-year period between Christ's ascension and the destruction of the Old Covenant Temple in AD 70. He makes it clear that these latter-day "mockers" were *Covenant apostates*: familiar with Old Testament history and prophecy, they were Jews who had abandoned the Abrahamic Covenant by rejecting Christ. As Jesus had repeatedly warned (cf. Matt. 12:38-45; 16:1-4; 23:29-39), upon this evil and perverse generation would come the great "Day of Judgment" foretold in the prophets, a "destruction of ungodly men" like that suffered by the wicked of Noah's day (2 Pet. 3:5-7). Throughout His ministry Jesus drew this analogy (see Matt. 24:37-39 and Luke 17:26-27). Just as God destroyed the "world" of the antediluvian era by the Flood, so would the "world" of first-century Israel be destroyed by fire in the fall of Jerusalem.

In his first epistle, Peter wrote that "the end of all things has come near" for those reading his letter (1 Pet. 4:7). This "end" is not a reference to the end of the world but the end of the old covenant. Was Peter mistaken? Of course not. Was Jesus wrong in His prediction that the temple would be destroyed before the passing away of the generation to whom He was speaking (Matt. 24:2)? Since the New Testament says that certain prophetic events were said to be "near" and were to take place before "this generation" passed away (Matt. 24:34), the passing of nearly 2,000 years with no fulfillment is a contradiction and is deserving of mocking.

Peter and Jude were describing what was on the near horizon, the passing of the old covenant represented by the temple that was then standing in Jerusalem and its destruction in AD 70. The 2 Peter 3 passage deserves more attention than I can give it here.[13]

> Here's the trump card. Jesus said to watch for when the Jews regained Jerusalem (see Luke 21:24). That happened in 1967, after 2,000 years of the Jews not having a homeland, they stepped into Jerusalem, bringing into culmination all the signs of the times.

Luke 21:24 doesn't say anything about the Jews regaining Jerusalem after the AD 70 judgment. The Jews were living in Israel at the time the prophecy was given. The burden of proof is on futurists to show the passage refers to the *regathering* of Jerusalem at some distant time. There isn't a verse in the New Testament that says anything about Jews returning to their land. Nothing is said about Israel becoming a nation again. Those who appeal to the "fig tree" of Matthew 24:32 do so out of desperation. It's not about renewed nationhood for Israel but "evidence that summer is near.... The signs in this passage, accordingly, are not the revival of Israel, but the great tribulation."[14]

During the time leading up to and including the destruction of Jerusalem in AD 70, Jews were killed by the sword, they were led captive into all the nations, and Jerusalem was trampled underfoot

---

13. Gary DeMar and David Chilton, "What Does Peter Mean by the Passing Away of Heaven and Earth? A Study of 2 Peter 3": https://bit.ly/48qHerH..

14. John F. Walvoord, *Matthew: Thy Kingdom Come* (Chicago, IL: Moody, [1974] 1980), 191-192.

by the Gentiles (see Luke 17:22-37). Comfort chose 1967 for the time **"when the Jews regained Jerusalem,"** but others before him chose 1917 and 1948. In the first edition of *The Beginning of the End*, which was published in 1972, Tim LaHaye wrote:

> Carefully putting all this together, we now recognize this strategic generation. *It is the generation that 'sees' the four-part sign of verse 7* [in Matt. 24], *or the people who saw the First World War.* We must be careful here not to become dogmatic, but it would seem that these people are witnesses to the events, not necessarily participants in them. That would suggest they were at least old enough to understand the events of 1914-1918, not necessarily old enough to go to war.[15]

A number of things changed in LaHaye's 1991 revised edition of *The Beginning of the End*. The "strategic generation" has been modified significantly. It's no longer "the people who saw the First World War."

> Carefully putting all this together, we now recognize this strategic generation. *It is the generation that "sees'" the events of 1948.* We must be careful here not to become dogmatic, but it would seem that these people are witnesses to the events, not necessarily participants in them.

The change from 1917 to 1948 gave LaHaye more time before this new generation passed away.[16] The 1948-1988 connection was all the rage in the early 1970s, especially with the publication of Hal Lindsey's *Late Great Planet Earth* in 1970.

> The most important sign in Matthew has to be the restoration of the Jews to the land in the rebirth of Israel. Even the figure of speech "fig tree" has been a historic symbol of national Israel. When the Jewish people, after nearly 2,000 years of exile, under relentless persecution, became a nation again on 14 May 1948 the "fig tree" put forth its first leaves. Jesus said that this would indicate that He was "at the door," ready to return.

---

15. Tim LaHaye, *The Beginning of the End* (Wheaton, IL: Tyndale House Publishers, 1972), 165, 168. Emphasis added.

16. Tim LaHaye, *The Beginning of the End*, rev. ed. (Wheaton, IL: Tyndale House Publishers, 1991), 193. Emphasis added.

Then He said, "Truly I say to you, *this generation* will not pass away until all these things take place" (Matthew 24:34, NASB). What generation? Obviously, in context, the generation that would see the signs—chief among them the rebirth of Israel. A generation in the Bible is something like forty years. If this is a correct deduction, then within forty years or so of 1948, all these things could take place. Many scholars who have studied Bible prophecy all their lives believe that this is so.[17]

The late Chuck Smith, then pastor of Calvary Chapel and founder of the worldwide Calvary Chapel system of churches, went a step further than Lindsey: "That generation that was living in May 1948 shall not pass away until the second coming of Jesus Christ takes place and the kingdom of God established upon the earth. How long is a generation? Forty years on average in the Bible.... Where does that put us? It puts us right out at the end. We're coming down to the wire."[18] Smith wrote the above in 1976!

Comfort closed his short article with the following: "**Don't test God's patience. You had better get right with Him today, before it's too late**." What if someone offers the following in response?

"You know, I've tested the prophetic system of date setting that you are using to call me to get right with God. I've noticed that the prophetic goal posts are moved each time a definitive prediction does not come to pass. First it was 1917, then 1948, and now it's 1967. How is it possible for me to be certain about what you claim God wants me to do based in part on a prophetic system that does not have a very good track record? My reading of the NT shows that Jesus claimed that He was going to return in some capacity before that present generation passed away. Other NT passes describe prophetic events that are said to take place 'shortly' because 'the time is near.' If these things did not take place as they are stated, then Jesus was mistaken. If He was mistaken on this issue, then it's most likely that He was mistaken on other issues as well."

---

17. Hal Lindsey, *The Late Great Planet Earth* (Grand Rapids, MI: Zondervan, 1970), 53-54.
18. Chuck Smith, *Snatched Away* (Costa Mesa, CA: Maranatha Evangelical Association of Calvary Chapel, 1976), 21.

Ray Comfort is not helping the cause of the gospel by bringing up the same failed arguments about how the end is near based on certain signs. It's been done to death. There is a long history of prophetic speculators who tried to make the case for a near end time. There are hundreds of examples.[19] In 1926, Oswald J. Smith wrote *Is the Antichrist at Hand?* The following copy appears on the cover:

> The fact that this book has run swiftly into a number of large editions bears convincing testimony to its intrinsic worth. There are here portrayed startling indications of the approaching end of the present age from the spheres of demonology, politics and religion. No one can read this book without being impressed with the importance of the momentous days in which we are living."

Smith identified the antichrist as Benito Mussolini. John Warwick Montgomery writes that after Mussolini's death in 1945 "Smith himself tried to buy up all the remaining copies of the book to destroy them."[20] It's time that prophetic speculation stop.

19. Gumerlock, *The Day and the Hour.*

20. John Warwick Montgomery, "Prophecy, Eschatology, and Apologetics," *Looking into the Future: Evangelical Studies in Eschatology*, ed. David W. Baker (Grand Rapids, MI: Baker Academic, 2001), 366.

# CHAPTER 10

# "Just Like the Days of Noah"

To help His listeners better understand the timing and circumstances of the events leading up to and including the destruction of the temple before their generation passed away, Jesus draws on a familiar Old Testament judgment event—the flood. Jesus, teaching by analogy, shows how the coming of the flood waters during Noah's generation and His own coming in judgment against Jerusalem are similar (Luke 17:22-37). Noah's flood is not an end of the world analogy. How do we know? Because Jesus said, speaking of Himself, "but first He must suffer many things and be rejected by this generation" (17:25). Every time Jesus uses the phrase "this generation, it always means the generation to whom He was speaking. Jesus isn't jumping over nearly 2,000 years of history. There is a link between His suffering, the rejection by many in His own generation (Acts 2:22-23, 40), and the flood analogy of judgment. Joel McDurmon writes:

> To those who may be tempted to argue ... that "this generation" refers to something other than the generation to whom Jesus was speaking ... something more general or more future ... the context here in Luke 17:25 makes it clear that Jesus' "this generation" would be the same generation which rejected Him and caused Him to suffer.[1]

In Matthew's gospel we read about "**those days** which were before the flood" and "**the day** that NOAH ENTERED THE ARK" (Matt. 24:38). Similarly, there were *days* before the coming of the Son of Man who prophesied judgment on the temple and city of Jerusalem and the *day* of the coming of the Son of Man. The same people were involved in

---

1. Joel McDurmon, *Jesus v. Jerusalem: A Commentary on Luke 9:51-20:26, Jesus' Lawsuit Against Israel* (Powder Springs, GA: American Vision Press, 2011), 113.

both the "days before" and "the day of" the Son of Man. Those who "were eating and drinking" and "marrying and giving in marriage" were the same people who were shut out on "the day that Noah entered the ark." They were all a part of Noah's generation.

Noah entered the ark on a single day similar to the way Jesus as the Son of Man came on the "clouds of heaven with power and great glory" (Matt. 24:30), a day and hour known only to the Father (24:36). "Some shall be rescued from the destruction of Jerusalem, like Lot out of the burning of Sodom: while others, no ways perhaps different in outward circumstances, shall be left to perish in it."[2]

Jesus said His coming "will be just like the days of Noah" (24:37). The people were doing normal things—"eating and drinking" and "marrying and giving in marriage." Jesus told His audience that life would be going on as usual when He returns in judgment against the temple and city of Jerusalem. Jesus did not describe evil behavior like drunkenness and sexual sins like "'exchanging mates' or 'wife swapping,'" contrary to what prophecy writers like M. R. DeHaan and Jack Van Impe claim.[3] "Marrying and given in marriage" is a phrase to describe, well, "marrying and giving in marriage" (see Matt. 22:30; Luke 17:27-28). People did it in Jesus' day and people do it today. Men and women marry and parents give their daughters away in marriage. There's nothing untoward about it. D. A. Carson's comments are helpful:

> That the coming of the Son of Man takes place at an unknown time can only be true if in fact life seems to be going on pretty much as usual—just as in the days before the flood (v. 37). People follow their ordinary pursuits (v. 38). Despite the distress, persecutions, and upheavals (vv. 4-28), life goes on: people eat, drink, and marry. There is no overt typological usage of the Flood as judgment here, nor any mention of the sin of that generation.[4]

---

2. Thomas Newton, *Dissertations on the Prophecies, Which Have Remarkably Been Fulfilled, and at This Time are Fulfilling in the World* (London: J.F. Dove, 1754), 379.

3. Jack Van Impe, *The Great Escape: Preparing for the Rapture, the Next Event on God's Prophetic Clock* (Nashville, TN: Word, 1998), 127.

4. D. A. Carson, "Matthew," *The Expositor's Bible Commentary*, gen. ed., Frank E. Gaebelein (Grand Rapids, MI: Zondervan, 1984), 8:509. Also see N. T. Wright, *Jesus and the Victory of God* (Minneapolis, MN: Fortress Press, 1996), 365-366.

Support for Carson's interpretation can be found in Luke's account of the time just before Sodom's destruction: "It was the same as happened in the days of Lot: they were eating, they were drinking, they were buying, they were selling, they were planting, they were building; but on the day that Lot went out from Sodom it rained fire and brimstone from heaven and destroyed them all" (Luke 17:28). Buying, selling, planting, and building describe life going on as usual without any regard to an impending judgment.

> The picture here is on normal life, eating and drinking at meals and parties, getting married and giving their children in marriage.... In itself it is not a negative picture, but these were people obsessed with their daily lives, giving no thought whatsoever to their obligations to God. All this was to change when "Noah entered the ark," but then it was too late.[5]

Are dispensationalists willing to say that these activities "connote moral corruption"? Darrell L. Bock attempts this interpretation even though he admits that the idea of "moral corruption ... is not emphasized in Luke's description."[6] Of course not since buying, selling, planting, and building are common everyday actions that can describe any period of history and any type of people. It's the time indicator of "this generation" (their generation: Matt. 24:33-34) that identifies who is in view.

No one disputes that Noah and Lot lived in a time of moral corruption that brought judgment. Jesus' point, however, is that the people in Noah and Lot's day went on with their lives as if the promise of imminent judgment was an idle threat (see 2 Peter 3:3-4). Notice the audience reference: "Therefore, beloved, since **you** look for **these** things" (2 Pet. 3:14). Peter is not describing a distant event but one that was soon to take place (1 Peter 4:7). The same is true of those who were told Jesus would return in judgment within a generation (Matt. 24:34). The use of the second person plural ("you") throughout Matthew 24 is evident of this fact (vv. 1, 3, 4, 6, 9, 26, 32, 33, 34).

---

5. Grant R. Osborne, *Matthew: Zondervan Exegetical Commentary on the New Testament* (Grand Rapids, MI: Zondervan, 2010), 904. Also see Alfred Plummer, *An Exegetical Commentary on the Gospel According to Saint Matthew* (Grand Rapids, MI: Eerdmans, 1953), 340.

6. Darrell L. Bock, *Luke: Baker Exegetical Commentary on the New Testament*, 2 vols. (Grand Rapids, MI: Baker Books, 1996), 2:1432-1433.

## No Rapture Here!

Many futurists claim the phrase "took them all away" (24:39) refers to a rapture that is still in our future. On the contrary, "In the context of 24:37-39, 'taken' presumably means 'taken to judgment' (cf. Jer. 6:11 NASB, NRSV),"[7] or taken away "to their doom."[8] It's not about the rescue of the church from tribulation. The phrase ties the judgment of the world in Noah's day with the judgment of the Jews' world in their day that took place with the destruction of the temple in AD 70. Who was taken away in the judgment of the flood? Not Noah and his family. They were "left behind" to carry on God's work. John Gill writes in his commentary on this passage: "the whole world of the ungodly, every man, woman, and child" were taken away in judgment. Note who was left behind: "except eight persons only; Noah and his wife, and his three sons and their wives." And what does Gill say about those in the field?: They shall be taken away "by the eagles, the Roman army, and either killed or carried captive by them." The Bible gives its own commentary on the meaning of "took them all away." "Destroyed them all" (Luke 17:27, 29) is equivalent to "took them all away." Consider John F. Walvoord's comments on "took them away."

> An argument advanced by Alexander Reese and adopted by [Robert] Gundry is that the references in Matthew 24:40, 41 should be interpreted as referring to the rapture. These verses state, "Then shall two be in the field; the one shall be taken, and the other left. Two women shall be grinding at the mill; one shall be taken and the other left."
>
> Here both Gundry and Reese violate the rule that the context should determine the interpretation of a passage. Both Gundry and Reese concede that the context deals with judgment such as characterized the time of Noah. According to Matthew 24:39 those living at that time "knew not until the flood came, and took them all away, so shall also the coming of the Son of Man be." Those taken away were taken away in judgment.

7. Craig S. Keener, *The IVP Bible Background Commentary: New Testament* (Downers Grove, IL: InterVarsity Press, 1993), 115.

8. Osborne, *Matthew*, 904.

\* \* \* \* \*

Claiming that those taken in verses 40 and 41 are taken away in the rapture, Gundry in discussing the parallel passage in Luke 17:34-37, ignores verse 37. There two are pictured in the same bed, with one taken and the other left. Two are grinding together, and one is taken and the other left. Two are in the field, one is taken and the other left. Then, in verse 37, the question is asked, "Where, Lord?" The answer is very dramatic: "And He said unto them, Wherever the body is, there will the eagles be gathered together." It should be very clear that the ones taken are put to death and their bodies are consumed by the vultures. If the ones taken are killed, then verses 40, 41 of Matthew 24 speak of precisely the same kind of judgment as occurred in the flood where the ones taken were taken in judgment. [9]

Walvoord writes in another place:

Because at the rapture believers will be taken out of the world, some have confused this with the rapture of the church. Here, however, the situation is the reverse. The one who is left, is left to enter the kingdom; the one who is taken, is taken in judgment."[10]

But like Reese and Gundry, Walvoord ignores the time texts that run throughout Matthew 24-25, claiming that they refer to a distant coming of Christ. Since there was a judgment where Jews were in fact "taken away in judgment" by the Roman armies, it makes much more sense to place the timing of the event to the temple's destruction and Jerusalem's judgment in AD 70 since the Jesus tells His disciples that "not one stone here will be left upon another, which will not be torn down" (Matt. 24:2). Jesus was not describing a supposed future rebuilt temple; He was describing what was going to happen to the temple that they could see with their own eyes: "not one stone **here**."

---

9. John F. Walvoord, *The Blessed Hope and the Tribulation: A Historical and Biblical Study of Posttribulationism* (Grand Rapids, MI: Zondervan, 1976), 89, 90. Also see David L. Turner, *Matthew: Baker Exegetical Commentary on the New Testament* (Grand Rapids, MI: Baker Academic, 2008), 590.

10. John F. Walvoord, *Matthew: Thy Kingdom Come* (Chicago, IL: Moody Press, 1974), 193.

## After a Long Time

Another line of evidence offered by those who believe that events following Matthew 24:34 refer to a yet future personal and physical return of Jesus is the meaning given to "after a long time" (24:48; 25:19) and the "delay" by the bridegroom (25:5). On the surface these examples seem to indicate that two different events are in view, one near (the destruction of Jerusalem) and one distant (the second physical coming of Christ). This is the view of Stephen F. Hayhow.

> Both parables, the parables of the virgins (vv. 1-13), and the parable of the talents (vv. 14-30), speak of the absence of the bridegroom/master, who is said to be "a long time in coming" (v. 5) and "After a long time the master of the servants returned..." (v. 19). This suggests, not the events of AD 70 which were to occur in the near future, in fact within the space of a generation, but a distant event, the return of Christ.[11]

Notice that the evil slave says, "My master is not coming for a long time" (Matt. 24:48). The evil slave then proceeds to "beat his fellow-slaves and eat and drink with drunkards" (24:49). But to the surprise of the "evil slave" the master returned when he least expected him (24:50). The master did not return to cut the evil slave's distant relatives in pieces (24:51); he cut *him* in pieces. The evil slave was alive when the master left, and he was alive when the master returned. In this context, a "long time" must be measured against a person's lifetime. In context, two years could be a long time if the master usually returned within six months.

The same idea is expressed in the parable of the "talents." A man entrusts his slaves with his possessions (25:14). The master then goes on a journey (25:15). While the master is gone, the slaves make investment decisions (25:16-18). We are then told that "after a long time the master of *those slaves* came and settled accounts *with them*" (25:19). In this context "a long time" is no longer than an average lifetime. The settlement is made with the same slaves who received the talents. In every other New Testament context, "a long time" means nothing more than an extended period of time (Luke 8:27; 23:8; John 5:6; Acts 8:11;

---

11. Stephen F. Hayhow, "Matthew 24, Luke 17 and the Destruction of Jerusalem," *Christianity and Society* 4:2 (April 1994), 4.

14:3, 28; 26:5, 29; 27:21; 28:6). Nowhere does it mean centuries or multiple generations.

The delay of the bridegroom is no different from the "long time" of the two previous parables. The bridegroom returns to the same two groups of virgins (25:1-13). The duration of the delay must be measured by the audience. The Bible defines "long time" for us: "Now a man was there who had been ill for **thirty-eight years**. "Jesus, upon seeing this man lying there and knowing that he had already been in that condition for a **long time**, said to him, 'Do you want to get well?'"

How is "long time" used elsewhere in Scripture? "Now a man was there who had been ill for thirty-eight years. Jesus, upon seeing this man lying there and knowing that he had already been in that condition **for a long time** [πολὺν ... χρόνον], said to him, 'Do you want to get well?'" (John 5:5-6). This biblical definition of "long time" fits the 40-year generational timeline specified by Jesus in Matthew 24 and 25.

This brief analysis helps us understand the "mockers" who ask, "Where is the promise of His coming?" (2 Peter 3:3-4). Peter was aware that Jesus' coming was an event that would take place before the last apostle died (Matt. 16:27-28; John 21:22-23). The doctrine of the soon return of Jesus was common knowledge (Matt. 24:34; 26:64; Phil. 4:5; Heb. 10:25; 1 John 2:18; Rev. 1:1, 3; 22:10). It is not hard to imagine that the passage of several decades would lead some to doubt the reliability of the prophecy, especially as the promised generation that would see and experience what Jesus had predicted was coming to a close. The horrendous events of AD 70 silenced the mockers.

Ray Comfort has also made comments about Gog and Magog being the fulfillment of Bible prophecy, a battle that takes place with bows and arrows, with soldiers riding horses and chariots, and wielding clubs. For Comfort and others, Iran is really the biblical Persia:

> I'm going to show you how Iran is hidden in Bible prophecy. The nation of Iran has finally come out of the closet. Never before has it openly attacked Israel. Like a camouflaged predator, it has remained snarling in the shadows, but it's never attacked.

If Iran is Persia, then Comfort does not know biblical history. "Haman sought to annihilate all the Jews, the people of Mordecai, who were found throughout the kingdom of Ahasuerus" (Esther 3:6).[12] The "prophecy" about Iran is so hidden that you won't find Iran mentioned in the Bible.

Comfort published the book *Russia Will Attack Israel* in February 1991. He quotes from the May 1982 *Reader's Digest* article "Countdown in the Middle East": "The Soviets are entrenched all around the rim of the Middle East heartland—In Afghanistan, South Yemen, Ethiopia, and Libya." The "Soviets" pulled out of Afghanistan. The Union of Soviet Socialist Republics (USSR) was dissolved on December 26, 1991. So much for prophetic prognostication! None of these failed predictions stopped Comfort from releasing *Volatile!: The Nations The Bible Says Will Attack Israel in the Latter Days* in 2024.

Comfort's *Russia Will Attack Israel* included a list of "PROPHETIC FACTS" (pages 17-35). The problem with these "facts" is that they describe what was to take place before that Apostolic generation passed away (Matt. 24:34). They don't have anything to do with current geopolitics. To get around this reality, Comfort argues for "double fulfillment or dual fulfillment." But what of "a threefold and fourfold sense"? John Owen comments, "If the Scripture has more than one meaning, it has no meaning at all."[13] What we do find in Scripture is the application of Old Testament references like Jezebel (Rev. 2:20), Sodom and Egypt (11:8), Babylon (17-18), and Gog and Magog (20:8). According to Revelation 20:8, Gog and Magog do not appear until after the thousand years. If this is a "dual fulfillment," it's at least a thousand years in the future.

It didn't take long to move from the April 8, 2024, solar eclipse to Gog and Magog ... again! You might remember that when Russia invaded Ukraine, we were warned that the Gog and Magog war was near. What this attack had to do with Russia and Israel is beyond my ability to understand since the Bible does not mention Ukraine. The Bible also does not mention a nation like the United States sending billions of dollars to Ukraine to help with the war effort. It seems the Bible is only so prophetic.

---

12. See my book *The Gog and Magog End-Time Alliance* Powder Springs, GA: American Vision, 2016).

13. Milton S. Terry, *Biblical Hermeneutics: A Treatise on the Interpretation of the Old and New Testaments* (New York: Phillips & Hunt, 1883), 445.

# CHAPTER 11

# Calculating the Number of the Beast

A reader left this comment on one of my posts about the number of the Beast in Revelation 13:18.

> The question is: Why should we use Hebrew gematria in a book that is written in Greek for the Greek speaking churches of Asia Minor?

Gematria is an interpretive method that assigns numerical value to letters, words, and phrases. Most of us are unfamiliar with this method since we have a separate alphabet and numbering system. Anybody familiar with the Bible understands that numbers are important. This is not to dismiss the idea that some, maybe many, Bible numbers have a deeper symbolic meaning, especially when the Bible tells us in the case of Revelation 13:18 to "calculate the number of the beast."

When trying to match up "six hundred and sixty-six" with a known historical figure, we need more than a plausible candidate; we need a relevant candidate. The first readers of Revelation were told to "calculate the number of the beast, for the number is that of a man; and his number is six hundred and sixty-six" (13:18). Since Revelation was written to a first-century audience ("these things must **shortly take place** ... for the **time is near** ... the hour of testing is **about to come** on the land.... Do not seal up the words of the prophecy of this book for the time is **near**": 1:1, 3; 3:10, 22:10), we should expect some first-century readers to have been able to calculate the number with relative ease and understand the result. They would have had few candidates from which to choose. It's unlikely that this number of a man identifies someone outside their time of reference. The same is true of the rest of the book.

Notice that the number is "six hundred and sixty-six," not three sixes. Tim LaHaye misidentifies the number when he writes, "The plain sense of Scripture tells us that it comprises the numbers: six, six,

six."[1] The three Greek letters that make up the number represent 600 (ἑξακόσιοι), 60 (ἑξήκοντα), and 6 (ἕξ).

## ΝΕΡΩΝ ΚΑΙΣΑΡ

Ancient numbering systems used an alphanumeric method. This is true of the Latin (Roman) system that is still common today: I = 1, V = 5, X = 10, L = 50, C = 100, D = 500, which, interestingly, adds up to 666.

Greek and Hebrew follow a similar numbering method but with each letter of the alphabet representing a number. The first nine letters represent 1-9. The tenth letter represents 10, with the nineteenth letter representing 100 and so on. Since the Revelation is written in a Hebrew context revealed to a Jew with numerous allusions to the Old Testament, we should expect the solution to deciphering the meaning of 666 to be Hebraic. "The reason clearly is that, *while [John] writes in Greek, he thinks in Hebrew,* and the thought has naturally affected the vehicle of expression."[2]

The "angel of the abyss" is described in two ways: "His name in Hebrew is Abaddon, and in the Greek he has the name Apollyon" (Rev. 9:11). Something similar is done with "Har-Magedon" (hill of Megiddo) or "Ar-Magedon" (city of Megiddo) (Rev. 16:16). Megiddo was an Old Testament city (1 Chron. 7:29), the place where King Josiah was killed (2 Chron. 35:20-27). There are references to Egypt and Sodom (Rev. 11:8), Jezebel (2:20), Balaam (2:14), Babylon (17-18), the attire of the high priest (17:4-5), etc.

> "Of the 404 verses of the book of Revelation, 278 are based directly on Old Testament language and thought. ... The author of Revelation does not intend to show that Old Testament predictions are fulfilled in events involving Christ and the church. Instead, he used Old Testament language to describe the situation facing his readers. He draws parallels between Old Testament events and ideas and the circumstances in which he and his readers find themselves."[3]

1. Tim LaHaye, *Revelation Unveiled*, rev. ed. (Grand Rapids, MI: Zondervan, 1999), 22-27.

2. R. H. Charles, *A Critical and Exegetical Commentary on the Revelation of St. John,* 2 vols. (New York: Charles Scribner's Sons, 1920), 1:cxliii.

3. Frank Pack, "The Old Testament and the Book of Revelation": http://goo.gl/iwNoZ1. For a comprehensive list, see Arnold G. Fruchtenbaum, "Old Testament References in the Book of Revelation": http://goo.gl/oY8eFx

In John's gospel, the place where Pontius Pilate sat down to judge Jesus was called "The Pavement," but John called attention to its Hebrew (Jewish Aramaic) name "Gabbatha" (John 19:13). In the same chapter, John wrote how Pilate had an inscription placed on the cross above Jesus' head written in "Hebrew, Latin, and in Greek" (John 19:20). Going from Greek to Hebrew was typical and expected since Jews spoke Hebrew or Jewish Aramaic which is very similar to Hebrew.[4]

So what name is behind the cryptic 666? When Nero Caesar's name is transliterated into Hebrew, which a first-century Jew would probably have done immediately, he would have gotten *Neron Kesar* or simply *nrwn qsr*, since Hebrew has no letters to represent vowels. (The *w* represents a long "o" sound and the *q* represents the "k" sound in Hebrew.) "It has been documented by archaeological finds that a first-century Hebrew spelling of Nero's name provides us with precisely the value of 666. Jastrow's lexicon of the Talmud contains this very spelling."[5] When we take the letters of Nero's name and spell them in Hebrew, we get the following numeric values: n = 50, r = 200, w = 6, n = 50, q = 100, s = 60, r = 200 = 666.

> Every Jewish reader, of course, saw that the Beast was a symbol of Nero. And both Jews and Christians regarded Nero as also having close affinities with the serpent or dragon . . . The Apostle writing as a Hebrew, was evidently thinking as a Hebrew.... Accordingly, the Jewish Christian would have tried the name as he *thought* of the name—that is *in Hebrew letters*. And the moment that he did this the secret stood revealed. No Jew ever thought of Nero except as "*Neron Kesar*."[6]

I have a coin that spells Nero's name as NERŌN. Coins were struck with the spelling ΝΕΡΩΝ ΚΑΙΣΑΡ ΣΕΒΑΣΤΟΣ[7] = "Neron Caesar Augustus." Richard Bauckham writes:

4. For a fully study of this topic, see William Henry Guillemard, *Hebraisms in the Greek Testament (Cambridge: Deighton, Bell and Co. and London: George Bell and Sons, 1879).*

5. Kenneth L. Gentry, Jr. *The Beast of Revelation*, rev. ed. (Powder Springs, GA: American Vision, 2002, chap. 3. Also see Charles, *A Critical and Exegetical Commentary on the Revelation of St. John*, 1:367.

6. Frederic W. Farrar, *The Early Days of Christianity* (New York: E. P. Dutton, 1882), 471.

7. See the image of the coin in Robert Hillegonds, *The Early Date of Revelation and the End Times* that reads ΝΕΡΩΝ ΚΑΙΣΡ ΣΕΒΣΤΟΣ (Fountain Inn, SC: Victorious Hope Publishing,

The solution to the riddle of 666 which has been most widely accepted since it was first suggested in 1831 is that 666 is the sum of the letters of Nero Caesar written in Hebrew characters as נרון קסר (נ = 50 + ר = 200 + ו = 6 + ן = 50 + ק = 100 + ס = 60 + ר = 200). Few of the many other solutions by gematria which have been proposed offer a *name*, which the phrase "the number of his name" (Rev. 13:17; 15:2) requires, and of those few which do, this seems eminently the most preferable.[8]

Israel P. Wayne quotes the following from Melchior De Vogue's *Syrie centrale. Architecture civile et religieuse du Ier au VIIe siècle* (1865-1877):

Neron Kesar (Nero the Emperor), was apparently the name by which the Christians of Asia spoke of the monster. Thus the coins of Asia bore the legend, Neron Kaiser, the form of the mystic number. There are inscriptions at Paymyra in which Nero's name and dignity are written exactly as in the cypher in the Apocalypse. [9]

A textual variant in some New Testament manuscripts has the number of the Beast as 616 based on the reading of *nrw qsr*—Nero Caesar— instead of "the Greek form Nerwn, ... so that the final ן is omitted from נרון, the numerical value becomes 616."[10]

## Solomon and 666

The Jews had seen the number six hundred and sixty-six before (not 6-6-6 but 600 + 60 + 6 = 666). Prior to Solomon's slide into apostasy, a description of his reign is given. One of the things said about him is that "the weight of gold which came in to Solomon in one year was 666 talents of gold" (1 Kings 10:14). From the number of shields (300) to

2016), v-vi. Another coin from *c.* AD 65-66 reads ΝΕΡΩΝ ΚΑΙΣΑΡ ΣΕΒΑΣΤ[ΟΣ].

8. Richard Bauckham, *The Climax of Prophecy: Studies on the Book of Revelation* (Edinburgh: T&T Clark, 1993), 387.

9. Israel P. Wayne, T*he Parousia: A Critical Study of the Scripture Doctrine of Christ's Second Coming; His Reign as King, the Resurrection of the Dead; and the General Judgment* (Portland, ME: Hoyt, Fogg, & Donham, 1879), 126, note.

10. Bauckham, *The Climax of Prophecy*, 387. Also see James Tabor, "Why 2K?: The Biblical Roots of Millennialism," *Bible Review* (December 1999): http://goo.gl/i7xBdj

the price of a horse imported from Egypt (150 shekels), we find round numbers, except when the number of gold talents is mentioned. From the point where we are told that 666 talents of gold came into Solomon's possession in one year, we read of Solomon's apostasy. First, Solomon violates the law regarding the accumulation of horses, chariots, wives, and gold (1 Kings 10:26; see Deut. 17:16-17).

> The law of Deuteronomy 17 forbad the king to multiply gold, women, and horses, but here we see Solomon do all three. In Revelation, the religious rulers of the "land" are called kings, the "kings of the land." The apostasy of the High Priest, and of the religious leaders of Israel, is thus linked to Solomon's sin. As Solomon lost his kingdom when the northern tribes rebelled after his death, so the Land Beast will lose his kingdom permanently when Jerusalem is destroyed.[11]

Second, Solomon sells himself to foreign interests by marrying foreign women to create political alliances (1 Kings 11:1-2). It is here that we see a parallel with Revelation 13. In their rejection of Jesus as the promised Messiah ("He came to His own, and those who were His own did not receive Him": John 1:11), the unbelieving Jews committed spiritual adultery with the nations (Roman Empire of nations) in the way that Solomon committed physical/spiritual adultery with the nations surrounding him:

> Now Solomon loved many foreign women along with the daughter of Pharaoh: Moabite, Ammonite, Edomite, Sidonian, and Hittite women, from the nations concerning which the LORD had said to the sons of Israel, 'You shall not associate with them, neither shall they associate with you, for they will surely turn your heart away after their gods.' Solomon held fast to these in love. And he had seven hundred wives, princesses, and three hundred concubines, and his wives turned his heart away (1 Kings 11:1-3).

James Jordan sums up the connection between Solomon and the apostate character of the Church's enemy in Revelation 13:

---

11. James Jordan, *A Brief Reader's Guide to Revelation* (Niceville, FL: Transfiguration Press, 1999), 36.

The number of the name (character) of the Sea Beast, then, means "apostate Solomon; apostate Jew." It is Solomon, not free under Yahweh's rule, but enslaved to Gentiles through illicit trade, the idol worshipping wiles of his women, and his lust for gold.[12]

It's possible, therefore, that 666 refers to both Nero and Solomon since the Sea Beast (Roman Empire under Nero) and the Land Beast (Israel as a "synagogue of Satan": Rev. 2:9; 3:9) cooperate in their desire to see the new covenant people of God destroyed. Those Jews who rejected Jesus (the greater David: Acts 2:25-36) embraced the apostasy of Solomon who did not follow after his father David.

Marrying foreign wives was similar to what the Jews did when they cried out at Jesus' trial before Pontius Pilate, the civil representative of Rome, "We have no king but Caesar" (John 19:15). They aligned themselves with Rome against Jesus. This made them true antichrists (2 John 2:7; 1 John 2:18-22; 4:2-3). They chose the bastard Barabbas ("son [bar] of a father [abba]") rather than the true son, Jesus (Son of the Father).

## Nero the Beastly Character

By all accounts, Nero had a reputation as an immoral beast. "According to the emperor Marcus Aurelius [121-180], 'To be violently drawn and moved by the lusts of the soul is proper to wild beasts and monsters, such as Phalaris and Nero were.'"[13] Other histories of the period offer a similar description. But for Christians, Nero was a beast because "he was the first emperor to persecute the church."[14]

Nero was an animalistic pervert. He kicked one of his pregnant wives to death. He murdered his mother. He set Christians on fire to serve as lamps for a dinner party. He would dress up as a beast and rape both male and female prisoners. And he was the covenant head of Rome—that great Satan.[15]

There is a long history of Christian commentators who have taught that John, through the Revelation received through Jesus, had Nero in mind

---

12. James Jordan, "The Beasts of Revelation (4)," *Studies in the Revelation* (April 1996), 2.

13. Bauckham, *The Climax of Prophecy*, 409.

14. Bauckham, *The Climax of Prophecy*, 411.

15. Douglas Wilson, "666" (July 13, 2005): http://bit.ly/StHTRq

as the fulfillment of what is taking place in Revelation 13 as the Sea Beast. Nero fits the historical circumstances since he was the Emperor of Rome from AD 54 through June of 68 and was a tyrant of first order. According to first-century Roman historian Tacitus (AD 56-117), Nero blamed the burning of Rome on Christians:

> Consequently, to get rid of the report, Nero fastened the guilt and inflicted the most exquisite tortures on a class hated for their abominations, called Christians by the populace.[16]

Nero committed numerous atrocities against Christians. Some Christians were "wrapped in animal skins and torn apart by dogs; others were crucified and set aflame after being soaked in oil. Nero threw open his gardens for the spectacle and drove about in his chariot."[17]

One of the reasons Nero was often identified as the Beast of Revelation 13 (the word "antichrist" is not used in Revelation) was because his name, when put into Hebrew letters, as a Jew would have done (Rev. 16:16), adds up to 666:

> Every Jewish reader, of course, saw that the Beast was a symbol of Nero. And both Jews and Christians regarded Nero as also having close affinities with the serpent or dragon.... The Apostle writing as a Hebrew, was evidently thinking as a Hebrew.... Accordingly, the Jewish Christian would have tried the name as he *thought* of the name—that is *in Hebrew letters*. And the moment that he did this the secret stood revealed. No Jew ever thought of Nero except as *"Neron Kesar."*[18]

Mark Wilson writes the following in his brief commentary on Revelation in the *Zondervan Illustrated Bible Backgrounds Commentary*: "Nero is the only first-century emperor whose name can be calculated to equal 666. Nero's Greek name *NERON KAISER* was inscribed on the obverse of coins from Ephesus, Sardis, and Laodicea during this period."[19] The *IVP Bible Background Commentary* states that identifying Nero as

---

16. Tacitus, *Annals,* 15:44

17. John Haralson Hayes, *Introduction to the Bible* (Louisville, KY: Westminster John Knox Press, 1971), 453.

18. Frederic W. Farrar, *The Early Days of Christianity* (New York: E. P. Dutton, 1882), 471.

19. Mark W. Wilson, "Revelation," *Zondervan Illustrated Bible Backgrounds Commentary,* gen. ed. Clinton E. Arnold (Grand Rapids, MI: Zondervan, 2002), 4:330.

the Beast and the number 666 is "the most popular proposal among scholars today."[20]

There's something else to consider. If the Greek word for *beast* (θηρίον = תריון) is translated "into Hebrew consonants, the numerical value comes out to 666. This appears to be what John means when he mentions in 13:18 'the number of the beast, for it is the number of a man, and his number is 666.'"[21]

## Conclusion

By paying attention to the specific time elements in Revelation and audience relevance, we can conclude that John's Beast with a name that adds up to 666 is long dead and gone. Today's end-time speculation is foolish and counter-productive and dilutes the Bible's message of the finished work of Jesus Christ and the end of the old covenant system that passed away with the destruction of the temple in AD 70. We should focus on the name of Jesus "and the name of His Father" (Rev. 14:1). The Lamb *has conquered* the Beasts of Revelation 13 and any beasts to follow.

---

20. Craig S. Keener, *The IVP Bible Background Commentary: New Testament* (Downers Grove, IL: InterVarsity Press, 1993), 799.

21. Bauckham, *The Climax of Prophecy*, 389.

# CHAPTER 12

# Refuting Charges of "Replacement Theology"

D r. Michael Brown, who holds a Ph.D. in Near Eastern Languages and Literatures from New York University and has served as a professor at a number of seminaries and hosts the nationally syndicated, daily talk radio show, *The Line of Fire*, has recently written an article entitled "A Deadly, Anti-Israel, Theological Error."[1]

And what is this error? According to Dr. Brown, it's "the idea that God is finished with the Jewish people as a nation and that the church has replaced Israel in God's plan." It's "not only a serious theological error," Dr. Brown writes. "It is a deadly one as well."

Unfortunately, the charge of "Replacement Theology" has become a catchall phrase that is used without much precision and is often used to describe anybody that does hold to any number of prophetic positions about the end times. Personally, I don't know anybody who believes that God is finished with the Jewish people. Jews are becoming Christians every day, and there are many Jews who are dying without Christ every day. This has always been the case. It was the case leading up to the destruction of the temple in AD 70 (Matt. 24:1-2).

It seems, however, that the accusation of "Replacement Theology" is leveled against people who believe the Bible teaches that there is a single covenant that includes Jews and Gentiles as Ephesians 3:6 indicates: "The Gentiles are co-heirs, members of the same body, and partners of the promise in Christ Jesus through the gospel" (also see Gal. 3:26-29; 4:23, 28). This does not mean that Jews cease to be Jews or that Jews will never be saved. It does mean, however, that the promises made to Israel are fulfilled in the person and work of Jesus Christ. In his book *Our Hands Are Stained with Blood,* Dr. Brown wrote the following:

---

1. Michael Brown, "A Deadly, Anti-Israel, Theological Error." Charisma News. Accessed 03/31/14. https://bit.ly/45hTDg0

It would not have been a problem if Gentile Christians had simply said: "God has expanded the borders of Israel! Now we are included among the covenant people since we are the spiritual seed of Abraham. And we look forward to the day when the Lord will restore the physical seed of Abraham too! The Old Testament 'Church' consisted of Israel alone, but the New Testament 'Church' consists of Israel and us. Together we are the new Israel!" Many devout Christians have held to this belief—and there is much truth in it—without for a moment thinking that God's promises to the natural children were ever in doubt.[2]

God's promises to Israel are not in doubt, but to maintain that they have been postponed for nearly 2,000 years only to be realized when Israel encounters another holocaust when two-thirds of the Jews living in Israel will be slaughtered and only a remnant saved, is not an answer to the claim "that God is finished with the Jewish people as a nation." I have more to say about this topic later in this chapter.

It's obvious from the Bible that God is not going to restore every "physical seed of Abraham." If God were going to do that, then why bother with the gospel? Paul does not mean by "in this way all Israel will be saved" (Rom. 11:26) that every Jew without exception throughout history (the diachronic[through time] view) will one day be saved. Paul is writing about a "remnant" of his countrymen (11:5). Even so, Paul states unequivocally that God has not rejected His people (11:1). What evidence does He give?

For I too am an Israelite, a descendant of Abraham, from the tribe of Benjamin. God has not rejected His people whom He foreknew. Or don't you know what the Scripture says in the Elijah section—how he pleads with God against Israel? Lord, they have killed Your prophets and torn down Your altars. I am the only one left, and they are trying to take my life! But what was God's reply to him? I have left 7,000 men for Myself who have not bowed down to Baal (11:1-4).

Paul's own salvation is *prima facie* evidence that God had not rejected Israel even though not every Israelite was or will be saved. The way

2. Michael L. Brown, *Our Hands are Stained with Blood: The Tragic Story of the "Church" and the Jewish People* (Shippensburg, PA: Destiny Image Publishers, 1992), chap. 13.

that God saved a remnant in Elijah's day, God was saving a remnant in Paul's day: "In the same way, then, there is also at the **present time** a remnant chosen by grace."

Paul wasn't projecting an event in the distant future. He was describing God's faithfulness to His covenant promises "at the present time," that is, in Paul's own day. As we'll see, God was demonstrating this fact beginning with Pentecost when "Jews from every nation under heaven" (Acts 2:5-11) embraced Jesus as the fulfillment of God's promises made to Abraham long ago. Jesus said to "the Jews" of His day, "Your father Abraham rejoiced to see My day, and he saw it and was glad" (John 8:57).

## Martin Luther *On the Jews and Their Lies*

Dr. Brown begins his argument on the dangers of "Replacement Theology" in his article by referencing anti-Jews from history, for example, John Chrysostom (347-407) and Martin Luther (1483-1546). Dr. Brown's book *Our Hands Are Stained with Blood* is a much more thorough study of how the Jews have been treated throughout history. It's very troubling reading, but not all of the anti-Jewish culprits in the book can be associated with "Replacement Theology," as he seems to do with this quotation from his article:

> Luther's murderous words were put into action by none other than Adolf Hitler, beginning the night of November 9th, 1938, which is called Krystallnacht, the Night of Broken Glass, when, according to Nazi officer Reinhard Heydrich, "815 [Jewish] shops [were] destroyed, 171 dwelling houses set on fire or destroyed ... 119 synagogues were set on fire, and another 76 completely destroyed ... and those seriously injured were also numbered at 36...."
>
> This is a direct result of a theology that was dead wrong helping to justify deadly actions. (The Nazis were obviously not true Christians, but it was centuries of "Christian" anti-Semitism in Europe that helped make the Holocaust possible.)

Anti-Semitism, even the "Christian" variety described by Dr. Brown, cannot and should not be attributed to "Replacement Theology" as the designation is often used today. There are people who truly do believe that the Church replaces Israel who are not in any way anti-Semitic that would lead them to persecute Jews or stand by while they are being persecuted. After rehearsing the evils of the Nazi holocaust, Dr. Brown reduces his rhetoric a bit by qualifying his claims with the following:

> To be sure, there are fine Christians today who embrace this same theological error (called Replacement Theology or Supersessionism, meaning that the church has replaced or superseded Israel), and they are absolutely not anti-Semites and they would never sanction the persecution of the Jewish people in Jesus' name. And they totally repudiate hateful quotes like these just cited.

If this is such a dangerous doctrine, and there are people who hold to it, then why haven't they become virulent anti-Semites that burn synagogues and kill millions of Jews today? We know who's doing this, and it's not Christians who claim that the church replaces Israel in redemptive history.

Could it be that Dr. Brown is committing a fallacy of causation?: "after this (the holocaust), therefore because of this (Luther's 1543 treatise *On the Jews and Their Lies*)"?[3] Is it possible that "Replacement Theology," as Dr. Brown understands it, didn't have anything to do with these evil acts? If "Replacement Theology" is the catalyst for such actions, then how do we explain the tens of millions of non-Jews who were murdered in the 20th century, millions of whom were Christians? Evil people do evil things and they don't need a theological reason for justification.

Hitler was concerned with racial purity not theology. This is an important distinction to make. Did Hitler exploit Luther's comments? He may have, but Hitler also exploited Christianity generally. In *Mein*

---

3. Compare with Martin Luther, *That Jesus Christ Was Born a Jew* (1523). Excerpts published by Council of Centers on Jewish-Christian Relations: http://goo.gl/DD4LWb. In 1516, Luther wrote the following in his commentary on Romans: "Many people are proud with marvelous stupidity when they call the Jews dogs, evildoers, or whatever they like, while they too, and equally, do not realize who or what they are in the sight of God. Boldly they heap blasphemous insults upon them, when they ought to have compassion on them and fear the same punishment for themselves." Quoted in Carter Lindberg, "Tainted Greatness: Luther's Attitudes Toward Judaism and their Historical Reception," *Tainted Greatness: Antisemitism and Cultural Heroes*, ed. Nancy A. Harrowitz (Philadelphia: Temple University Press, 1994), 17.

*Kampf*, Hitler wrote, "And the founder of Christianity made no secret indeed of his estimation of the Jewish people. When He found it necessary, He drove those enemies of the human race out of the Temple of God." Following the logic of "it was because of Luther," atheists have made a similar logical leap, "it was because of the Bible." When have politicians not appealed to religion to gain the support of the people? Think about the number of people who use the Bible to justify same-sex marriage, the welfare state, and socialism, not to mention various cults.

## Hitler and the Churches

As Hitler gained power, he turned against the church. Churches in Nazi Germany were "confined as far as possible to the performance of narrowly religious functions, and even within this narrow sphere were subjected to as many hindrances as the Nazis dared to impose." This is the evaluation of a 1945 report published by the Office of Strategic Services (OSS), the precursor to the CIA. It was called *The Nazi Master Plan: The Persecution of the Christian Churches* and was prepared for the War Crimes Staff. It offered the following summary: "This study describes, with illustrative factual evidence, Nazi purposes, policies and methods of persecuting the Christian Churches in Germany and occupied Europe."

Where did the strategic plan begin? "Implementation of this objective started with the curtailment of religious instruction in the primary and secondary schools with the squeezing of the religious periods into inconvenient hours, with Nazi propaganda among the teachers in order to induce them to refuse the teaching of religion, with vetoing of ... religious text books, and finally with substituting [a] Nazi *Weltanschauung* [worldview] and 'German faith' for Christian religious denominational instruction.... At the time of the outbreak of the war ... religious instruction had practically disappeared from Germany's primary schools."

When Martin Niemoeller used his pulpit to expose Adolf Hitler's radical politics, "He knew every word spoken was reported by Nazi spies and secret agents."[4] Leo Stein describes in his book *I Was in Hell with Niemoeller* how the Gestapo gathered evidence against Niemoeller:

---

4. Basil Miller, *Martin Niemoeller: Hero of the Concentration Camp*, 5th ed. (Grand

Now, the charge against Niemoeller was based entirely on his sermons, which the Gestapo agents had taken down stenographically. But in none of his sermons did Pastor Niemoeller exhort his congregation to overthrow the Nazi regime. He merely raised his voice against some of the Nazi policies, particularly the policy directed against the Church. He had even refrained from criticizing the Nazi government itself or any of its personnel. Under the former government his sermons would have been construed only as an exercise of the right of free speech. Now, however, written laws, no matter how explicitly they were worded, were subjected to the interpretation of the judges.[5]

In a June 27, 1937 sermon, Niemoeller told those in attendance that they had a sacred duty to speak out on the evils of the Nazi regime no matter what the consequences: "We have no more thought of using our own powers to escape the arm of the authorities than had the Apostles of old. No more are we ready to keep silent at man's behest when God commands us to speak. For it is, and must remain, the case that we must obey God rather than man."[6] A few days later, he was arrested. His crime? "Abuse of the pulpit."

The "Special Courts" set up by the Nazis made claims against pastors who spoke out against Hitler's policies. Niemoeller was not the only one singled out by the Gestapo. "Some 807 other pastors and leading laymen of the 'Confessional Church' were arrested in 1937, and hundreds more in the next couple of years."[7] A group of Confessional Churches in Germany, founded by Pastor Niemoeller and other Protestant ministers, drew up a proclamation to confront the political changes taking place in Germany that threatened the people "with a deadly danger. The danger lies in a new religion," the proclamation declared. "The church has by order of its Master to see to it that in our people Christ is given the honor that is proper to the Judge of the world.... The First Commandment says 'Thou shalt have no other gods before me.' The new religion is a rejection of the

Rapids, MI: Zondervan, 1942), 112.

5. Leo Stein, *I Was in Hell with Niemoeller* (New York: Fleming H. Revell, 1942), 175.

6. Quoted in William L. Shirer, *The Rise and Fall of the Third Reich* (New York: Simon and Schuster, 1960), 239.

7. Shirer, *The Rise and Fall of the Third Reich*, 239.

First Commandment."[8] Five hundred pastors who read the proclamation from their pulpits were arrested.

Then there is Dietrich Bonhoeffer (1906-1945), a German Lutheran pastor, theologian, and founding member of the Confessing Church. "Bonhoeffer became known for his staunch resistance to the Nazi dictatorship. He strongly opposed Hitler's euthanasia program and genocidal persecution of the Jews. He was also involved in plans by members of the Abwehr (the German Military Intelligence Office) to assassinate Adolf Hitler. He was arrested in April 1943 by the Gestapo and executed by hanging on April 1945 while imprisoned at a Nazi concentration camp, just 23 days before the German surrender."[9]

## Racial Purity and Two-Kingdom Theology

Hitler only cared about theology when he could use it to promote his pure race ideas. As far as I can find, he did not promote the belief that the church replaced Israel. His deep seated anti-Semitism did not allow him to acknowledge that Jews had anything to do with Christianity. Carl Trueman writes the following:

> Race as we think of it today is really a concept of relatively modern provenance, something that arguably emerges in the nineteenth century as interest grew in biology, evolution etc. The ideology of the Holocaust was undoubtedly racist in this sense: the Nuremberg laws of 1935, which effectively paved the way in judicial terms for what became the Final Solution, made it clear that conversion to Christianity did not exempt someone: for the Nazis the matter was one of blood (albeit built on completely fallacious science) not of religion. For Luther, however, Judaism was a religious category. He had no real grasp of racial identity and no concern for the kind of racial issues which dominated Nazi ideology.[10] ... This does not make his hate any more acceptable, but it does mean that the road

---

8. Quoted in Eugene Davidson, *The Trials of the Germans: An Account of the Twenty-Two Defendants before the International Military Tribunal at Nuremberg* (Columbia, MO: University of Missouri Press, [1966] 1997), 275.

9. For a moving portrait of this anti-Nazi dissident, see Eric Metaxas, *Bonhoeffer: Pastor, Martyr, Prophet, Spy* (Nashville: Thomas Nelson, 2010).

10. Carl Trueman, "Luther and the Jews II: The Context," Reformation 21.

between Luther and Auschwitz is a complicated one which defies direct and simplistic attempts to make him one of the primary historical culprits.[11]

In reality, it was Luther's two-kingdom theology that led to the rise of Hitler and the Nazi regime. This is an important point: "the reorganized Protestant churches and the newly established Nazi-submissive German Evangelical Church acquiesced to Nazification of the churches, being influenced by nationalism and **their traditional obedience to state authority.**" If Christians had been involved in government decades before, Germany would never have had a Hitler. In 19th-century Germany, a distinction was made between the realm of public policy managed by the State and the domain of private morality under the province of the gospel. Religion was the sphere of the inner personal life, while things public came under the jurisdiction of the "worldly powers" that could not be questioned by those in the church sphere.

Redemption was fully the province of the church while the civil sphere was solely the province of the State. "Religion was a private matter that concerned itself with the personal and moral development of the individual. The external order—nature, scientific knowledge, statecraft—operated on the basis of its own internal logic and discernible laws."[12] Christians were told that the church's sole concern was the *spiritual* life of the believer. "The Erlangen church historian Hermann Jorda declared in 1917 that the state, the natural order of God, followed its own autonomous laws while the kingdom of God was concerned with the soul and operated separately on the basis of the morality of the gospel."[13]

This view is very much like what Christians are being taught today. It has neutralized them in the name of the authority of the Bible. How many times have Christians heard, there's a separation between church and state, Jesus didn't get mixed up in politics, our citizenship is in heaven, do not judge, you can't impose your morality on other people, God's kingdom is not of this world, render unto Caesar the things that are Caesar's, etc?[14]

---

11. Carl Trueman, "Luther and the Jews III: Lessons," Reformation 21.

12. Richard V. Pierard, "Why Did Protestants Welcome Hitler?," *Fides et Historia*, X:2 (Spring 1978), 13

13. Pierard, "Why Did Protestants Welcome Hitler?," 14.

14. Gary DeMar, *Myths, Lies, and Half-Truths* (Powder Springs, GA: American Vision, 2010).

Here's a sample of some German theological thinking that shaped the mindset of the nation and paved the way for a dictator like Hitler to gain power:

- **Christian Ernst Luthard** wrote in 1867: "The Gospel has absolutely nothing to do with outward existence but only with eternal life, not with external orders and institutions which could come in conflict with the secular orders but only with the heart and its relationship with God.... It is not the vocation of Jesus Christ or of the Gospel to change the orders of secular life and establish them anew. ... Christianity wants to change man's heart, not his external situation."[15]

- **Rudolf Sohm** (1841-1917), speaking to a convention on the main Christian social action group, the Inner Mission, asserted: "The Gospel frees us from this world, frees us from all questions of this world, frees us inwardly, also from the questions of public life, also from the social question. Christianity has no answer to these questions." The issues of public life, he wrote, "should remain untouched by the proclamation of the Gospel, completely untouched."[16]

- **Wilhelm Hermann** (1846-1922) declared in the 1913 edition of his book on ethics that the state was a product of nature and that it could not be love but only self-assertion, coercion, and law.... Once the Christian understood the moral significance of the state, then "he will consider obedience to the government to be the highest vocation within the state. For the authority of the state on the whole, resting as it does upon authority of the government, is more important than the elimination of any shortcomings which it might have."

- **Robert Benne** makes the following good points on the effects of this type of thinking: "There are two serious theological problems here. For one, the affirmation of the Sovereign God as Creator, Sustainer, and Judge of all is forgotten. The God whose will is revealed in the commandments and in

15. Quoted in Carl E. Braaten, *Principles of Lutheran Theology*, 2nd ed. (Minneapolis: Fortress Press, 2007), 152.

16. Quoted in Carl E. Braaten, *Principles of Lutheran Theology*, 152.

his involvement in history is somehow expunged from the political world. Along with this denial of God's involvement in history is the elevation of the gospel to such a height that it has no relevance to ordinary life. The gospel addresses only the inner man about eternal life, not the whole man who is embedded in God's history."[17]

None of this is to dismiss Luther's harsh rhetoric, not only against the Jews, but against other individuals and groups (e.g., the Papacy and Anabaptists). For example, in his 1523 treatise *That Jesus Christ Was Born a Jew*, he described "our fools, the popes, bishops, sophists, and monks" as "crude asses' heads."

## An Overdone Rhetorical Device

So, is Dr. Brown's serious charge against "Replacement Theology" accurate? If you want to end a debate over eschatology, just charge your opponent with holding to "Replacement Theology." It's the theological equivalent of calling someone a racist and a mild way of saying a person is an anti-Semite. Dr. Brown is not the only one to do this. Hal Lindsey started the ball rolling with his 1989 book *The Road to Holocaust*.[18] Here's a typical internet analysis of the topic:

> One of the most dangerous and subversive doctrines held by adherents of Preterism is the view that in AD 70, at the destruction of Jerusalem by the Roman armies, God's covenant nation of Israel was superseded by the Christian church.[19]

Not to be outdone:

> There is a *demonic cancer* coursing through the life blood of the Church of Jesus Christ and its name is REPLACEMENT THEOLOGY.

Certainly less strident than "demonic," another prophecy pundit describes the position as "a *heresy*."[20] A watchdog website warns,

---

17. *Good and Bad Ways to Think about Religion and Politics* (Grand Rapids, MI: Eerdmans, 2010), 22.

18. Hal Lindsey, *The Road to Holocaust* (New York: Bantam Books, 1989).

19. Brian Simmons, "Preterism and Replacement Theology."

20. John E. Young, "Clear View: Replacement Theology."

"There is a powerful movement afoot called Replacement Theology which states that the church is Israel and the promises given to Israel were primarily for the church. This movement is incurring the wrath of God...."[21] These types of indictments are not only found on the internet. Noted Old Testament scholar Walter Kaiser once wrote, "Replacement theology is just plain *bad news* for both the Church and Israel."[22] He doesn't explain why.

Anyone familiar with the Bible knows that Christianity does not "supersede Judaism." The genealogies found in Matthew and Luke clearly show that Jesus is "the son of David, the son of Abraham" (Matt. 1:1). The first New Covenant believers were from the nation of Israel (Luke 1-2) with hints of a later expanded redemptive role for Samaritans (John 4:7-45), Greeks (John 12:20-22), the nations (Luke 2:32), and the broader world (John 3:16; 4:42).

## To the Jew First and a Better Everything

"To the Jew first" (Rom. 1:16) predominates in the New Testament: For example, "Now there were Jews living in Jerusalem, devout men, from every nation under heaven" (Acts 2:5). The promises that had been made to Israel were being fulfilled in the events of Pentecost and beyond:

> Now when they heard this, they were pierced to the heart, and said to Peter and the rest of the apostles, "Brethren, what shall we do?" Peter said to them, "Repent, and each of you be baptized in the name of Jesus Christ for the forgiveness of your sins; and you will receive the gift of the Holy Spirit. For the promise is for you and your children and for all who are far off, as many as the Lord our God will call to Himself." And with many other words he solemnly testified and kept on exhorting them, saying, "Be saved from this perverse generation!" So then, those who had received his word were baptized; and that day there were added about three thousand souls. They were continually devoting themselves to the apostles' teaching and to fellowship, to the breaking of bread and to prayer. Everyone kept feeling a sense of awe; and many wonders and signs were taking place through

---

21. Anonymous, "Replacement Theology."
22. Quoted by Thomas Ice in "What is Replacement Theology?"

the apostles. And all those who had believed were together and had all things in common; and they began selling their property and possessions and were sharing them with all, as anyone might have need. Day by day continuing with one mind in the temple, and breaking bread from house to house, they were taking their meals together with gladness and sincerity of heart, praising God and having favor with all the people. And the Lord was adding to their number day by day those who were being saved (Acts 2:37-47).

Peter's message was to "all the house of Israel" (Acts 2:36; see Matt. 10:6, 23; 15:24). When these Israelites asked, "Brethren, what shall we do?" (2:37), Peter told them: "For the promise is for **you** and **your children**, and for **all who are far off**, as many as the Lord God shall call to Himself" (2:39). Israel's spiritual destiny is the same as it is for non-Israelites: Repent and believe in Jesus! But it's "to the Jew first," not to the Jews only (Rom. 1:16; John 4:22; Acts 3:26), or when the gospel goes to the Gentiles, the Jews no longer matter.

No one said anything about a delay in the promises that had been made to Israel centuries before. In fact, Peter clearly informed his audience that the promises were for them and their children (Acts 2:38). There is no mention of the land, a rebuilt temple, the reinstitution of animal sacrifices, or anything else related to the shadows of the Old Covenant. In fact, "for all who were owners of land or houses" sold them (4:34). They possessed something better, the forgiveness of their sins (2:38) and a better inheritance (Heb. 11:8-16).

Jesus is "the mediator of a better covenant, which has been enacted on better promises" (Heb. 8:6). What would they rather have, land, a stone altar and temple, the cutting of their flesh, and yearly bloody sacrifices, or forgiveness of sins, a sinful priesthood, the power of the Holy Spirit (Acts 1:8), and Jesus who intercedes as a mediator for them daily? The answer is obvious as the book of Hebrews makes clear in multiple chapters.

## A Jewish Church

The first church was made up exclusively of Jews (Acts 8:1). As anyone can see, there is nothing said or indicated that the church replaced

Israel since Israel made up the church. In fact, Dr. Brown agrees with this assessment:

> Let's go back to the Book of Acts. The early Church was exclusively Jewish. It was almost *ten years* before a group of Gentiles received the gospel, and this created shock waves in Jerusalem.[23]

God kept His promise to Israel by sending His only begotten Son. As the above passages show, God did not reject His people. Jews were being saved by the thousands throughout the entire world. At the same time, there were Jews who were rejecting Jesus as the promised redeemer. Consider the following from Acts 13:46-52:

> But when the Jews saw the crowds, they were filled with jealousy and began to oppose what Paul was saying by insulting him. Then Paul and Barnabas boldly said: "It was necessary that God's message be spoken to you first. But since you reject it and consider yourselves unworthy of eternal life, we now turn to the Gentiles! For this is what the Lord has commanded us: 'I have made you a light for the Gentiles to bring salvation to the ends of the earth.'" When the Gentiles heard this, they rejoiced and glorified the message of the Lord, and all who had been appointed to eternal life believed. So the message of the Lord spread through the whole region. But the Jews incited the prominent women, who worshiped God, and the leading men of the city. They stirred up persecution against Paul and Barnabas and expelled them from their district. But they shook the dust off their feet against them and went to Iconium. And the disciples were filled with joy and the Holy Spirit."

This passage is in keeping with all we see in the New Testament. The Jews were the first to hear the gospel. The Jews were the first to believe. The Jews were the first to make up the New Covenant church. When the gospel went to the Gentiles, the Gentiles did not replace Israel. The Gentiles were grafted into an already growing New Testament assembly of believers made up of those from "the house of Israel."

---

23. Brown, *Our Hands are Stained with Blood*, chap. 8.

## Church, Assembly, Congregation

The church does not replace Israel since the church is made up of Jews and Gentiles. The entire idea of "Replacement Theology," those who advocate for it and those who denounce it, is a theological construct built on the foundation of confusion based on the meaning of the word "church." The Greek word *ekklēsia*, most often translated "church," was not new to the New Testament. It's the Greek equivalent of the Hebrew word *qahal* and means "assembly" or "congregation." It's the way William Tyndale wanted to translate *ekklēsia* in his English translation but was forced to the point of death by the Roman Catholic leadership to translate it as "church."

One of the requirements of the translators of the King James Version was that *ekklēsia* had to be translated as "church" according to the *Rules to be Observed in the Translation of the [King James] Bible*: "The old Ecclesiastical Words to be kept, *viz.* the Word *Church* not to be translated *Congregation &c.*"[24]

As William Stafford writes, it was understood by the laity and church officials that "it was the clergy who were the *ecclesia*, the church."[25] But as Tyndale saw it, "the church was not the clergy, nor was it the hierarchical, legal, and ceremonial edifice sustaining the clergy, but rather the congregation of all who responded to the word of God."[26]

The Hebrew translation of the New Testament translates the Greek *ekklēsia* as *qahal* meaning assembly or congregation. The TLV Bible translation, published by the Messianic Jewish Family Bible Society, translates Matthew 16:18 as "community" and 18:17 as "Messiah's community" and not "church." With this background, we can understand why Stephen could describe "the children of Israel" as the "*ekklēsia* in the wilderness" (Acts 7:37-38).

In Hebrews 2:12 there is a direct quotation from Psalm 22:22. The Old Testament Psalm used the word *qahal* and the Septuagint translated it as *ekklēsia*:

---

24. Quoted in David Daniell, *The Bible in English: It's History and Influence* (New Haven, CT: Yale University Press, 2003), 439.

25. William S. Stafford, "Tyndale's Voice to the Laity" in *Word, Church, and State: Tyndale Quincentenary Essays*, 105.

26. Stafford, "Tyndale's Voice to the Laity," 106.

> I will tell of Your name to my brethren;
> In the midst of the assembly [*qahal*] I will praise You.

The Septuagint (LXX), the Greek translation of the Hebrew Old Testament, translates *qahal* in Psalm 22:22 as *ekklēsia*. Hebrews 2:12 reads this way in the King James Version:

> I will declare thy name unto my brethren,
> in the midst of the church [*ekklēsia*]
> will I sing praise unto thee.

The *ekklēsia* was identified with Israel long before the inauguration of the New Testament Church (*ekklēsia*).

## The Gentiles Also

The first Christians were Jews. The gospel was preached to "Israel" (Acts 2:22, 26). We later learn that the gospel extends "also to the Greek" (Rom. 1:16) as Peter's encounter with Cornelius shows (Acts 10). Notice Peter's evaluation of these events and the response of his fellow Jews:

> "And as I began to speak, the Holy Spirit fell upon them just as *He did* upon us at the beginning. And I remembered the word of the Lord, how He used to say, 'John baptized with water, but you will be baptized with the Holy Spirit.' Therefore if God gave to them the same gift as *He gave* to us also after believing in the Lord Jesus Christ, who was I that I could stand in God's way?" When they heard this, they quieted down and glorified God, saying, "Well then, God has granted to the Gentiles also the repentance *that leads* to life" (Acts 11:15-18).

"The Gentiles *also*." Gentile believers were grafted into the Jewish assembly of believers and were given "the same gift," the Holy Spirit (see Acts 1:8; 2:38). Jews and Gentiles together making "the two into one new man" (Eph. 2) made up the "congregation of God." The charge of "Replacement theology" obscures the obvious. The charge is a tactical red herring to get people's attention away from what the New Testament shows about the relationship between the promises of the Old Covenant and their fulfillment in the New Covenant with Israel and how Gentiles are grafted in to an Israelite assembly (*ekklēsia*) of believers.

How is this even close to a replacement? It's not. The "Replacement Theology" epithet is dispensationalism's trump card in any debate over eschatology because it implies anti-Semitism. Once the charge is made, all rational discourse ceases. Dispensationalism has established a false Israel-Church distinction that leads to the claim that anyone who is not a dispensational premillennialist is either anti-Semitic or, to use a less pejorative term, "anti-Judaism." A quick reading of the New Testament will show that no one makes the case that there is a church-Israel distinction. There are Jews and Gentiles, but there is one people of God. There aren't two olive trees; there's one olive tree (Rom. 11:17-24).

## Israel Replaced by the Church

As I've shown, there is no church-Israel distinction since the first members of the church (*ekklēsia*) were the believing remnant of Israelites (Acts 2-3) and Gentiles who were grafted into this Jewish believing remnant. The promises made to Israel were fulfilled in Jesus. Believing this does not make anybody an anti-Semite. Is there a future for Israel? Sure there is, either with or without Jesus Christ. The same is true for everybody. Does any of this mean that Israel does not have a right to the land of Israel? Not at all. Do some people believe that the Jews don't have a right to the land? Yes. Most of them are Muslims who hardly believe in "Replacement Theology."

There are a number of passages that Dr. Brown and other Christians point to in support of the belief that there is a future national restoration still in store for ethnic Israel. Personally, I do not believe the New Testament teaches such a view. Does this mean that there is not a *redemptive* future for Jews? Not at all. Is it necessary for there to be a national restoration for Israel in order **not** to be anti-Semitic? Does a national restoration for Israel mean salvation for Israel? The New Testament doesn't say anything about a national restoration of Israel, and yet Jews were being saved by the thousands in the first century.

National salvation for the Jews doesn't seem to have taken place since Israel became a nation again in 1948. In terms of the Bible and recent history, there does not seem to be a correlation between national restoration and salvation, and yet individual Jews are being saved every day around the world.

Then there is the belief that God has no regard for Israel as a nation this side of the "rapture." Those who hold this view share Dr. Brown's premillennial view. For example, John R. Rice held this view:

> Thus the trouble in Jerusalem, and the dispersion of Jews among all the nations of Jerusalem throughout this whole age, is simply a continuation of the punishment of God upon the whole race of Jews.[27]

Did this include Martin Luther's anti-Semitic writings, the pogroms against the Jews, and current Islamic threats to "wipe Israel from the map"? Are Jews still under God's judgment during the time when the Church supersedes Israel until the "rapture"? In 1950, Rice made it clear that Israel becoming a nation again prior to the rapture is prophetically inconsequential, and those who take the position that Israel's new national status is a fulfillment of Bible prophecy are teaching "heresy."[28]

> [T]he custom has grown up among a lot of premillennial Christians of looking for Christ's return because we have had the first or second world war, or of looking for Christ's return because Zionists and infidel Jews have established the modern nation Israel in Palestine. Some are moved more by newspaper accounts than by the plain command of the Lord Jesus.[29]

Thomas Ice, a co-author with prophecy writers Tim LaHaye and Mark Hitchcock, states that the Church replaced Israel this side of the rapture: "We dispensationalists believe that **the church has superseded Israel during the current church age**, but God has a future time in which He will restore national Israel 'as the institution for the administration of divine blessings to the world.'"[30]

Individual Jews like individual Gentiles have not lost the blessings of the gospel forever. Jews and Gentiles at this very moment can embrace Jesus as their savior. There were believing and unbelieving Jews and Gentiles in Jesus' day, and there are believing and unbelieving

---

27. John R. Rice, *The King of the Jews: A Commentary on the Gospel According to Matthew* (Murfreesboro, TN: Sword of the Lord Publishers, 1955), 369.

28. John R. Rice, *We Can Have Revival Now* (Greenville, SC: Bob Jones University Press, 1950), 41.

29. Rice, *We Can Have Revival Now*, 43.

30. Thomas Ice, "The Israel of God," The Thomas Ice Collection: http://goo.gl/4u5hNBl

Jews today. National status doesn't have anything to do with being in or out of Christ. Just like the temple never saved anybody; national restoration won't save anyone. "But as many as received Him, to them He gave the right to become children of God, even to those who believe in His name, who were born, not of blood nor of the will of the flesh nor of the will of man, but of God" (John 1:12-13).

## The Slaughter of Millions of Jews

What I found curious is that Dr. Brown does not deal with the views of dispensationalists who envision a future Jewish holocaust as part of their prophetic system based on Zechariah 13:8-9:

"It will come about in all the land," Declares the LORD,
"That two parts in it will be cut off and perish;
But the third will be left in it.
"And I will bring the third part through the fire,
Refine them as silver is refined,
And test them as gold is tested.
They will call on My name,
And I will answer them;
I will say, 'They are My people,'
And they will say, 'The LORD is my God.'"

While Dr. Brown quotes several passages from Zechariah (1:14-15; 8:23; 12:10; 13:1; 14:4-9, 16) in his book *Our Hands are Stained with Blood*, he does not quote 13:8-9.

Why is this important? At the 2012 Democratic National Convention, Mark Alan Siegel, who served as the chairman of Florida's Palm Beach County Democratic Party, told an interviewer the following about what he thought of Christian and Jewish relationships:

The Christians just want us to be there so we can be slaughtered and converted and bring on the second coming of Jesus Christ. The worst possible allies for the Jewish state are the fundamentalist Christians who want Jews to die and convert so they can bring on the second coming of their Lord. It is a false friendship. They are seeking their own ends and not ours. I don't believe the fundamentalists urging a greater Israel are friends of the Jewish state.

It wasn't too long before the video of the interview went viral and Mr. Siegel was forced out of his position. Where did Mr. Siegel get such crazy ideas? It's a prevalent view among dispensational prophecy writers. "The period of great tribulation between the two phases of Jesus' Second Coming is portrayed by dispensationalists as a time of horrific suffering and destruction of the Jewish people."[31]

On the September 18, 1991 edition of the "700 Club," Sid Roth, host of "Messianic Vision," stated that "two-thirds of the Jewish people [living in Israel] will be exterminated" during a future Great Tribulation. He bases this view on Zechariah 13:8-9. He argued that incidents of Blacks turning against Jews in New York City were a prelude to a coming great persecution.[32]

Pat Robertson asked Roth: "You don't foresee some kind of persecution against Jews in America, do you?" Roth responded: "Unfortunately, I believe God foresees this." Roth believes that the end (pre-tribulation rapture) is near. Roth believes that Jews are destined to suffer based on a futurized interpretation of Zechariah 13:8-9.[33] He claims that today's anti-Semitism is a prelude to an *inevitable* future Jewish tribulation that will result in another holocaust. The reality of violent acts against Jews is all part of Israel's prophetic history based on the parenthesis view that is fundamental to dispensational premillennialism.

Hal Lindsey describes the judgment against Israel in AD 70 as a "picnic" compared to a super-holocaust that will lead to the slaughter of two-thirds of the Jews living in Israel.[34]

Kay Arthur, another dispensational author, has stated publicly that what lies ahead for Israel will make Hitler's Holocaust look like

---

31. Stephen R. Haynes, *Reluctant Witnesses: Jews and the Christian Imagination* (Louisville: Westminster John Knox Press, 1995), 162.

32. Dr. Brown reported on these events in the Preface to his book *Our Hands are Stained with Blood*: "Although it sounds more like a nightmare than reality, enraged mobs of young New York Blacks staged anti-Jewish riots in September 1991, screaming, 'Heil Hitler! Kill the dirty Jews!' They looted Jewish stores, vandalized Jewish schools, ransacked Jewish synagogues—even killed a Jewish student, wounding several others as well." Can an incident like this be blamed on "Replacement Theology"? One thing does not have to do with the other.

33. Zechariah was describing a future holocaust. It was fulfilled in AD 70 with the destruction of Jerusalem and the slaughter of 1,100,000 Jews at the hands of the Romans.

34. Hal Lindsey, *The Road to Holocaust* (New York: Bantam Books, 1989), 220.

"a Sunday school picnic." In her novel, *Israel My Beloved*, the heroine is standing before a future scene where the Valley of Jehoshaphat is littered with the dead. This is based on her understanding of Zechariah 13:8-9 that only a third of Israel will survive "the fire just as Zechariah promised."[35] During the future Great Tribulation, Israel is the target of God's wrath:

> Auschwitz was nothing compared to this.[36] ... I've watched as men, women, and children writhe in agony—an agony beyond the Crusades, the Inquisitions, the pogroms. Beyond the horrors of Sobibor, Treblinka, Auschwitz—all the death camps combined.... We have experienced an agony beyond any horror the human mind can envision ... beyond even Hitler.[37]

Let's not forget Jack Van Impe's *Israel's Final Holocaust* in which he writes that when the prophecy clock starts ticking again after the "rapture," it "will be traumatic days for Israel. Just when peace seems to have come, it will be taken from her and she will be plunged into another bloody persecution, ... a devastating explosion of persecution and misery for Israel...."[38]

Consider what Thomas Ice writes in his article "What do you do with a future National Israel in the Bible?"[39] Like Dr. Brown, Ice believes "that Old Testament promises made to national Israel will literally be fulfilled in the future. This means the Bible teaches that God will return the Jews to their land before the tribulation begins (Isa. 11:11-12:6; Ezek. 20:33-44; 22:17-22; Zeph. 2:1-3). This has been accomplished and the stage is set as a result of the current existence of the modern state of Israel." Then he goes on to write the following:

> The Bible also indicates that before Israel enters into her time of national blessing she must first pass through the fire of the tribulation (Deut. 4:30; Jer. 30:5-9; Dan. 12:1; Zeph. 1:14-18).

---

35. Kay Arthur, *Israel, My Beloved: A Novel* (Eugene, OR: Harvest House, 1996), 433

36. Arthur, *Israel, My Beloved*, 431.

37. Arthur, *Israel, My Beloved*, 434.

38. Jack Van Impe with Roger F. Campbell, *Israel's Final Holocaust* (Nashville: Thomas Nelson, 1979), 37.

39. Thomas Ice, "What do you do with a future National Israel in the Bible?": https://bit.ly/4c1DTRM

Even though the horrors of the Holocaust under Hitler were of an unimaginable magnitude, the Bible teaches that a time of even greater trial awaits Israel during the tribulation. **Anti-Semitism will reach new heights, this time global in scope, in which two-thirds of world Jewry will be killed (Zech. 13:7-9; Rev. 12).** Through this time God will protect His remnant so that before His second advent "all Israel will be saved" (Rom. 11:36).

In reality, it's "all that's left of Israel [that] will be saved."

In his book *Blow the Trumpet in Zion,* published by the same company that published Dr. Brown's book, Richard Booker writes:

> What is this terrible tribulation that awaits the Jews? Moses said it would take place in the "latter days." It is the last seven years of this age just prior to the coming of Messiah Jesus to earth. The Bible says this will be a time of suffering such as the world has never known.
>
> *****
>
> The Antichrist will march his troops into Israel and for a short period of time will occupy Jerusalem. Every nation will support his retaliation against Israel for their disturbing world peace. **The Antichrist will kill two-thirds of all the Jews. This could mean that up to ten million Jews could be killed.** The Antichrist will plunder the beloved city of Jerusalem, and one-half of the citizens will be forced into exile.[40]

In a December 2, 1984 sermon, the late Jerry Falwell said the following: "Millions of Jews will be slaughtered at this time but a remnant will escape and God will supernaturally hide them for Himself for the last three and a half years of the Tribulation, some feel in the rose-red city of Petra."

Charles Ryrie writes in his book *The Best is Yet to Come* that during this post-rapture period Israel will undergo "the worst bloodbath in Jewish history."[41] The book's title doesn't seem appropriate considering that during this period of time most of the Jews will die!

---

40. Richard Booker, *Blow the Trumpet in Zion* (Shippensburg, PA: Destiny Image Publishers, 1985), 112, 118.

41. Charles C. Ryrie, *The Best is Yet to Come* (Chicago, IL: Moody Press, 1981), 86.

John Walvoord follows a similar line of argument: "Israel is *destined* to have a particular time of suffering which will eclipse any thing that it has known in the past.... The people of Israel ... are placing themselves within the vortex of this future whirlwind which will destroy the majority of those living in the land of Palestine."[42]

Arnold Fruchtenbaum states that during the Great Tribulation "Israel will suffer tremendous persecution (Matthew 24:15-28; Revelation 12:1-17). As a result of this persecution of the Jewish people, two-thirds are going to be killed."[43]

Barry Horner claims that "quite a few [non-premillennialists], by their derogatory manner have inferred that they would be delighted if the Arabs would push Israel into the Mediterranean Sea, repossess Palestine, and thus vindicate their Eschatology!"[44] He doesn't identify these people or offer supporting documentation, but I'll assume that he can produce the documentation if asked to do so. I can produce the following from Dr. Paige Patterson, president of Southwestern Baptist Theological Seminary and a *dispensational premillennialist*:

> The present state of Israel is not the final form. The present state of Israel will be lost, eventually, and Israel will be run out of the land again, only to return when they accept the Messiah as Savior.[45]

It's not advocates of "Replacement Theology" that promote the idea that Israel must be kicked out of the land but someone who holds a prophetic view similar to that of Dr. Brown. Given Dr. Patterson's end-time scenario, if Israel finds herself in a war with her neighbors, should Christians support Israel and thereby interfere with God's plan for Israel or should they intervene? This is not a hypothetical question when we look at what happened during World War II.

How do dispensationalists respond to a future Jewish holocaust during the tribulation period." It's really quite simple. Not only will

---

42. John F. Walvoord, *Israel in Prophecy* (Grand Rapids, MI: Zondervan, 1962), 107, 113. Emphasis added.

43. Arnold G. Fruchtenbaum, "The Little Apocalypse of Zechariah," *The End Times Controversy: The Second Coming Under Attack,* eds. Tim LaHaye and Thomas Ice (Eugene, OR: Harvest House, 2003), 262.

44. Barry Horner, *Future Israel: Why Christian Anti-Judaism Must be Challenged* (Nashville: Broadman & Holman, 2007), xviii.

45. Stated on Dallas, Texas, radio program (KCBI) in a debate with me on May 15, 1991.

millions of Jews be killed but billions of people around the world also will die. The following is from Ron Rhodes' book *Bible Prophecy Under Siege*:

> Preterists charge pretribulationists with barbarism for holding to the belief that two-thirds of the Jews will die during the tribulation period. Zechariah 13:8 tells us, In the whole land, declares the Lord, two thirds shall be cut off and perish, and one third shall be left alive." DeMar criticizes Tim LaHaye for this view on the verse: "Why isn't LaHaye warning Jews now living in Israel about this predetermined holocaust by encouraging them to leave Israel until the conflagration is over? Indeed, we find those who hold to LaHaye's position supporting relocation efforts of Jews to the land of Israel that will mean certain death for a majority of them because it's a 'fulfillment of Bible prophecy.'"
>
> Thomas Ice responds to DeMar by pointing out that "about three-fifths of the entire earth's population will be killed during the course of the seven-year tribulation, many of them believers (Rev. 6:9-11). Hence, it is unfair to accuse LaHaye of teaching a Jewish holocaust when, in fact, a holocaust will come upon the entire world—killing both Gentiles and Jews. Let's also be clear that LaHaye did not "write the letter," so to speak. He is simply the mail carrier. In other words, LaHaye did not write the scripture which prophesies the deaths of two-thirds of the Jews. Rather, he is simply delivering the message of what scripture teaches in Zechariah 13:8.

This is a crazy argument since God did not send His Son into the world to condemn the world, but rather so that the world through Him would be saved. The Zechariah 13 judgment was local and applied to Israel. It was a judgment that could be escaped on foot. It was not a worldwide judgment. The same is true of Revelation 6 because it is parallel to Matthew 24 which was a judgment on that generation alone. For example, in his commentary on Revelation, James Hamilton writes, "the opening of the seals in Revelation 6 corresponds to what Jesus describes in the Olivet Discourse in the Synoptic Gospels."[46]

---

46. Hamilton, "An Interview with Dr. James Hamilton." For further discussion of this point, see James M. Hamilton, Jr., *Revelation: The Spirit Speaks to the Churches* (Wheaton,

If the Olivet Discourse describes events leading up to and including the destruction of Jerusalem that took place within a generation in AD 70, then Revelation must be given a similar interpretation. Even if it's not, and refers to events in the seven-year period after the "rapture of the church," as dispensationalists claim, there is no way that falling stars should be interpreted as physical stars that hit the earth.

## "Hands Off" While Hitler Acted Against the Jews

Dwight Wilson, author of *Armageddon Now!*, who describes himself as "a third-generation premillenarian who has spent his whole life in premillennialist churches, has attended a premillennialist Bible college, and has taught in such a college for fourteen years,"[47] argues that some noted premillennialists advocated a "hands off" policy regarding Nazi persecutions of the Jews during World War II. Since, according to dispensational views regarding Bible prophecy, "the Gentile nations are permitted to afflict Israel in chastisement for her national sins," there is little that should or could be done to oppose it. Wilson writes, "It is regrettable that this view allowed premillennialists to expect the phenomenon of 'anti-Semitism' and tolerate it matter-of-factly."[48]

Wilson describes "premillenarian views" opposing "anti-Semitism" in the mid-thirties and thereafter as "ambivalent."[49] There was little moral outcry "among the premillenarians ... against the persecution, since they had been expecting it."[50] He continues:

> Another comment regarding the general European anti-Semitism depicted these developments as part of the on-going plan of God for the nation; they were "Foregleams of Israel's Tribulation." Premillennialists were anticipating the Great Tribulation, "the time of Jacob's trouble." Therefore, they predicted, "The next scene in Israel's history may be summed up in three words: purification through tribulation." It was

IL: Crossway, 2012), 166-167. Also, Louis A. Vos, *The Synoptic Traditions in the Apocalypse* (Kampen, Netherlands: J.H. Kok N. V., 1965), 181-188.

47. Dwight Wilson, *Armageddon Now!: The Premillenarian Response to Russia and Israel Since 1917* (Grand Rapids, MI: Baker Book House, 1977), 13.

48. Wilson, *Armageddon Now!*, 16.

49. Wilson, *Armageddon Now!*, 94.

50. Wilson, *Armageddon Now!*, 94.

clear that although this purification was part of the curse, God did not intend that Christians should participate in it. Clear, also, was the implication that He did intend for the Germans to participate in it (in spite of the fact that it would bring them punishment) . . . and that any moral outcry against Germany would have been in opposition to God's will. In such a fatalistic system, to oppose Hitler was to oppose God.[51]

Wilson maintains that it was the view of a predicted Jewish persecution prior to the Second Coming that led to a "hands off" policy when it came to speaking out against virulent "anti-Semitism." "For the premillenarian, the massacre of Jewry expedited his blessed hope. Certainly he did not rejoice over the Nazi holocaust, he just fatalistically observed it as a 'sign of the times.'"[52]

Premillennialist James M. Gray of the Moody Bible Institute believed in the authenticity of the *Protocols of the Elders of Zion*. He defended Henry Ford when Ford published installments of the *Protocols* in his self-funded *Dearborn Independent* newspaper. In a 1927 editorial in the *Moody Bible Institute Monthly*, Gray claimed that Ford "had good grounds for publishing some of the things about the Jews.... Mr. Ford might have found corroborative evidence [of the Jewish conspiracy] had he looked for it."[53]

As time went on, Gray was coming under increasing pressure to repudiate the *Protocols* as a forgery. Not only Gray, but *Moody Bible Institute Monthly* was being criticized by the evangelical *Hebrew Christian Alliance* for not condemning the manufactured *Protocols*. Gray grew indignant and once again voiced his belief that the *Protocols* were authentic. He did this in the *Moody Bible Institute Monthly*. Gray, of course, pointed out that "Moody Bible Institute had always worked for the highest interests of Jews by training people to evangelize them."[54]

Even so, Gray went on to assert that "Jews were at least partly to blame for their ill treatment." He supported this contention by referring his readers to an article written by Max Reich, a faculty member at the

51. Wilson, *Armageddon Now!*, 94. Emphasis added.

52. Wilson, *Armageddon Now!*, 95.

53. Timothy P. Weber, *Living in the Shadow of the Second Coming: American Premillennialism, 1875-1982* (Grand Rapids, MI: Zondervan/Academie, 1983), 189.

54. Weber, *Living in the Shadow of the Second Coming*, 189.

Moody Bible Institute. Reich wrote: "Without religion, the Jew goes down and becomes worse than others, as a corruption of the best is always the worst corruption."[55]

Charges of "anti-Semitism" were not abated by Gray's attempts at clarification. His views concerning the Jews remained. "By the beginning of 1935, Gray was fending off charges from the *American Hebrew and Jewish Tribune*, the *Bulletin of the Baltimore Branch of the American Jewish Congress*, and even *Time* magazine that persons connected with Moody had been actively distributing the *Protocols*."[56]

Of course, Gray was not the only dispensationalist who vouched for the veracity of the *Protocols* and had negative (anti-Semitic) things to say about the Jews. Arno C. Gaebelein, an editor of the *Scofield Reference Bible*, believed that the *Protocols* were authentic, that they accurately revealed a "Jewish conspiracy." His *Conflict of the Ages*[57] would be viewed today as an anti-Semitic work because it fostered the belief that communism had Jewish roots and that the Bolshevik revolution of 1917 had been masterminded by a group of well-trained Jewish agitators.

At the same time that Gaebelein was using anti-Semitic rhetoric, he had a thriving evangelistic ministry to Jews in New York City. Why the double-mindedness? Dispensationalism expects both the persecution and salvation of the Jews.[58] This is why George Marsden could write that "fundamentalists between [World War I and II] could be both pro-Zionist and somewhat anti-Semitic, favoring the return of the Jews to Israel, which would lead eventually to their conversion; yet in the meantime especially distrusting apostate Jews."[59]

## Summary

First, in what we've seen, "Replacement Theology" is often used as a rhetorical club in opposition to theologians who take issue with the

---

55. Quoted in Weber, *Living in the Shadow of the Second Coming*, 190.

56. Weber, *Living in the Shadow of the Second Coming*, 189.

57. Arno C. Gaebelein, *The Conflict of the Ages: The Mystery of Lawlessness: Its Origin, Historic Development and Coming Defeat* (New York: Publication Office "Our Hope," 1933).

58. Timothy P. Weber, "A Reply to David Rausch's 'Fundamentalism and the Jew,'" *Journal of the Evangelical Theological Society* (March 1981), 70.

59. George M. Marsden, *Fundamentalism and American Culture: The Shaping of Twentieth Century Evangelicalism: 1870-1925* (New York: Oxford University Press, 1980), 187-188, note 15.

claim that the promises made to Israel have been fulfilled related to the return of the Israelites from Assyrian and Babylonian captivity, the person and work of Jesus Christ, and events from Pentecost and the destruction of the temple in AD 70. The charge of "Replacement Theology" is a cover for the more pejorative "anti-Semitism" because most people who believe the promises have been fulfilled are not anti-Semitic and do not claim that ethnic Jews are no longer Jews and don't have a right to the land of Israel.

Second, Christians who do not believe that there are yet to be fulfilled certain prophesies have not opened the flood gates of Jewish persecution. The examples cited by Dr. Brown do not show a causal relationship, even with someone like Martin Luther.

Third, Dr. Brown ignores the view of dispensationalists and some premillennialists that teach Israel must undergo another holocaust, what Charles Ryrie describes as "Israel's greatest bloodbath."

Fourth, during World War II, non-Replacement Theology advocates, many of whom were dispensationalists, took a "hands off" approach to Israel because their prophetic system taught that Israel would have to go through a period of "purification through tribulation."

CHAPTER 13

# Isaiah 11:11-12 and the Recovery of Israel "The Second Time"

While commenting on a few Facebook posts, I got some pushback from Gavin Potter and Jackie Alnor, the wife of the late William "Bill" Alnor (1954-2001). The topic was eschatology. I was called "ignorant" and "heretical" for not believing that we are living in the last days and Jesus is going to "rapture" the church "soon" because all the signs point to the fact that the "rapture" is "near."

Dispensationalism teaches that there are no signs before the "rapture" of the church. Since we are living in the "church age" (according to dispensational teaching), no one can make any predictions about the last days. The "rapture" is said to be an "any moment" event. There can't be any prophetic signs during the church age according to dispensationalism since the church age was God's Plan B after Israel rejected Jesus as the Messiah. The prophetic clock starts ticking again when God "raptures" the church.

Bill wrote the book *Soothsayers of the Second Advent* that was published in 1989. As books like these go, it's OK. I found parts of it helpful. One of the shortcomings of *Soothsayers of the Second Advent* is that it is encumbered by a dispensational premillennial paradigm, and as a result, the author forces that paradigm on passages that have nothing to do with the so-called "end times" or "last days"

After I made a few comments on Gavin Potter's Facebook post and Jackie Alnor's comments (that offered no exegetical rebuttal to any of my points), I decided to re-read Bill Alnor's 1989 book. When I opened it, I noticed that I had taken a few notes on Isaiah 11:11:

Then it will happen on that day that the Lord will again recover the second time with His hand the remnant of His people, who will remain, from Assyria, Egypt, Pathros, Cush, Elam, Shinar,

Hamath, and from the islands of the sea. And He will lift up a standard for the nations and assemble the banished ones of Israel, And will gather the dispersed of Judah from the four corners of the land.

Bill Alnor claimed that this prophecy (and others) referred to "the return of the Jews to Palestine in the latter days."[1]

Does Isaiah 11:11-12 refer to a distant return of Israel back to their land, or did it have a past fulfillment in view? No Jew reading Isaiah 11 in Isaiah's day, during the time of the exile, and the return under the decree of Cyrus (2 Chron. 36:22-23; Ezra 1:1-4), would ever have considered such an interpretation given that the chapter mentions Assyria, Shinar, the Philistines, Edom, Moab, "and the sons of Ammon" (vv. 11, 14). These people groups existed at the time when the prophecy was given, and the fulfillment was expected when those people groups would still exist. New Testament scholar William Hendriksen writes:

"[T]hose who believe that *now*, in the twentieth century AD [and 21st century], these Philistines, Edomites, Moabites, and Ammonites must still be destroyed or plundered or subjected will have a hard time even *finding* them!"[2]

This prophecy was fulfilled when the people of Israel returned to their land, rebuilt the temple, and reestablished the priesthood and the sacrificial system after their 70-year exile.

"Thus says Cyrus king of Persia, 'The Lord, the God of heaven, has given me all the kingdoms of the earth and He has appointed me to build Him a house in Jerusalem, which is in Judah. Whoever there is among you of all His people, may his God be with him! Let him go up to Jerusalem which is in Judah and rebuild the house of the Lord, the God of Israel; He is the God who is in Jerusalem. Every survivor, at whatever place he may live, let the men of that place support him with silver and gold, with goods and cattle, together with a freewill offering

---

1. William M. Alnor, *Soothsayers of the Second Advent* (Old Tappan, NJ: Fleming H. Revell, 1989), 48-50.

2. William Hendriksen, *Israel and the Bible* (Grand Rapids, MI: Baker Book House, 1968), 21.

for the house of God which is in Jerusalem" (Ezra 1:2-3; cp. Ezek. 38:13).

Why does Bill Alnor skip over this history and claim that the prophecies regarding Israel's return to the land were only fulfilled in the 20th century, specifically in 1948? Israel became a nation again after Isaiah's prophecy when the Jews returned to the land as God had promised they would after 70 years (Dan. 9:1-2; 2 Chron. 36:21-22; Ezra 1:1-4; Jer. 25:11-12; 29:10; Zech. 7:5).

Note what Isaiah 11:1 states: "Then it will happen on that day that the Lord will again recover **the second time** with His hand the remnant of His people...." If what was revealed to Isaiah was to be the "second time," then when was the first time? Alnor and other futurists argue that the first time was when the Jews returned after the captivity, and the second time is when Israel became a nation again in 1948.

Isaiah tells us in the same chapter something about the first time:

And there will be a highway from Assyria
For the remnant of His people who will be left,
Just as there was for Israel
**In the day that they came up out of the land of Egypt** (11:16).

If the second gathering of the remnant back to the land comes by way of Assyria, and Assyria does not exist today, the first return was when Israel "came up out of the land of Egypt." Alnor and other dispensationalists dismiss or don't consider the Egyptian exodus as the first-time Israel was recovered and brought into the Promised Land. Hendriksen comments:

The fact that Isa. 11:11 refers to a *second* recovery has nothing whatever to do with recent events, for according to the context the *first* recovery or exodus was the one under Moses. It was the return from the house of bondage (11:16). Hence, the second recovery was fulfilled when in stages, the Jews returned from the Assyrian-Babylonian captivity, and were established in their own land. All this took place long, long ago. There is, accordingly, no justification for interpreting these prophecies as if they referred to events happening in the twentieth century."[3]

---

3. Hendriksen, *Israel and the Bible*, 21.

We know that Israel returned in belief from their post-Babylonian and earlier Assyrian captivity in the events recorded in Ezra and  miah. "The sons of Israel were in the cities, the people gathered together as one man in Jerusalem" (Ezra 3:1). The Jews considered themselves to be an "escaped remnant" by God's grace.

> But now for a brief moment grace has been *shown* from the LORD our God, to leave us an escaped remnant and to give us a peg in His holy place, that our God may enlighten our eyes and grant us a little reviving in our bondage. For we are slaves; yet in our bondage our God has not forsaken us, but has extended lovingkindness to us in the sight of the kings of Persia, to give us reviving to raise up the house of our God, to restore its ruins and to give us a wall in Judah and Jerusalem (Ezra 9:8-9).

This is a description of a believing remnant returning according to God's promise a second time. They admit their "great guilt" (Ezra 9:13-15): "behold, we are before You in our guilt, for no one can stand before You because of this." This can't be said about what took place in 1948 or what's going on in Israel today.

> Now while Ezra was praying and making confession, weeping and prostrating himself before the house of God, a very large assembly, men, women and children, gathered to him from Israel; for the people wept bitterly. Shecaniah the son of Jehiel, one of the sons of Elam, said to Ezra, 'We have been unfaithful to our God and have married foreign women from the peoples of the land; yet now there is hope for Israel in spite of this. So now let us make a covenant with our God to put away all the wives and their children, according to the counsel of my lord and of those who tremble at the commandment of our God; and let it be done according to the law. Arise! For this matter is your responsibility, but we will be with you; be courageous and act.' Then Ezra rose and made the leading priests, the Levites and all Israel, take oath that they would do according to this proposal; so they took the oath (10:1-5).

God would not have regathered Israel if they had not first been faithful:

> Remember the word which You commanded Your servant Moses, saying, "If you are unfaithful I will scatter you among the

peoples; but if you return to Me and keep My commandments and do them, though those of you who have been scattered were in the most remote part of the heavens, I will gather them from there and will bring them to the place where I have chosen to cause My name to dwell" (Neh. 1:8-9).

The people were so moved because of God's loving kindness to them that they "were weeping when they heard the words of the law" (Neh. 8:9-10). No such thing happened in 1948. Israel did not return believing. In fact, the Jews returned with no regard for Jesus Christ. Compare this with what we read in the book of Acts of how the remnant of Israel embraced Jesus as the promised Messiah (Acts 2:21, 37-47).

The "four corners of the earth" or "land" in Isaiah 11 presents no difficulty since the Israelites that were taken into captivity were often sold to other neighboring nations (Ezek. 27:13; Joel 3:7; Amos 1:6, 9). The use of "four corners" means the same thing as it does today—the four points of the compass.

Bill Alnor, Jackie Alnor, Gavin Potter, and other modern-day prophecy writers who believe that Israel becoming a nation again, returning to their land in unbelief, is a fulfillment of Bible prophecy do not rightly interpret Scripture. If such a singular prophetic witness is so significant, we must wonder why Jesus and the New Testament biblical writers never mentioned a third return.

If the land was so important to Jews after the "it is finished" (John 19:30) work of Jesus on the cross and His subsequent resurrection, ascension, and enthronement, then why did "all who were owners of land or houses" sell them? (Acts 4:34; 2:35). The world was now open to the gospel. Jews and Gentiles were now one new person in Christ:

> Therefore remember that formerly you, the Gentiles in the flesh, who are called "Uncircumcision" by the so-called "Circumcision," which is performed in the flesh by human hands—remember that you were at that time separate from Christ, excluded from the commonwealth of Israel, and strangers to the covenants of promise, having no hope and without God in the world. But now in Christ Jesus you who formerly were far off have been brought near by the blood of Christ. For He Himself is our peace, who made both groups into one and broke down the barrier of the dividing wall,

by abolishing in His flesh the enmity, which is the Law of commandments contained in ordinances, so that in Himself He might make the two into one new man, thus establishing peace, and might reconcile them both in one body to God through the cross, by it having put to death the enmity. AND HE CAME AND PREACHED PEACE TO YOU WHO WERE FAR AWAY, AND PEACE TO THOSE WHO WERE NEAR; for through Him we both have our access in one Spirit to the Father. So then you are no longer strangers and aliens, but you are fellow citizens with the saints, and are of God's household, having been built on the foundation of the apostles and prophets, Christ Jesus Himself being the corner stone, in whom the whole building, being fitted together, is growing into a holy temple in the Lord, in whom you also are being built together into a dwelling of God in the Spirit (Eph. 2:11-22).

Being in Christ means that Gentiles are included in the "Commonwealth of Israel." The Alnors and their fellow dispensationalists want to rebuild the wall and divide Jews and Gentiles and make Gentiles strangers once again. This is a false gospel.

What should we make of the earlier section of Isaiah 11 about animals—predators and prey - being reconciled?

And the wolf will dwell with the lamb,
And the leopard will lie down with the young goat,
And the calf and the young lion and the fatling together;
And a little boy will lead them.

Also the cow and the bear will graze,
Their young will lie down together,
And the lion will eat straw like the ox.

The nursing child will play by the hole of the cobra,
And the weaned child will put his hand on the viper's den.

Animals are often used to represent people and nations. Jesus is the "Lamb of God (John 1:29). Jesus the Lamb (Rev. 14:1) is contrasted with the Beasts of Revelation 13:2, 11. Paul mentions "savage wolves" that "will come in among you, not sparing the flock" (Acts 20:29; see Ezek. 22:27). Jesus warns, "Beware of the false prophets, who come to you in sheep's clothing, but inwardly are ravenous wolves" (Matt. 7:15). Jesus describes Herod Antipas as "that fox" (Luke 13:32).

The book of Daniel depicts the nations as wild and ferocious animals. There is the vision of the four beasts in Daniel 7 that represent "four kingdoms that will rise from the earth" (v. 17). Nebuchadnezzar is turned into an animal because of his rebellion against God (Dan. 4:28-33).

That animals, most of them unclean, represent nations is made clear when Peter encounters an array of unclean animals that he is told to "kill and eat" (Acts 10:13). These unclean animals—the nations— were now designated by God as clean: "What God has cleansed, no *longer* consider unholy" (10:15). What was Peter's response?: "God has shown me that I should not call any man unholy or unclean" (10:28). This was confirmed when "the gift of the Holy Spirit had been poured out on the Gentiles also" (10:45). The animals represented people.

There's also this: "Behold, I have given you authority to tread on serpents and scorpions, and over all the power of the enemy, and nothing will injure you" (Luke 10:19). Adam Clarke comments:

> "To tread on serpents," etc.—It is possible that by serpents and scorpions our Lord means the scribes and Pharisees, whom he calls serpents and a brood of vipers, Matthew 23:33, ... because, through the subtlety and venom of the old serpent, the devil, they opposed him and his doctrine; and, by trampling on these, it is likely that he means, they should get a complete victory over such: as it was an ancient custom to trample on the kings and generals who had been taken in battle, to signify the complete conquest which had been gained over them.

Therefore, Paul could write, "The God of peace will soon crush Satan under your feet. The grace of our Lord Jesus be with you" (Rom. 16:20; see Josh. 10:24).

What's being revealed to Isaiah is a time when the nations will embrace the promised Redeemer and be reconciled. They will do so because of the "shoot [that] will spring from the stem of Jesse, and a branch from his roots will bear fruit" (Isa. 11:1). Jesus is the "horn of salvation" for Israel "in the house of David" (Luke 1:69) that will result in "salvation" from Israel's enemies, ... from the hand of all who hate" Israel (1:71, also v. 74). Jesus was to be "a light of revelation to the nations, and the glory of ... Israel" (2:32; Isa. 9:2).

After citing several Old Testament passages of how the Gentiles fit into God's redemptive plan (Rom. 15:7-11), Paul references Isaiah 11:10: "*Again Isaiah says, 'THERE SHALL COME THE ROOT OF JESSE, AND HE WHO ARISES TO RULE OVER THE GENTILES, IN HIM SHALL THE GENTILES HOPE'*" (Rom. 15:12). And what follows in Isaiah 11 are the verses about prey (Jews) and predators (the nations) lying down together and not devouring one another.

How will this happen? Because being in Christ makes us "new creatures": "Therefore if anyone is in Christ, *he is* a new creature; the old things passed away; behold, new things have come (2 Cor. 5:17)."

CHAPTER 14

# A Critique of
# *Bible Prophecy*
# *Under Siege*

In 2019 I wrote a review and critique of Ron Rhodes' book *Jesus and the End Times* titled "Repetitive Prophecy Books Keep Getting It Wrong." Rhodes' book from Harvest House, *Bible Prophecy Under Siege: Responding Biblically to Confusion About the End Times,* is mostly a defense of pretribulationalism. Rhodes claims that while all eschatological positions have problems (agreed), he argues that "pretribulationalism has the fewest difficulties when compared to midtribulationalism, posttribulationalism, the pre-wrath view, the partial rapture view, and the preterist view." (8-9) I'll lay may cards on the table early: There is no such biblical doctrine known as the prretribulational "rapture of the church." Each of these rapture positions assumes the legitimacy of other prophetic doctrines that also lack biblical support. There is no verse in the New Testament that says the church will be taken off the earth before, anytime during, before the wrath of God is poured out, or at the end of a seven-year period. Not a single verse! I found the following from Rhodes curious:

> With millions vanishing off the planet in the blink of an eye, people all over the world will be grasping for answers. This event will probably make global headlines. Videos of people vanishing will no doubt go viral on the internet. (32)

The New Testament does not say anything like what Rhodes and others claim. This is pure inference to support a doctrine that has no specific proof texts. Given that description, no one in nearly 2,000 years would have ever conceived of such a scenario given the paucity of biblical support. Rhodes appeals to Revelation 18:20 as evidence that the "saints" must "include the church." (34) The "saints and apostles and "prophets" were martyrs. They didn't make it to heaven in a rapture. This would have included Stephen, James the brother of Jesus, and most likely Paul and Peter, and who knows how many others who perished during that Apostolic generation in that past "great tribulation" (Matt. 24:21).

Anyone familiar with the pre-trib view knows that there are no signs that precede it, otherwise the "rapture" could not always be "imminent," that is, at any moment through the past 2,000 years. But Rhodes writes "that the signs of the times [our times] are relevant to us because these signs are an indicator of the end times." (44). If this is true, then the "rapture" couldn't have been at any moment in the past because it's only **today's signs** that indicate the "rapture" is near. He expands on his point:

> Many wonder what the relationship is between the signs of the times and the rapture. After all, the signs of the times deal specifically with the tribulation period. Here is the significance: If we witness the stage currently being set for a prophecy relating to the future tribulation period (such as the rebuilding of the Jewish temple, or the development of a one-world-government, or the movement toward globalism), since the rapture precedes the tribulation period. *If the tribulation is near, then the rapture is even nearer.*" (45)

On page 208, Rhodes writes what is a contradiction when compared to what he wrote on page 45: "The term *imminent* means 'ready to take place' or 'impending.' The New Testament teaches that the rapture is imminent—that is, there is nothing that must be prophetically fulfilled before the rapture.... The rapture is a signless event that can occur at any moment." He can't have it both ways.

Notice that Rhodes uses the word "near." Does his use of "near" have the same meaning of "near" in Revelation 1:3 and 22:10 and James 5:9? I'll deal with this question when I evaluate his comments from Chapter 6 of his book.

I deal with the "any moment rapture" belief system and how it is rarely followed by pre-tribbers in my book *Ten Popular Prophecy Myths Exposed and Answered.* According to the any-moment rapture doctrine, the rapture could have taken place anytime in the past 2,000 years. If this is true, then why are modern-day technologies (e.g., bar and QR codes, RFID readers, and nuclear weapons) said to be found in prophetic books like Zechariah (14:12) and Revelation (13:16-18)?

As with all the rapture views, the "seven-year tribulation period" is fundamental to all rapture positions. It's odd, therefore, that the book of Revelation never mentions "seven years," and yet chapters 4-19 are said to be about the seven-year tribulation period. The number "seven" is used many times in Revelation, but never "seven years." Seems odd. I deal with this point in my book *Last Days Madness*.

The "wrath" mentioned in 1 Thessalonians 5:9 was described by Paul in 2:16. Paul was not describing some far distant wrath; he was describing a wrath that was imminent for his time. Note the audience references (you, them, your countrymen, the Jews) and the timing (has come):

> For **you**, brethren, became imitators of the churches of God in Christ Jesus that are in Judea, for **you** also endured the same sufferings at the hands of **your own countrymen**, even as they *did* **from the Jews**, who both killed the Lord Jesus and the prophets, and drove us out. They are not pleasing to God, but hostile to all men, hindering us from speaking to the Gentiles so that they may be saved; with the result that they always fill up the measure of their sins. **But wrath has come** [aroist/past tense] **upon them to the utmost** (vv. 14-16).

Rhodes and others use 1 Thessalonians 4-5 to support a series of yet future events. But it's clear from what Paul states in the fourth and fifth chapters of Thessalonians that a coming wrath was on the horizon: "**We** who are alive" (1 Thess 4:15) and "For God has not destined **us** for wrath" (5:9). The "wrath" in chapter two of 1 Thessalonians is the same "wrath" in chapter five. Same wrath but different outcomes.  miah Nisbett offers a helpful commentary:

> It is a remarkable fact, that the Apostle, in his first epistle to the Thessalonians, denominates the Jews as *a nation*, as the *common enemies of mankind*; and that by their flagitious [vicious] conduct in *killing the Lord Jesus and their own Prophets*, and their *forbidding them to speak to the Gentiles that they might be saved*, they were proceeding εις το αναπληρωσαι [*eis to anaplērōsai*] *completely to fill up the measure of their iniquities* [1 Thess. 2:16; also Acts 7:51-52], as a vessel or measure is filled up till it can hold no more; and that, in consequence of their extreme wickedness, *wrath was coming upon them to the uttermost*. So,

in Matthew 23, our Lord describes, with great particularity and minuteness, the flagitious character of the Rulers of the Jews, charging them with crimes of the deepest dye, and towards the close of the chapter, he has this remarkably striking expression, delivered in the form of a prediction—*Ye will fill up yourselves the measure of your Fathers, i.e., of the Iniquities of your Fathers* [Matt. 23:32].[1]

For Rhodes, the pre-trib rapture is the lynch pin of his prophetic system, and as I mentioned earlier, there is no verse that anyone can turn to support the doctrine. First Thessalonians 4:13-18, the go-to verses used to support the "rapture," does not mention seven years, "the" antichrist, a great tribulation, or the reestablishment of Israel as a nation. Revelation 4:1 does not support the pre-trib rapture of the church. It was John and only John who was told to "come up here" and was "in the Spirit" (vv. 1-2), not the church. If he was physically taken up, he later returned to earth. That's not indicative of the "rapture" doctrine. John wrote that he was their "brother and fellow-partaker in the tribulation" (1:9).Rhodes argues that "the word 'church(es)' is used 19 times in the first three chapters of Revelation" as if to say the church around the world in the future. He extrapolates from this claim by arguing that "in the section dealing with the tribulation—chapters 6-18—not a single mention is made of the church. The church is then mentioned again in Revelation 22:16; where John addresses the first-century church. Why isn't the church mentioned in Revelation 6-18? *Because the church isn't there!*" (196) This is a horrible and fundamentally flawed argument.

Revelation states that it was written "to the seven churches" (1:4, 11), "the angels of the seven churches" (1:20), individually named first-century churches—"the **church in** Ephesus ... Smyrna ... Pergamum ... Thyatira ... Sardis ... Philadelphia ... Laodicea" (2:1, 8, 12, 18, 3:1, 3:7, 14)—and churches (plural) generally (2:7, 11, 17, 23, 29; 3:6, 13, 22). A future worldwide "church" is not in view. The Christians in those first-century historical churches were not raptured. Rhodes and his fellow-dispensationalists must insert a gap in time between Revelation 4 and 19 that is now nearly 2,000 years long.

---

1. Nehemiah Nisbett, *The Destruction of Jerusalem, the Mysterious Language of St. Paul's Description of the Man of Sin, and the Day of the Lord* (Powder Springs, GA: American Vision, [1787 and 1808] 2023), 105.

Let's not forget that Rhodes' interpretation claims that **the** antichrist is the predominate figure in Revelation, that he takes over the world for a specified number of years, but if this is so, why isn't the word "antichrist" found anywhere in Revelation? Counting the number of times a word appears or does not appear is not a good apologetic for an eschatological position. If the word "church" is not mentioned after Revelation 3 and this is significant, then the complete absence of the word "antichrist" should also be significant. Let's not forget how the seven-year tribulation period is manufactured by separating the 70$^{th}$ week from the other 69 weeks and placing a gap between them (Dan. 9:24-27). For those who are interested in a refutation of the "gap theory," see my book *Last Days Madness*. The rapture doctrine is dealt with in *The Rapture and the Fig Tree Generation* written by Frank Gumerlock and me.

Rhodes muddies the prophecy waters with a chapter on "replacement theology," that the "church replaces" Israel as if the New Testament's use of the word *ekklēsia*, translated as "church," is something new in the New Testament. *Ekklēsia* is a common Greek word that's found in the Greek translation of the Old Testament, in Matthew 18:17, the book of Acts, and elsewhere in the New Testament. William Tyndale translated *ekklēsia* as "congregation" and "assembly" in his 1526 English translation. The 1537 "Matthew Bible" also translated *ekklesia* as "congregation." Stephen uses *ekklēsia* in Acts 7:38 as "the *ekklēsia* in the wilderness," a reference to Israel. The KJV translates the verse as "the church in the wilderness" and does the same in Hebrews 2:12. The *ekklēsia* in Acts 5:11 was made up exclusively of Jews. The same is true of "the church in Jerusalem" (8:1, 3). I cover this topic more thoroughly in my book *Ten Popular Prophecy Myths Exposed and Answered*. There is no replacement of Israel by the *ekklesia*. The *ekklesia* was a body of believing Christians made up of Jews and non-Jews.

Instead of rehashing refuted critiques of pretribulationalism, I want to spend time on Rhodes' interaction with preterism. I'll give him credit for the attempt but not the result. Preterism is an eschatological view that argues that the prophecies of the Bible predicted events that have already been fulfilled in history.

Rhodes begins in chapter 5 with "Examining the Preterist Case for an Early Date of Revelation" where he appeals to Revelation 11:1-2 and the measuring of the temple by John:

> Then there was given me a measuring rod like a staff; and someone said, "Get up and measure the temple of God and the altar, and those who worship in it. Leave out the court which is outside the temple and do not measure it, for it has been given to the nations; and they will tread under foot the holy city for forty-two months.

If Revelation was written in the mid-AD 90s as Rhodes contends, then there would not have been a temple to measure since it was destroyed in AD 70. Since the New Testament doesn't say anything about a rebuilt temple, then logically this seems to refer to the rebuilt temple in Jerusalem that was completed in AD 63, the same temple Jesus said not one stone would be left upon another (Matt. 24:1-3).

Rhodes argues that "John is mystically transported to the future vision and speaks about future events that will one day unfold (see Revelation 1:10, 19; 4:1)." But Revelation 1:19 states that these "future events" were "about to [*mellō*] take place" (Rev. 1:19). Robert Young in his *Concise and Critical Commentary on the New Testament* explains the Greek word used in Revelation 1:19: "WRITE] at once [therefore], the things thou didst perceive ... are about to happen after (*or* with) these." The prophetic events John was seeing in his day were followed by events that were "about to happen." Rhodes assumes a gap while Young and others do not.

Rhodes then argues that "reference to a temple by a spokesman for God does not require the actual existence of a temple." (82) This is curious for someone who claims to interpret the Bible literally and believes a future physical temple will be built again in Jerusalem. If this is true, then this supposed future temple also may not actually exist. It's purely visionary and symbolic. This is a dilemma for a prophetic view that claims the temple will be rebuilt again even though the New Testament does not say anything about another rebuilt temple.

Rhodes continues with this statement: "*If both Daniel and Ezekiel prophesied about a temple when there was no temple in existence in their day, couldn't we expect John to follow the same pattern?*" (82, italic in original). John is not prophesying about a future rebuilt temple. It was a temple in existence either symbolically or physically in his day. The temple he was told to measure had worshippers. This means it was an earthly temple. Jesus was found in the temple in Jerusalem, discussing with the elders and asking them questions when he was twelve years old (Luke 2:41-52). He had left the temple that was under construction when He declared its destruction (Matt. 24:1-3). Paul was thrown out of the temple (Acts 21:30-31). Before AD 70, when the temple was destroyed, it was a functioning temple. The New Testament does not say anything about another temple. The burden of proof is on Rhodes and his fellow dispensationalists to prove otherwise from Scripture. Jesus is the temple (John 2:19-21), and by extension, Christians are the temple (2 Cor. 6:16), likened to "living stones" (1 Pet. 2:4-8), with Jesus being the "chief cornerstone" (Matt. 21:42; Eph. 2:20).

Comparing John's measuring the temple to Ezekiel's temple is a mistake that dispensationalists often make. Ezekiel does not measure the temple because it did not exist because it was a visionary temple. Notice what Ezekiel's prophecy states:

> So He brought me [Ezekiel] there; and behold, **there was a man whose** appearance was like the appearance of bronze, **with a line of flax and a measuring rod in his hand**; and he was standing in the gateway (Ezek. 40:1-3).

Ezekiel does not measure the temple. Thomas Ice made a similar mistake:

> **Ezekiel, during a similar vision of a Temple (Ezek. 40-43) was told to measure that Temple. When Ezekiel saw and was told to measure a Temple** there was not one standing in Jerusalem (Preterists agree). Thus, there is no compulsion whatsoever to conclude that just because a temple is referenced in Revelation 11 that it implies that there had to be a physical Temple standing in Jerusalem at the same time.[2]

John measures an actual physical temple that was operational.

Rhodes references Mark Hitchcock, an advocate for the Domitian date for the composition of Revelation around AD 95, and writes, "Mark Hitchcock suggests that an early date ultimately makes the book of Revelation irrelevant for most Christians" (86). If the events prophesied in Revelation are yet to be fulfilled, then it's been irrelevant for Christians for nearly 2,000 years! In addition, following his logic, the entire Bible would be irrelevant for Christians because most of

---

2. Thomas Ice, "The Date of the Book of Revelation" (May 2009).

it is preterist, that is, the events have already taken place as the Old Testament and New Testament clearly show.[3]

In *I Don't Have Enough Faith to Be an Atheist* by Norman Geisler and Frank Turek, they write that "most if not all [the New Testament] books were written before AD 70."[4] Consider the following:

> Well, here's the problem for those who say the New Testament was written after 70—there's absolutely no mention of the fulfillment of this predicted tragedy anywhere in the New Testament documents. This means most, if not all, of the documents must have been written prior to 70.[5]
>
> * * * * *
>
> So if we would expect tragedies such as Pearl Harbor and 9/11 to be mentioned in the relevant writings of today, we certainly should expect the events of AD 70 to be cited somewhere in the New Testament (especially since the events were predicted by Jesus). But since the New Testament does not mention these events anywhere and suggests that Jerusalem and the temple are still intact, we can conclude reasonably that most, if not all, of the New Testament documents must have been written prior to 70.[6]

There are many internal and external proofs for the pre-AD 70 composition of Revelation. Many of the late-date arguments are based on external evidence that is not convincing. For an update on the

---

3. On the dating question, see Robert Hillegonds, *The Early Date of Revelation and the End Times* (Fountain Inn: SC: Victorious Hope Publishing, 2016).

4. Norman L. Geisler and Frank Turek, *I Don't Have Enough Faith to Be an Atheist* (Wheaton, IL: Crossway, 204), 237.

5. Geisler and Frank, *I Don't Have Enough Faith to Be an Atheist*, 238. A similar argument is made by Chuck Missler: "Many scholars now believe that the Gospels were written before Paul's first imprisonment of 57-60 AD, and that virtually all of the New Testament books were written before Jerusalem's destruction. (Risto Santala, *The Messiah in the New Testament in the Light of Rabbinical Writings*, 47-48.) There is no hint in the New Testament of Nero's persecutions after 64 AD, nor of the execution of James, the Lord's brother, in 62 AD There is not the slightest mention of the Jewish revolt against the Romans which began in 66 AD, nor of the destruction of Jerusalem in 70 AD These historic events would have been irresistible in making many of the arguments in the New Testament documents." (http://www.khouse.org/articles/2000/205/)

6. Geisler and Turek, *I Don't Have Enough Faith to Be an Atheist*, 238-239.

external evidence for the pre-AD 70 composition of Revelation, I suggest readers consult Francis X. Gumerlock's "External Evidence for an Early Date of Revelation: Ten Early Date Traditions in Ancient Christianity."[7] Gumerlock's study is based on his own Latin translation work. While external evidence is helpful, it is not unanimous or authoritative. Here is Gumerlock's conclusion:

> Regarding our brothers, like Philip Schaff, who in the early twentieth century made the claim that the Domitianic dating of Revelation was the *only* tradition of early Christianity, latitude can be shown for their inaccurate statements; perhaps the patristic texts illustrating the variety of opinions prevalent in the early church and middle ages were not readily available to them. But now that so many of these texts have been brought to light, it seems to me that in the twenty first century there is no excuse for making the assertion that the church fathers were all agreed on the Domitianic date of Revelation, or that such dating was the exclusive view of the early church. For, in dating the Apocalypse before 70 AD, at least ten different traditions from ancient and medieval Christianity have been preserved.

Rhodes' book does not plow any new ground. His arguments are dated, incomplete, and often inaccurate, all designed to support the already refuted pretribulational and dispensational views. He does not reference any of the latest scholarship dealing with the dating issue. James Jordan writes about the insufficiency of the source work of the early Church Fathers.

> We have to remember that we only have a few Church Fathers to draw on. Often Christian scholars have strained mightily to build on evidence from these writings, writings of men clearly not familiar with the facts in other instances. Many of the Fathers were new converts to the faith who wrote apologetics, and who did not know much about Christianity (as can be seen when we compare them with the teachings of the New Testament). What we don't have are reams of sermons preached by pastors in local churches during the first two centuries, and

---

7. https://bit.ly/4d9QfbI

that is the kind of material that would give us an accurate picture of the early church....

Jordan's point is something to keep in mind. We have tens of thousands (maybe millions) of sermons, books, commentaries, and articles on any number of biblical topics. This is not the case when we read the writings of some of what second and third century writers wrote. There remain many works that have not been translated into English and most likely many sermons that were never transcribed and published. This is why the ultimate standard is the Bible.

Eschatology is about timing. If we misread passages that mention timing, we can be seriously wrong in our interpretation and application of prophetic events. The history of bad prophetic timing is a long one. One of the key elements of a preterist interpretation of when prophetic events will take place or have taken place is the meaning of words like "near," "at hand," "shortly," "quickly," and "long time." The following is from *Bible Prophecy Under Siege*:

> Depending on the context, biblical words can carry different nuances of meaning—especially in New Testament Greek, which is a particularly rich language. Examples include "soon" (Greek: *tachos*) and "near" (Greek: *eggus* [pronounced *engus*]) as related to the fulfillment of Bible prophecy. Let's consider the details. (91)

He then lists verses in Revelation that "indicate a 'soon' fulfillment of prophecy (Revelation 1:1, 3; 22:6, 6, 10, 12, 20)." Because preterists argue that Revelation was revealed to John "in the mid-60s AD," therefore, "this 'soon' fulfillment must refer to AD 70, when Jesus 'came' in judgment against Jerusalem through the Roman army." (91-92)

Rhodes does a good job describing the preterist position on this point. He quotes Hank Hanegraaf, Kenneth Gentry, and me. He could have quoted many others going back centuries, but he does not. It's not like we're the only three people who hold or held the preterist position. We didn't make it up sometime in the 20th century. Charles Spurgeon mentions preterism in his book *Commenting and Commentaries*: "1. Preterists. The prophecies contained in the Apocalypse were fulfilled with the destruction of Jerusalem and the fall of heathen Rome. This is the view of *Bossuet, Grotius, Hammond, Wetstein, Eichhorn, Ewald, De Wette, Lücke,* and others, among whom is the

American expositor, *Moses Stuart.*"[8] Not surprisingly, Rhodes turns to the early church for support for his view that he claims refutes the preterist argument. His first stop is the Didache that he argues "dates to the end of the first century and the beginning of the second" (92). Let's assume he is correct; this does not mean that the pre-trib rapture position is correct. Far from it, since pre-tribulationalism is a 19th century doctrinal invention. In Didache 16, there are 12 references to Matthew 24-25 (24:4, 10-13, 21, 24, 30, 31, 42, 44, and 25:31). The crucial time text of Matthew 24:34 ("this generation will not pass away") is not quoted, but a form of Matthew 24:30 is: "The Lord shall come and all His saints with Him. Then shall the world see the Lord coming upon the clouds of heaven" (16:7-8).

The verses quoted from Matthew 24-25 in Didache 16 obviously refer to future events from the perspective of the author(s). Of course, if the Didache was written before the destruction of Jerusalem in AD 70 then it supports preterism. The Didache is not Scripture and does not teach a pre-trib rapture prior to a seven-year time of tribulation. Moreover, the claim that it was written after AD 70 is not conclusive. In the authoritative work *The Apostolic Fathers*, we read the following:

> A remarkably wide range of dates, extending from before AD 50 to the third century or later, has been proposed for this document…. The Didache may have been put into its present form as late as 150, though a date considerably closer to the end of the first century seems more plausible. The materials from which it was composed, however, reflect the state of the church at an even earlier time. The relative simplicity of the prayers, the continuing concern to differentiate Christian practice from Jewish rituals (8.1), and in particular the form of church structure—note the twofold structure of bishops and deacons (cf. Phil. 1:1) and the continued existence of traveling apostles and prophets alongside a resident ministry—*reflect a time closer to that of Paul and James (who died in the 60s) than Ignatius (who died sometime after 110)*.[9]

---

8. Charles Haddon Spurgeon, *Commenting and Commentaries* (London: The Banner of Truth Trust, [1876] 1969), 198.

9. Michael W. Holmes, ed., *The Apostolic Fathers: Greek Texts and English Translations*, rev. ed. (Grand Rapids, MI: Baker Books, [1992] 1999), 247-248. Emphasis added.

The definitive work on the Didache was written by the French-Canadian Jean-Paul Audet who concluded "that it was composed, almost certainly in Antioch, between 50 and 70,"[10] "contemporary with the first gospel writings."[11] Andrew Louth writes that many scholars would date the Didache "earlier than the New Testament itself."[12] Aaron Milavec's 1000-page study of the Didache also places its composition sometime between AD 50 and 70.[13] His essay "Synoptic Tradition in the Didache Revisited"[14] concludes:

> Should Didache scholars come to accept the thesis of this essay, the way would be open for an early date of the **Didache** and for its interpretation as well as a well-integrated and self-contained religious system that must be allowed to speak for itself. Matthew's Gospel can no longer be called upon to amplify or to distort the unique voice of the **Didache**. A new era of **Didache** studies would thus lie open before us.

For further study of the dating of the Didache, see *New Testament Eschatology: What the Early Church Believed about Bible Prophecy.*[15] As I mentioned earlier, one of my criticisms is that the scholarship of *Bible Prophecy Under Siege* is out of date and seems to work hard to ignore contrary historical and exegetical evidences. Rhodes uses sources from his own perspective and has not taken the time to consult works outside his pre-trib bubble. For example, in addition to not investigating the latest scholarly works on the Didache, there is no interaction with Jonathan Bernier's *Rethinking the Dates of the New Testament* published in 2022. Bernier concludes that "1 Clement was written no earlier than 64 and no later than 70," and that The

---

10. John A. T. Robinson, *Redating the New Testament* (Philadelphia: Westminster Press, (1976), 323.

11. Jean-Paul Audet, *La Didachè: Instructions des Apôtres* (Paris: Gabalda, 1958), 187-210.

12. Andrew Louth, *Early Christian Writers* (London: Penguin Books, 1968), 189.

13. Aaron Milavec, *The Didache: Faith, Hope, and Life of the Earliest Christian Communities, 50-70 C.E.* (Mahwah, NJ: Paulist Press, 2003). Also see E. Earle Ellis, *The Making of the New Testament Documents* (Boston: Brill Academic Publishers, 2002), 55.

14. https://bit.ly/3SfHYLc

15. Gary DeMar and Francis X. Gumerlock, *New Testament Eschatology: What the Early Church Believed about Bible Prophecy* was originally titled *The Early Church and the End of the World* that was originally published in 2006. This new edition includes a chapter on the Nicene Creed.

Didache has a date range from "no earlier than 45 and no later than 125."[16] In both cases, they could have been written before AD 70. This counters Rhodes' assertion that "[i]t is telling that there are no first- or second-century preterists that lend support to the 'soon' viewpoint of preterists" is presumptive (93). We need to keep in mind that there's very little extant written material of any kind from the first century. The works of Josephus are a standout example of a secular historical sources that scholars have turned to understand the history of the Jews, including the events surrounding the destruction of Jerusalem. In his book *Paradise Restored,* David Chilton includes material in an appendix "Josephus and the Fall of Jerusalem" that shows parallels with what we read in the Olivet Discourse.[17]

Rhodes appeals to Justin Martyr who is just another non-biblical historical source, as is Eusebius (260/265-339) who argues for a preterist interpretation of the Olivet Discourse. Thomas Ice, who is quoted favorably by Rhodes, stated: "There is early preterism in people like Eusebius. In fact, his work *The Proof of the Gospel* is full of preterism in relationship to the Olivet Discourse."[18] The works of the early church are a mixed bag. This is why dispensationalist author John D. Hanna, who served as Professor of Historical Theology and Research Professor of Theological Studies at Dallas Theological Seminary, is honest enough to admit that it's "not an easy task to piece together a picture of what early Christians thought about the end times.... [since] our sources for their thought in this area are relatively limited."[19] While historical sources are interesting and sometimes helpful, the Bible is the standard.

One of the problems with Rhodes' defense of pre-tribulationalism is that he relies on outdated works and worn out and refuted arguments. He's counting on the fact that most readers will not spot what he's left out and won't be aware of counter arguments. Check out the "Notes" section of *Bible Prophecy Under Siege*. It is filled with support works

---

16. Jonathan Bernier, *Rethinking the Dates of the New Testament: The Evidence for Early Composition* (Grand Rapids: Baker Academic, 2022), 250-251.

17. David Chilton, *Paradise Restored: A Biblical Theology of Dominion* (Dallas, GA: Dominion Press, [1985] 2023).

18. Thomas Ice, "Update on Pre-Darby Rapture Statements and Other Issues": audio tape (December 1995).

19. *Our Legacy: The History of Christian Doctrine* (Colorado Springs: NAVPRESS, 2001), 305.

from fellow pre-trib writers. He should have at least interacted with Jonathan Bernier's *Rethinking the Dates of the New Testament* who is neither a pre-tribulationalist nor a preterist.

In the final analysis, we must evaluate words like "near," "at hand," "shortly," "quickly," and "long time" in terms of how the New Testament uses them. It surprised me that Rhodes did not use examples from Scripture to make his case on how these time words are used in other contexts. This is a major weakness in his arguments.

Rhodes writes, "If the preterist view is wrong, as futurists believe it is, then how is the word 'soon' to be interpreted?" (93) Good question. He offers some ways interpreters have tried to get around the obvious meaning of time indicators by first appealing to someone from the 6th century who argued that "soon" must be interpreted in terms of "the timelessness and eternality of God." (93), but God being timeless and eternal does not change the meaning of how words like "soon, "near," and "shortly" are used in everyday speech in the New Testament. God is communicating to us in language we can understand. There aren't special "prophecy words."

Another alternative he suggests is "that 'soon' is a relative term." (94) Who says? Does the New Testament use *tachos* and *engus* as relative terms in other places? To support his claim, one would think that Rhodes would give us some examples. He doesn't. He tells his readers what 19th-century Bible commentator Albert Barnes says, but Rhodes never demonstrates from specific verses where the words appear outside of Revelation and how they are used. I can find many commentators who disagree with Barnes. Paul says, "examine everything" (1 Thess. 5:21). The Bereans "searched the Scriptures" (Acts 17:11). Here's the challenge: Look up every use of the words "near," "shortly," and "quickly" to see how they are used elsewhere in the New Testament and plug in Rhodes' "relative terms" definition to see if it makes sense.

In Rhodes' critique of preterism, his next line of defense is to turn to Greek scholars. I'm OK with this approach, but there's nothing in the definitions from the lexicons and dictionaries that Rhodes mentions that supports his position. The three sources he uses state that the Greek word *tachos* means "soon," "quick," "swift," or "speedy." Here is Rhodes' interpretation:

Given this, the word need not mean that the events in Revelation would occur soon from John's vantage point (in the first century) but can simply mean that when the events first begin to transpire, they will unfold *quickly, speedily,* and *swiftly.* Hence, these words in Revelation refer not to *soon events* but to *swiftly unfolding events.*

"*Can* simply mean"? The question is, what do they mean in context? It's true that *tachos* refers to speed. The Greek word *tachos* is followed by an action that is not delayed. Consider the following verses.

- **Matthew 5:25:** "Make friends quickly [ταχὺ] with your opponent at law while you are with him on the way, in order that your opponent may not deliver you to the judge, and the judge to the officer, and you be thrown into prison." (Jesus didn't say make friends, but to do it quickly or something worse may befall him.)

- **Matthew 28:7-8:** "'And go quickly [ταχὺ] and tell His disciples that He has risen from the dead; and behold, He is going before you into Galilee, there you will see Him; behold, I have told you.' And they departed quickly [ταχὺ] from the tomb with fear and great joy and ran to report it to His disciples." (The entire point is to move fast at that time with the report.)

- **Luke 15:22:** "But the father said to his slaves, 'Quickly [ταχὺ] bring out the best robe and put it on him and put a ring on his hand and sandals on his feet.'" (There is no hint of a delay with this request. There is no, "when you decide to do it, do it fast.")

- **Luke 16:6:** "And he said, 'A hundred measures of oil.' And he said to him, 'Take your bill, and sit down quickly [ταχέως] and write fifty.'" (Could the distant relatives of this person still be waiting for this to happen?)

- **Luke 18:8:** "I tell you that He will bring about justice for them quickly [τάχει]." (Speedy justice is the point of the story. The end result of the speed is justice at that time and place.)

- **John 11:29:** "And when she heard it, she arose quickly [ταχὺ], and was coming to Him." (It's not that she was fast in the way she approached Jesus but her rising and subsequent action occurred at the same time. There was no delay.)

- **John 11:31**: "The Jews then who were with her in the house, and consoling her, when they saw that Mary rose up quickly [ταχέως] and went out, followed her, supposing that she was going to the tomb to weep there." (Did she rise up quickly, thought about it for a time, and later went out?)
- **John 13:27**: "And after the morsel, Satan then entered into him. Jesus therefore said to him, 'What you do, do quickly [τάχιον].'" (Does anyone believe Judas delayed in any way? We know he didn't.)
- **Acts 12:7**: "And behold, an angel of the Lord suddenly appeared, and a light shone in the cell; and he struck Peter's side and roused him, saying, 'Get up quickly [τάχει].' And his chains fell off his hands." (Should we read this as, "When Peter decided to get up, he would do it quickly"? Impossible, since he was to follow the angel out of the prison past the guards without delay.)
- **Acts 22:18**: "and I saw Him saying to me, 'Make haste, and get out of Jerusalem quickly [τάχει], because they will not accept your testimony about Me.'" (A delay would bring harm to them.)
- **Acts 25:4**: "Festus then answered that Paul was being kept in custody at Caesarea and that he himself was about to leave shortly [ἐν τάχει]." (Again, there was no delay. He left shortly.)
- **Galatians 1:6**: "I am amazed that you are so quickly [ταχέω] deserting Him who called you by the grace of Christ, for a different gospel." (There's nothing relative in this use of quickly, otherwise Paul's statement would have been meaningless.)
- **Philippians 2:19**: "But I hope in the Lord Jesus to send Timothy to you shortly [ταχέως], so that I also may be encouraged when I learn of your condition." ("Hope deferred makes the heart grow sick..." [Prov. 13:12]).
- **Philippians 2:24**: "and I trust in the Lord that I myself also shall be coming shortly [ταχέως]." (How would the Philippians have understood Paul's use of "shortly"? Are they still waiting?)
- **2 Thessalonians 2:2**: "that you may not be quickly [ταχέως] shaken from your composure or be disturbed either by a spirit

or a message or a letter as if from us, to the effect that the day of the Lord has come." (The point of Paul's admonition is that certain beliefs were being quickly questioned.)

Did you notice that a specific action followed the use of *tachos* in each of the verses listed above? Since this is an established fact, why is *tachos* (often translated as "soon") interpreted in a different way in Revelation 1:1 and 22:6? And what about 2:16, 3:11, 11:14, and 22:7? Rhodes will argue that some of the events in the early chapters happened soon, but based on Revelation 1:19, some events take place "after these things" but not necessarily soon after. As was pointed out above, the Greek word *mellō* is used. *Mellō* is also used in 2:10: "Do not fear what you are **about to** suffer...." The things that were to follow "the things which are" (happened at the time Revelation was written and shown to the seven historical churches) were "about to take place" (1:19). It's regrettable that *mellō* is not translated in 1:19 when it's translated twice in 2:10 as "about to." Why is that? Because the implications of events that were "about to happen" in Revelation do not fit the futurist's interpretation that those prophetic events are still unfulfilled.

> "Things which must shortly come to pass," must be said in general of the contents of this entire book, and not, as some have supposed, of the first three chapters only. "Shortly" can have no other and no less meaning than *very soon*. This sense of the original Greek words is absolute and decisive. It is only serious trifling with God's words to say that *"shortly"* may mean a thousand years distant, or two and three thousand, according as the exigencies of some preconceived scheme of interpretation may require. Why should not God be permitted to be his own interpreter and give his own views in regard to the *time* of the events here foretold? The rule of fair common sense must be, that whatever God may say in *explanation* of his own prophecies—*e.g.*, as to the *time* of their fulfillment, must be taken in its plain and most obvious sense. Else how does it *explain* any thing?—Angels were largely employed in making these revelations to John, and made them chiefly (as the word *"signify"* indicates) by the use of signs, symbols....[20]

20. Henry Cowles, *The Revelation of John; With Notes, Critical, Explanatory, and Practical;*

Rhodes appeals to Revelation 3:10 to support the pre-trib rapture view:

> This verse reveals that church saints will be kept from the actual time period of testing, not just the testing itself.... That Revelation 3:10 refers to a rapture before this future period of worldwide testing is implied in verse 11: "I am coming soon. Hold fast what you have, so that no one may seize your crown." The phrase "I am coming soon" apparently refers to the imminence of the rapture...." (195)

There's so much wrong with his explanation that I don't know where to begin. First, notice how he applies the meaning of "soon ... to the imminence of the rapture." Wait a minute! Didn't Rhodes tell us that "soon" in Revelation doesn't really mean "soon" as the word is normally understood? Suddenly "soon" does really mean "soon" for Rhodes. His view is that when these prophetic events occur, they *"will all happen quickly!"* (97). As we saw earlier, that's not how the word *tachos* is used elsewhere in the New Testament. Also note that he uses the word "apparently" because nothing is said about the church being taken to heaven in the "rapture." He reads into the passage an unproven assumption.

Second, he says this period of testing is global. Where does it state that? You might say, "It's right there in the text: 'the whole world.'" Revelation 3:10 does not use the Greek word *kosmos* but *oikoumenē*. The use of *oikoumenē* instead of *kosmos* indicates that the events that were about to unfold were confined to the political boundaries of the Roman Empire. *Oikoumenē* is used many times in the New Testament and refers to limited geography. Rome didn't and couldn't tax the "whole world" (Luke 2:1), and it's highly unlikely that there was a famine over the entire planet at that time (Acts 11:28). That's why Luke uses *oikoumenē* in both cases. The men preaching the gospel in Thessalonica did not "upset the world" as we know it today. It was a segment of the world (*oikoumenē*) that was spreading through the Roman Empire (17:6). We know this because they were charged with acting "contrary to the decrees of Caesar, saying that there is another king, Jesus" (17:7).

Third, the Greek word *mellō*, "about to," is used. As we saw, the same word is used in 1:19 and 2:10. Latin scholar Francis X. Gumerlock writes that

---

*Designed for Both Pastors and People* (New York: D. Appleton and Company, 1880), 53-54.

many comments from medieval commentaries ... attributed the 'tribulation coming upon the whole earth' (Rev. 3:10) to the persecution of Christians in the early church, rather than a great tribulation at the end of the world. ... "Nerses of Lambron wrote a commentary in the Armenian language around 1180 AD. On Rev. 3:10 it reads: 'By "the hour of trial" he means that which shortly and rapidly was about to occur from the impious kings of the Romans against the Christians, from which he promises to save them.'" ... "On Rev. 3:10, about the 'hour of testing' or [*sic*] tribulation coming upon the whole earth,' Ralph of Laon, Hugh of Saint Cher, and Nicholas of Gorran interpreted it as a time of testing that immediately followed the emperor Nero, who died in 68 AD.

The following is from Moses Stuart's commentary on Revelation:

Μελλούσης ἔρχεσθαι [*mellousēs erxesthai*], *is about to come*, or which is speedily coming; for so μέλλω usually signifies, being employed to designate the proximate future. —Οἰκουμένην ὅλης [*oikoumenēn holēs*], *the whole world* [*oikoumenē*]; comp. πᾶσαν τὴν οἰκουμένην [*pasan tēn oikoumenēn*] in Luke 2:1, where possibly it means *Judea*, but probably the whole Roman empire. At any rate, the phrase is often used indefinitely for a wide extent of country; and so it may designate the whole Roman empire. Here the most probable meaning is the same, or at least the whole region of the Roman Asia Minor, or the whole country around the region of Philadelphia.... Γῆς [*gēs*, land] is most evidently here synonymous with οἰκουμένης ὅλης [*oikoumenēs holēs*/whole inhabited world]; and κατοικοῦντας ἐπὶ τῆς γῆς [*katoikountas epi tēs gēs*] dwelling upon the land: Rev. 11:10; 17:2, 8]; is a common Hebraistic idiom for designating the inhabitants of a country.[21]

Fourth, note the use of "quickly" or "soon" in Revelation 3:11. If this has not happened, then how was this a warning to "the churches" in John's day?[22] How would the people in those seven churches have understood

---

21. Moses Stuart, *Commentary on the Apocalypse*, 2 vols. (New York: Allen, Morrill and Wardwell, 1845), 2:94-95.

22. "But this coming can not be the final one or the last judgment, because that coming was then certainly remote, and Jesus never indicated the time when it should occur

what they read? Notice the use of "the hour of testing." John wrote the following in 1 John 2:18:

> Children, **it is the last hour**; and just as you heard that antichrist is coming, **even now** many antichrists have appeared; from this **we know that it is the last hour**.

If these refer to the same "hour," then that hour is past because Revelation was written before the destruction of Jerusalem that took place in AD 70, and John wrote, "It is the last hour." Not the last hour of the end of the world but the end of the impending judgment Jesus mentioned in the Olivet Discourse and elsewhere. The generation was known (their generation), but the "day and the hour" were not known (Matt. 24:34-36).

After *tachos*, Rhodes mentions the Greek word *engus* which means "near" or "at hand." Once again, instead of considering how *engus* is used elsewhere in the New Testament, Rhodes appeals to some of his dispensational colleagues like Norman Geisler and Mark Hitchcock. Geisler states that *engus* "is a relative term like 'short' and 'long.'" He continues with, "there are clear biblical examples where a 'short' time was really a long time for us. Hebrews 10:37 says Jesus would come in just 'a little while,' and it has been nearly 2,000 years since then, and He has not come yet." (97) "A short time was really a long time." Really? And what is typical, when the consistent use of "near" doesn't fit their system, an appeal is made to 2 Peter 3:8, "what is long for us is short for God," as Geisler puts it. Hebrews 10:37 is very emphatic : "very, very little" (μικρὸν ὅσον ὅσον/*mikron hoson hoson*). Compare this with what Jesus says to His disciples:

> "A **little while**, and you no longer are going to see Me; and again a **little while**, and you will see Me." So some of His disciples said to one another, "What is this that He is telling us, 'A **little**

(Mark 13: 32). For reasons more fully given in my notes on 1:7, it may be supposed to refer somewhat definitely to Christ's coming to destroy Jerusalem, considered as the first great persecuting anti-Christian power, the general thought being—I am about to make special manifestations of my presence and power in retributive vengeance on the present persecutors of my people, and also for the salvation of my faithful friends.—This coming will be an hour of crisis and of stern conflict: therefore hold fast thy profession; stand firmly for Jesus; a few days of terrible struggle —and then, if faithful, thy crown is made sure; but one hour's apostasy will be at the cost of thy crown!" Cowles, *The Revelation of John*, 80.

**while**, and you are not going to see Me; and again a little while, and you will see Me'; and, 'because I am going to the Father'?" So they were saying, "What is this that He says, 'A **little while**'? We do not know what He is talking about." Jesus knew that they wanted to question Him, and He said to them, "Are you deliberating together about this, that I said, 'A **little while**, and you are not going to see Me, and again a **little while**, and you will see Me'?"

Jesus would be crucified, dead, and buried, but He would be raised from the dead, and His disciples would see Him again after His resurrection. "Little while" is not relativized.

Hebrews 10:37 described what was on the horizon for that generation. The author of Hebrews mentions he "who has trampled under foot the Son of God and has regarded as unclean the blood of the covenant by which he was sanctified and has insulted the Spirt of grace" (10:29). This is reminiscent of what we read in Acts 2:23 with Peter's message to his Jewish audience (2:5): "you nailed [Jesus] to a cross by the hands of godless men and put Him to death." In Hebrews 10:30 we find, "the Lord will judge His people." Also see 1 Corinthians 2:6-8 and Matthew 23:31-36. The author of Hebrews is not describing some distant relativized generation. John Owen offers this comment:

> Of the first sort were the Jews, who slew him, who murdered him, and cast him out of the vineyard, and thereon continued their hatred against the gospel and all that made profession thereof. He was to come to "destroy those murderers, and to burn their city" [Matt. 22:7]; which fell out not long after the writing of this epistle, and is properly intended in this place. See Matthew 24:3; Matthew 24:27; Matthew 24:30; 2 Peter 3:4; Jude 1:14; Revelation 1:7; Mark 14:62; James 5:7-8. For hereon ensued the deliverance of the church from the rage and persecution of the Jews, with the illustrious propagation of the gospel throughout the world.

I'll add the comments of John Brown from his well-respected commentary on Hebrews republished by The Banner of Truth Trust and recommended as one of the finest commentaries on Hebrews:

It cannot refer to His first coming in the flesh, for that was already past. It cannot refer to His second coming in the flesh, for that is even yet future, after the lapse of nearly eighteen centuries; whereas the coming here mentioned was a coming just at hand. But though these are the only comings of the Son of God in the flesh, they are by no means the only comings that are mentioned in Scripture: His coming in the dispensation of the Holy Spirit; and His coming for the destruction of His Jewish enemies, and the deliverance of His persecuted people.... [As to] the second, in Matt. xxiv. 27: "For as the lightning cometh out of the east, and shineth even unto the west; so shall also the coming of the Son of man be." It is the last of these that there is a reference in the passage before us. Jesus Christ had promised, that's when He came to execute vengeance on His enemies of the Jewish nation. His friends should not only be preserved from the calamity, but obtain deliverance from their persecutions: "When these things begin to come to pass, then look up, and lift up your heads; for your redemption draweth nigh" [Luke 21:28]. This coming was to take place before that generation passed away [Matt. 24:34]. More than thirty years had already elapsed; and within eight or nine years—"a little while"—the prediction was accomplished.[23]

James Stuart Russell references commentators whose interpretations are like those of John Brown. While Jesus uses the Greek word *mikron* (little) for something that was to happen soon, we find in Hebrews 10:37 very, very, little while "and will not delay."

This statement looks in the same direction as the preceding. The phrase, 'he that shall come' [ὁ ἐρχόμενος] is the customary designation of the Messiah,—'the coming One.' That coming was now at hand. The language to this effect is far more expressive of the nearness of the time in the Greek than in English: 'Yet a very, very little while;' or, as Tregelles renders it, 'A little while, how little, how little!' The reduplication of the thought in the close of the verse,—'will come, and will not tarry,' is also indicative of the certainty and speed of the

23. John Brown, *An Exposition of Hebrews* (1862), 484-485.

approaching event. Moses Stuart's comment on this passage is,— 'The Messiah will speedily come, and, by destroying the Jewish power, put an end to the sufferings which your persecutors inflict upon you,' comp. Matt. xxiv.'[24] This is only part of the truth; the Parousia brought much more than this to the people of God, if we are to believe the assurances of the inspired apostles of Christ.[25]

John Owen and Rhodes cite James 5:7-9 to support their views. Who is correct? Earlier, Rhodes called on Albert Barnes to make his case. Here's what Barnes says about James 5:

For the coming of the Lord draweth nigh—Compare Revelation 22:10, 12, 20; the notes at 1 Corinthians 15:51. It is clear, I think, from this place, that the apostle expected that that which he understood by "the coming of the Lord" was soon to occur; for it was to be that by which they would obtain deliverance from the trials which they then endured. See James 5:7.... The most natural interpretation of the passage, and one which will accord well with the time when the Epistle was written, is, that the predicted time of the destruction of Jerusalem Matthew 24:30 was at hand; that there were already indications that that would soon occur; and that there was a prevalent expectation among Christians that that event would be a release from many trials of persecution, and would be followed by the setting up of the Redeemer's kingdom.... The destruction of Jerusalem and of the temple would contribute to that by bringing to an end the whole system of Jewish types and sacrifices;... The Epistle was written, it is supposed, some ten or twelve years before the destruction of Jerusalem,... and it is not improbable that there were already some indications of that approaching event."

---

24. Moses Stuart, *Commentary on the Epistle to the Hebrews*, 2nd ed. (New York: Flagg, Gould, and Newman, 1833), 481.

25. *The Parousia: The New Testament Doctrine of Our Lord's Second Coming*, reprint ed. (Grand Rapids, MI: Baker Books, [1887] 1983), 274-275. *The Parousia* was first published in 1878 with the title, *The Parousia: A Critical Inquiry into the New Testament Doctrine of Our Lord's Second Coming*.

I will add the comments of Henry Cowles, "The time is indeed very short, this time of your trial; for when, under the sweep of terrific judgments, the proud city Jerusalem shall fall, all persecution from bigoted Jews will cease. Even now the signs suffice to show that her day of judgment is near, and can not tarry long."[26]

As with *tachos*, *engus* is used many times in the New Testament in numerous contexts and means that a person, event, or location is locally near. The Greek word *engus*, often translated "at hand," "is an adverb of time formed from two words: *en* ('in, at') and *guion* ('limb, hand'). Hence the meaning is literally 'at hand.' The Arndt and Gingrich *Lexicon* offers one word, 'near,' as the meaning.[27] Thayer expands on the idea of the word: 'of Time; concerning things imminent and soon to come to pass.'[28] He lists Revelation 1:3 and 22:10 in his series of examples. The word is used frequently of chronologically near events, such as approaching summer (Matt. 24:32), the Passover (Matt. 26:18; John 2:13; 11:55), the Feast of Tabernacles (John 7:2), etc."[29]

Rhodes argues (quoting fellow-dispensationalist Mark Hitchcock) that since *engus* is found in Revelation 22:10 that it can't have the meaning of "near" as the word is used repeatedly in the New Testament, because it would mean that all of Revelation has been fulfilled. That's a problem he'll have to deal with because that's what *engus* means in every other context. Because such an interpretation does not fit his system does not mean it's not true. There would have been an opportunity for God to make it clear to John that the events described in Revelation after chapter 3 were not near. But He didn't do that. He repeated: "things which must shortly take place" (22:6); "I am coming quickly" (22:7); "Do not seal up the words of the prophecy of this book, for the time is near" (22:10; cp. Dan. 12:4); "I am coming quickly" (22:12); "Yes, I

---

26. *The Epistles to the Hebrews* (New York: D. Appleton, and Company, 1878), 108.

27. W. F. Arndt and F. W. Gingrich, eds., *A Greek-English Lexicon of the New Testament and Other Early Christian Literature*, 4th ed. (Chicago: University of Chicago, 1957), 213.

28. Joseph Henry Thayer, ed., *Greek English Lexicon of the New Testament* (New York: American Book, 1889), 164. Some of Thayer's examples are: "the coming of the Lord is at hand" (James 5:8); "the time is at hand" (Luke 21:8) "the day is at hand" (Rom. 13:12); "the end is at hand" (1 Peter 4:7).

29. Kenneth L. Gentry, Jr., *Before Jerusalem Fell: Dating the Book of Revelation* (Bethesda, MD: International Scholars Press, [1989] 1997), 140.

am coming quickly" (22:20). Jesus did not say, "When I come it will be fast." His "fast coming" is related to the nearness of that coming.

Revelation is a book of symbols and signs (1:1: sign-ified).[30] For example, Rhodes appeals to Revelation 19:11-21 to support his contention that it's a description of "the second coming of Christ" (98).

> And I saw heaven opened, and behold, **a white horse**, and He who sat on it is called Faithful and True, and in righteousness He judges and wages war…. And **the armies which are in heaven**, clothed in fine linen, white *and* clean, were following Him on white horses…. From His mouth comes a sharp sword…. (vv. 11-14)

If Acts 1:11 is said to be the description of the Second Coming (He "will come in just the same way"), then how does what we read in Revelation 19 fit with that description? Jesus did not ascend to heaven riding a horse accompanied by "armies." The symbolic vision of Jesus' coming riding a horse with a sword coming out of His mouth fits with the promised coming in Judgment that Jesus described in the Olivet Discourse.

Rhodes moves next to Matthew 24 and begins with, "many evangelicals believe Christ was simply saying that those people who witness the signs stated earlier in Matthew 24—such as the abomination of desolation (verse 15) and 'the great tribulation' (verse 21)—will see the coming of Jesus Christ within *that* generation." (99). Since Rhodes references R.C. Sproul and me, one would assume he would explain how we came to our conclusions. It's not as if I and others have not written extensively on the topic. Instead at looking how Matthew uses the phrase "this generation" elsewhere in the New Testament, he argues that the reason Matthew 24:34's use of "this generation" does "not refer to Christ's contemporaries" is "because that generation did not witness 'all these things' of which Jesus so clearly spoke. Only the generation that witnesses *those specific prophetic things* will not pass away until all the events of the tribulation period are literally fulfilled." Again, Rhodes' prophetic system forces him into this conclusion.

In his two pages of explanation as to why "this generation" does not mean the generation of Jesus' day, Rhodes did not reference a single verse in the synoptic gospels where the same phrase is used (Matt. 11:16-19;

---

30. Σημαίνω (*sēmainō*): "to give a sign."

12:39, 41, 42; 16:4; 17:17; 23:36; Mark 8:12; Luke 7:31; 11:29, 30, 31, 32, 50, 51; 17:25; 21:32). Instead, he calls on Darrell Bock and Thomas Ice, two people from his own prophetic camp, for scholarly support. I've listed the comments of dozens of commentators going back to the second and fourth centuries and including those in the 21st century on Matthew 24:34 in my book *Wars and Rumors of Wars* who disagree. There were many more I could have listed. Bock says that "what Jesus is saying is that the generation that sees the beginning of the end, also sees the end." (100). Of course, that's not what the text states. Rhodes references Matthew 24:32 (the parable of the fig tree) and 24:34 (this generation) but not verse 33. I wonder why? Because this verse tells us who would see "all these things," and it's not some distant generation: "Even so **you** too, when **you see all these things**, recognize that He [or it][31] is near, at the doors." The "you" is them. Compare what Jesus said in Matthew 24:33 with 26:64: "Jesus said to him [Caiaphas], 'You have said it yourself; nevertheless I tell you [plural], hereafter you [plural] will see THE SON OF MAN SITTING AT THE RIGHT HAND OF POWER, and COMING ON THE CLOUDS OF HEAVEN.'" This is another example of Rhodes not presenting an accurate description of the preterist interpretation by leaving out crucial information.

Rhodes then appeals to Matthew 16:27-28. I and others have dealt extensively with these verses.[32] Once again, he leaves out some essential information. Curiously, he does not quote the verses, but I will:

> For the Son of Man is **about to** [*mellō*] come in the glory of His Father with His angels, and WILL THEN REPAY EVERY MAN ACCORDING TO HIS DEEDS. Truly I say to you, **there are some of those who are standing here who will not taste death until they see** the Son of Man coming in His kingdom.

Rhodes says that 16:27 refers to the transfiguration, an event that happened about a week later. This means he interprets it in a preterist fashion as fulfilled prophecy! Some partial and all full preterists interpret verse 16:27 as applying to the judgment on Jerusalem in AD 70. Consider these comments from Bible expositor Adam

---

31. Or "it." See Gary DeMar, *Wars and Rumors of Wars*, updated ed. (Powder Springs, GA: American Vision, 2023), 156-160.

32. See chapter 17 of this book.

Clarke (1762-1832), a British Methodist theologian, about the timing component of the verse.

> For the Son of man shall come in the glory of his Father—This seems to refer to Daniel 7:13-14. "Behold, one like the Son of man came—to the ancient of Days—and there was given him dominion, and glory, and a kingdom, that all people, and nations, and languages should serve him." This was the glorious Mediatorial kingdom which Jesus Christ was now about to set up, by the destruction of the Jewish nation and polity, and the diffusion of his Gospel through the whole world. If the words be taken in this sense, the angels or messengers may signify the apostles and their successors in the sacred ministry, preaching the Gospel in the power of the Holy Ghost. It is very likely that the words do not apply to the final judgment, to which they are generally referred; but to the wonderful display of God's grace and power after the day of Pentecost.[33]

Many commentators interpret 16:27 as applying to the Second Coming, an event that's in our future but others apply it to the events of that generation.[34] Jesus said in verse 28, "there are some of those who are standing **here** who will not taste death until they see the Son of Man coming in His kingdom." Of those who were standing there, who died between Matthew 16:28 and 17:1? No one. Why would Rhodes leave out this important fact? Here's what R.C. Sproul says about Matthew 16:27-28:

> With these words, Jesus uttered a prophecy, but not about an event that would take place hundreds or thousands of years

---

33. "There be some [16:28]—which shall not taste of death—This verse seems to confirm the above explanation, Clarke writes [16:27], as our Lord evidently speaks of the establishment of the Christian Church after the day of Pentecost, and its final triumph after the destruction of the Jewish polity; as if he had said, 'Some of you, my disciples, shall continue to live until these things take place.' The destruction of Jerusalem, and the Jewish economy, which our Lord here predicts, took place about forty-three years after this: and some of the persons now with him doubtless survived that period, and witnessed the extension of the Messiah's kingdom; and our Lord told them these things before, that when they came to pass they might be confirmed in the faith, and expect an exact fulfillment of all the other promises and prophecies which concerned the extension and support of the kingdom of Christ."

34. See chapter 17 of this book.

later.... It would happen within the lifetimes of at least some of the disciples.[35]

Henry Alford states that Matthew 16:27-28 refers *"to the destruction of Jerusalem, and the full manifestation of the Kingdom of Christ by the annihilation of the Jewish polity...."*[36]

Henry Hammond offers a harmony of Matthew 16:27-28, John 21:18-23, and Matthew 24 and their relationship to Jesus' judgment on Jerusalem.

The nearness of this to the story of Christ's Transfiguration, makes it probable to many, that this coming of Christ is that Transfiguration of his, but that cannot be, because the 27th verse of the son of man's coming in his glory with his Angels to reward, &c. (to which this verse clearly connects) cannot be applied to that. And there is another place, John 21:23 (which may help to the understanding of this) which speaks of a real coming, and one principal person (agreeable to what is here said of some standing here) that should tarry, or not die, till that coming of his. And that surely was fulfilled in John's seeing the ... famous destruction of the Jews, which was to fall in that generation, Matthew 24, that is, in the lifetime of some there present, and is called the Kingdom of God, and the Coming of Christ, and by consequence here most probably the son of man's coming in his kingdom, ... that is, his coming in the exercise of his Kingly office, to work vengeance on his enemies, and discriminate the faithful believers from them.[37]

---

35. R.C. Sproul, *Mark: An Expositional Commentary* (Orlando, FL: Reformation Trust, 2011), 205 and *Luke: An Expositional Commentary* (Sanford, FL: Ligonier Ministries, 2020), 275-276. Sproul states the following in his commentary on Matthew where he tells his readers that the fulfillment is found in Matthew 24 which he says "also contains a very controversial time-frame reference" (page 456). "I acknowledge again that the entire Olivet Discourse is very difficult, and this passage [24:35] especially so. Yet I continue to believe that the most natural way to understand this text is to regard everything Jesus said as to taking place in that generation, including His coming in judgment upon the chosen nation of Israel." *Matthew: An Expositional Commentary* (Sanford, FL: Ligonier Ministries, 2019), 656.

36. Henry Alford, *The New Testament for English Readers* (Chicago: Moody Press, [1886] n.d.), 122. Alford, like other commentators, adds to what Jesus said and claims that the near coming "was a type and earnest of the final coming of Christ." There is nothing in Matthew 16:27-28 that references a coming that was emphatically near and one that is still distant.

37. Henry Hammond (1605-1660), *A Paraphrase, and Notations Upon All the Books of the*

John Lightfoot states, in a parallel gospel, that "**his coming in glory should be in the lifetime of some that stood there** [Mark 9:1]."[38] This comment matches Matthew 16:27, "**coming in the glory** of His Father." Charles Spurgeon gets it right: "If a child were to read this passage I know what he would think it meant: he would suppose Jesus Christ was to come, and there were some standing there who should not taste death until really and literally he did come. This, I believe, is the plain meaning."[39]

Jack P. Lewis offers a helpful comprehensive commentary on Matthew 16:27-28:

> [27] The call of Jesus to self-sacrifice is clearly premised upon the coming judgment for all men. Accompanied by **angels** (Matt. 25:31; cf. 1 Thess. 4:16; 2 Thess. 1:7; *1 Enoch* 54:6, the **Son of man** is to pay each man according to his deeds. Judgment according to deeds is a prevalent biblical concept (Ps. 62:12; Prov. 24:12; Rom. 2:6; 2 Cor. 5:10; cf. Sirach 35:19 and *1 Enoch* 45:3; 69:27).
>
> [28] ....To **taste death** (Mark 9:1; Luke 9:27; John 8:52; Heb. 2:9; *Biblical Antiquities of Philo* 48:1) is to experience death. Jesus clearly predicted the **Son of man coming in his kingdom** (cf. 13:41) within the life of those then living. The statement is likely a reference to Jesus' entering his reign which took place at his exaltation to the right hand of God following the resurrection, which was proclaimed at Pentecost. The coming "with power" (Mark 9:1) and "seeing the kingdom" (Luke 9:27) must focus on Pentecost (cf. Acts 1:8; 2:1ff.). After

---

*New Testament*, 7th ed. (London: John Nicholson, [1653] 1702), 74-75. For similar comments on John 21:18-21, see John Gill, *Exposition of the Old and New Testaments*, 9 vols. (London: Mathews and Leigh, 1809), 8:135.

38. John Lightfoot, *A Commentary on the New Testament from the Talmud and Hebraica: Matthew—1 Corinthians*, 4 vols. (Peabody, MA: Hendrickson Publishers, [1859] 1989), 2:422. Lightfoot goes on to comment, "In that phrase, 'in the last times,' Isa. ii.2; Acts ii.17; 1 Tim. iv,1; 2 Pet. iii.3; that is, in the last times of that city and dispensation." See Appendix A.

39. Spurgeon, "An Awful Premonition" in *12 Sermons on the Second Coming of Christ* (Grand Rapids, MI: Baker Book House, 1976), 5.

Pentecost the kingdom is spoken of in the New Testament as a reality (Col. 1:13; Heb. 12:28; Rev. 1:9).[40]

In conclusion, *Bible Prophecy Under Siege* follows a dispensational premillennial script. It's as if the prophetic works in existence that have credibility are only those published in the past 150 years and pertain to a dispensational premillennial hermeneutic. In addition to the weak exegetical arguments found in *Bible Prophecy Under Siege*, Rhodes ignores numerous commentators going back centuries that follow a preterist interpretation. Here are three examples from a mid-18th century commentary:

- [Rev. 1:3] *For the Time is at Hand:*] The Beginning of the Accomplishment of the Things here written is at Hand. —The civil Wars of the *Romans*, and the Destruction of the *Jewish* State, were probably Things which were meant by *the Time is at hand*."[41]
- [Rev. 3:10] I also will keep thee from the Hour of Temptation, which all come upon all the World, &c.] By all the World here [where the Greek words *oikoumenē* and *mellō*[42] are used], as in other Places of the New Testament, is meant the Roman Empire, as Ch. ii. 6,—The Temptation here spoken of, must either mean some great Evil which was gathering, and ready to break over the whole Roman Empire; or an approaching Storm of Persecution; which is called a Temptation, because by Persecution Men are tempted to deny their Faith, or Religion. The Persecution raised against the Christians the Emperor

---

40. Jack P. Lewis, *The Gospel According to Matthew: Part II*, 13:53-28:20 (Austin, TX: Sweet Publishing Co., 1976), 2:42-43.

41. Robert Goadby [1721-1778], *An Illustration of the Holy Scriptures, by Notes and Explications on the Old and New Testament. In which The Useful observations of former Commentators will be made Use of; the different Translations of the Bible into various Languages taken Notice of, to explain difficult Texts; And The Observations of the most learned Men applied, which such new Notes added, as will greatly explain the Nature and Spirit of the Holy Scriptures, shew the Gracious Design of God in every Part of them, unfold the Sublime Truths they teach, more particularly that great and wonderful Mystery of the Redemption of Mankind by Jesus Christ; clear the seeming difficult Accounts of Things found therein, and set to View the great use, Improvement, and Delight, we may gather from them*, 5th ed., 2 vols. (London: [1759] 1772 ), 2:916.

42. "About to."

Nero, is here supposed to be meant. Hour is put for any Time, even a very long Space: See John v. 25 ["long time" is around 38 years], 1 John ii, 18 ["we know it is the last hour"]. This Persecution was intended to try the Christians, whether they would be faithful to their Profession. But Christ was free to give this Church of Philadelphia a Promise that he would preserve it from this Persecution, as having received Proofs of its, Fidelity already.[43]

- "St. Paul speaks of false prophets, as being among the Corinthians; calling them deceitful workers, who transformed themselves into Apostles of Christ. In the 2d epistle to the Thessalonians, he mentions one whom he characterizes as the Man of Sin, whose coming would be after the working of Satan, with all power and signs, and lying wonders, and with all deceivableness of unrighteousness in them that perish. St. John assured those to whom he wrote, that many antichrists and many false prophets, were already gone out into the world [1 John 2:18, 22]; whereby they knew it was the last time, or the time when the Jewish polity was arrived to its utmost period, and Jerusalem would be destroyed. St. Peter also mentions some false teachers, who would bring in damnable or destructive heresies, even denying the Lord that bought them, and bring upon themselves swift destruction."[44]

There are even earlier works going back more than 1,500 years:

- [1] But of wars in Jerusalem is He speaking; for it is not surely of those without, and everywhere in the world; for what did they care for these? And besides, He would thus say nothing new, if He were speaking of the calamities of the world at large, which are happening always. For before this, were wars,

---

43. *An Illustration of the Holy Scriptures*, 923.

44. miah Nisbett, *The Prophecy of the Destruction of Jerusalem, An Attempt to Illustrate Various Important Passages in the Epistles and of the New Testament from Our Lord's Prophecies of the Destruction of Jerusalem, and from Some Prophecies of the Old Testament to Which is Added an Appendix Containing Remarks upon Dr. MacKnight's Commentary and Notes on the two Epistles to the Thessalonians* (1787). Republished as *The Destruction of Jerusalem, the Mysterious Language of St. Paul's Description of the Man of Sin, and the Day of the Lord*, ed. Gary DeMar (Powder Springs, GA: American Vision, 2023), 40.

and tumults, and fightings; but He speaks of the Jewish wars coming upon them at no great distance, for henceforth the Roman arms were a matter of anxiety. Since then these things also were sufficient to confound them, He foretells them all.

- [2] Therefore He saith, they shall come not by themselves or at once, but with signs. For that the Jews may not say, that they who then believed were the authors of these evils, therefore hath He told them also of the cause of their coming upon them. "For verily I say unto you," He said before, "all these things shall come upon this generation," having made mention of the stain of blood on them."

- [3] For, "Then," saith He, "let them which be in Judea flee into the mountains." Then, When? When these things should be, "when the abomination of desolation should stand in the holy place." Whence he seems to me to be speaking of the [Roman] armies. Flee therefore then, saith He, for thenceforth there is no hope of safety for you.[45]

- "But our Master did not prophesy after this fashion; but, as I have already said, being a prophet by an inborn and every-flowing Spirit, and knowing all things at all times, He confidently set forth, plainly as I said before, sufferings, places, appointed times, manners, limits. Accordingly, therefore, prophesying concerning the temple, He said: "See ye these buildings? Verily I say to you, There shall not be left here one stone upon another which shall not be taken away [Matt. 24:3]; and this generation shall not pass until the destruction begin [Matt. 24:34]...." And in like manner He spoke in plain words the things that were straightway to happen, which we can now see with our eyes, in order that the accomplishment might be among those to whom the word was spoken.[46]

- "And when those that believed in Christ had come thither from Jerusalem, then, as if the royal city of the Jews and the whole land of Judea were entirely destitute of holy men, the judgment of God at length overtook those who had committed

---

45. John Chrysostom of Antioch (347-407), *Homilies*.
46. *Clementine Homilia*, 3:15.

such outrages against Christ and his apostles, and totally destroyed that generation of impious men."[47]

The list could go on to cover centuries. The position that Rhodes presents had its start in the 19th century and was codified in the *Scofield Reference Bible* that was first published in 1909 and later revised in 1917 and has been a perennial best seller.

47. Eusebius, *Ecclesiastical History*, Book III, Chapter 5.

# CHAPTER 15

# Pure Language–Hebrew

Is the Modern Hebrew Language a Fulfillment of Bible Prophecy? Prophecy writer Grant Jeffrey (1948-2012) gave some reasons why he believed the incontrovertible truth that Jesus' coming was about to take place. One piece of supposed evidence that caught my attention was his use of Zephaniah 3:9-10 and the claim that the revival of the Hebrew language under the work of Eliazar Ben-Yehuda (1858-1922) in the late 19th and early 20th centuries is a fulfillment of Zephaniah's prophecy. There is no doubt that Ben-Yehuda's work to revive Hebrew as an everyday spoken language was a major accomplishment, but does it have anything to do with prophecy and the modern state of Israel?

I first came across the argument that Ben-Yehuda's work is a prophetic fulfillment of Zephaniah 3:9-10 when I was preparing for my debate in June of 2010 with Jim Fletcher, the author of the 2009 book *It's the End of the World as We Know It [and I feel fine]*:

> You can walk through any city in Israel today and you will hear Israelis who come from a hundred different nationalities speaking one language. In Zephaniah 3:9 the Lord had predicted, 'I will return unto you a pure language.' A hundred years ago when Ezra Ben-Yehuda began to revive Hebrew, people thought he was crazy. But now you can walk through those cities in Israel where you hear them speak one language, and it's Hebrew. You don't hear people today speak Babylonian. You don't hear them speak Assyrian. You hear them speak Hebrew. So that's a dramatic example of fulfilled prophecy.

The claim is made by Jeffrey and Fletcher that Zephaniah 3:9-10 refers to the return of Jews from around the world to Israel and that they will speak a purified Hebrew language. Not only is this passage not referring to modern-day Israel or the Hebrew language spoken today, pure Hebrew or not, it's not talking about Israel ancient or modern.

Keep in mind that Hebrew was not a lost language. It was used by scholars and in liturgical settings for centuries. Early English translators of the Bible knew Hebrew. Take a look at John Lightfoot's 17th-century four-volume work *A Commentary on the New Testament From the Talmud and Hebraica,* first published between 1658 and 1674, as just one example. *Hebraica* refers to the Hebrew language. There's the 1640 *Bay Psalm Book,* the first book printed in America at Cambridge, Massachusetts, that was translated from Hebrew.

After doing more research on the subject, I found that Fletcher most likely took his "pure language" claim verbatim from Jeffrey. Prophecy enthusiasts will find an argument like this convincing. They have been conditioned to believe that any scrap of evidence put forth by prophecy "experts" is key evidence that the return of Jews to their land in 1948 was a fulfillment of Bible prophecy. The problem is, there is not a single verse in the New Testament that says anything about Israel returning to the land. And there's nothing in Zephaniah 3:9-10 that supports Jeffery's argument from his books *The Signature of God* and *Triumphant Return* that the modern Hebrew language is a fulfillment of Bible prophecy.

The main problem with Jeffery's argument is in the translation of the passage he saw as evidence of the fulfillment of Bible prophecy related to the return of the Jews to their land. It's ironic that Jeffrey mentioned the "pure language" of Hebrew but never bothered to look at the Hebrew text or the context of the prophecy.

The King James Version translates Zephaniah 3:9, "For then will I turn to the people a pure language, that they may all call upon the name of the LORD, to serve him with one consent." *The Living Bible,* as it often does, interprets rather than translates: "At that time I will change the speech of my returning people to pure Hebrew so that all can worship the Lord together." The words "pure Hebrew" are not found in the Hebrew text. In a note, the editors of *The Living Bible* state: "Literally, '... I will change the speech of the peoples to a pure speech....' See Isaiah 19:18." O. Palmer Robertson comments: "The singular form of the term *lip (śāpāh)* in Scripture often means 'language' (Gen. 11:1, 6, 7, 9; Ps. 81:6 [Eng. 5]; Isa. 19:18; Ezek. 3:5-6). But the idea of a 'purified language' confuses imageries. The rendering of the phrase so that it reads 'they will speak pure Hebrew' hardly can be justified."[1] The Hebrew word often translated "language" is

---

1. O. Palmer Robertson, *The Books of Nahum, Habakkuk and Zephaniah,* NICNT (Grand Rapids: Eerdmans, 1990), 328.

the word "lip," and in some contexts refers to "confession" rather than the language someone speaks.

"Returning people" is an interpretation, not a translation. It is not a reference to the Jews returning to their land, either after the Babylonian captivity hundreds of years before the time of Christ or in 1948. The context refers to the nations surrounding Israel, "from beyond the rivers of Ethiopia..." (Zeph. 2:10). These aren't dispersed Israelites. Even the dispensational-oriented *Liberty Bible Commentary* understands the Zephaniah 3:9 passage this way:

> The people in view are the remnant of the Gentiles who survived God's judgment because of their conversion. Jehovah will give them a pure language ... so they can call upon the true Jehovah.[2]

John Hannah, a professor of historical theology at the dispensational Dallas Theological Seminary, puts the passage in its proper historical context:

> Zephaniah predicted that the nations will be renewed both morally (v. 9) and spiritually (v. 10). The purifying **of the lips of the peoples** does not mean they will speak a new language (as the KJV seems to imply by its trans. "a pure language"). Instead it means the renewal of once-defiled speech. One's lips represent what he says (the words spoken by his lips), which in turn reflect his inner life (cf. Isa. 6:5-7)[3].... As a result the nations, turning to reverential trust in God, will **call on the name of the LORD and** will evidence their dependence on Him by their united service (**shoulder to shoulder**).[4]

Albert Barnes offers a helpful commentary:

---

2. Paul R. Fink, "Zephaniah," *Liberty Bible Commentary: Old Testament*, eds. Edward E. Hinson and Woodrow Michael Kroll (Lynchburg, VA: The Old-Time Gospel Hour, 1982), 1781.

3. "Then I said, 'Woe is me, for I am ruined! Because I am a man of unclean lips, and I live among a people of unclean lips; for my eyes have seen the King, the Lord of hosts.' Then one of the seraphim flew to me with a burning coal in his hand, which he had taken from the altar with tongs. He touched my mouth with it and said, 'Behold, this has touched your lips; and your iniquity is taken away and your sin is forgiven'" (Isa. 6:5-7). This is hardly a description of Isaiah speaking pure Hebrew after his lips were touched.

4. John D. Hannah, "Zephaniah," *The Bible Knowledge Commentary: Old Testament*, eds. John F. Walvoord and Roy B. Zuck (Wheaton, IL: Victor Books, 1983), 1533.

I will turn—Contrary to what they had before, "to the people," literally, "peoples," the nations of the earth, "a pure language," literally, "a purified lip." It is a real conversion, as was said of Saul at the beginning 1 Samuel 10:9; "God" (literally) "turned to him another heart." Before the dispersion of Babel the world was "of one lip," but that, impure, for it was in rebellion against God. Now it shall be again of "one lip;" and that, "purified." The purity is of faith and of life, "that they way call upon the Name of the Lord," not as heretofore on idols, but that every tongue should confess the one true God, Father Son and Holy Spirit, in Whose Name they are baptized. This is purity of faith. To "call upon the Name of the Lord Jesus" Acts 22:16; Romans 10:13 is the very title of Christian worship; "all that called upon the Name" of Jesus, the very title of Christians Acts 9:14, Acts 9:21; 1 Corinthians 1:2....

God gave back one pure language, when, on the Day of Pentecost, the Holy Spirit, the Author of purity, came down in fiery tongues upon the Apostles, teaching them and guiding them "into the whole truth" John 16:13, and to "speak to everyone in his own tongue, wherein he was born, the wonderful works of God" Acts 2:8, Acts 2:11. Thenceforth there was to be a higher unity than that of outward language. For speech is not the outer sound, but the thoughts which it conveys and embodies. The inward thought is the soul of the words. The outward confusion of Babel was to hinder oneness in evil and a worse confusion. At Pentecost, the unity restored was oneness of soul and heart, wrought by One Spirit, whose gift is the one Faith and the one Hope of our calling, in the One Lord, in whom we are one, grafted into the one body, by our baptism Ephesians 4:3-6. The Church, then created, is the One Holy Universal Church diffused throughout all the world, everywhere with one rule of Faith, "the Faith once for all delivered unto the saints," confessing one God, the Trinity in Unity, and serving Him in the one law of the Gospel with one consent.

One by one the passages that dispensationalists claim are a fulfillment of Bible prophecy are collapsing under the weight of exegetical scrutiny.

The following from Larry Walker reinforces the interpretation that the revival of modern Hebrew is not what is being discussed:

> The lips or language that had become impure through use in idol worship will become purified so that all may in unison call on the name of the Lord. The reference to lips, the organ of speech, includes the heart behind the language; as Keil, 156, notes, "Purity of the lips involves or presupposes the purification of the heart." The outpouring of the Holy Spirit on the day of Pentecost brought about purification and renewal of heart and lips resulting in a widespread calling on the name of the Lord (Ac 2:21).[5]

Adam Clarke (1762-1832), who spent 40 years writing his commentary on the Bible, makes similar arguments:

> The *pure language,* ספה ברורה *saphah berurah,* may here mean the *form of religious worship.* They had been before *idolaters:* now God promises to restore his *pure worship* among them. The word has certainly this meaning in Ps 81:5; where, as God is the speaker, the words should not be rendered, "I heard a language which I understood not," but, "I heard a religious confession, which I approved not." See Isa 19:18; Ho 14:3; and see Joe 2:28, where a similar promise is found.[6]

Again, "[t]he term *lip* often means 'language' (Gen. 11:1), but here it seems rather to denote the organ of speech. Comp. Is. 6:5, 7, 'I am a man of unclean lips … lo, this hath touched thy lips, and thine iniquity shall depart.'"[7]

Bible commentaries I checked offer the same interpretation. "'Lip' is singular in Hebrew and probably refers to the 'speech' of the Gentile nations which have defiled their lips by the worship of false gods. In the future their speech would be pure as they called on the name of the

---

5. Larry L. Walker, "Zephaniah," in *The Expositor's Bible Commentary: Daniel-Malachi* (Revised Edition), ed. Tremper Longman III and David E. Garland, vol. 8 (Grand Rapids, MI: Zondervan, 2008), 688.

6. Adam Clarke, "Zephaniah," *The Holy Bible, Commentary and Critical Notes* (Baltimore: John J. Harrod, 1834).

7. A. B. Davidson, *The Books of Nahum, Habakkuk and Zephaniah with Introduction and Notes,* The Cambridge Bible for Schools and Colleges (Cambridge: Cambridge University Press, 1896), 132.

Lord."[8] The interpretation of Zephaniah 3:9 in *The Twelve Minor Prophets* commentary by The Soncino Press, a Jewish publishing company based in the United Kingdom, states, "*a pure language.* Better, 'a pure lip'; human lips will not be contaminated by the mention of idolatrous gods, but will only mention (*call upon*) the name of God in prayer."[9]

The New Testament puts the above points in perspective: "If you confess with your **lips** that Jesus is Lord and believe in your heart that God raised him from the dead, you will be saved. For one believes with the heart and so is justified, and one **confesses with the mouth** and so is saved (Rom. 10:9-10). That's what a "pure lip" is, a true confession of Jesus as Lord and Savior, not the revival of the Hebrew language.

---

8. Kenneth L. Barker, *Micah, Nahum, Habakkuk, Zephaniah*, vol. 20, The New American Commentary (Nashville: Broadman & Holman Publishers, 1999), 488.

9. S.M. Lehrman, "Zephaniah," *The Twelve Prophets*, ed. A. Cohen (London: The Soncino Press Ltd., 1948), 248.

# CHAPTER 16

# Matthew 24:21: Future or Past Great Tribulation?

How should Matthew 24:21 be interpreted when 24:34 says, "This generation will not pass away until all these things that place"? "All these things" include "a great tribulation, such as has not occurred since the beginning of the world until now, nor ever will." Commentators agree. "This verse is a supporting statement of the previous verses in this paragraph [in Matt. 24], reiterating the distress of those days. The verse utilizes hyperbole, typical of the apocalyptic genre. Although the language is hyperbolic, the horrors of Jerusalem's destruction as reported by Josephus were severe."[1] R.T. France comes to a similar conclusion:

> Josephus' lurid description of the horrors of the siege
> (*War* 5.424-438, 512-518, 567-572; 6.193-213) shows that, while
> v. 21 uses the hyperbolic language of apocalyptic (cf. Dan 12:1;
> Joel 2:2; 1QM 1:11-12; *Test. Mos.* 8:1; Rev 16:18), it is an assessment
> which would have been agreed by those involved in the events.[2]
> In passing, we should note that "nor ever will be again" confirms
> that this passage is about a historical event, not about the end
> of the world! The horror was in fact "cut short" by the Roman
> capture of the city after five months, bringing physical relief to
> those who had survived the famine in the city.[3]

Its fulfillment had to have taken place before the passing away of "this generation" (Matt. 24:34), their generation. The language is like what is found in Ezekiel 5:9,[4] a form of rhetorical hyperbole that was used

---

1. Douglas Mangum, ed., *Lexham Context Commentary: New Testament*, Lexham Context Commentary (Bellingham, WA: Lexham Press, 2020), Matt. 24:15-22.

2. Josephus himself, who was a witness to the events he described, claims that none of the disasters since the world began can compare to the fate of Jerusalem (*War* 1.12).

3. R. T. France, *The Gospel of Matthew*, The New International Commentary on the New Testament (Grand Rapids, MI: Eerdmans, 2007), 915.

4. "Verses 8-9 [in Ezekiel 5] give the principal statement of God's verdict. He would

about events that took place under the Old Covenant. Notice the use of the phrase "your abominations."

> And I will do among you what I have not done and the like of which I will never do again because of all your abominations.

Ezekiel described what was going to happen in Israel's near future. If this was true, how could there be a greater retribution based on Israel's abominations? William Greenhill explains the use of forceful language in comparison to the action of the Jews in terms of what they did:

First, "I will do in thee that which I have not done.' Had not God dealt severely with the old world, with Sodom and Gomorrah, with the Egyptians whom he drowned? Yes, he had; but their sins being not so grievous as the Jews' [sins], their judgments were not so great. The sorest was that of Sodom, and Lam. iv. 6, "The punishment of the iniquity of the daughter of my people is greater than the punishment of the sin of Sodom" that was overthrown in a moment, it was a sharp but short punishment; Jerusalem had severity and length of time, therefore it is added, ver. 9, "They that be slain with the sword are better than they that be slain with hunger," their judgment is easy.

But was not the siege of Samaria as sad a judgment as this executed against Jerusalem? 2 Kings vi. 28, 20, there the women ate their own children, and suffered great distress through famine.

*Ans.* The women ate their children, but it came not to that extremity, as that the fathers should eat their sons, and the sons the fathers, as here it was. And,

Secondly, that was not taken as Jerusalem was, and burned, many put to the sword, many carried into captivity.

This part of the verse you see cleared; that which respects the time to come is more difficult: "I will not do any more the like." Did God do his utmost now ? did he not do as much or

---

execute the judgments pronounced in the Mosaic covenant on Jerusalem in the sight of the nations. *Never again would God execute a judgment like this.* He would withdraw himself from the sanctuary (v. 11b; cf. 10:4; 11:22-23) to pour out his judgment without pity. One-third of the inhabitants of Jerusalem would die in the city through disease and famine; one-third would die by the sword." Ralph H. Alexander, "Ezekiel," *The Expositor's Bible Commentary*, gen. ed. Frank E. Gaebelein, 12 vols. (Grand Rapids, MI: Zondervan, 1986), 6:773. Emphasis added.

more against Jerusalem and its inhabitants, for putting Christ to death ? When Titus besieged Jerusalem, did they not eat their children, one another, die with famine? did not the plague and sword destroy? ran not their blood down the streets, out at the gates, and affected their very enemies? came not the wrath of God upon them to the utmost? I Thess. ii. 16; and said not the Lord Christ, Matt. xxiv. 21, that there should be at that time such "tribulation as was not from the beginning of the world, nor ever should be?" how then is it truth in our prophet, that God saith, "I will not do any more the like?"

*****

Some interpreters conceive the words, "that which I have not done, and whereunto I will do no more the like," to be a usual phrase amongst the Hebrews to set out the greatness of the judgment.[5]

Jesus appropriated the language from Ezekiel and applied it to the prophesied coming judgment on Jerusalem that would take place before their generation passed away (Matt. 24:34). The judgment was greater because the crime was greater, and no other crime could be greater. It was only those in that generation who "crucified the Lord of glory" (1 Cor. 2:8). Let's recall what Peter said at Pentecost:

"Men of Israel, listen to these words: Jesus the Nazarene, a man attested to you by God with miracles and wonders and signs which God did through Him in your midst, just as you yourselves know—this Man, delivered over by the predetermined plan and foreknowledge of God, you nailed to a cross by the hands of lawless men and put *Him* to death" (Acts 2:22-23).

The punishment fit the crime.

Similar hyperbole is found elsewhere in Scripture. Could there have been two kings in the southern kingdom of Judah who were the greatest kings Judah ever had? Logic would dictate that there can only be one greatest king but any number of great kings. But the Bible tells us that there were two kings who were the "greatest." How can this be?

---

5. William Greenhill, *An Exposition of Ezekiel* (Carlisle, PA: Banner of Truth Trust, [1647-1667], 1994), 145-146.

- "He [Hezekiah] trusted in the LORD, the God of Israel; **so that after him there was none like him among all the kings of Judah, nor among those who were before him**" (2 Kings 18:5).
- "And before him [Josiah] **there was no king like him** who turned to the LORD with all his heart and with all his soul and with all his might, according to the law of Moses; **nor did any like arise after him**" (2 Kings 23:25).

In 2 Kings 18:5 it is written of Hezekiah that there would be no king after him who would show the same devotion to the Lord as he showed. When we get an assessment of Josiah's reign, which *followed* Hezekiah's reign, we are informed that "there was no king like him who turned to the LORD." How can Hezekiah's reign be the greatest (when considering the reign of a future king like Josiah) and Josiah's reign be the greatest (when considering the reign of a past king like Hezekiah)? Is this a contradiction? The phraseology is obviously hyperbolic, emphasizing complete devotion to the Lord and His law. The authors of these biblical books did not see them as contradictions. They were following a common literary style of their day.

Of King Solomon God said, "Behold, I have given you a wise and discerning heart, so that there has been no one like you before you, **nor shall one like you arise after you**" (1 Kings 3:12). As we just saw, both Hezekiah and Josiah are singled out as the best of the best. Keep in mind that these descriptions come from the biblical writers. These kings are not describing themselves and the splendor of their kingly exploits.

In addition, we learn from the New Testament that one arose after Solomon, Hezekiah, and Josiah who was wiser and more discerning than the three of them. Jesus says of Himself, "The Queen of the South shall rise up with this generation at the judgment and shall condemn it, because she came from the ends of the earth to hear the **wisdom of Solomon**; and behold, **something greater than Solomon is here**" (Matt. 12:42). Jesus surpasses Solomon, Hezekiah, and Josiah, and yet each of them had been described as the greatest.

Similar language is used to describe judgments brought on nations by God. Jesus follows this Hebrew method of stressing the impact of the calamity by using hyperbole in Matthew 24:21 that was familiar to the hearers and readers of the Hebrew and Greek translations of the Old Testament.

- "There had never been so many locusts, **nor would there be so many again**" (Ex. 10:14; compare with Joel 1:1-4).
- "There shall be a great cry in all the land of Egypt, **such as there has not been before and such as shall never be again**" (Ex. 11:6).
- "For under the whole heaven **there has not been done anything like what was done to Jerusalem**" (Dan. 9:12; compare with 12:1).
- "A day of darkness and gloom, a day of clouds and thick darkness. As the dawn is spread over the mountains, so there is a great and mighty people; **there has never been anything like it, nor will there be again after it to the years of many generations**" (Joel 2:2).

One Facebook writer posted that World War II was much worse than the judgment on Israel in that generation. Was Jesus describing a world-wide tribulation? Not according to Matthew 24:16-20. Here is Luke's description. "For there will be **great distress** upon the earth [Gk: τῆς γῆς : *tēs gēs*: the land] and wrath against **this** people [Gk: λαῷ τούτῳ: *laō toutō*]. They will fall by the edge of the sword and be led captive among all nations, and Jerusalem will be trampled underfoot by the Gentiles, until the times of the Gentiles are fulfilled" (Luke 21:23-24; see 19:41-44). The Great Tribulation consisted of a series of local events that could be escaped on foot. A person's cloak was important (Ex. 22:26; Deut. 24:13; Matt. 5:40; Luke 6:29-30). Flat roofs were a common building practice (Luke 5:17-20). The Sabbath was still operating (Acts 1:12), but only in Israel in the first century. We live in a much larger world today where the Sabbath is not generally observed or enforced.

If Jerusalem is utterly destroyed (with no stone on another, v. 44 [in Luke 19]) then its socio-religious role is also decimated. If Jerusalem is no longer the center of the world, then the status distinctions it embodied and propagated are no longer definitive. In this light, the citation of Isaiah 56:7 in v. 46, "My house shall be a house of prayer" is telling, for it runs counter to the eschatological vision of all peoples coming to Jerusalem to worship Yahweh and paves the way for a mission that is centrifugal rather than centripetal (Cf. Acts 1:8).[6]

Gregory Stevenson says that to the Jew, "the destruction of the temple could be seen as tantamount to the destruction of the nation." Josephus remarked, "there was left nothing to make those that came thither believe it had ever been inhabited" (*Wars*, 7.1.1, para 3). In his commentary on Matthew 24, Adam Clarke estimates that some 1,357,000 people perished during the war, including an estimated 1.1 million in Jerusalem. In addition to what the Romans did, many thousands were killed by Jewish zealots that ended up prolonging the war fighting over limited food supplies. Josephus describes the carnage:

> And now, since his soldiers were already quite tired with killing men, and yet there appeared to be a vast multitude still remaining alive, Caesar gave orders that they should kill none but those that were in arms, and opposed them, but should take the rest alive. But, together with those whom they had orders to slay, they slew the aged and the infirm; but for those that were in their flourishing age, and who might be useful to them, they drove them together into the temple.... [B]ut of the young men he chose out the tallest and most beautiful, and reserved them for the triumph; and as for the rest of the multitude that were above seventeen years old, he put them into bonds, and sent them to the Egyptian mines. Titus also sent a great number into the provinces, as a present to them, that they might be destroyed upon their theatres, by the sword and by the wild beasts; but those that were under seventeen years of age were sold for slaves." (*Wars*, 6.9.2).

Hank Hanegraaff notes, Jesus "was not literally predicting that the destruction of Jerusalem would be more cataclysmic than the catastrophe caused by Noah's flood. Rather, He was using apocalyptic hyperbole to underscore the distress and devastation that would be experienced when Jerusalem and its temple were judged." Their trusted and privileged covenantal order was going to be judged. In terms of God's covenant relationship with Israel, the events surrounding that

---

6. Joel Green, *The Gospel of Luke* (New International Commentary on the NT) (Grand Rapids, MI: Eerdmans, 1997), 682.

generational judgment could not be repeated because God's covenant with Israel had been forever altered, and the crime of crucifying Jesus was a single occurrence. Note what Jesus said to the religious leaders when He was on the Mount of Olives:

> "Therefore, I say to **you**, the kingdom of God will be taken away from **you** and given to a nation, producing the fruit of it. And he who falls on this stone will be broken to pieces; **but on whomever it falls, it will scatter him like dust**." And when the chief priests and the Pharisees heard His parables, **they understood that He was speaking about them** (21:43-45).

Because the Bible is literature, we should expect to find numerous literary devices, especially figures of speech (e.g., simile, metaphor, personification, anthropomorphism, hyperbole). When Jesus says, "I am the door" (John 10:9), no one forces the text to mean that Jesus is adorned with hinges.[7]

Jesus used hyperbole in Matthew 21:21-22 when He said, "Truly I say to you, if you have faith and do not doubt, you will not only do what *was done* to the fig tree, but even if you say to this mountain, 'Be taken up and cast into the sea,' it will happen." Mark quotes Jesus, "It is easier for a camel to go through the eye of a needle than for a rich man to enter the kingdom of God" (Mark 10:25)." Jesus said, "Everything is possible for him who believes" (Mark 9:23). We're back to casting that mountain into the sea. "Everything"? The Pharisees said of Jesus, "the whole world has gone after Him" (John 12:19). That statement is like what we find in Matthew 24:21.

---

7. The following author does not see Jesus' words as hyperbole. "*For there shall be*, &c. This verse contains the reason for the foregoing directions. Unless they succeeded in escaping from the city, they would share in tribulation such as the world had never witnessed. *Great tribulation.* Compare Luke 21: 23, 24. In this expression are included all the excesses, horrors, and carnage which attended the siege and fall of the city. *Such as was not,* &c. Hardly can this be deemed hyperbolical, when the reality of those dreadful atrocities and horrors of the siege of Jerusalem are taken into account, and which, as Bloomfield remarks, have never to this day been paralleled. This form of expression is found in Ex. 10:14; 11: 6; Dan. 12:1; Joel 2:2. *No, nor ever shall be.* The negation in the original is exceedingly emphatic, and forbids attributing to our Lord in this passage, the language of exaggeration." John J. Owen, *A Commentary, Critical, Expository, and Practical, on the Gospels of Matthew and Mark* (New York: Leavitt & Allen, 1857), 315.

Jesus used hyperbole when He mentioned a plank being in one's eye while attempting to remove the splinter in a brother's eye (Matt. 7:3-4). If this was not hyperbole, the lesson would be rejected as being impossible. We use hyperbole in everyday speech with very little misunderstanding. "This book weighs a ton," or "I'm so hungry I could eat a horse."

We get so caught up in trying to defend the Bible against skeptics that we forget the Bible is literature. To interpret the Bible literally is to interpret it according to its literature. The Bible is translatable and applicable because it uses everyday speech. It's not a book of scientific formulations. You don't have to defend the Bible because the dimensions of a circle do not line up with our view of scientific or mathematical accuracy regarding Pi (1 Kings 7:23).[8] Round numbers are accurate enough and used repeatedly in the Bible. So are very large numbers. Kenneth Gentry has this to say about the "thousand years" in Revelation 20:

> The fact that he has an army as large as "the sand of the seashore" (Rev 20:8b) should not make us believe that this is the vast majority of the human race. This is a hyperbolic statement in an enormously symbolic book. And this figure is a common ancient image used of large-scale armies in (Jos 11:4; Jdg 7:12; 1 Sa 13:5; 2 Sa 17:11), various local populations (1 Ki 4:20; Isa 10:22; 48:19; Jer 15:8; 33:22; Hos 1:10), the patriarchs' offspring (Ge 22:17; 32:12), and so forth. In fact, the 1 Sam 13:5 reference specifically mentions only 30,000 chariots and 6,000 horsemen accompanying Philistia's army. In 2 Sam 17:11 the writer is referring to early Israel's own army, which could hardly approach this enormous number literally. In Jeremiah God speaks against Jerusalem warning that "their widows will be more numerous before Me / Than the sand of the seas" (Jer 15:8a). Sandy (2002: 41)[9] notes that prophets often "express emotion rather than exactness ... in order to shock listeners...."[10]

---

8. Harold Lindsell, *The Battle for the Bible* (Grand Rapids, MI: Zondervan, 1976), 165-167.

9. D. Brent Sandy, *Plowshares & Pruning Hooks: Rethinking the Language of Biblical Prophecy and Apocalyptic* (Downers Grove, IL: InterVarsity, 2002).

10. Kenneth L. Gentry, Jr., *The Divorce of Israel: A Redemptive-Historical Interpretation of Revelation*, 2 vols. (Acworth, GA and Vallecito, CA: Tolle Lege Press/Chalcedon Foundation,

G.K. Beale mentions that there are numerous "Jewish traditions about the nature and length of the future messianic reign ... from 40 to 365,000 years."[11] Similar hyperbolic language is found early in the Bible:

- "The LORD your God has multiplied you, and behold, **you are this day like the stars of heaven in number**" (Deut. 1:10).

- "Where can we go up? Our brethren have made our hearts melt, saying, 'The people are bigger and taller than we; **the cities are large and fortified to heaven**. And besides, we saw the sons of the Anakim there'" (1:28).

- "They came out, they and all their armies with them, **as many people as the sand that is on the seashore**, with very many horses and chariots" (Josh. 11:4).

- "Now the Midianites, the Amalekites, and all the people of the east were lying in the valley **as numerous as locusts**; and **their camels were without number, as numerous as the sand on the seashore**" (Judges 7:12).

- "The king [Solomon] made silver and gold as common in Jerusalem as stones, and cedar as plentiful as sycamore-fig trees in the foothills" (2 Chron. 1:15).

- "I am weary with my sighing / Every night I make my bed swim / I flood my couch with my tears" (Psalm 6:6).

- "You blind guides, who strain out a gnat and swallow a camel!" (Matt. 23:24).

- "So the Pharisees said to one another, 'See, this is getting us nowhere. Look how the whole world [κόσμος/*kosmos*] has gone after Him!'" (John 12:19; cp. Matt, 4:4 and Luke 4:4).

After David killed Goliath, the women in Israel met King Saul and sang, "Saul has slain his thousands, and David his tens of thousands" (1 Sam. 18:7). Up to this point, David had killed only one man!

> If writers using hyperbole were saying more than they intended, is this to be understood as error? No. Error is not reflected by hyperbole because ... hyperbole is generally readily understood

---

2024), 2:1593-1594.

11. G.K. Beale, *The Book of Revelation*, NIGCNT (Grand Rapids, MI: Eerdmans, 1999), 1018-1019.

by the reader as an exaggerated statement given for emphasis or impact. Therefore the readers are not misled.[12]

Jesus' disciples would have understood His use of hyperbole, and even if they didn't, Jesus was the truth teller not their understanding of what He said. Often those in Jesus' audience and His disciples didn't understand His statements (e.g., John 6:41-65). This was true of the "teacher of Israel" (3:1-21). Since Jesus mentioned the destruction of the temple and used sun, moon, and stars language, they would have interpreted His words against the background of the Scriptures of their time (Isa. 13:10, 13, 17; 24:19, 21, 23; 30:26; 34:4).

Using the Bible as our guide, we will see that the language used by Jesus in Matthew 24:21 is found in several places in the Bible to describe extraordinary events related to distinguished governance, national judgment, and personal misfortune.

> When you come across a saying of Jesus that uses exaggerated terminology, what you need to do is say, "This must be especially important, because He is using exaggerated language. This must be so important to Him that He is evoking language to show its importance, and in many ways it is these things that give us the flavor of the heart of Jesus much more than the non-exaggerated language.[13]

R. H. Charles comments that the phrase in Matthew 24:21 "is a stock eschatological expression. It is first found in Dan. xii.1; then in 1 Macc. ix.27; next in Ass. Mos. viii. 1, and subsequently in Rev. xvi. 18."[14] If there is an impending worldwide Great Tribulation based on Matthew 24:21 as futurists maintain, then Egypt will suffer a greater tribulation than she suffered during the time of the ten plagues. But this would go against the absolutist language of Exodus 11:6: "Moreover, there shall be a great cry in all the land of Egypt, such as there has not been *before* and such as shall never be again." According to those

---

12. Roy B. Zuck, *Basic Bible Interpretation: A Practical Guide to Discovering Biblical Truth* (Colorado Springs: David C. Cook, 1991), 156.

13. Robert H. Stein, "Hermeneutics of Exaggeration: Part 2: https://bit.ly/488M12o

14. R.H. Charles, *A Critical History of the Doctrine of a Future Life in Israel, in Judaism, and in Christianity or Hebrew, Jewish, and Christian Eschatology from Pre-Prophetic Times till the Close of the New Testament Canon* (London: Adam and Charles Black, 1899), 329, note 1.

who believe in a coming great tribulation as part of the end times, "one fourth of the world's population"[15] will perish during this expected affliction. This means that a fourth of Egypt's 114,239,913 (28 million) people will die. Surely there were not millions of first-born sons who died in Egypt at the time of the Exodus.

Hyperbole is God's way of making a definitive point of the utmost seriousness. It's no different from the way we use hyperbole today. Today's prophecy "experts" are oblivious to how the Bible uses various literary devices. To make Bible prophecy relevant, they force it to comply with modern concepts and technology. Bows and arrows and riders must mean missiles and missile launchers and horses in Ezekiel 38 and 39 must mean horsepower while chariots must refer to tanks.

A side point is needed here for advocates of dispensationalism and the pre-tribulation "rapture of the church" who claim that it was/is always imminent. This means that the "rapture" could have taken place any time during and after the events in the book of Acts. Anyone who claims the Bible is describing nuclear weapons (e.g., Isa. 2:19; Zech. 14:12; Rev. 8:10-11) as part of a post-rapture event has an interpretive problem. Such weapons did not exist. If the "rapture" was an any moment event, let's say in the 13th century, how could the above passages be referring to nuclear weapons?

Nineteenth-century prophecy "experts" are some of the worst, far outpacing Hal Lindsey's locusts of Revelation 9:1-12 that could be Vietnam-era—from the 1970s—"Cobra helicopters."[16] Robert H. Ellison,[17] in an insightful study of prophecy writer John Cumming (1807-1881), makes the following observation: "[Cumming] asserts that it is 'neither hasty nor irrelevant' to compare 'ancient prophecy' with

15. John F. Walvoord, *Israel in Prophecy* (Grand Rapids, MI: Zondervan/Academie, [1962] 1988), 110.

16. "I have a Christian friend," Lindsey writes, "who was a Green Beret in Viet Nam. When he first read this chapter he said, "I know what those are. I've seen hundreds of them in Viet Nam. They're Cobra helicopters! That may be conjecture, but it does give you something to think about! A Cobra helicopter does fit the sound of 'many chariots.' My friend believes that the means of torment will be a kind of nerve gas sprayed from its tail." Hal Lindsey, *There's a New World Coming: A Prophetic Odyssey* (Santa Ana, CA: Vision House Publishers, 1973), 138-139.

17. Robert H. Ellison, "John Cumming and His Critics: Some Victorian Perspectives on the End Times," *Leeds, Centre Working Papers in Victorian Studies: Platform Pulpit Rhetoric*, ed. Martin Hewitt, vol. 3 (Horsforth, Leeds: Leeds Centre for Victorian Studies, 2000), 83, note 20.

daily press reports and states that 'This use of the modern newspaper is all the originality I claim.'"[18] Here are some examples of Cumming's "newspaper exegesis" as detailed by Ellison:

> Cumming's use of current events to interpret ancient Scripture gets rather ingenious at times. He claims, for example, that Daniel's phrase 'And knowledge shall be increased' [Dan. 12:4] can also be translated 'And knowledge shall be flashed along', a rendering which anticipates the telegraph, the 'mysterious whispering wire'[19] that can transmit a message to 'the most distant capital of Europe' in less than an hour's time. Even more inventive is his interpretation of the prophecy he sees in Isaiah 18:1-2—'Woe to the land . . . beyond the rivers of Ethiopia: That sendeth ambassadors by the sea, even in vessels of bulrushes upon the waters'. He asserts that the phrase 'vessels of bulrushes' is literally 'vessels of that which drinks water', a phrase which many have perplexed the translators working in 1611 [when the King James version of the Bible was published] but which can now be seen as a reference to the steamship, a 'vessel whose . . . motive force from beginning to end, is water'.[20]

Cumming also saw "railway traveling"[21] to be a reference to "many shall run to and fro" (Dan. 12:4) even though trains don't "run" and neither did the people who took the trains. Seeing some forms of technology as the fulfillment of Bible prophecy can get outdated very fast. We need to read and interpret the Bible in its covenantal context.

J. L. Martin's *The Voice of the Seven Thunders: Lectures on the Apocalypse*, outpaces them all:

> "And the number of the army of the horsemen were two hundred thousand thousand and I heard the number of them" [Rev. 9:16]

---

18. Robert H. Ellison, "John Cumming and His Critics: Some Victorian Perspectives on the End Times," *Leeds, Centre Working Papers in Victorian Studies: Platform Pulpit Rhetoric*, ed. Martin Hewitt, vol. 3 (Horsforth, Leeds: Leeds Centre for Victorian Studies, 2000), 83, note 20.

19. John Cumming, *Behold, the Bridegroom Cometh: The Last Warning Cry with Reasons for the Hope That Is in Me* (London: James Nisbet & Co., 1865), 357-358. Also see pages 189-190.

20. Ellison, "John Cumming and His Critics," 77.

21. Quoted in Ellison, "John Cumming and His Critics," 79.

The four angels are two hundred millions. Two hundred thousand thousand are just two hundred millions, and that is just about the fighting force of the whole world [of the 19th century]. We have a few more than one billion inhabitants on the earth,[22] and in a few centuries past the average population on the globe has not varied much from one billion. But of that billion, about five hundred millions (one half) are females, leaving an average population of male inhabitants of about five hundred millions, and of that number about one-half are minors, leaving about two hundred and fifty millions of adult males on the earth at a time. But of that number of adult males, about one-fifth are superannuated—too old to fight. These are statistical facts. This leaves exactly John's two hundred millions of fighting men on earth. And when we prove a matter mathematically, we think it is pretty well done.

*****

But when let loose, John tells us how they fought. We are now in the time of the sounding of the sixth angel's trumpet as certain as that the nations of earth are loosed to fight and there is no power to prevent them from it. "And thus, I saw the horses in the Vision and them that sat on them having breastplates of fire and of jacinth and brimstone, and the heads of the horses were as the heads of lions and out of their mouths issued fire and smoke and brimstone." The heads of the horses, including the rider, were as the heads of lions.

John is pointing to the modern mode of fighting on horseback [in the 19th century], with the rider leaning forward, which, to his sight, and to the sight of one looking on at a distance, would appear as the great mane of the lion; the man leaning on his horse's neck. He would, in fighting with firearms, have to lean forward to discharge his piece, lest he might shoot down his own horse that he was riding. In John's day, the posture was very different.... Now, I want to ask my friendly hearers if it is not as literally fulfilled before our eyes as anything can be? Are not all nations engaged in this mode of warfare? Do they not kill men with fire and smoke and brimstone?... Do you not know that

---

22. There are ~8 billion today.

this is just ignited gunpowder? Do not all men know without calling in a chemist that it is precisely the chemical division of gunpowder when ignited—fire smoke and brimstone?

*****

Could an uninspired man in the last of the first century have told of this matter? Could he have known unless he had been inspired that soon after the darkest time of the dark ages when these greedy preachers hurt the men that had not the knowledge of God's Word, that the nations would all be let loose from that mighty power that bound them and engage in the fight with fire and smoke and brimstone? It is unreasonable to think that an uninspired man could have foretold it; it is utterly impossible.[23]

The problem with Martin's conclusion is that he got the timing wrong like so many interpreters before him and after him.

The English translator of the *Works of Josephus* comments about what Jesus predicted in Matthew 24:1-34: "That these calamities of the Jews, who were our Saviour's murderers, were to be the greatest that had ever been since the beginning of the world, our Saviour had directly foretold, Matthew 24:21; Mark 13:19; Luke 21:23-24; and that they proved to be such accordingly, Josephus is here a most authentic witness."[24]

---

23. (Bedford, IN: James M. Mathes, 1878), 149-150, 151, 152-153.

24. William Whiston, "Preface" to *The Wars of the Jews*, in *The Works of Josephus* (Peabody, MA: Hendrickson Publishers, 1987), 544 note c. "The temple and the city were made desolate. Jesus told His disciples that all these things would come upon "this generation." The savagery, slaughter, disease, and famine (mothers eating their own children) were monstrous (cf. Jos. Wars V, 424-38 [x.2-3]), "unequaled from the beginning of the world until now," and, according to Jesus, "never to be equaled again." There have been greater numbers of deaths—six million in the Nazi death camps, mostly Jews, and an estimated twenty million under Stalin—but never so high a percentage of a great city's population so thoroughly and painfully exterminated and enslaved as during the fall of Jerusalem." D. A. Carson, *The Gospel According to John* (Grand Rapids, MI: Eerdmans, 1991), 501.

# CHAPTER 17

# Are There Two Comings Separated by 2,000 Years?

"For the Son of Man is about to come in the glory of His Father with His angels; and WILL THEN RECOMPENSE EVERY MAN ACCORDING TO HIS DEEDS. Truly I say to you, there are some of those who are standing here who will not taste death until they see the Son of Man coming in His kingdom." (Matt. 16:27)

Screenwriter Dan O'Bannon, who wrote the screenplay for the 1979 film *Alien*, had inspirational help from other sci-fi films like the film *The Thing from Another World* (1951) and *Forbidden Planet* (1956). Anyone familiar with these films will note some of the thematic similarities between those and other films. O'Bannon was honest enough to admit, "I didn't steal *Alien* from anybody. I stole it from *everybody!*"[1]

Like O'Bannon, I'm not ashamed to admit that most of my work is "borrowed" from what many people have researched and published over the centuries. What follows will show that not everyone agrees with the interpretation that Matthew 16:27 refers to a future physical coming of Jesus. To prove this point, I suggest you look at William E. Biederwolf's *The Millennium Bible* that lists nine different interpretations and states that "'*shall come*' ... is not a simple future, and '[John Peter] Lange is inclined to see in its meaning that the event is impending , i.e., He shall come—is about to come.'" Here is Lange's comment from his commentary on Matthew: "Μέλλει γὰρ [Emphatically placed at the beginning of the sentence.]"[2] As I'll show, the Greek word *mellō* is an important timing word that is often not translated.

---

1. Quoted in Chris Nashawaty, *The Future Was Now: Madmen, Mavericks, and the Epic Sci-Fi Summer of 1982* (New York: Flatiron Books, 2024). 31.

2. "Matthew," *Lange's Commentary on the Holy Scriptures*, 4th ed. (New York: Charles Scribner and Co., 1865), 304.

Debates continue over which biblical passages refer to the AD 70 judgment coming of Jesus and those that refer to what is commonly called the yet Second Coming of Jesus. As I have repeatedly pointed out, there is no unanimous agreement among scholars on this question, especially among those who signed the "Three Questions Letter" that was sent to me to affirm specific creedal and confessional statements or else! Kenneth Gentry argues that Matthew 16:27 and 28 describe two comings separated by nearly 2,000 years (so far).[3] Almost any commentary you pick up will admit that these two verses (also found in Mark and Luke) are difficult to interpret. Honest students of Scripture should be free to study the topic without being labeled a "heretic" for arguing that both verses refer to events surrounding that first-century destruction of Jerusalem in AD 70 that included the dismantling of the temple (Matt. 24:1-3). Douglas Wilson is honest enough to admit that he is "not finally settled" but is "strongly inclined to take Matthew 16:27 as a 70 AD reference because of the 'not taste death' reference in the next verse."[4]

Gentry takes a different approach by describing himself "as an orthodox preterist." Does this mean that anyone who does not interpret Matthew 16:27 the way he does is not "orthodox"? Here's how he expresses his position:

> As an orthodox preterist, I hold that this passage brings together the AD 70 judgment and the Final Judgment. As orthodox preterists argue (following most conservative, evangelical theologians in general), the AD 70 destruction of the temple is a dramatic judgment of God in itself. But it is also a typological foretaste of the universal Final Judgment, which it pictures through the local judgment on Israel. (This is much like the Israel's Old Testament exodus event being an important act in itself, while serving as a type of coming redemption through Christ.)[5]

---

3. Ken Gentry, "Matt. 16:27-28: AD 70 and the Final Judgment" (July 31, 2018): https://bit.ly/4h69MMU

4. Wilson stated this to Michael Sullivan in response to a question. See Sullivan's "A Full Preterist Response to Kenneth Gentry's Article 'Matt. 16:27-28: AD 70 and the Final Judgment—Will the REAL 'Orthodox Preterist' Please Stand Up?!?" (August 3, 2024): https://bit.ly/3U2UluL

5. Gentry, "Matt. 16:27-28: AD 70 and the Final Judgment."

Gentry shows by his comment that there is no agreement of two comings in Matthew 16:27-28. Yes, many evangelical commentators state that Matthew 16:27 is a Second Coming passage. Surprisingly, Gentry declares, "Many scholars see v. 28 as simply repeating v. 27, using different words." This means that by his own admission "many scholars" disagree with him that two comings are described in verses 27 and 28. While he does not tell us who these "many scholars" are, I'll list some of them. I'll start with contemporary author Keith Mathison who edited the book *When Shall These Things Be? A Reformed Response to Hyper-Preterism* that includes a chapter by Gentry and himself. Mathison states the following in his book *Postmillennialism: An Eschatology of Hope*:

> There is a distinct parallel between the language of 2 Thessalonians 1:7-9 and Matthew 16:27-28, which describes a coming of the Son of Man for judgment within the lifetime of some of His disciples.[6]

"A coming," not two comings separated by thousands of years. He expands on the above comments in his 2009 book *From Age to Age: The Unfolding of Biblical Eschatology*. Mathison notes that some interpret Matthew 16:27 as a reference to a yet future coming of Jesus. He then argues that "a more likely ... possibility is that the judgment Jesus is referring to in verse 27 is the judgment referred to in Daniel 7:9-10, a heavenly judgment of the 'beasts/nations' that is directly related to Jesus receiving of the Kingdom of God from the father, an event that occurs in connection with his first advent."[7]

In his chapter titled "The Eschatological Time Texts of the New Testament" in the book *When Shall These Things Be?*, Mathison states the following with some equivocation:

> [I]t is possible that Jesus did say (in Matthew 10:23, 16:27-28, and 24:34) that the coming of the Son of Man would occur within the lifetime of those who heard him speak, but that it does not refer to his second coming from heaven to earth.... Even if such texts as Matthew 10:23, 16:27-28; and 24:30 refer to something that happened in the first century, we cannot

---

6. (Phillipsburg, NJ: Presbyterian and Reformed, 1999), 228.
7. (Phillipsburg, NJ: Presbyterian and Reformed, 2009), 366.

automatically assume that Acts 1 [verses 9-11] is referring to the same thing.[8]

There's this from Adam Clarke (1762-1832):

Verse 27. *For the son of man shall come in the glory of his father*] this seems to refer to Dan. vii. 13, 14. "Behold one like the Son of man came—to the Ancient of days—and there was given him dominion, and glory, and a kingdom that all people, and nations, and languages, should serve him this was the glorious mediatorial kingdom, which Jesus Christ was now about to set up, by the destruction of the Jewish nation and polity, and the diffusion of his gospel throughout the whole world. If the words be taken in this sense, the angels or messengers may signify the apostles and successors in the sacred ministry, preaching the Gospel in the power of the Holy Ghost. It is very likely that the words do not apply to the final judgment, to which they are generally referred; but to the wonderful display of God's grace and power after the day of Pentecost.

Henry Hammond (1605-1660) has this to say on Matthew 16:27:

[v. 27] For there shall be a solemn visitation among the Jews, a time of judgment on them … wherein there shall be a visible discrimination between those which cleave fast to Christ, and those which do not, and so likewise on all mankind, either in particular visitation upon kingdoms, or at the day of doom. [v. 28] And of this coming of mine against my enemies, and to the relieving of them that adhere to me, I tell you assuredly, that some that are here perfect, John by name [John 21:], shall live to see it, that is, that he shall not die till that remarkable coming of Christ in judgment upon his crucifiers, the visible destruction of the Jewish S[t]ate.

miah Nisbett writes that to understand Matthew 16:28, "we need only go back to the 27th verse" where "the coming of the Son of Man in the

---

8. Mathison, ed., *When Shall These Things Be? A Reformed Response to Hyper-Preterism* (Phillipsburg, NJ: Presbyterian and Reformed, 2004), 182, 185. Richard L. Pratt, Jr., should be commended for listing some preterist works that take a position contrary to the topic of *When Shall These Things Be?* (148, note 25).

former [v. 27]," and "His coming in His kingdom, in the latter of these verses [v. 28], clearly determines the connection between the two."[9] This means if verse 28 refers to events surrounding Jerusalem's destruction, a view Gentry holds, then so does verse 27.

Several commentators have taken the approach that Jesus predicted His coming was near, but He was wrong. For example, Frederick Dale Bruner asserts that "Jesus' expectation of the time of judgment of 'every' person is *soon*: 'The Son of Man is just about (*mellei*, placed at the head of the sentence for emphasis) ... to come. We now know that this expectation, in its earliest and strict sense, was mistaken: the Son of Man did not come just then in the glory of his angels for judgment."[10]

Bruner believes Matthew's Gospel was written after AD 70. If this is true (I don't believe it is), then why was such a "mistake" left in the gospels? Here is Bruner's response:

> But what is perhaps as surprising is that an author of a late-first-century canonical Gospel included this expectation in his record. Some find this a mark of the evangelist's character: "What does it profit a person if one makes one's hero infallible to the whole world and loses one's integrity?" We believe authors who include mistakes of their heroes.[11]

Following this line of argument would mean that when Matthew wrote about a coming Messiah figure in several places (Matt. 10:23; 16:27-28; 24:34), and two other Gospel writers did the same, they were describing a flawed, mistaken, and misguided Messiah (Mark 13; Luke 17:22-37; 19:37-44; 21:5-36). If Jesus was mistaken so many times, what other things was He mistaken about? Bruner continues about Matthew 16:28:

---

9. Nehemiah Nisbett (d. 1812), *The Destruction of Jerusalem, the Mysterious Language of St. Paul's Description of the Man of Sin, and the Day of the Lord* (Powder Springs, GA: American Vision, 2023), 31. Nisbett has a lengthy discussion of the relationship between verses 27 and 28 in Matthew 16 from his 1811 book *The Triumphs of Christianity over Infidelity Displayed. Or the Coming of the Messiah, the True Key to the Right Understanding of the Most Difficult Passages in the New Testament*. Nisbett's work shows that the debate over the relationship between Matthew 16:27 and 28 is not new.

10. *Matthew, A Commentary*, 2 vols. (Dallas, TX: Word Publishing, 1990), 2:596. Bruner spends a great deal of time on this claim in his book *The Christbook* (1987) and on Matthew 16:28 and Matthew 24:34 in his Matthew commentary.

11. Frederick Dale Bruner, *The Churchbook: Matthew 13-28*, revised and expanded ed., 2 vols. (Grand Rapids, MI: Eerdmans, 2004), 2:158-159.

"If … (the *Parousia*-second Coming) was in Matthew's mind when he wrote v. 28, as many important interpreters believe it was (and in combination with v. 27 this view is reinforced, then either Jesus or Matthew's representation of Jesus was mistaken, for Jesus' Second Coming has not yet occurred. Bonnard, 252,[12] believes the variety of interpretations betrays the church's embarrassment at having an unfulfilled saying of Jesus in her records, and he suggests that instead of attempting to reinterpret the text we should admire the fidelity of the earliest church in preserving here "the memory of a word of Jesus that was already belied by the facts at the moment of its literary fixation in the gospel."[13]

This is an untenable and illogical position to take, especially by commentators who believe Matthew's gospel was written after AD 70. Why leave this "mistake" in all the gospel records if they were trying to present Jesus as the long-awaited prophesied Messiah?[14] Jesus clearly specified that their generation would not pass away before His promised coming (e.g., Matt. 24:34), but He did not know the day and hour. He was not referring to His so-called Second Coming but a definitive time within that generation when that judgment would happen. Luke's version reinforces the idea of specificity by stating, "when you see Jerusalem surrounded by armies, then know that her desolation is near" (21:20). Mounce admits that "the apparent meaning of these verses [Matt. 16:27-28] is that the second advent will occur during the lifetime of the disciples. History has demonstrated that this interpretation is inadequate."[15] But that's what Jesus said would take place!

Gentry, like Bruner and other commentators, contend that *parousia* refers to Jesus' second physical coming. For example, as Gentry now believes, the use of *parousia* in Matthew 24:27 refers to the Second Coming and not the coming of Jesus in judgment in AD 70. But here's

---

12. Pierre Bonnard, *L'évangile selon Saint Matthieu* (Delachaux & Niestlé, 1992).

13. Bruner, *The Churchbook*, 2:162.

14. A few commentators argue that "mistakes" make the gospel accounts more "authentic." Craig Keener is an example of this claim in his *A Commentary on the Gospel of Matthew* (Grand Rapids, MI: Eerdmans, 1999), 435.

15. Robert H. Mounce, *Matthew,* Understanding the Bible Commentary Series (Grand Rapids, MI: Baker Books, 2011), 165.

what he wrote in 1999 in his published debate with Thomas Ice: "Jesus warns His followers that He will *not* appear bodily in the first-century judgment (vv. 23, 25-26). Nevertheless, He will 'come' in judgment like a destructive lightning bolt against Jerusalem (v. 27). This coming, however, is a providential *judgment coming,* a Christ-directed, rather than a miraculous, visible, bodily coming."[16]

Gentry changed his position in his 2010 book *The Olivet Discourse Made Easy.*[17] He now argues that Matthew 24:27 refers to another coming in addition to the coming that took place before that Apostolic generation passed away. But other partial preterist commentators disagree. For example, John Gill states in his comments on Matthew 24:27 that it "must be understood not of his last coming to judgment … but of his coming in his wrath and vengeance to destroy that people, their nation, city, and temple."

Adam Clarke also interprets Matthew 24:3 and 27 as describing Jesus' coming to that generation related to a judgment coming that took place in AD 70: "*What shall be the sign of thy coming* [*parousia*]? viz. to *execute* these judgments upon them [the *destruction* of the *city, temple,* and *Jewish state*].… It is worthy of remark that our Lord, in the most particular manner, points out the very *march* of the Roman army: they entered into Judea on the EAST, and carried on their conquest WESTWARD, as if not only the extensiveness of the ruin, but the very route which the army would take, were intended in the comparison of the *lightning issuing from the east, and shining to the west.*"

## Not Very *'Mellō'*

As has already been pointed out by Bruner and others, Matthew 16:27 includes the Greek word *mellō*. Gentry interpreted *mellō* as a crucial time indicator, that is, events that were "about to" take place for his defense of a pre-AD 70 date for the composition of Revelation in his book *Before Jerusalem Fell.*[18] He has since changed his view on the

---

16. Gentry spends nearly two pages making his AD 70 judgment argument coming by Jesus in *The Great Tribulation: Past or Future?* (Grand Rapids, MI: Kregel Publications, 1999), 53-55. He says something similar in his book *Perilous Times: A Study in Eschatological Evil* (1999).

17. (Draper, VA: Apologetics Group Media, 2010), 102 and note 27.

18. "The relevant phrases read: 'the things which are about to occur' (Rev. 1:19) and

meaning of *mellō* in some verses because the timing aspect does not fit with his partial preterist view. For example, the Christians in the church at Smyrna "need these words of comfort and exhortation, for they are 'about to' (*melleis*) suffer tribulation. As Jesus says, the devil is 'about to (*mellei*) cast some of you into prison' (2:10).... The phrase 'about to come' is *tēs mellousēs erchesthai,* which suggests nearness, as we see in the use of *mellō* in 2:10; 3:16; 6:11."[19] Within the span of three chapters (1:19; 2:10 [twice]; 3:10), Gentry translates *mellō* two different ways. Back to Matthew 16:27:

> In v. 27 [of Matt. 16] the coming is indeterminate, simply stating that "the Son of Man is going to come." Here *mellō* ('be destined to') is followed by the present infinitive *erchomai* ('come').' This results in the statement meaning that he 'will certainly come.' But it provides no indication of when that might be.[20]

'being about to come' (Rev. 3:10).... Certainly it is true that the verb μέλλω [*mellō*] can indicate simply 'destined,' or it can be employed in a weakened sense as a periphrasis for the future tense. Nevertheless, when used with the aorist infinitive—as in Revelation 1:19—the word's preponderate usage and preferred meaning is: "be on the point of, be about to." The same is true when the word is used with the present infinitive, as in Rev. 3:10. The basic meaning in both Thayer and Abbott-Smith is: "to be about to." Indeed, "Μέλλειν [*mellein*] with the infinitive expresses imminence (like the future)."... All of this is particularly significant when the contexts of these two occurrences of μέλλω [*mellō*] in Revelation are considered: the words appear in near proximity with statements made up of the two other word groups indicating 'nearness.' Revelation 1:19 is preceded by Revelation 1:1 and 1:3 (which contain representatives of both the τάχος [*tachos*] and ἐγγύς [*engus*] word groups). Revelation 3:10 is followed by Revelation 3:11 (which contains a representative of the τάχος [*tachos*] word group). Clearly, then, the Revelation 1:19 and 3:10 references hold forth an excited expectation of soon occurrence." Gentry, *Before Jerusalem Fell: Dating the Book of Revelation* (Powder Springs, GA: American Vision, 1998), 141-142.

He changed his position in his two-volume Revelation commentary: "When Jesus speaks of 'the things which will take place after these things,' he uses the verb *mellō,* which can mean 'are about to, in the sense of nearness in time. Yet this term often implies mere futurity, sometimes with the connotation of divine determination (BAGD 500, 501). This is the preferred interpretation among translators (KJV, NKJV, NAB, NASB, NIV, NJB, RSV, NRSV, ESV) and commentators (Swete 21; Caird 26; Mounce 62; Beale 156; Witherington 82; Osborne 97; Boxall 44). Though John's basic concern in Revelation is with the near term (see Excursus 1 at 1:1), we probably should not translate the word *mellō* as emphasizing nearness, since it seems intentionally to be avoiding the clearer language already appearing in the context (1:1, 3)." Kenneth L. Gentry, Jr., *The Divorce of Israel: A Redemptive-Historical Interpretation of Revelation,* 2 vols. (Acworth, GA and Vallecito, CA: Tolle Lege Press and Chalcedon Foundation, 2024), 1:351.

19. Gentry, *The Divorce of Israel,* 1:351, 435, 484.

20. Gentry, "Matt. 16:27-28: AD 70 and the Final Judgment" (July 31, 2018): https://bit.ly/4h69MMU

If this is true, then no one can be dogmatic about applying Matthew 16:27 to the Final Judgment/Second Coming of Jesus since he could have "certainly come" before that generation passed away. In Mark 8:38 we find "For whoever is ashamed of Me **in this adulterous and sinful generation**, the Son of Man will also be ashamed of him when He comes in the glory of His Father with the holy angels." If "it is appointed for men to die once and after this judgment," then when is that "adulterous and sinful generation" judged? (Heb. 9:27)

John Lightfoot (1602-1675) says it happened to that generation in that generation:

> [O]ur savior had said in the last verse of the former chapter [8:38], "Whosoever shall be ashamed of me and of my words in this adulterous and sinful generation; of him also shall the Son of man be ashamed, when he cometh in the glory of his father with the holy angels" [compare with Matt. 16:27], to take punishment of that adulterous and sinful generation. And he suggests, with good reason, that his coming in glory should be in the lifetime of some that stood there."[21]

Commentator William Plummer includes the following in a footnote.

> "'His words are generally so interpreted (of His personal visible return), and this seems at first their obvious meaning. Yet it is doubtful whether all the language which is so interpreted is not better understood as oriental imagery describing the accompaniments of His coming in the conversion of multitudes to faith in Him, and in the downfall of Judaism as the representative of true religion' (Burton and Matthews)."[22]

Jesus said the following at His trial before Caiaphas and others in attendance: "'But I tell you, from now on you [plural] will see the Son of Man seated at the right hand of Power and coming on the clouds of heaven'" (Matt. 26:64). This looks like a comment that's parallel with what we find in Matthew 16:27. It's the enthronement of Jesus and a judgment by Jesus on that generation.

---

21. *A Commentary on the New Testament from the Talmud and Hebraica: Matthew—1 Corinthians*, 4 vols. (Peabody, MA: Hendrickson Publishers, [1859] 1989), 3:422.

22. Alfred Plummer, *An Exegetical Commentary on the Gospel According to St. Matthew*, 237, n. 2.

Not everyone would agree with Gentry's interpretation of *mellō* in Matthew 16:27. For example, in *Gnomon Novi Testamenti, or Exegetical Annotations on the New Testament,* published in 1742, Johann Albrecht Bengel states, "Μέλλει ἔρχεσθαι, *is about to come)* A stronger expression than ἐλεύσεται *will come.*[23]

Alexander B. Bruce, in his commentary on the Gospels in *The Expositors Greek Testament* series, concludes that "μέλλει points to something near and certain; note the emphatic position" (1:227) used for emphasis.

Davies and Allison's commentary on Matthew in the International Critical Commentary series comment, "Our evangelist has also added (in anticipation of v. 28; …) μέλλει…. Although μέλλω need not imply imminence … more often than not it does in the First Gospel (2:13; 17:12, 22; 24:6). That nearness is intended in 16:27, where the verb is editorial, is strongly suggested by what follows, v. 28, which is an assertion about the Son of man coming in the near future…. In fact, v. 28 can be viewed as explicating the μέλλει of v. 27."[24]

There is ample evidence of many commentators applying 16:27-28 to that Apostolic generation, for example Sylvanus Cobb:

"These two verses conclude the course of conversation which Jesus, at that sitting, held with his disciples. He here re-affirmed the certainty of that judgment of which he had repeatedly spoken to them, and also to his enemies, before,—and to which he referred at verse 25. And he expressly affirmed that this judgment should come during the lifetime of some of his hearers. Of course he spoke of the judgment which involved the dissolution of the Jewish church and state….The assumption that what is meant in these verses by the Son of man coming in the glory of his Father, and in his kingdom, referred to the transfiguration noted in the beginning of the next chapter, is a species of trifling with the Scriptures hardly worthy of notice…. All these events,— the fulfillment of Jesus' prophecies, the visible manifestation of God's providence in behalf of his cause and church, and the

---

23. Johann Albrecht Bengel, *Gnomon of the New Testament,* ed. M. Ernest Bengel and J. C. F. Steudel, trans. James Bandinel and Andrew Robert Fausset (Edinburgh: T&T Clark, 1860), 1:331.

24. W. D. Davies and Dale C. Allison, *Matthew* (T&T Clark, 1991), 2:675.

dissolution of the power of that people who were, directly, and indirectly by instigating the Gentiles, his chief persecutors, involved a more extensive and permanent establishment of his cause and kingdom in the world. Though, in a sense, the Christian dispensation may be said to have commenced when Christ entered upon his public ministry, yet there was a lapping, as it were, of the two dispensations. Visibly and historically, the Christian age commenced when it supplanted the Jewish age, on the dissolution of the Jewish polity. This was, in an eminent New Testament sense, *the coming of the Son of man in his kingdom.*"[25]

Robert Young, compiler of *Young's Analytiacal Commentary* and *The Concise Critical Comments on the Holy Bible* states: "27. SHALL COME,] *lit.* 'is about to come,' in 40 years."

Zachary Pearce (1690-1774) states the following on Matthew 16:25, 27-28: "This is meant of the time of the destruction of the Jewish state. Pearce does not see two comings separated by an extended period of time.[26] His comment on 16:27 states, "This is meant of his coming to visit and punish the Jews, as in ver. 25. See ch. xxiv. 30 and xxvi. 64. And Daniel vii. 13 and Rev. 1:7."

James Stuart Russell has a lengthy discussion of Matthew 16:27-28 in his book *The Parousia* (32-33):

"[T]he coming here spoken of is the Parousia, the second coming of the Lord Jesus Christ.... His coming was to be *glorious*—'in his own glory;'[27] 'in the glory of his Father;' 'with

---

25. *The New Testament of Our Lord and Saviour Jesus Christ; with Explanatory Notes and Practical Observations* (Boston: 1864), 48.

26. *A Commentary, with Notes, on the Four Evangelists and the Acts of the Apostles; Together with a New Translation of St. Paul's First Epistle to the Corinthians, With a Paraphrase and Notes.* ... Published from the original manuscripts, by John Derby, ... In two volumes. ... 1777: Vol. 1:117-118.

27. Lightfoot remarks, "Christ's pouring down his vengeance in the destruction of that city and people, is called his 'coming in his glory,' and his 'coming in judgment'; and as the destruction of that city and nation is charactered in Scripture, as the destruction of the whole world;—so, there are several passages, that speak of the nearness of that destruction, that are suited according to such characters. Such is that in I Cor. x. 11, 'Upon us the ends of the world [αἰώνων/*aiōnōn*] are come.'—I Pet. iv. 7, 'The end of all things is at hand.'—Heb. x. 37, 'Yet a little while; and he that shall come, will come, and will not tarry.' And to the very same tendency, may this be, in the words of the text: 'Behold, the Judge standeth before the door' (James 5:9]. As, also, that in the verse before [5:8], 'The coming of the Lord draweth

the holy angels.' ... the object of His coming was to judge that 'wicked and adulterous generation' (Mark 8:38), and 'to reward every man according to his works.'... His coming would be the consummation of 'the kingdom of God;' the close of the æon; 'the coming of the kingdom of God with power.'... this

---

**THE PAROUSIA TO TAKE PLACE WITHIN THE LIFETIME OF SOME OF THE DISCIPLES**

| Matt. 16:27-28 | Mark 8:38-9:1 | Luke 9:26-27 |
|---|---|---|
| For the Son of man shall come in the glory of his Father with his Angels; and then he shall reward every man according to his works. | Whosoever therefore shall be ashamed of me and of my words in this adulterous and sinful generation; of him also shall the Son of man be ashamed, when he cometh in the glory of his Father with the holy angels. | For whosoever shall be ashamed of me and of my words, of him shall the Son of man be ashamed, when he shall come in his own glory, and in his Father's, and of the holy angels. |
| Verily I say unto you, there be some standing here, which shall not taste of death, till they see the Son of man coming in his kingdom. | And he said unto them, Verily I say unto you, That there be some of Them that stand here which shall not taste of death, till they have seen the kingdom of God come with power. | But I tell you of a truth, there be some standing here, which shall not taste of death, till they see the kingdom of God. |

---

coming was expressly declared by our Saviour to be *near*. Lange justly remarks that the words, μέλλει γάρ, are 'emphatically placed at the beginning of the sentence; not a simple future, but meaning, The event is impending that He shall come; He is about to come.' [See Lange in loc.]...The inference therefore is, that the

---

nigh.'" John Lightfoot, "Sermon on James 5:9" in *The Whole Works of the Rev. John Lightfoot,* ed. John Rogers Pitman, 13 vols. (London: 1822), 6:380. Take note of what John writes: "we saw His glory, glory as of the only *Son* from the Father, full of grace and truth" (John 1:14). Seeing Jesus' "glory" is not an end-time event. When Jesus acted, his "glory" was seen. The same is true when He came in judgment against Jerusalem that resulted in the destruction of the temple and the scattering of the Jews who remained in the city.

Parousia, or glorious coming of Christ, was declared by Himself to fall within the limits of the then existing generation,—a conclusion which we shall find in the sequel to be abundantly justified."

Milton Terry offers the following parallel chart and commentary:

| Matt. 16:27-28 | Mark 8:38-9:1 | Luke 9:26-27 |
|---|---|---|
| "For the Son of man is about to come in the glory of His Father with His angels and WILL THEN REPAY EVERY PERSON ACCORDING TO HIS DEEDS. Truly I say to you, there are some of those who are standing here who will not taste death until they see the Son of Man coming in His kingdom." | "For whoever is ashamed of Me and My words in this adulterous and sinful generation, the Son of Man will also be ashamed of him when He comes in the glory of His Father with the holy angels." And Jesus was saying to them, "Truly I say to you, there are some of those who are standing here who will not taste death until they see the kingdom of God when it has come with power." | "For whoever is ashamed of Me and My words, the Son of Man will be ashamed of him when He comes in His glory, and the glory of the Father and of the holy angels. But I say to you truthfully, there are some of those standing here who will not taste death until they see the kingdom of God." |

All sorts of efforts have been made to evade the simple meaning of these words but they all spring from the dogmatic prepossession that the coming of the Son of man in his glory must needs be an event far future from the time when the words were spoken. Some have understood that the reference is to the transfiguration which all three synoptists record immediately afterward. But two decisive objections stand in the way of such a reference: (1) that event occurred only six or eight days afterward, and (2) it could not with any propriety be called a coming of the Son of man in the glory of his Father with the angels, or coming in his kingdom. Others have distinguished between Christ's coming in the glory of his Father with the angels and his coming in his kingdom or the coming of his kingdom. But we incline to the belief that very few can be fully persuaded, with the above Gospel-parallels before them, that our Lord meant to be understood as speaking of two events centuries apart. Had this been his intention he might certainly have employed language less ambiguous and less likely to confuse the minds of his disciples. The plain teaching of the passage is that before some of those who heard him speak should die the Son of man would come in glory, and his kingdom would be established in power. And this teaching is in strict accord with what is taught in Matt xxiv and its parallels in Mark and Luke.[28]

As the above comments show, Gentry's argument does not hold water. There are many fine commentators who interpret Matthew 16:27 as an indicator of an "about to" coming that's linked with 16:28. Albert Pigeon's 13-page list of commentators on how they translate and interpret *mellō* shows that there is a diversity of opinion on the interpretation of Matthew 16:27. There is a comprehensive study of this topic in Andrew Perriman's book *The Coming of the Son of Man: New Testament Eschatology for an Emerging Church* (2005). Based on the above works, Matthew 16:27-28 is not a solid argument that two comings separated by nearly 2,000. I've included additional examples below.

## Frederic W. Farrar's *The Early Days of Christianity*[29]

It was to this event, the most awful in history — "one of the most awful eras in God's economy of grace, and the most awful revolution in all God's religious dispensations"[30] — that we must apply those prophecies

---

28. Milton Terry, *Biblical Apocalyptics: A Study of the Most Notable Revelations of God and of Christ* (New York: Eaton & Mains, 1898), 221.

29. (London: Cassell & Company, Limited, 1891), 489.

30. Bp. Warburton's *Julian*, i. p. 21. ["This therefore being one of the most important eras in the economy of grace, and the most awful revolution in all God's religious dispensations; we see the elegance and propriety of the terms in question, to denote *so great an event*, together with the *destruction of Jerusalem*, by which it was effected: for in the whole prophetic language, the change and fall of principalities and powers, whether *spiritual* or *civil*, are signified by the shaking of heaven and earth, the darkening the sun and moon, and the falling of the stars; as the rise and establishment of *new ones* are by processions in the clouds of heaven, by the sound of trumpets, and the assembling together of hosts and congregations [Matt. chap. xxiv]. Thus much, therefore, being premised, we enter directly on our subject; it being now seen, that the truth of Christianity must stand or fall with the ruin or the restoration of the temple at Jerusalem; for if that temple should be rebuilt for the purpose of Jewish worship, Christianity could not support its pretensions; nor the Prophets, nor Jesus, the truth of their predictions." (William Warburton's *Julian* [2nd ed.] in *The Works*

of Christ's coming in which every one of the Apostles and Evangelists describe it as *near at hand.*[31] To those prophecies our Lord Himself fixed these three most definite limitations — the one, that before that generation passed away all these things would be fulfilled;[32] another, that some standing there should not taste death till they saw the Son of Man coming in His kingdom;[33] the third, that the Apostles should not have gone over the cities of Israel till the Son of Man be come.[34] It is strange that these distinct limitations should not be regarded as a decisive proof that the Fall of Jerusalem was, in the fullest sense, the Second Advent of the Son of Man which was primarily contemplated by the earliest voices of prophecy.

## Jay E. Adams' *The Christian Counselor's Commentary: The Gospels of Matthew and Mark*

### MATTHEW 16:27-28

Mention of the future of eternal life and the rewards He will give out at his coming suggests the more immediate coming in 70 AD that some of the disciples would live to see occur. That would be the coming of Christ when His empire would take the place of the Jewish state, eventually to be followed by the overthrow of the Roman Empire (v. 28). Future certainties are the impetus to live as one should in the here and now.[35]

### MARK 8:38-9:1

Having mentioned the coming of Christ **with his holy angels in judgment upon that adulterous and sinful generation** which rejected the son of man who came to redeem his own (8:38). Mark now continues the discussion in the ninth chapter. He declares that **some standing**

---

*of Right Reverand William Warburton*, 12 vols. (London: 1811), 8:47-48.]

31. Acts ii. 16-20, 40; iii. 19-21; 1 Thes. iv. 13-17 ; v. 1-16; 2 Thess. i. 7-10; 1 Cor. i:7; x:11; xv. 21; xvi. 22 ; Rom. xiii 11, 12; Phil. iii. 20; iv. 6; 1 Tim. iv. 1 ; 2 Tim. Iii. 1; Heb. i. 2; x. 25, 37; James v. 3, 8, 9; 1 Pet. ii. 7; 2 Pet. iii 12; 1 J. ii. 18.

32. Matt. xxiv. 34.

33. Matt. xvi. 28.

34. Matt. x. 23.

35. *The Christian Counselor's Commentary: The Gospels of Matthew and Mark* (Woodruff, SC: Timeless Texts, 1999), 138.

**there** would not die before that judgment of apostate Judaism would occur at the **coming** of the new **empire of God in power**. Of course, this happened in 70 AD. Many counselees refuse to listen to warnings of this sort about the greater judgment yet to come. If biblical warnings are ignored it is at the peril of those in the generation when it occurs.[36]

## Spiro Zodhiates, *Evangelical Commentary on Matthew*[37]

For the Son of man **is about** [*mellei*, the present infinitive of *mellō*..., to be imminent] **to come** [*erchesthai*, the present infinitive of *erchomai*...] in the glory of His Father with his angels....

## Michael Wilkins, "Matthew," *The Holman Commentary on the Bible*[38]

Behind the expression "is going to come" (16:27) is the verb *mellō*, meaning I am about to come," which is ambiguous regarding timing. It can indicate something that is going to be undertaken soon. For example, if it is used in the predictions of Jesus' forthcoming crucifixion (17:12, 22; 20:22), and it was earlier used to refer to Herod's impending search fort the baby Jesus (2:13) and to announce the arrival of John the Baptist as the prophesied Elijah (11:14). But the verb can also refer to an indeterminate time, such as the time of judgment that John the Baptist said was "about to come" (3:7), the age to come (12:32), or the wars and rumors of wars that the disciples were about to hear throughout this age until the end (24:6).

## Samuel Lee, *Eschatology, Or, the Scripture Doctrine of the Coming of the Lord, the Judgment, and the Resurrection*[39]

Here are two facts that have greatly embarrassed commentators:

---

36. *The Christian Counselor's Commentary: The Gospels of Matthew and Mark.*

37. Chattanooga, TN: AMG Publishers, 2006.

38. *The Holman Commentary on the Bible: The Gospels* gen. ed. Jeremy Royal Howard (Nashville, TN: Broadman & Holmam Publishing Group, 2013), 278.

39. Samuel Lee, *Eschatology; or, The Scripture Doctrine of The Coming of the Lord, the Judgment, and the Resurrection* (Boston: J. E. Tilton and Co., 1859), 17-19, 251. Also see pages 124-125 and 251. Republished by American Vision (2025).

1. The Son of Man would *soon*,—during the life of some who heard him,—come in his kingdom—in the glory of his Father with his angels. "Shall come," μέλλει ἔρχεσθαι, *is now about to come.*

2. His "coming" would imply his elevation to the office of Judge of all men. "Then," that is, when he comes and receives his kingdom, he would reward *every man* according to his works....

To make these verses refer to the "Final Judgment," considered as a great fact coming in immediate sequence to the "end of the world," and the closing up of the history of the race on the earth, is to violate the plainest laws of language. More than eighteen hundred years [now nearly 2,000] have elapsed since this language was uttered, and the world is now standing and the Judgment therefore yet future.... So that he has judged men—given them not only law but award, ever since he was constituted "the Son of God in power," or, in his own words (Matt. 16:27), "rewarded every man according to his works."

## Peter J. Leithart, *The Gospel of Matthew Through New Eyes: Jesus as Israel*[40]

[T]he Son of Man will eventually come to "recompense every man according to his doing" (Matt. 16:27; cf. Psalm 62:12). Jesus assures the disciples that this vindication will come within the lifetime of some of the disciples (Matt. 16:28)."

## Thomas Stackhouse, *New History of the Holy Bible from the Beginning of the World to the Establishment of Christianity*[41]

Our Savior's Words are these: *Verily I say unto you, there are some of them, who are standing here, who shall not taste of Death, until they see the Son of Man coming in his Kingdom*, Matth. xvi. 28. Some *Interpreters* both *ancient* and *modern*, understand this Passage of our Lord's

---

40. (West Monroe: LA: Athanasius Press, 2018), 2:77.

41. *The History of the Holy Bible from the Beginning of the World to the Establishment of Christianity*..., 2 vols. (London: 1744), 1:1319. Also see the 1817 three-volume edition, 3:142.

*Transfiguration* on the Mount, in which there was some *Glimpse* of *the Glory of his Father*, and the Attendance of *Angels*; but, besides that this happened too soon (no more than six Days) after these Words were spoken, to need the Expression of *some of them not seeing Death* until it came to pass, which must at least denote some Distance of Time; 'tis very plain, that, at this wonderful Sight, none of the three Apostles could behold Christ *coming in his Kingdom*, because his Kingdom did not commence, till after his *Resurrection*, when *all Power both in Heaven and Earth was given him*, Matth. xxviii. 18.

Others imagine that the Passage relates to the great Day of Judgment, because 'tis said, that Christ will *reward every Man according to his Work*, Chap. xvi. 27. But then, on the other Hand, it may be alleged, that there was none in the Company *then standing there*, who was not to die, or to *taste of Death* (which is the *Jewish* Phrase) long before the Coming *of that great and terrible Day of the Lord*: And therefore, others have concluded, that *This Coming of Christ in his Kingdom* relates to another Event, viz. The Destruction of the *Jewish* Church and Nation, wherein our Lord may properly enough be said to *come in the Glory of his Father, and with his Angels, and to reward the Jews in destroying them*, and *Christians* in preserving them, *according to their Works*.

This happened above forty years after our Savior's Death, when some of the Company (as particularly *John the Evangelist* was) might be then alive, and Witnesses of the Accomplishment of our Lord's Menaces against that devoted City and Nation. This is the *popular* Interpretation at present, but I cannot see, why the other Parts of our Saviors' *Exaltation* may not be taken into the Account; for, as he began to enter upon his Kingdom by his *Resurrection*, and *Ascension* into Heaven, for his sending the Holy Ghost upon the *Apostles*, as well as the terrible Judgment, which he brought upon the *Jewish* Nation, may all be looked upon as the Effects and Consequences of his glorious Reign. *Whitby's* and *Beausobre's* Annotations, and *C[h]almer's* Commentary.

| Matt. 16:27-28 | Mark 8:38-9:1 | Luke 9:26 | Matt. 25:31 | Matt. 19:28 | Rev. 1:7 |
|---|---|---|---|---|---|
| "For the Son of man is about to come in the glory of His Father with His angels and then He will reward each according to his works. Assuredly, I say to you, there are some standing here who shall not taste death till they see the Son of Man coming in His kingdom." | "For whoever is ashamed of Me and My words in this adulterous and sinful generation, of him the Son of Man also will be ashamed when He comes in the glory of His Father with the holy angels. And he said to them, Assuredly, I say to you that there are some standing here who will not taste death till they see the kingdom of God present with power." | "Whoever is ashamed of Me and My words, of him the Son of Man will be ashamed when He comes in His *own* glory, and in *His* Father's, and of the holy angels. But I tell you truly, there are some standing here who shall not taste death till they see the kingdom of God." | "When the Son of Man comes in His glory, and all the holy angels with Him, then He will sit on the throne of His glory." | "So Jesus said to them, Assuredly I say to you, that in the regeneration, when the Son of Man sits on the throne of His glory, you who have followed Me will also sit on twelve thrones, judging the twelve tribes of Israel." | "Behold, He comes with the clouds, and every eye shall see Him, even they which have pierced Him, and all the tribes of the land shall wail because of Him. Yea. Amen." |

# CHAPTER 18

# Anti-Postmillennialists Make a Weak Case

There's a scene in the 1993 film *Searching for Bobby Fischer* where Josh Waitzkin, played by Max Pomeranc, is being taught that the complexities of chess require knowing more than where the pieces on the board are at any given moment and what the next move should be. A master chess player should determine "where they will be in one, two, three, and many moves ahead."

Ben Kingsley's character, Bruce Pandolfini, wants Josh to learn to see these necessary moves before he commits his tactical approach. To accomplish this, he sets up the pieces on the board for Josh to show how checkmate can be accomplished in four moves. He tells Josh, "Don't move until you figure it out in your head." Josh says he can't do it unless he can physically move the pieces. Pandolfini tells Josh, "Clear the lines of lint in your head, one at a time, and the king will be left standing alone, like a guy on a street corner. Here, I'll make it easier for you."

He makes it "easier" by sending them tumbling to the floor with his arm, leaving only the empty board for Josh to contemplate over.[1]

After deliberating over the empty 64 squares for a short time, Josh figures it out and tells Pandolfini his first move.

A similar process needs to be performed when dealing with a topic like eschatology in general and postmillennialism in particular. In a way, we are playing with a chessboard that's been set up by competitors and pieces that can only move in terms of pre-mandated rules. Sounds like the effect accomplished by "The Kragle," a weapon used by Lord Business to freeze LEGO world. Eschatologists have the board rigged by gluing down some of the pieces so they can't be moved … or challenged. One of the main stationary pieces is a reliance on Revelation 20 to make it about "the millennium." Does Revelation 20 describe what

---

1. Watch the video clip here: https://youtu.be/QNVWY5jUIbc

283

we think of as a "millennium," a utopian period of good government, great happiness, and prosperity because of the physical presence of Jesus ruling from Jerusalem? The word "millennium" does mean a thousand years, derived from the Latin *mille*, thousand, and *annus*, year. Revelation 20 does not describe what we generally think of as "the millennium" except for the thousand years.

The prophetic chess game must be played around these immovable pieces that from the start seemingly discount postmillennialism based on Revelation 20. In traditional systematic theology and the topic of eschatology, the word "postmillennial" is derived from the belief that Jesus returns after (post) the thousand years of Revelation 20. The better word is "kingdom," "The time has come," Jesus said. "The kingdom of God has come near. Repent and believe the good news!" (Mark 1:14). Was Jesus mistaken? How would that be possible? Was the promise postponed? There is no indication that it was.

Postmillennialists teach that Jesus Christ establishes His kingdom through His preaching and redemptive work beginning in the first century and that He equips Christians with the gospel, empowers the church by the Spirit, and charges the church with the Great Commission (Matt. 28:19) to disciple all nations. This is the message of the Bible. Revelation 20 doesn't describe such a view, and neither does it describe the view that Jesus will reign on the earth for a thousand years. Such beliefs are imported into the chapter. The book of Acts ends with, "Now Paul stayed two full years in his own rented lodging and welcomed all who came to him, preaching the kingdom of God and teaching things about the Lord Jesus Christ with all openness, unhindered" (28:30). Paul did not say anything about a thousand years.

It's unfortunate that so much discussion about the kingdom is obscured by debates about the Revelation 20 and the millennium. Benjamin B. Warfield lamented that nothing "seems to have been more common in all ages of the Church than to frame an eschatological scheme from this passage [Rev. 20], imperfectly understood, and then to impose this scheme on the rest of Scripture *vi et armis* [by force of arms]."[2]

---

2. Benjamin B. Warfield, "The Millennium and the Apocalypse," *The Princeton Theological Review* 2 (October 1904), 3. Reprinted in *Selected Shorter Writings of Benjamin B. Warfield—1*, ed. John E. Meeter (Nutley, NJ: Presbyterian and Reformed, 1970), 356.

It's still necessary, however, to deal with objections to the moniker "postmillennialism" because of so much history with the word. Dr. Greg L. Bahnsen's article "The *Prima Facie* Acceptability of Postmillennialism," that first appeared in *The Journal of Christian Reconstruction: Symposium on the Millennium* in 1976-1977, offers a shortlist of what some critics have said about the acceptability of postmillennialism as a biblical doctrine:

> Alva J. McClain says of postmillennialism: "This optimistic theory of human progress had much of its own way for the half-century ending in World War I of 1914. After that the foundations were badly shaken; prop after prop went down, until today the whole theory is under attack from every side. Devout Postmillennialism has virtually disappeared."[3]

J. Barton Payne's *Encyclopedia of Biblical Prophecy* mentions post-millennialism only once, and only in a footnote which parenthetically declares "two world wars killed this optimism."[4] *Merrill F. Unger dismisses postmillennialism in short order, declaring: "This theory, largely disproved by the progress of history, is practically a dead issue."*[5]

John F. Walvoord told us, "In eschatology the trend away from postmillennialism became almost a rout with the advent of World War II" because it forced upon Christians "a realistic appraisal of the decline of the church in power and influence."[6] *Hence he says that "In the twentieth century the course of history, progress in Biblical studies, and the changing attitude of philosophy arrested its progress and brought about its apparent discard by all schools of theology. Postmillennialism is not a current issue in millenarianism."*[7] *He accuses it of failing to fit the facts of current history, of being unrealistic, and of being outmoded and out of step.*[8]

---

3. "Premillennialism as a Philosophy of History," in W. Culbertson and H. B. Centz, eds., *Understanding the Times* (Grand Rapids: Zondervan Publishing House, 1956), 22.

4. *Encyclopedia of Biblical Prophecy* (New York: Harper and Row, 1973), 596.

5. "Millennium," *Unger's Bible Dictionary* (Chicago: Moody Press, revised 1961), 739.

6. John F. Walvoord, *The Millennial Kingdom* (Grand Rapids: Zondervan Publishing House, 1959), 9.

7. Walvoord, *The Millennial Kingdom*, 9.

8. Walvoord, *The Millennial Kingdom*, 18.

Jay E. Adams (1929-2020), who was a partial preterist and held to the early date for the writing of Revelation,[9] recognizes postmillennialism as a "dead issue" with conservative scholars, since it predicts a golden age while the world awaits momentary destruction; he agrees with the above authors that the "advent of two World Wars ... virtually rang the death knell upon conservative postmillennialism."[10] Adams offers his opinion that [Loraine] Boettner's long-range postmillennialism "is too difficult to grant when Christians must face the fact of hydrogen bombs in the hands of depraved humanity."[11]

Hal Lindsey's *The Late Great Planet Earth* captures well the attitude of these previous writers, stating that "there used to be" a group called "postmillennialists" who were greatly disheartened by World War I and virtually wiped out by World War II. Lindsey's (poorly researched) conclusion is this: "No self-respecting scholar who looks at the world conditions and the accelerating decline of Christian influence today is a 'postmillennialist.'"[12]

Bahnsen described these types of criticisms as "newspaper exegesis," that is, reading the Bible through the lens of current events. First Mussolini and then Hitler was the antichrist. Bar codes (and now QR codes) and computer chips are the mark of the beast. The locusts in Revelation 9:1-12 were Vietnam-war-era helicopters. The following is from a prophecy book written by Hal Lindsey in 1973:

> I have a Christian friend who was a Green Beret in Viet Nam. When he first read this chapter he said, "I know what those are. I've seen hundreds of them in Viet Nam. They're Cobra helicopters! That may be conjecture, but it does give you something to think about! A Cobra helicopter does fit the sound of "many chariots." My friend believes that the means of torment will be a kind of nerve gas sprayed from its tail.[13]

---

9. Jay E. Adams, *Preterism: Orthodox or Unorthodox?* (Stanley, NC: Timeless Texts, 2003).

10. Jay E. Adams, *The Time is at Hand* (Nutley, NJ: Presbyterian and Reformed, 1970), 2.

11. Adams, *The Time is at Hand*, 4. See Loraine Boettner's *The Millennium* first published in 1957 and republished in a revised edition in 1984.

12. Hal Lindsey (with C. C. Carlson), *The Late Great Planet Earth* (Grand Rapids, MI: Zondervan, 1970), 176.

13. Hal Lindsey, *There's a New World Coming: A Prophetic Odyssey* (Santa Ana, CA: Vision House Publishers, 1973), 138-139.

I suspect that over the centuries Bible commentators interpreted much of what we read in Revelation in terms of the news of their own time.[14] Consider just five examples:

- Katharine R. Firth's *The Apocalyptic Tradition in Reformation Britain, 1530-1645* (1979).
- Christopher Hill's *Antichrist in Seventeenth-Century England* (1971).
- David Brady's *The Contribution of British Writers between 1560 and 1830 to the Interpretation of Revelation 13.16-18* (1983).
- James H. Moorhead's *World Without God: Mainstream American Protestant Visions of the Last Things, 1880-1925* (1999).
- Ronald L. Numbers and Jonathan M. Butler, eds., *The Disappointed: Millerism and Millenarianism in the Nineteenth Century* (1987).

There is a long history of forcing prophetic texts from Scripture to fit current events, and there is also a long history of abject failure. For example, John Gill (1697-1771) interpreted the locusts as the main competing religions of his day: "And their faces were as the faces of men; which may be expressive of the affable carriage of Mahomet [Muhammad], and his followers, especially to the Christians, and of his great pretensions to holiness and religion, and of the plausible and insinuating ways, and artful methods, used by him, to gain upon men; and being applied to the clergy of the church of Rome, may denote their show of humanity, and their pretended great concern for the welfare of the souls of men, their flatteries, good words, and fair speeches, with which they deceive the simple and unwary."

The biblical approach is to study how locusts are depicted in the Old Testament and pay attention to the time element in Revelation (e.g., 1:1, 3; 22:10). Sometimes locusts are literal (Ex. 10:4, 12-15) and sometimes symbolic of armies (Judges 6:5; 7:12; Joel 2:4-5). Audience relevance precludes any claim that they are or will be helicopters or millions of drones, otherwise the Bible's revelation was irrelevant for God's people who first received it, and such irrelevance has continued

---

14. Gary DeMar, *Doomsday Déjà Vu: How Prophecy "Experts" Have Led People to Question the Authority of the Bible*: https://bit.ly/3Y1vnNy

for thousands of years, and will continue to be because technology is always changing. If, for example, atomic weapons are what's described in Zechariah 14:12 and 2 Peter 3:12, how were these descriptions to be understood by people who first read these accounts?

John Walvoord's book *Armageddon, Oil and the Middle East Crisis* went through numerous updated editions since it was first published in 1974 with the latest edition's title changed to *Armageddon, Oil, and Terror: What the Bible Says about the Future* (2007). Why was the title changed? Because current events changed.

Imagine what newspaper or internet exegesis would have been like in the first century. Peter and others were beaten and thrown in prison (Acts 4:1-3; 5:17-18). Stephen was martyred (7:54-60). Saul ravaged the church in Jerusalem, "entering house after house; and dragging off men and women" and putting "them in prison" (8:3). James, the brother of John, was executed (12:2-3). Some Jews took an oath to kill Paul (23:12, 30). Paul describes in his second letter to the Corinthians all the anti-postmillennial things that happened to him nearly 2,000 years ago:

> Are they servants of Christ?—I speak as if insane—I more so; in far more labors, in far more imprisonments, beaten times without number, often in danger of death. Five times I received from the Jews thirty-nine *lashes.* Three times I was beaten with rods, once I was stoned, three times I was shipwrecked, a night and a day I have spent in the deep. *I have been* on frequent journeys, in dangers from rivers, dangers from robbers, dangers from *my* countrymen, dangers from the Gentiles, dangers in the city, dangers in the wilderness, dangers on the sea, dangers among false brethren; *I have been* in labor and hardship, through many sleepless nights, in hunger and thirst, often without food, in cold and exposure. Apart from *such* external things, there is the daily pressure on me *of* concern for all the churches. Who is weak without my being weak? Who is led into sin without my intense concern? (11:23-29).

Who could have imagined the impact Christianity would have on the world given the fact that a small band of disciples, most of whom were martyred within 40 years of Jesus' death, resurrection, and ascension, and that Christianity would outlast and supplant the Roman Empire whose accomplishments are now tourist attractions?

Apply the historical criticisms of the above postmillennial critics to 2,000 years of history beginning with the first century and persecution (2 Tim. 3:11), tribulation (1 Thess. 1:5-6), and martyrdom (John 21:18-19). World conditions were not very encouraging when it came to the advance of Christianity through the centuries. If the historical logic of postmillennial (kingdom) critics is sound, there should have been a steady decline of Christianity from day one.

> Christianity has not survived for almost two thousand years because it is culturally irrelevant. It captured and then transformed the dying Roman Empire in the fourth century. It laid the foundations of modern science during the late medieval period (1000-1500), and developed it in the early modern period (1500-1700). Kings governed in the name of Christianity, and others were overthrown in the name of Christianity. It is proper to speak of Christian civilization, but for well over a century, such language has seemed out of date. And so it is, for our civilization today is humanistic, not Christian. This is the heart of mankind's problems.[15]

A few years ago, I spoke at a conference on postmillennialism in Torrance, California, on the topic, "Evidence that Postmillennialists are Winning the Prophecy Debate." I only got through a small portion of what I prepared. Ken Gentry also spoke. Kirk Cameron was there at my invitation. He gave a great talk about his prophetic pilgrimage. Sorry to say, the recording of my talk did not turn out. This is why I bring my own recording devices.

While waiting at the airport to board the redeye back to Atlanta, I came across the following post on Facebook: "Prof. D. J. Engelsma gives a devastating rebuke to the Postmil notion of 'Christianizing the world.'" The poster asked for comments. Here was my first comment: "David Engelsma is fixated on the common grace argument. That's a Christian Reformed Church amillennial problem. Engelsma uses almost no Scripture. His eschatology is closer to dispensationalism."

---

15. Gary North, *Liberating Planet Earth: An Introduction to Biblical Blueprints* (Fort Worth, TX: Dominion Press, 1987), 1-2.

I later added this comment, and for this chapter I've added more:

The Common Grace amils that Engelsma condemns share his prophetic position: "These common grace Dutch scholars and their North American academic disciples have all been amillennialists. As amillennialists, they believe that Satan's earthly kingdom and influence will expand over time until Jesus comes with His angels in final judgment. This assertion of the cumulative, visible triumph of Satan's kingdom in history is inherent in all amillennialism. This view of New Testament era history *defines* amillennialism. Amillennialism, as with premillennialism's view of everything that takes place prior to the millennium, is essentially a reversed form of postmillennialism: *postmillennialism for Satan's kingdom.*"[16] (Gary North, *Millennialism and Social Theory*, 82). This is Engelsma's position as well.

Typically, Englesma spends more time on creeds and confessions than he does on Scripture. Instead of offering a detailed counter exegesis to a preterist interpretation of Matthew 24, he assumes, like dispensationalists, that it is a prophetic description of end-time events: "This interpretation of Matthew 24 is basic to the postmillennial denial of apostasy, Antichrist, and great tribulation for the church in the future," he writes. "For in the light of this explanation of Matthew 24, the postmillennialist goes through the entire New Testament rigorously applying all prediction of such things to the destruction of Jerusalem." When a prophetic passage is about a soon coming judgment, then yes, the AD 70 destruction of Jerusalem is in view, and Prof. Engelsma doesn't give any exegetical evidence to the contrary. He also seems to be unaware of the biblical definition of antichrist (2 John 7), their number, and when they were alive (1 John 2:18, 22).

While creeds and confessions are important, they are not equal to Scripture. The Westminster Confession of Faith Chapter 31 says as much:

III. All synods or councils, since the apostles' times, whether general or particular, may err; and many have erred. Therefore

---

16. Gary North, *Political Polytheism: The Myth of Pluralism* (Tyler, TX: Institute for Christian Economics, 1989), 139.

they are not to be made the rule of faith, or practice; but to be used as a help in both.

In fact, the WCF was changed on an eschatological issue: the antichrist. The original WCF identified the papacy as the antichrist. Here is the original version from Chapter 25:

VI. There is no other head of the Church but the Lord Jesus Christ. Nor can the Pope of Rome, in any sense, be head thereof; but is that Antichrist, that man of sin, and son of perdition, that exalts himself, in the Church, against Christ and all that is called God.

Here's the American revised version:

6. There is no other head of the church but the Lord Jesus Christ. Nor can the pope of Rome, in any sense, be head thereof.

Prof. Engelsma is fond of quoting confessional statements while giving little regard to biblical exegesis in his article "Jewish Dreams" that appeared in the January 15, 1995, issue of *The Standard Bearer*. Have we become Romanists by having tradition interpret Scripture? An article titled "Creedal Amillennialism" argues against postmillennialism by referencing creeds and confessions. It concludes with, "To reject amillennialism, whether for postmillennialism or premillennial-dispensationalism, is necessarily to reject the Reformed creeds. But the Reformed creeds, in this critical matter of the doctrine of the last things and the return of Christ, are biblical."[17] We wouldn't know that by reading his article or the creeds because they don't present any exegesis.

Recently, an article appeared in the theological journal *Themelios* with the title "Postmillennialism: A Biblical Critique"[18] written by Jeremy Sexton. The following is the conclusion to his critique.

In view of the exegetical implausibility, theological shortcomings, and spiritual hazards of postmillennialism, believers should eschew "Jewish dreams that there will be a golden age on earth before the Day of Judgment" (Second Helvetic Confession XI)

---

17. Ron Cammenga, "Creedal Amillennialism": https://bit.ly/4h7HjGf
18. Volume 48, Issue 3 (December 2023): https://bit.ly/3SImupz

and keep a lookout for Christ's imminent[19] second coming (Matt 24:36-25:13; Luke 12:40; Rom 13:12; Jas 5:8; 1 Pet 4:7; 2 Pet 3:12; 1 John 2:18; Rev 1:1, 3; 2:16; 3:11; 22:6-7, 10, 12, 20), knowing that our eschatological "salvation" is ever "ready to be revealed" (1 Pet 1:5). Triumphalist expectations about what must transpire on earth before Jesus comes back diminish the comfort and motivation to godliness that stem from loving and anticipating his near return (Mark 13:32-37; Phil 3:20; 4:5; 1 Thess 1:10; 4:15-18; 5:6-11; 2 Tim 4:8; Titus 2:11-13; Heb 10:24-25; Jas 5:9; 2 Pet 3:10-12; 1 John 3:2-3). As long as the Father continues to delay (Matt 24:48; 25:5, 19; 2 Pet 3:4) the paradoxically fixed day of the parousia (Matt 24:36; Acts 1:7; 17:31) to allow more time for repentance (2 Pet 3:8-9) and to complete the divinely preset amount of suffering and martyrdom assigned to the church (Col 1:24; Rev 6:11), we must hasten that final day by living godly lives (2 Pet 3:11-12).[20] And we must use the borrowed

---

19. "QUESTION. 'Should not the speedy coming of the Lord be anticipated at all times, or as 'possible at any time; that no generation of believers should regard it as impossible in theirs,'" as Archbishop Trench avers?'

ANSWER. Where in the Scriptures is the second coming of the Lord represented as continually imminent, so that it may occur at any moment? It was imminent before A. D. 70, but that does not make it always imminent. If it was imminent then, it is not imminent now. If the expressions and phrases which assert its nearness were true then, they are not true now; and if they are true now, they were not true then. This demonstrates the error of all believers in the future sudden appearance of our Lord, in using terms and phrases to prove its *present* imminence, after the lapse of more than eighteen centuries, which, when employed by our Lord and his apostles, did teach the imminence of his coming. The words 'quickly,' 'at hand,' 'in a little while,' etc., mean *soon* or they do not. If they do, then, as God is faithful, the event came to pass long ago. If they do not, then they are of no possible value to prove it near today. What was true for the apostles may not be true for us. What was applicable to their case may have no application whatever to ours. Good 'ethical' effects can flow only from the truth. It cannot benefit one to believe that the second coming of the Lord is imminent unless in fact it is. Nothing has caused more skepticism than this very insistence on the near approach of the parousia, and the reiterated failure of such prophecies. The infidelity and loss of respect for the Bible on the part of many of the followers of William Miller, when they found that his calculations were fallacious, were fearful. Time after time has been set, only to pass without the event occurring. A Boston paper admitted, years ago, that ten times it had fixed the time for the Lord's coming, and as many times was, of course, disappointed. What can such a course produce in many minds but despondency, and then utter incredulity?" 179-180.

20. Richard J. Bauckham, "The Delay of the Parousia," *TynBul* 31 (1980): 3-36; David

time to deepen and widen the victory of the Great Commission achieved by the apostles, eagerly anticipating the redemption of our bodies and continually praying, "Come, Lord Jesus!" (Rev 22:20; cf. 1 Cor 16:22; Westminster Confession of Faith XXXIII.III).

When I read the author's conclusion, I was immediately struck by how far off-base he is. It's as if he has not done much study of preterist arguments. He mentions Douglas Wilson on Revelation 19 and adds a footnote from Peter J. Leithart's two-volume commentary on Revelation.[21] It's because of his failure to tackle preterist interpretations of Bible prophecy that his critique can only be two legs of a three-legged stool. Timing is everything. Let's begin with 1 Peter 1:5 where we find "the salvation ready to be revealed in the last time." Ready for whom? For Peter's intended audience. What last time? In 1 Peter 4:7 we read, "the end of all things has drawn near [perfect indicative active]." Near for whom? For the recipients of Peter's letter. Note what follows 1 Peter 1:5:

> In this you greatly rejoice, even though **now for a little while**, if necessary, **you** have been distressed by various trials, so that the proof of your faith, being more precious than gold which perishes though tested by fire, may be found to result in praise, glory, and honor at the revelation of Jesus Christ (vv. 6-8).

"A little while" is not sometime in the ongoing distant future.

I don't like the term "postmillennialism" because the moniker depends too much on the millennial language from Revelation 20, specifically, the "one thousand years." As I mentioned earlier in this chapter, I prefer the biblical language of "kingdom" (Mark 1:15; Acts 28:23, 31; Rev. 1:9). In addition, before the kingdom or "the millennium" can be studied, the topic of preterism must be dealt with. Unfortunately, Sexton does not offer a studied evaluation of at least some aspects of preterism, and yet the future of eschatological studies depends on a deep dive into preterism.

---

L. Mathewson, *Where Is the Promise of His Coming? The Delay of the Parousia in the New Testament* (Eugene, OR: Cascade, 2018); Thomas R. Schreiner, *1, 2 Peter, Jude*, NAC 37 (Nashville: B&H, 2003), 389-391.

21. Peter J. Leithart, *Revelation 12-22*, ITC (New York: T&T Clark, 2018), 269-298.

Sexton's arguments are like those of Engelsma who references a few Bible passages, but only as props to support an already accepted confessional statement they believe excludes postmillennialism from the status of orthodoxy. Proof-texting and confession-citing are not substitutes for biblical exegesis.

Engelsma calls postmillennialism a "heresy." Is he willing to include, for example, John Owen, the principal author of the postmillennial Savoy Declaration, Jonathan Edwards, Charles Hodge, A. A. Hodge, B. B. Warfield, Marcellus Kik, and John Murray as heretics because of their postmillennial beliefs?

Consider A. A. Hodge (1823-1886), son of Princeton professor Charles Hodge (1797-1878). The younger Hodge served as Professor in Systematic Theology at Princeton Seminary from 1877 until his death in 1886. He made the case that "the kingdom of God on earth is not confined to the mere ecclesiastical sphere, but aims at absolute universality, and extends its supreme reign over every department of human life."[22] The implications of such a methodology are obvious: "It follows that it is the duty of every loyal subject to endeavour to bring all human society, social and *political*, as well as ecclesiastical, into obedience to its law of righteousness."[23]

In addition, he had no problem teaching that there are *political* implications to the preaching and application of the gospel. Consider the following:

> It is our duty, as far as lies in our power, immediately to organize human society and all its institutions and organs upon a distinctively Christian basis. Indifference or impartiality here between the law of the kingdom and the law of the world, or of its prince, the devil, is utter treason to the King of Righteousness. The Bible, the great statutebook of the kingdom, explicitly lays down principles which, when candidly applied, will regulate the action of every human being in all relations. There can be no compromise. The King said, with regard to all descriptions of moral agents in all spheres of activity, "He that is not with me

---

22. A.A. Hodge, *Evangelical Theology: Lectures on Doctrine* (Carlisle, PA: The Banner of Truth Trust, [1890] 1990), 283.

23. Hodge, *Evangelical Theology*, 283. Emphasis added.

is against me." If the national life in general is organized upon non-Christian principles, the churches which are embraced within the universal assimilating power of that nation will not long be able to preserve their integrity.[24]

In addition to a lack of rigorous exegesis and ignoring Reformed advocates of postmillennialism, Engelsma also fails to reference the Westminster Confession of Faith and its Larger and Shorter catechisms and instead quotes Peter Toon's *interpretation* of the assembly's work. Engelsma is selective in the way he presents the confessional statements of the church. He chooses what suits his purpose.

In the *Larger Catechism* of the WCF the kingship of Christ is said to be evidenced by Christ's "overcoming all their enemies, and powerfully ordering all things for his own glory" (*LC, Q.* 45). Thomas Ridgeley (*c.* 1667-1734), in his massive commentary on the *Larger Catechism*, published between 1731 and 1733, gives a decidedly post-millennial interpretation of the Assembly's position:

We freely own, as what we think agreeable to scripture, that as Christ has, in all ages, displayed his glory as King of the Church, so we have ground to conclude, from scripture, that the administration of his government in this world, before his coming to judgment, will be attended with greater magnificence, more visible marks of glory, and various occurrences of providence, which shall tend to the welfare and happiness of his church, in a greater degree than has been beheld or experienced by it, since it was planted by the ministry of the apostles after his ascension into heaven. This we think to be the sense, in general, of those scriptures, both in the Old and New Testament, which speak of the latter-day glory.[25]

The *Shorter Catechism* is no less postmillennial. "Christ executeth the office of a king, in subduing us to himself, in ruling and defending us, and in restraining and conquering all his and our enemies" (*SC, Q.*

---

24. Hodge, *Evangelical Theology*, 283-284.

25. Thomas Ridgeley, *Commentary on the Larger Catechism*, previously titled *A Body of Divinity: Wherein the Doctrines of the Christian Religion are Explained and Defended, Being the Substance of Several Lectures on the Assembly's Larger Catechism* (Edmonton, AB Canada: Still Waters Revival Books, [1855] 1993), 1:562.

26). The evidence of His exaltation is made visible to His Church when He does "gather and defend his church, and subdue [her] enemies" (*LC, Q.* 54).

The *Larger Catechism* in the second petition of the Lord's Prayer states, "we pray, that the kingdom of sin and Satan may be destroyed, the gospel propagated throughout the world, the Jews called, [and] the fullness of the Gentiles brought in ... and that he would be pleased so to exercise the kingdom of his power in all the world, as may best conduce to these ends" (*LC, Q.* 191).

None of these examples squares with Engelsma's notion that "the church in the end-time will be a persecuted church, not a triumphalist church" (173). Paul says that "all who desire to live godly in Christ Jesus will be persecuted" (2 Tim. 3:12). Just before this verse Paul tells Timothy:

> Just as Jannes and Jambres opposed Moses, so these *men* [see verses 1-7] also oppose the truth, men of depraved mind, rejected in regard to the faith. But **they will not make further progress; for their folly will be obvious to all**, just as Jannes's and Jambres's folly was also. Now you followed my teaching, conduct, purpose, faith, patience, love, perseverance, persecutions, *and* sufferings, such as happened to me at Antioch, at Iconium *and* at Lystra; **what persecutions I endured, and out of them all the Lord rescued me!** (vv. 8-11).

The answer to *LC* Question 191 is almost identical to that of The Savoy Declaration (26.5), which Engelsma condemns! It seems, therefore, that the Helvetic Confession is out of step with the other great confessional statements of the Reformed churches.

Prof. Engelsma insists that passages like Matthew 24, 2 Thessalonians 2, and 2 Timothy 3 address conditions near the time when Jesus returns at the end of history. While this view is popular today, especially among dispensationalists, it cannot survive exegetical scrutiny. There is a great deal of biblical and historical evidence to demonstrate that these passages refer to conditions leading up to and including the destruction of Jerusalem in AD 70.

Postmillennialists do not do their work in an exegetical vacuum. I devoted hundreds of pages of detailed exegesis to Matthew 24-25 in *Last Days Madness* and Matthew 24:1-34 in *Wars and Rumors of*

*Wars*. More than fifty pages were devoted to 2 Thessalonians 2 in *Last Days Madness*. I also discuss Titus 2:13 in detail. In each case I showed that these passages, and many more like them, refer to events of the first century. Moreover, I was able to demonstrate that numerous non-postmillennial Bible commentators agree with me.

Prof. Engelsma claims that the solemn duty of the Protestant Reformed Churches "from the soon-coming Christ [is] to expose the hopes of postmillennialism as 'Jewish dreams,'" language taken from the amillennial Helvetic Confession of Faith. The "soon-coming Christ"? Prof. Engelsma sounds more like Hal Lindsey, Dave Hunt, and Tim LaHaye than a Reformed Christian when he concludes his article with these words.

> Be prepared for the Antichrist!
> Hope for the second coming of Christ!
> Hope *only* for the second coming of Christ!

So, if a new Hitler rises, "Hope *only* for the second coming of Christ!" Don't work to keep him from rising or stop him if he and his minions gain control? Englesma doesn't seem to understand the biblical definition of antichrist (1 John 2:22; 2 John 7), how there were many of them alive in John's day. Their existence was evidence that "it was the last hour" (1 John 2:18). Jesus said that the day and hour of His judgment coming before that generation passed away was unknown (Matt. 24:36), but the generation was known; it was that Apostolic generation (24:34).

Dave Hunt, an anti-Reformed author, wrote *How Close Are We?: Compelling Evidence for the Soon Return of Christ* in 1993 that's still in print. The church has been preaching the "soon-return of Christ" for centuries. This doctrine has been the bane of Reformed theology, the benefit of dispensationalism, and the ruin of our nation.

Jesus said that He would return in judgment before the last apostle died (Matt. 16:27-28; cf. John 21:18-23). Jesus promised His disciples that He would return in judgment to destroy the temple before their generation passed away (Matt. 24:1-2, 34). The Thessalonians knew the identity of the man of lawlessness and the restrainer. The man of lawlessness was restrained in Paul's day and ("you know what restrains him **now**"), "the mystery of lawlessness is **already at work**," and the temple that was destroyed in AD 70 was still standing, Paul wrote

(2 Thess. 2:6-7). The "is" was then. It is evident, therefore, that Paul described events that the Thessalonians were familiar with.

Revelation 1:1 and 22:6 state that the events laid out in Revelation "must shortly take place." The time was said to be "near" (1:3; 22:10) for those who first read the apocalypse (Ἀποκάλυψις/*Apokalypsis*). "Must shortly take place" for whom? Jesus said that He was coming "quickly" (22:7). Not just fast when He comes, but quickly in terms of the meaning of the word "near," confirmed with what was said in the first chapter, "the time is near" (22:10). Revelation was written nearly two-thousand years ago. If words mean anything, then the events of Revelation are now history.

Prof. Engelsma can follow the dispensationalists and claim that these time indicators are fluid and do not necessarily mean what they seem to mean, or he can deal with them honestly and get back to doing exegetical work and quit relying on the confessions to do his thinking for him. Until Prof. Engelsma deals with *exegetical* issues, the only ones who will listen to him will be those who already agree with him, a number that is steadily declining in his tiny denomination.

"Jewish dreams" are what the Jews in Jesus' day had. They wanted a war-like conquering Messiah who would set the world right by force. Postmillennialism knows of no such Messiah.

CHAPTER 19

# Are Luke 17 and Matthew 24 Describing Two Comings of Jesus?

A post on a Facebook page had an interesting discussion on Luke 17 and its relationship to Matthew 24-25 and Greg L. Bahnsen's view of that relationship. Dr. Bahnsen took the view that Luke 17:22-37 refers to the Second Coming while Matthew 24:1-34 refers to the judgment on Jerusalem that took place before that first-century generation passed away (24:34). Kenneth Gentry agrees with Dr. Bahnsen. According to Bahnsen and Gentry, verses after Matthew 24:35 refer to the Second Coming.

This is not a new debate. A great deal of material related to eschatology has resurfaced thanks to the internet. For example, miah Nisbett (d. 1812) dealt with the relationship between Luke 17 and Matthew 24 in *The Triumphs of Christianity over Infidelity Displayed* (1797/1802).[1] See his parallel chart at the end on this chapter (313).

I discuss the argument of a division in Matthew 24 separating events related to the destruction of Jerusalem in AD 70 and the claim that verse 35 serves as a transition text to a prophecy related to physical coming of Jesus that is still to take place. Since I cover the content of this view in my book *Last Days Madness*, I won't repeat all that I've written there. It is important to note that one of the reasons I believe Luke 17 and Matthew 24 through verse 41 are describing the same event—the judgment on Jerusalem and not the Second Coming—is the ordering of specific prophetic events related to Matthew 24:35-36:

> Heaven and earth will pass away, but my words will not pass away. But of that day and hour no one knows, not even the angels of heaven, nor the Son, but the Father alone.[2]

---

1. https://bit.ly/3MN0eII
2. Adam Clarke comments, that "nor the Son" is "taken in a *causative, declarative,* or

299

Bahnsen and Gentry argue, along with many others, that verse 35 refers to the physical heaven and earth while I and others believe it refers to the covenant relationship with Israel (e.g., Isa. 51:15-16; Jer. 4:23-31) described as heaven and earth.

John Gill shows why there is no transition to the end of the world after Matthew 24:36:

> **"But of that day and hour knoweth no man:** Which is to be understood, not of the second coming of Christ, the end of the world, and the last judgment; but of the coming of the son of man, to take vengeance on the Jews, and of their destruction; for the words manifestly regard the date of the several things going before, which only can be applied to that catastrophe, and dreadful desolation: now, though the destruction itself was spoken of by Moses and the prophets, was foretold by Christ, and the believing Jews had some discerning of its near approach; see (Hebrews 10:25) yet the exact and precise time was not known: it might have been: calculated to a year by Daniel's weeks, but not to the day and hour; and therefore our Lord does not say of the year, but of the day and hour no man knows; though the one week, or seven years, being separated from the rest, throws that account into some perplexity; and which perhaps is on purpose done, to conceal the precise time of Jerusalem's destruction: nor need it be wondered at, notwithstanding all the hints given, that the fatal day should not be exactly known beforehand; when those who have lived since, and were eyewitnesses of it, are not agreed on what day of the month it was; for, as Dr. Lightfoot observes, Josephus [*De Bello Jud.* l. 6. c. 26.] says, "that the temple perished the 'tenth' day of 'Lous,' a day fatal to the temple, as having been on that day consumed in flames, by the king of Babylon."[3]

---

*permissive* sense; and that it means here, *make known*, or *promulge*, as it is to be understood in 1 Corinthians 2:2 ["For I determined to know nothing among you except Jesus Christ, and Him crucified"]. This intimates that this secret was not to be *made known*, either by *men* or *angels*, no, not even by the Son of man himself; but it should be *made known* by the Father only, in the execution of the purposes of his *justice*. I am afraid this only *cuts* the knot, but does not *untie* it." Adam Clarke, "Mark," *Clarke's Commentaries*, Mark 13:32.

3. John Gill, *Exposition of the Bible* (Matthew 24:36). Also, "V. 36.—*But of that day—*

The following comments from other commentators show that there is no multi-millennial gap after Matthew 24:34 that leads to the dissolution of the physical cosmos or minimally Planet Earth and its attendant atmosphere:

> Verse 36. 'Of that day and hour knoweth no man, no, not the angels of heaven, but my Father only.' St. Mark has it: 'Neither the Son, but the Father;' but the sense is the same. Some men of great learning and eminence have thought that our Lord is here speaking, not of the destruction of Jerusalem, but of that more solemn and awful one of the day of judgment. But I can by no means think that the Evangelists are such loose, inaccurate writers, as to make so sudden and abrupt a transition, as they are here supposed to do; much less to break through the fundamental rules of good writing, by apparently referring to something which they had said before; when in reality they were beginning a new subject, and the absurdity of the supposition will appear more strongly, if it is recollected that the question of the disciples was, 'When shall these things be?' 'Why,' says our Saviour, 'of that day and hour knoweth no man, no, not the angels of heaven, but my Father only.'"[4]

*****

To suppose, on the contrary, that these verses were intended to describe *the final Judgment of the world*, is indeed violently to sever them from their manifest connection — not only with

---

*knoweth no man,*] Deut. 32:34. Lightfoot. Τῆς ἡμέρας ἐκείνης, it is shown by Hammond in a note on Heb. 10:25. refers in very many passages to the day of this destruction of the Jews. Zech. 14:1. gives the force of the expression. See Luke 17:24. 30. 19:43. Acts 2:20. 1 Cor. 1:7, 8. 3:13. 1 Thess. 5:2. 2 Thess. 1:10. 2 Pet. 1:19. 3:10. Rom. 13:11. 1 John 2:18. compare ver. 34. of this chapter. It may have a respect also to the day of judgment. The day and hour means the precise time. The general time of the destruction was certainly known to our Lord. Hammond. Le Clerc." Heneage Elsley, *Annotations on the Four Gospels, and the Acts of the Apostles*: Compiled and Abridged for the Use of Students, 5th ed. (London: C. & J. Rivington, 1824), 1:391.

4. miah A. Nisbett, *The Triumphs of Christianity over Infidelity Displayed; Or the Coming of the Messiah, the True Key to the Right Understanding of the Most Difficult Passages in the New Testament... A Full Answer to the Objection of Mr. Gibbon, That Our Lord and His Apostles Predicted the Near Approach of the End of the World in Their Own Times* (Printed for the Author by J. Atkinson [1797] 1802), 30.

the preceding verses — but, as will presently appear, from the subsequent context; which, in the strongest terms which language can convey, asserts that all the things which he had before been describing, would be in *that generation*. It would be to violate all the rules of probability and just criticism and to charge the Evangelical Historians with such a confusion of ideas and such a perversion of language as would render them utterly unworthy of any regard; for, as the learned University Preacher has very justly observed—"whenever the same word is used in the same sentence—or in different sentences, not far distant from each other; we ought to interpret it precisely, in the same sense, unless either that sense should involve a contradiction of ideas—or the Writer expressly inform us that he repeats the word in a fresh acceptation."[5]

Adam Clarke agrees with the above assessment:

> **But of that day and hour]** ωρα, here, is translated *season* by many eminent critics, and is used in this sense by both sacred and profane authors. As the *day* was not known, in which Jerusalem should be invested by the Romans, therefore our Lord advised his disciples to pray that it might not be on a *Sabbath*; and as the *season* was not known, therefore they were to pray that it might not be in the *winter*; Mt 24:20.[6]

John Owen comes to a similar conclusion:

> We are thrown back again upon the context to determine its reference, and that, as we have seen, points clearly to his coming to destroy Jerusalem. That the precise time of this event is referred to, is evident from the words *that day and hour*, as we say the *hour and minute* (Alford). Our Lord had predicted in general terms his coming to destroy Jerusalem. It was to be soon. The race of men then living [Matt. 24:33-34], were not all to pass away before its accomplishment. But the precise day and hour was known only to Him, with whom the future was as the past. The disciples were not, therefore, to expect any more

---

5. Nisbett, *Triumphs of Christianity*, 112.
6. Adam Clarke, "Matthew," *Clarke's Commentaries*.

definite revelation in respect to the precise time, than what had just been given in v. 34.[7]

Similar to the way the dissolution of the old heavens and earth referred to the Old Covenant world of Judaism, the creation of the new heavens and new earth described in Isaiah 65:17-25 and Revelation 21-22 do not refer to the creation of a new physical creation, a depiction of the eternal state, since women are still giving birth and people continue to die (65:20). This is an old and respected view taught by John Owen,[8] John Lightfoot, John Brown, among others. Here's Lightfoot's interpretation:

> That the destruction of Jerusalem is very frequently expressed in Scripture as if it were the destruction of the whole world, Deuteronomy 32:22; "A fire is kindled in mine anger, and shall burn unto the lowest hell" (the discourse there is about the wrath of God consuming that people; see verses 20, 21), "and shall consume the earth with her increase, and set on fire the foundations of the mountains." Jeremiah 4:23; "I beheld the earth, and lo, it was without form and void; and the heavens, and they had no light," &c. The discourse there also is concerning the destruction of that nation, Isaiah 65:17; "Behold, I create new heavens and a new earth: and the former shall not be remembered," &c. And more passages of this sort among the prophets. According to this sense, Christ speaks in this place; and Peter speaks in his Second Epistle, third chapter; and John, in the sixth of the Revelation; and Paul, 2 Corinthians 5:17 ["Therefore if anyone is in Christ, *he is* a new creation; the old things passed away; behold, new things have come"], &c.

Paul's comment that the person who undergoes the new birth—being "born from above" (John 3:3)—is a "new creation" does not describe a physical change in the Christian. He or she is the same physically but renewed redemptively. The same is true of what we find in Revelation 21 as Gentry points out:

---

7. John J. Owen, *Commentary on Matthew and Mark* (New York: Leavitt & Allen, 1864), 325.

8. John Owen, "Providential Changes, An Argument for Universal Holiness," in William H. Goold, ed., *The Works of John Owen*, 16 vols. (London: The Banner of Truth Trust, 1965-68), 9:134.

In Revelation 21-22 we find much spiritual new-creation imagery reflecting the original historical creation. John presents this spiritual new creation in terms of the original physical Edenic beginning. He includes a new heaven and earth (21:1; Ge 1:1), a bride (21:2; Ge 2:22-24), a river (22:1; Ge 2:10), fruit trees (22:2; Ge 1:11), and so forth. Without a doubt Isaiah 65:17 (and 66:2) stands "behind the wording of Rev. 21:1" (Beale 1041): **Then I saw a new heaven and a new earth** (21:1a). Isaiah's passage reads: "For behold, I create new heavens and a new earth; / And the former things will not be remembered or come to mind."

*****

Furthermore, John seems clearly to pull Isaiah's context into his presentation. Immediately after Isaiah 65:17, the prophet refers to Jerusalem (v. 18) as does John in Revelation 21:2. And Isaiah 65:19b declares "there will no longer be heard in her / The voice of weeping and the sound of crying," which parallels Revelation 21:4. Thus, "there is unanimous agreement among scholars" that Revelation 21:1 reflects Isaiah's famous passage (Mathewson 33). That being so, we must recognize that Isaiah 65:17 speaks of pre-eternal, redemptive glory *in history*. Thus, Isaiah is picturing the coming of the new-covenant era. Note that though God creates a new heavens and a new earth, Isaiah also mentions aspects of this new order that cannot apply to the eternal realm. There will be infants, which necessitates birth (contra Mt 22:30ff).

*****

If Isaiah can use the new-creation motif to describe Israel's historical exodus from Babylon, surely John can do so for new covenant Christianity's exodus from Judaism to form the new covenant body.[9]

Following Gentry, the use of "heaven and earth" does not always refer to the physical heaven and earth. Similarly, in Matthew 5:18 Jesus said not a single jot or tittle of the law would pass away if heaven and earth

---

9. Kenneth L. Gentry, Jr., *The Divorce of Israel: A Redemptive-Historical Interpretation of Revelation* 2 vols. (Vallecito, CA: Chalcedon and Tolle Lege, 2024), 2:1620-1622 .

remained. But we know from what we read in the letter to the Hebrews that much of what is designated as the ceremonial law was in the process of passing away (Heb. 8:13). This means that Jesus in Matthew 5:18 and 24:35-36 most likely was not referring to the dissolution of the physical heavens and earth and the renewal of the same. The following is from John Brown:

> If the words [of Jesus in Matthew 5:17-19], however, are carefully examined, they will be found to contain in them, not an indefinite declaration of the inviolable authority of the law, but a declaration of the inviolable authority till a certain period, till certain events had taken place,—"till heaven and earth pass,"—"till all things be fulfilled." "Heaven and earth passing away," understood literally, is the dissolution of the present system of the universe, and the period when that is to take place, is called the "end of the world." But a person at all familiar with the phraseology of the Old Testament Scriptures, knows that the dissolution of the Mosaic economy, and the establishment of the Christian, is often spoken of as the removing of the old earth and heavens, and the creation of a new earth and new heavens.[10]

To be clear, Gentry does not agree with this conclusion since he maintains that 2 Peter 3:10-13 refers to the actual burning and melting of the physical heavens and earth. For a contrary view, see David Chilton and Gary DeMar "What Does Peter Mean by the Passing Away of Heaven and Earth?: A Study of 2 Peter 3."[11]

It's significant that if there is no gap in time after Matthew 24:36 where events are yet to be fulfilled, the verses that follow track chronologically and are part of the previous signs of the discourse. This means that rest of the events in chapter 24, and in my estimation all of chapter 25, apply to the same generational judgment that were fulfilled before that generation passed away. We can see this when we turn to Luke 17:22-37 where identical signs are found that line up with what we find in Matthew 24. The difference between Matthew 24 and

---

10. John Brown, *Discourses and Sayings of Our Lord* (Edinburgh: The Banner of Truth Trust, [1852] 1990), 1:171-172.

11. bit.ly/48qHerH

Luke 17 is the order of the events in relation to Matthew 24:35-36, a characteristic of the passages that are difficult to explain if the order of events is important. Bahnsen and Gentry do not consider the ordering of events to be significant since Matthew and Luke often differ. I and others disagree.

Taking Matthew 24 as the standard, Luke places the Noah's ark analogy (Luke 17:26-27) found in Matthew 24:37-39 before the events of Matthew 24:17-18 ("let him who is on the housetop not go down"), verse 27 ("for just as the lightning comes from the east"), and verse 28 ("wherever the corpse is, there the vultures will gather").

If the five prophetic events of Matthew 24 found in Luke 17:22-37 are numbered 1-2-3-4-5, Luke's numbering of the same events would be 2-4-1-5-3. It seems odd that Jesus would mix the events of two comings separated by 2000 years in the same discourse. How confusing it would have been for those who first heard and later read what Jesus said later in the 21st chapter of Luke's Gospel. The chart on the next page (307) offers some visual help. Note that sections 2 and 4 from Luke 17 appear before Matthew 24:35-36.

J. Marcellus Kik, in his book *Matthew 24*, and Gentry and Bahnsen maintain that Matthew 24:35-36 are transitional texts that separate the judgment coming of Jesus of that generation (24:1-34) from the Second Coming (24:36-25:46). That can't be if Jesus places the events of Luke 17:23-24 and 26-27 before the supposed dissolution of heaven and earth.

Dr. Bahnsen's most significant argument is his interpretation of Luke 17:22 is that those in Jesus' audience would "long to see one of the days of the Son of Man, and you [referring to them] will not see it." Bahnsen says that this differs from what we find Jesus saying in Matthew 24 where we read that "relief WILL be granted, for the elect's sake" since the tribulation will be shortened. In Luke's version, "although people WANT the relief, it will not be given." This last phrase applies to those who rebelled against Roman and got caught in the conflagration. Those who believed Jesus and acted on His words fled to the mountains (Matt. 24;16; Luke 21:20-21).

The context of Luke 17:22-37 is found in verses 20-21 when the Pharisees questioned Jesus about "when the kingdom of God was coming." Jesus answered, "The kingdom of God is not coming with signs to be observed; nor will they say, 'Look, here' or, 'There!' For

# Are Luke 17 and Matthew 24 Describing Two Comings of Jesus?

## Matthew 24:1-41

## Luke 17:20-37

**1**

"Whoever is on the housetop must not go down to get the things out that are in his house. Whoever is in the field must not turn back to get his cloak" (24:17-18).

**2**

"They will say to you, 'Look there! Look here!' Do not go away, and do not run after them. For just like the lightning, when it flashes out of one part of the sky, shines to the other part of the sky, so will the Son of Man be in His day" (17:23-24).

**2**

"So if they say to you, 'Behold, He is in the wilderness, do not go out, or, 'Behold, He is in the inner rooms, do not believe them For just as the lightning comes from the east and flashes even to the west, so will the coming of the Son of Man be" (24:26-27).

**4**

"And just as it happened in the days of Noah, so it will be also in the days of the Son of Man: they were eating, they were drinking, they were marrying, they were being given in marriage, until the day that Noah entered the ark, and the flood came and destroyed them all" (17:26-27).

**3**

"Wherever the corpse is, there the vultures will gather" (24:28).

> Heaven and earth will pass away, by My words will not pass away. But of that day and hour no one knows, not even the angels of heaven, nor the Son, but the Father alone." (Matt. 24:35-36)

**4**

"For the coming of the Son of Man will be just like the days of Noah. For as in those days before the flood they were eating and drinking, marrying and giving in marriage, until the day that Noah entered the ark, and they did not understand until the flood came and took them all away; so will the coming of the Son of Man be" (24:37-39).

**1**

"On that day, the one who is on the housetop and whose goods are in the house must not go down to take them out; and likewise the one who is in the field must not turn back. (17:31)

**5**

"There will be two women grinding at the same place; one will be taken and the other will be left. Two men will be in the field; one will be taken and the other will be left" (17:35-36).

**5**

"Then there will be two men in the field; one will be taken and one will be left. Two women will be grinding at the mill; one will be taken and one will be left" (24:40-41).

**3**

"And answering they said to Him, Where, Lord?' And He said to them, Where the body is, there also the vultures will be gathered" (17:37).

behold, the kingdom of God is in your midst." Others translate the phrase as "within you." Either way, it was a present reality. Darrel L. Bock notes:

> "[T]the kingdom of God is in your midst." This phrase is one of the most discussed in Luke's Gospel. It is one of the few statements of Jesus that puts the kingdom in the present. In fact, so unprecedented is this statement that some argue the idea is really futuristic. The idea is, The kingdom is as good as present, since I am here. You need not miss it when it comes (Nolland[12] 1993:853-54; Mattill[13] 1979:198-201).

> But a futuristic meaning is unlikely here. The verb that normally takes a futuristic present is *erchomai,* not *eimi,* which is the verb in verse 21. Thus Luke's shift of verbs in this context is significant, as is his shift of tenses. Moreover, the verb is placed in an emphatic position in the Greek text. More important, the remark about signs in verses 20-21 is specifically denied if a future sense exists, for Jesus appears to go on and enumerate the signs![14]

Joel McDurmon's comments do a good job explaining the historical and theological context:

> The question shows that the Pharisees had understood Jesus to be preaching about something imminent for them. Jesus' interactions with them up to this point all indicated a great change, a great division, a coming judgment. He had even rebuked the people explicitly earlier for not discerning the times (12:54-59), He preached parables about the Kingdom (13:18-21), and He had warned them all about being locked out of the Kingdom while others had entered (13:28-29). He, in fact, had just rebuked a group of Pharisees for not discerning the

---

12. John Nolland, *Luke 9:21-18:34,* Word Biblical Commentary (Dallas: Word, 1993), vol. 35B, 858.

13. A.J. Mattill, Jr., *Luke and the Last Things: A Perspective for the Understanding of Lukan Thought* (Dillsbor, NC: Western North Carolina Press, 1979), 198-201.

14. Darrell L. Bock, *Luke,* The IVP New Testament Commentary Series (Downers Grove, IL: InterVarsity Press, 1994), Lk 17:20-37.

nature of the Kingdom which had been preached since John the Baptist (16:16-17). So they were certainly on the right subject.

But just like so much of what they did in relation to Jesus, they proved that they missed the point of His teaching. The Kingdom of God had been preached since John, not because it was yet to come, but *because He was here now.* There was a great momentous event on the near horizon, true, but this was not the coming of the Kingdom. Jesus made it clear much earlier in this journey that with Him the Kingdom had in fact arrived: "But if it is by the finger of God that I cast out demons, then the Kingdom of God *has come upon you*" (Luke 11:20). Now He reminds the Pharisees of this reality again: "the kingdom of God is in the midst of you" (17:21). But He does not correct their misunderstanding of the thing they could watch out for, they could observe, and which would come upon them outwardly in the near future—the destruction of Jerusalem. For this warning, He turns again privately to His disciples (17:22ff). Why? Because the Pharisees were too blind to see Him; they would remain in their blindness and fall under judgment. Jesus' withholding of information from them goes right back to the whole idea of speaking in parables: the non-elect were not allowed to understand, and not allowed to receive the clear witness of the truth (Luke 8:9-10, 18). They were *appointed* to destruction (Jude 4)....

[T]he disciples receive special instruction as to the nature of the *visible* coming judgment. Many will be looking for Christ after Christ is gone (thus there would be many false Christs in that interim period, Matt. 24:5; Luke 21:8), and of all people who had a keen interest in His arrival, the disciples would be most anxious, for they would be among the few who knew for sure He was coming back in their lifetimes. So Jesus makes sure to insulate them against false Christs. He does this by teaching them about the true nature of the coming destruction He has been preaching about [in Luke 17:22-37]....

[Noah and Lot] were forewarned men who were prepared for a coming judgment and got out when the time came. The others were all taken by surprise by a massive cataclysmic judgment. Here Jesus sees fit to give His disciples this warning, but not unto the multitudes or the Pharisees. This was a warning to the elect remnant only, for only they would get out."

In addition to this lesson which we have already covered earlier, it is important to note Jesus' prediction, "But first he must suffer many things and be rejected by this generation" (17:25). This verse will have great importance later when we hear Jesus referring again to "this generation." To those who may be tempted to argue there that "this generation" refers to something other than the generation to whom Jesus was speaking—something more general or more future—the context here in Luke 17:25 makes it clear that Jesus' "this generation" would be the same generation which rejected Him and caused Him to suffer.

The main lesson here, however, is to the disciples: the day of the Son of Man will not require strained observation or secret knowledge of His whereabouts. Rather, it would be as visible and clear to everyone as lightning streaking all the way across the sky. The key was that the disciples would be prepared for this, but faithless Israel would not; for the remnant already knew the hidden Kingdom that had come among them, and would thus be prepared for the great revealing in judgment to come. To the Pharisees that Kingdom was invisible, and they would still be looking for it when the great judgment came upon them.[15]

This means that not seeing one of the days of the Son of Man is about not seeing the manifestation of the kingdom the way the Pharisees envisioned it and possibly the way the disciples anticipated it, a rescue from Roman oppression and a full vindication of the righteousness of Israel. What they would see was a judgment on unbelievers and a way of escape for believers and even unbelievers (Luke 21:21; Matt. 24:16-20). Jesus is speaking to His disciples of that generation.

---

15. Joel McDurmon, *Jesus v. Jerusalem: A Commentary on Luke 9:51-20:26, Jesus' Lawsuit Against Israel* (Powder Springs, GA: American Vision, 2011), 111-113.

As events proceeded from bad to worse in the leadup to the rebellion of the Jews and the response from the Romans, life was going on as normal (Matt. 24:28, 38-41) but with serious signs of trouble. When the time got closer, the disciples who remained in the city would "long to see one of the days of the Son of Man" but they would not see it (Luke 17:22) because there was going to be "great tribulation' (Matt. 24:21-22). Jesus warned them that there would be those who would claim "'Look there! Look here! Do not go away, and do not run after *them*" (17:23). The temptation would be to seek relief by the physical return of the Messiah to rescue them. But it would not happen (21:8; Matt. 24:24-26). Jesus' coming would be in judgment upon the temple and city. The only immediate remedy would be a physical escape to the mountains outside of the city (Luke 21:20-24; Matt. 24:15:20). Albert Barnes offers a similar interpretation that Jesus:

> takes occasion to direct the minds of his disciples to the days of vengeance which were about to fall on the Jewish nation. Heavy calamities will befall the Jewish people, and you will desire a deliverer.... Such will be the calamities of those times, so great will be the afflictions and persecutions, that you will greatly desire *a deliverer*—one who shall come to you in the character in which *you have expected* the Messiah would come, and who would deliver you from the power of your enemies; and at that time, in the midst of these calamities, people shall rise up pretending *to be* the Messiah,[16] and to be able to deliver you. In view of this, he takes occasion to caution them against being led astray by them.... *Ye shall not see it*—You shall not see such a day of deliverance—such a Messiah as the nation has expected, and such an interposition as you would desire.[17]

That tribulation was indeed great. Jesus had predicted it with attendant details and had tied the timing to their generation. All who were living then would have to live through it, but it would not go on forever or beyond the confines of the city of Jerusalem. The tribulation period was

---

16. "Many false Christs, according to Josephus, appeared about that time, attempting to lead away the people." Albert Barnes, *Notes on the New Testament: Luke & John*, ed. Robert Frew (London: Blackie & Son, 1884-1885), 124.

17. Barnes, *Notes on the New Testament: Luke & John*, 124.

shortened and geographically limited (Matt. 24:22; see Luke 18:1-8). It's a mistake to claim that what Jesus described was "worldwide" and "inescapable."[18] The tribulation could be escaped on foot (Matt. 24:16-20; Luke 21:20-24).

---

The following is from miah A. Nisbett's *The Triumphs of Christianity over Infidelity Displayed; Or the Coming of the Messiah, the True Key to the Right Understanding of the Most Difficult Passages in the New Testament... A Full Answer to the Objection of Mr. Gibbon, That Our Lord and His Apostles Predicted the Near Approach of the End of the World in Their Own Times* (Printed for the Author by J. Atkinson [1797] 1802), 133-136.

For the most cursory view of these two opposite columns [next page->] , no doubt can well be entertained, that the subject treated of, by both the Evangelists, is one and the same. And, from a closer inspection; various interesting and important observations, very naturally arise, which seem, in the strongest manner, to confirm the reasoning, which has been adopted, in the examination of Matthew 24 and the parallel chapters of Mark and Luke; which will, at the same time, very fully prove, how much those Writers have mistaken the design of those chapters, who have referred them, to any other event, than to the destruction of Jerusalem, and to the full manifestation, by that awful event, of the true nature of the Messiah's character, as opposed to his being a temporal Prince, who was to raise the Jews to a state of unexampled prosperity.

---

18. Joel B. Green, *The Gospel of Luke*, The New International Commentary on the New Testament (Grand Rapids, MI: Wm. B. Eerdmans Publishing Co., 1997), 631.

| | |
|---|---|
| **The Questions of the Disciples**<br>*Matthew 24:3*<br>When will these things happen, and what [will be] the sign of Your coming? | **The Question of the Pharisees**<br>*Luke 17:20*<br>Now having been questioned by the Pharisees as to when the kingdom of God was coming… |
| **The Answer**<br>*Matthew 24:27*<br>For just as the lightning comes from the east and flashes even to the west, so will the coming of the Son of Man be. | **The Answer**<br>*Luke 17:24*<br>For just like the lightning, when it flashes out of one part of the sky, shines to the other part of the sky, so will the Son of Man be in His day. |
| **Cautions against Deception**<br>*Matthew 24:4-5, 23-25*<br>See to it that no one misleads you. For many will come in My name, saying, 'I am the Christ,' and will mislead many. … Then if anyone says to you, 'Behold, here is the Christ,' or 'There [He is,]' do not believe [him.] For false Christs and false prophets will arise … Behold, I have told you in advance. | **Cautions against Deception**<br>*Luke 17:20-22*<br>The kingdom of God is not coming with signs to be observed; nor will they say, "Look, here [it is!]" or, "There [it is!]" For behold, the kingdom of God is in your midst. And He said to the disciples, "The days will come when you will long to see one of the days of the Son of Man, and you will not see it." |
| **The suddenness of the coming of the Son of Man**<br>*Matthew 24:37-39*<br>For the coming of the Son of Man will be just like the days of Noah. For as in those days before the flood they were eating and drinking, marrying and giving in marriage, until the day that Noah entered the ark, and took them all away; so will the coming of the Son of Man be. | **The suddenness of the coming of the Son of Man**<br>*Luke 17:26-27, 30*<br>And just as it happened in the days of Noah, so it will be also in the days of the Son of Man: they were eating, they were drinking, they were marrying, they were being given in marriage, until the flood came and destroyed them all. … It will be just the same on the day that the Son of Man is revealed. |
| **Particular Directions how to conduct themselves when calamity should come upon them**<br>*Matthew 24:17-18, 40-41*<br>Whoever is on the housetop must not go down to get the things out that are in his house. Whoever is in the field must not turn back to get his cloak. … Then there will be two men in the field; one will be taken and one will be left. Two women [will be] grinding at the mill; one will be taken and one will be left. | **Particular Directions how to conduct themselves when calamity should come upon them**<br>*Luke 17:31, 34-35*<br>On that day, the one who is on the housetop and whose goods are in the house must not go down to take them out; and likewise the one who is in the field must not turn back. … I tell you, on that night there will be two in one bed; one will be taken and the other will be left. There will be two women grinding at the same place; one will be taken and the other will be left. |
| **General Reason for these Cautions and Directions**<br>*Matthew 24:28*<br>Wherever the corpse is there the vultures will gather. | **General Reason for these Cautions and Directions**<br>*Luke 17:37*<br>Where the body [is,] there also the vultures will be gathered. |

# CHAPTER 20

# Does Eschatology Matter More than Six Literal Days of Creation?

K en Ham, who is a Young Earth Creationist (YECist), says the church opened a door for the exodus of youth beginning in the 19th century when it taught that "the age of the Earth is not an issue as long as you trust in Jesus and believe in the resurrection and the Gospel accounts." Ham concedes that "salvation is not conditioned on what you believe about the age of the Earth and the six days of creation." He admits that there "are many who believe in millions of years and are Christians." Even so, the Genesis issue does matter, he argues, "because salvation does rise or fall on the authority of Scripture. The message of the Gospel comes from these words of Scripture." There is no direct biblical evidence that establishes the age of the Earth when compared to direct evidence that God created the heavens and earth (Gen. 1:1; Col. 1:16; 1 Tim. 4:4; Heb. 11:3).

Old Earth Creation (OEC) advocates believe in the authority and integrity of the Bible as much as YECists do. By their own admission, YECists note that well-respected Bible-believing theologians, Christian scientists,[1] and scholars from different fields[2] did not and do not believe the Bible teaches a young earth. (Personally, I believe the Bible does not deal with the topic of the age of the earth. The fact that God is the creator is fundamental to both the Old and New Testaments with no mention of the Earth's age.) Charles Spurgeon (1834-1892) had this to say about the age of the earth:

> Can any man tell me when the beginning was? Years ago we thought the beginning of this world was when Adam came upon it; but we have discovered that thousands of years before

---

1. David Snoke, *A Biblical Case for an Old Earth* (Grand Rapids, MI: Baker Books, 2006).
2. https://bit.ly/4f7zoXZ

that God was preparing chaotic matter to make it a fit abode for man, putting races of creatures upon it, who might die and leave behind the marks of his handiwork and marvelous skill, before he tried his hand on man.[3]

I don't know anyone who would accuse Spurgeon of not holding up the authority and integrity of the Bible.

In the book edited by Terry Mortenson and Thane Ury, *Coming to Grips with Genesis*, the following is found: "The Baptist 'Prince of Preachers,' Charles Spurgeon (1834-1892), uncritically accepted the old-earth geological theory (though he apparently did not realize that the geologists were thinking in terms of millions of years.)"[4] Further digging will show that Spurgeon did believe in an old earth, "many millions of years" old:

In the 2d verse of the first chapter of Genesis, we read, "And the earth was without form, and void; and darkness was upon the face of the deep. And the Spirit of God moved upon the face of the waters." We know not how remote the period of the creation of this globe may be—**certainly many millions of years before the time of Adam**. Our planet has passed through various stages of existence, and different kinds of creatures have lived on its surface, all of which have been fashioned by God. But before that era came, wherein man should be its principal tenant and monarch, the Creator gave up the world to confusion. He allowed the inward fires to burst up from beneath, and melt all the solid matter, so that all kinds of substances were commingled in one vast mass of disorder.[5]

Take note that this sermon was preached before Darwin's publication of *On the Origin of Species* in 1859.

---

3. Charles H. Spurgeon, "Election," *The New Park Street Pulpit*, 6 vols. (Grand Rapids, MI: Zondervan [1856] 1963), 1:311-322. No. 41-42, preached on September 2, 1855, on 2 Thessalonians 2:13-14. The online version can be found at https://bit.ly/4dMfkcj

4. Terry Mortenson and Thane Ury, *Coming to Grips with Genesis: Biblical Authority and the Age of the Earth* (Green Forest, AR: New Leaf Publishing, 2008), 96.

5. Charles Spurgeon, "The Power of the Holy Ghost," *The New Park Street Pulpit*, 1:230. No. 30 preached on June 17, 1855, on Romans 5:13. The online version can be found at https://bit.ly/3zOCjG5

As mentioned above, there are many modern-day evangelical, Bible-believing scholars who hold to an old-earth position. Gleason L. Archer (1916-2004), who was a staunch defender of the inspiration and authority of the Bible, held the old-earth position[6] as did Arthur Custance (1910-1985) in his book *Without Form and Void*,[7] "described by John C. Whitcomb, one of the chief opponents of the OEC view, as *the* definitive work on the Gap Theory, also known as the Restitution Theory." The *Scofield Reference Bible* teaches the gap theory, which necessitates an old earth:

1. "Jer. 4.23-26, Isa. 24.1 and 45.18 clearly indicate that the earth had undergone a cataclysmic change as the result of a divine judgment. The face of the earth bears everywhere the marks of such a catastrophe."[8]

2. "Relegate fossils to the primitive creation, and no conflict of science with the Genesis cosmogony remains."[9]

Clarence Larkin,[10] another dispensationalist, held the old earth position, as did Finis Dake (1902-1987). Since *The Scofield Reference Bible* was first published in 1909, and it is the most widely distributed study Bible in the world,[11] why is it only in the past few decades that we are seeing young people leaving the church? There are other reasons, and as I hope to show it's not the age of the earth but the end of planet earth and the escape from it that has garnered the attention of millions of Christians. I could just as easily take the other end of the dog and claim that it's the last book of the Bible that's causing young people to abandon Christianity. The age of the earth is not the problem; it's eschatology. For nearly 200 years, Christianity has been dominated by a prophetic belief system that discounts the future by repeatedly claiming that "Jesus is coming back in our generation!" Numerous failed

---

6. Gleason L. Archer, *The New International Encyclopedia of Bible Difficulties* (Grand Rapids, MI: Zondervan, 2001).

7. https://custance.org/Library/WFANDV/index.html

8. Comments on Genesis 1:2 in the 1945 edition of *The Scofield Reference Bible*.

9. Comments on Genesis 1:11 in the 1945 edition of *The Scofield Reference Bible*.

10. Clarence Larkin, *Dispensational truth or God's Plan and Purpose in the Ages* (Philadelphia: Rev. Clarence Larkin Estate, 1918), 21-24.

11. Arno C. Gaebelein, T*he History of the Scofield Reference Bible* (New York: Our Hope Publicans/Loizeaux Brothers, 1941), 11.

predictions have led many Christians to question the reliability of the Bible. Young people notice examples of failed prophetic speculation. Several generations of Christians have been caught up in "rapture fever."[12] Hal Lindsey's *The Late Great Planet Earth*, first published in 1970, argued that the so-called "rapture of the church" would take place sometime before 1988. The Left Behind series presented a prophetic model for millions of Christians to embrace.

So why does Ken Ham pick only old-earth creationism and not the entire dispensational system that is footnoted and codified in the works of Scofield, Larkin, Dake, and with books, articles, and podcasts?

I realize Answers in Genesis is a creation organization, so creation is its emphasis. Eschatology is also a big part of the Bible (broader in content than creation), why not mention it as well? Later in this article I deal with Ham's entry into the eschatology debate.

Bart Ehrman, author of numerous books critical of the New Testament, wrote that the catalyst for rejecting the authority of the Bible was not because of creation (although it might have played a role later); it was eschatology. His best-selling book *Misquoting Jesus* describes how he struggled to reconcile what he believed to be errors in the Bible.[13] His pilgrimage from Moody Bible Institute to Princeton changed him forever. His trek down the road to skepticism began with what he describes as "one of the most popular books on campus" at the time, Hal "Lindsay's [sic] apocalyptic blueprint for our future, *The Late Great Planet Earth*." Ehrman wrote that he "was particularly struck by the 'when'" of Lindsey's prophetic outline of Matthew 24. "When" is also the issue in the YEC/OEC debate. Why isn't the time factor an issue among YEC advocates since, as I will show, the interpretive principles are the same. There are specific biblical time indicators related to eschatology that are not found in creation.

Ehrman's story is not unusual. Michael Ruse, Professor of Philosophy at Florida State University and a self-professed "ex-Christian,"[14] devotes a

---

12. Francis X. Gumerlock, *The Day and the Hour* (Powder Springs, GA: American Vision, 2000).

13. Bart D. Ehrman, *Misquoting Jesus: The Story Behind Who Changed the Bible and Why* (New York: HarperCollins, 2005).

14. Michael Ruse, "Saving Darwinism from the Darwinians," *National Post* (May 13, 2000), B3.

chapter to the subject of eschatology in his book *The Evolution-Creation Struggle*.[15] He believes the interpretive methodology of dispensational premillennialism is inexorably linked to the way its advocates defend their position on creation. Creationists claim they interpret the Bible literally, but when they come to a prophetic passage like Matthew 24:34, they throw their literal hermeneutic to the wind. Don't you think young people notice this type of interpretive sleight of hand?

Consider the following comments on Matthew 24:34 from Henry M. Morris, a dispensationalist and a founding father of the modern-day, six-day creationist movement and the co-author of *The Genesis Flood* (1964) along with John C. Whitcomb. The comments on "this generation" come from Morris' creationist-themed *Defender's Study Bible* first published in 1995:

> The word "this" is the demonstrative adjective and could better be translated "that generation." That is, the generation which sees all these signs (probably starting with World War I) shall not have completely passed away until all these things have taken place (1045).

There are no World War I veterans alive today. Frank Buckles, the last American surviving veteran from World War I died February 28, 2011. He was 110.

Morris describes the use of "this" as a "demonstrative adjective," but it is better designated as a "near" demonstrative adjective identifying the proximate generation that will see the signs, that is, the generation to whom Jesus was speaking. In Greek and English, the near demonstrative (this) is contrasted with the far demonstrative (that). Greek language specialists make this very point:

> Greek grammars and lexicons recognize two demonstratives: near and distant. The near demonstrative, as the name denotes, points to someone or something "near," in close proximity. They appear as the singular word "this" and its plural "these." The distant demonstratives, as their name suggests, appear as "that" (singular), or "those" (plural).[16]

---

15. Michael Ruse, *The Evolution-Creation Struggle* (Cambridge, MA: Harvard University Press, 2005).

16. Cullen I K Story and J. Lyle Story, *Greek To Me: Learning New Testament Greek*

The near demonstrative "this" always refers to something contemporary, as the *Greek-English Lexicon of the New Testament and Other Early Christian Literature* makes clear: "[T]his, referring to something comparatively near at hand, just as *ekeinos* [that] refers to something comparatively farther away."[17] Prior to his comments in his *Defender's Study Bible*, Morris wrote the following extended comments on Matthew 24:34 in his book *Creation and the Second Coming*:

> In this striking prophecy, the words "this generation" has the emphasis of "*that* generation."[18] That is, that generation—the one that sees the specific signs of His coming—will not completely pass away until He has returned to reign as King.[19] Now if the first sign was, as we have surmised, the first World War, then followed by all His other signs, His coming must indeed by very near[20]—even at the doors! There are only a few people still living from that[21] generation. I myself was born just a month before the Armistice was signed on November 11, 1918. Those who were

---

*Through Memory Visualization* (New York: Harper, 1979), 74. "Sometimes it is desired to call attention with special emphasis to a designated object, whether in the physical vicinity or the speaker or the literary context of the writer. For this purpose the demonstrative construction is used.... For that which is relatively near in actuality or thought the immediate demonstrative [*houtos*] is used.... For that which is relatively distant in actuality or thought the remote demonstrative [*ekeinos*] is used." H. E. Dana and Julius R. Mantey, *A Manual Grammar of the Greek New Testament* (New York; Macmillan, 1957), 127-128, sec. 136.

17. William F. Arndt and F. Wilbur Gingrich, *A Greek-English Lexicon of the New Testament and Other Early Christian Literature*, 4th ed. (Chicago, IL: The University of Chicago Press, 1952), 600.

18. I received the following in an e-mail: "I will admit that the word 'this' has ALWAYS presented an obstacle to a full understanding of the Discourse. Have you ever considered this word COULD HAVE BEEN 'that' in the original [Manuscript]???? I believe from my reading that could have been possible" (November 12, 2007). Almost anything is possible, but there is no indication that the Greek word *ekeinos* was ever used. It's pure conjecture. The e-mailer's comments show the extremes some people will go to adopt to hold on to an interpretive system that has no biblical support.

19. There is nothing in Matthew 24 that says Jesus is going to return to reign as king on the earth.

20. Why does "near" mean "even at the doors" for Morris in his day, but it did not mean "near" for those living in the first century?

21. Notice how Morris uses the far demonstrative "that" to refer to a generation in the past. How would he have described the generation in which he was living? Obviously with the near demonstrative "this" to distinguish it from "that" *past* generation or any *future* generation.

old enough really to know about that first World War—"the beginning of sorrows"—would be at least in their eighties now. Thus, we cannot be dogmatic, we could very well now be living in the very last days before the return of the Lord.[22]

Consider the last sentence: "we could very well now be living in the very last days before the return of the Lord." When young people continually hear such things, they get discouraged and find solace and meaning elsewhere. Who wants to be part of a religion that is continually preaching false inevitable gloom and doom with the hope of a "rapture" that is always elusive? "A philosophy calling for an escape from time is not likely to involve itself in the battles of time."[23] Pretribulational dispensational David Schnittger pointed out the problem in 1986:

> Many in our camp have an all-pervasive negativism regarding the course of society and the impotence of God's people to do anything about it. They will heartily affirm that **Satan is Alive and Well on Planet Earth**, and that this must indeed be **The Terminal Generation**; therefore, any attempt to influence society is ultimately hopeless. They adopt the pietistic platitude: *"You don't polish brass on a sinking ship."* [Coined by dispensationalist J. Vernon McGee]. Many pessimistic pretribbers cling to the humanists' version of religious freedom; namely Christian social action and political impotence, self-imposed, as drowning men cling to a life preserver.[24]

Furthermore, how can young people believe in the authority and integrity of the Bible when there has been a long history (too many to list here) of repeated and failed attempts at date setting?

Matthew 24:33 tells us what audience Jesus had in view: "so, **you** too, when **you** see all **these** things, recognize that He is near, right at the door." It is obvious, and without any need for debate, that the first "you" refers to those who asked the questions that led to Jesus' extended

---

22. Henry Morris, *Creation and the Second Coming* (Green Forest, AR: Master Books, 1991), 183. Morris died on February 25, 2006, at the age of 87.

23. R. J. Rushdoony, *The One and the Many: Studies in the Philosophy of Order and Ultimacy* (Nutley, NJ: The Craig Press, 1971), 129.

24. David Schnittger, *Christian Reconstruction from a Pretribulational Perspective* Oklahoma City, OK: Southwest Radio Church, 1986), 7.

remarks (Matt. 24:2-4). The second "you" is the same audience. Jesus identified those who would "see all these things" by again using "you." If Jesus had a future generation in mind, He could have eliminated all confusion by saying, "when **they** see all these things, **they will** recognize that He is near, right at the doors. Truly I say to you, **that** generation will not pass away until all these things take place." Instead, Henry Morris and others must massage the text to support a future tribulation period.[25]

There is also the problem with the way Morris understands the meaning of "last days" in the notes of his *Defender's Study Bible*. He states, "this 'last days' prophecy of Joel was fulfilled at Pentecost only in a precursive sense" (1179). Peter says the events at Pentecost were a fulfillment of what Joel predicted (Joel 2:28-32): "**this** is **that** which was spoken by the prophet Joel" (Acts 2:17). The "this" referred to the supernatural events of Pentecost. Morris argued that "its complete fulfillment must await the time of the end.... Thus Peter's statement: 'This is that' (Acts 2:16) should be understood in the sense of 'This is like that'" (1179).[26] Once again, a literalist responds in a non-literal way because interpreting "this is that" literally would deny his futurist position.

What implications does this type of interpretation have for the issue of the authority and integrity of the Bible that Ken Ham rightly raises in his book *Already Gone: Why Your Kids Will Quit Church and How You Can Stop It*? How will we ever convince skeptics of the truthfulness of the Bible when it is distorted to defend interpretations where "this" means "that" and "this is that" means "this is *like* that"? Don't even get me started on words like "near," "shortly," "quickly," and "at hand." I wonder how YECists would respond to an OECist who applied Morris' interpretive methods to Genesis.

---

25. An example is found in Tim Demy and Gary Stewart, *101 Most Puzzling Bible Verses: Insight into Frequently Misunderstood Scriptures* (Eugene, OR: Harvest House, 2007), 105-106. They argue that there is no mention of an audience reference in Matthew 24:33, just that "The phrases 'this generation' and 'these things' are linked together by context and grammar in such a way that Jesus must be speaking of a future generation." This is the height of obfuscation. Jesus clearly identifies the audience: "when YOU see all these things." The "you" are those in Jesus' audience, the disciples that asked the questions in 24:3.

26. Thomas Ice argues in a similar way: "But this is [like] that which was spoken by the prophet Joel." He tries to explain the addition of "like" by claiming that "The unique statement of Peter ('this is that') is in the language of comparison and similarity, not fulfillment." Thomas Ice, "Acts," in Tim LaHaye, ed. *Prophecy Study Bible* (Chattanooga, TN: AMG Publishers, 2000), 1187.

So then, it's not the age of the earth that is driving some young people away, it's the fact that the Bible is not taught in a comprehensive way that has meaning for the here and now and future.

When I wrote my article "Why Young People are Leaving the Church" I knew it would generate some response. I was taken to task by a few YECists because I did not point out the dangers of OECism arguments and how they create serious theological problems such as disease and death before the fall. Some OECists attempt to answer this objection exegetically. YECists can and do disagree with OEC arguments, but they can't accuse OECists of not appealing to the Bible to make their case since appealing to the Bible and science are like the approach YECists take.

The claim that a church exodus among young people is the result of not teaching YECism is simplistic, unproven, and shortsighted. I pointed out in "Why Young People are Leaving the Church" that it is factually and apologetically a mistake to imply that OECists take a compromised position on biblical inspiration, authority, and integrity as compared to YECists. It gets YECists nowhere to argue otherwise and *vice versa*. I have fundamental problems with dispensationalists on the issue of eschatology, but I have never accused them of not believing the Bible.

In "Why Young People are Leaving the Church," I argued that there are exegetical and hermeneutical inconsistencies among YECists who are dispensationalists (e.g., Henry Morris, Tim LaHaye, and Ray Comfort) and among those who speak in churches and homeschool conventions about YECism (even though they themselves may not be dispensationalists). I contend that prophecy, because it is about the future, has a greater impact on people than does whether the earth is young or old. Some creation/prophecy writers[27] claim that not to believe in a global flood is a sign that the end is near based on 2 Peter 3:3-9. Since there are many who are questioning a belief in a global flood, so the argument goes, we must be living in the last days. As Morris pointed out in his book *Creation and the Second Coming*, there is no way to escape a creation-prophecy connection.

Ken Ham wrote a cordial response to my article "Why Young People are Leaving the Church" in which he characterized me as claiming

---

27. http://tinyurl.com/kp3n4b

"that creation and the age of the earth are secondary in importance to eschatology in leading to an exodus of young people from the church." Of course, I made no such point. They are *equally important*. To neglect either one is a mistake. I've written extensively on creation issues along with eschatology, ethics, America's Christian history, and apologetics. I have published books, articles, and podcasts to prove it. My emphasis has been on the ethical implications of evolution. That's why I wrote the book *Why It Might be OK to Eat Your Neighbor: If Atheism is Right Can Anything be Wrong?* I gave an early lecture on the topic at a creation conference at Coral Ridge Presbyterian Church sponsored by Ken Ham's Answers in Genesis organization.[28]

And if we're going on a percentage basis, there is more eschatology than creation in the Bible. After analyzing, cataloging, and commenting on every prophetic verse in the Bible, J. Barton Payne concluded in his *Encyclopedia of Biblical Prophecy* that 8,352 verses out of 31,124 total verses deal with prophecy of one type or another. That works out to twenty-seven percent of the Bible being predictive.[29] Tim LaHaye stated something similar that "one third of the Bible is prophecy."[30]

The Synoptic Gospels must consider prophecy very important since six chapters (Matt. 24-25; Mark 13; Luke 17, 19, and 21) and the entire book of Revelation deal with the subject. There are many other passages (Acts 2:17; 1 Thess. 4:13-18; 2 Thess. 2, etc.). When compared to eschatology, the New Testament says little or nothing about how old the Earth is. In terms of the load factor, eschatology wins hands down. So then, we must go "Back to Genesis" and "Forward to Revelation" with a consistent hermeneutic. This being the case, I find it difficult to understand why YECist ministries won't deal with the inherent interpretive problems that are found among so many YECists who are also dispensational. Once a person becomes a YECist, then what? He or she is taught that Jesus is going to return "soon," that Russia is set to invade Israel, the rapture must be "near" because Israel is back in

---

28. https://bit.ly/4gx9T3N

29. J. Barton Payne, *Encyclopedia of Biblical Prophecy: The Complete Guide to Scriptural Predictions and Their Fulfillment* (New York: Harper & Row, 1973).

30. Tim LaHaye, "Twelve Reasons Why This Could Be the Terminal Generation," *When the Trumpet Sounds*, eds. Thomas Ice and Timothy Demy (Eugene, OR: Harvest House, 1995), 428.

the land, the European Common Market is about to bring forth the predicted antichrist, we're headed for a cashless society, etc.[31] Does any of this sound familiar? It should; it's been standard fare for more than 150 years. How do arguments about how old the earth is counter these false prognostications?

Having said all of this, I don't believe the authors of *Already Gone* prove what they claim. The book could have made a better case for why so many of those surveyed devalue the Bible dealing with the statistic that a substantial majority of them—859 out of 1000—attend public schools! One hour of Sunday school (if they attend) and an hour at Youth Meeting (if they attend) each week can't make up for 30 hours of public-school instruction and peer associations within public schools. The humanists understand this, so why don't Christians? Charles Francis Potter, who signed the first *Humanist Manifesto*, stated as much in 1930:

> Education is thus a most powerful ally of Humanism, and every American public school is a school of Humanism What can the theistic Sunday-school, meeting for an hour once a week, and teaching only a fraction of the children, do to stem the tide of a five-day program of humanistic teaching?[32]

*Already Gone* is critical of the Sunday School system (as it should be), but the *real* problem is five days a week, six hours each day, 9 months of the year, 12+ years of public schools that are officially atheistic.

If these young people are typical evangelicals, the default position of most of the churches participants in the survey attended hold to dispensational premillennialism or some variation of it: Baptist (260), Church of God (84), Pentecostal (69), Assembly of God (66), Calvary Chapel (32), Bible Church (29), Community Church (38),[33] Christian Missionary Alliance (17), Evangelical Free Church (15), and Brethren (8).

---

31. These topics are covered in Gary DeMar, *Last Days Madness, Wars and Rumors of Wars,* and *The Gog and Magog End-Time Alliance* at AmericanVision.org

32. Charles Francis Potter, *Humanism: A New Religion* (New York: Simon and Schuster, 1930), 128. Quoted in David A. Noebel, J.F. Baldwin, and Kevin Bywater, *Clergy in the Classroom: The Religion of Secular Humanism* (Manitou Springs, CO: Summit Press, 1995), vi.

33. As far as I can tell, there may be a denomination called "Community Church," but it's more likely that it fits in the non-denominational category. In the research I've done, many of them are dispensational. Here's an example: https://bit.ly/48oUy1H

Lutherans are typically amillennial (136) as are Presbyterians (44). Both denominations hold an end-time view that is also culturally pessimistic. I suspect that most of these young people don't even know there is an alternative eschatological position that teaches that most prophetic texts that are taught are yet to be fulfilled were fulfilled in the first century. Since they attend public schools, they are aware that there is a major debate over creation and evolution. It's a hot topic in schools, the courts, magazines, TV specials, and news reports. There's almost no dissent among most of the churches represented in the survey on the end-time scenario made popular by writers like YECists Hal Lindsey, Tim LaHaye, and Ray Comfort and YECist schools like Liberty University and The Master's University.

In a survey that Left Behind publisher Tyndale did, "More than 50 percent of respondents ... said 'I'm anxiously expecting his return.'" So what topic do you think is having the biggest impact on young people? The Left Behind series, published from 1995 to 2007, was a publishing phenomenon that has sold around 100 million copies and were sold in every major bookstore chain. Seven titles in the adult series reached #1 on the bestseller lists for *The New York Times*, *USA Today*, and *Publishers Weekly*. It has been translated into many languages and generated spin-offs, films, audio dramatizations, graphic novels, a children's series, and computer games. There is not a single creation book that has sold anywhere near this number or has had the influence of books like Left Behind.[34] On statistics alone, I think it's clear that prophecy has had more of an impact on Christian beliefs than the debate over the age of the earth. Here are some of the questions that should be asked of young people.

1. Have you been taught Jesus is going to return "in your generation"?

2. Does such an end-time scenario affect your view of the future 10, 20, 30, or 40 years from now? Considering what you have been taught about Bible prophecy, do you think you will be here 40 years from now?

3. What did Jesus mean when He said, "this generation will not pass away until all these things take place"? Was He referring to a future generation or the generation of His own day?

---

34. For a critique of the Left Behind series, see my book *Left Behind: Separating Fact from Fiction*.

4. Are we seeing an increase in the number and magnitude of natural disasters, and are these signs of an approaching "rapture" of the church?

5. Are you aware that Bible skeptics point to Jesus' "failed" prediction to come back within a generation (Matt. 24:34) to be incontrovertible evidence that He was not a prophet, and the Bible is filled with mistakes?

6. Revelation says prophetic events given to John are to happen "shortly" (1:1) because the "time is near" (1:3). It's been nearly 2000 years. Do you think the Bible is mistaken? Should these and other time words ("at hand" and "quickly") be taken literally? If they shouldn't be taken literally, should the days of creation be taken literally since they deal with time as well?

7. The Bible says, in a prophetic passage, "that with the Lord one day is like a thousand years, and a thousand years like one day" (2 Pet. 3:8). Could this also apply to the days of creation?

8. Are you aware that 1917 (World War I), 1948 (Israel becoming a nation again), and 1967 (the Six-Day-War) have been used by prophecy writers to determine the beginning point of when the signs leading up to the rapture will begin? How can these dates be right if the Bible is true and the prophesied events have not taken place?

9. Does the fact that many prophecy writers (e.g., Hal Lindsey and the late Chuck Smith of Calvary Chapel) said the rapture would take place before 1988 have any bearing on the authority of the Bible? Does it bother you that they are still considered to be authorities and experts on Bible prophecy?

If YECists and OECists would take on the prophecy issue, I believe we would see a worldwide Christian cultural revival that would dwarf the Reformation and scare the Humanists. Evolutionists are not afraid of creationism; they are afraid of an optimistic eschatology that has this world application! They loved the Scofield Reference Bible because it turned millions of Christians into cultural pacifists. Even if most Christians became six-day creationists, most of them would still believe they are living in the last days, Jesus is coming soon to "rapture" His church, the antichrist is alive somewhere in the world today, the world is headed for a nuclear Armageddon, and we can't do anything to stop any of it because the world is a sinking Titanic.

After many years of avoiding the topic, Ken Ham decided to enter the debate over eschatology in a long Facebook post about the last days:

> We are in the last days! Ever since God's Son stepped into history to become Jesus Christ the God-man, we have been in the last days. We don't know how "last" we are. We just know we are more "last" than we were. We do know that one day Jesus will return and there will be a final judgment—and the last days will then end.
>
> It's fascinating that nearly 2,000 years ago, Peter (under the inspiration of the Holy Spirit) wrote about scoffers in the last days. As we read about these scoffers, we realize that there is "nothing new under the sun" (Ecclesiastes 1:9). The basic sin nature of man is the same today as it was 2,000 years ago—and as it was 6,000 years ago when our ancestor Adam rebelled against God.
>
> Peter explains that these scoffers in the last days will scorn those who believe Jesus is returning, and will exclaim, "Where is the promise of His coming? For since the fathers fell asleep, all things continue as they were from the beginning of creation." The philosophy of the scoffers is that physical processes just go on and on without any miraculous intervention (2 Peter 3:4). [35]

Ham ties his interpretation to today's persecution of Christians as evidence that Jesus' return may be near. Did Peter describe events of some unknown distant future? Not at all. There was a great tribulation in the first century (Matt. 24:21), [36] and Peter (John 21:18-19), John (Rev. 1:9), and Christians of that generation were a part of it.

Ham's view is not new. Brock Hollett in his book *Debunking Preterism* also appeals to 2 Peter 3 to explain that the mockers Peter mentions are still future. Here's Hollett's way of interpreting Peter's objection to the scoffers of his day:

---

35. For a thorough study of 2 Peter 3:3 see "What Does Peter Mean by the Passing Away of Heaven and Earth? A Study of 2 Peter 3" (https://bit.ly/48qHerH) and Gary DeMar, *Identifying the Real Last Days Scoffers* (Powder Springs, GA: American Vision Press, 2012). Especially chapter 10.

36. See chapter 16 of this book.

Peter reminded his readers that scoffers would cast aspersion on the prophetic certainty of the Lord's promise to return quickly. They will mock, "Where is the promise of his coming?" (2 Peter 3:4). The apostle responded to this charge by explaining that the *apparent* failure of Jesus to return quickly is not an *actual* failure to faithfully keep his promises. Furthermore, the fact that he did not return *immediately* does not indicate a failure to return *soon*. The apostle affirmed that the Lord "is not slow *as some count slowness*" (v. 9, emphasis added.)

Ham's position is similar to Hollett's. They line up with Morris's view in his 1991 book *Creation and the Second Coming* (132). I don't have the space to expand on the "flood" analogy only to say that the imagery is picked up in Daniel 9:26 related to the destruction of the temple that took place in AD 70: "And its end will come with a flood; even to the end there will be war [Matt. 24:6]; desolations are determined [23:38]." The "flood" is a reference to the invading armies that destroyed the temple as Jesus had predicted and took away some of the Jews as prisoners of war as described in Matthew 24:37-41:

> For the coming of the Son of Man will be just like the days of Noah. For as in those days which were before the flood they were eating and drinking, they were marrying and giving in marriage, until the day that Noah entered the ark, and they did not understand until the flood came and took them all away; so shall the coming of the Son of Man be. Then there shall be two men in the field; one will be taken, and one will be left. Two women will be grinding at the mill; one will be taken, and one will be left.[37]

It was a local judgment (Matt. 24:15-20). The same is true of how Peter uses the flood analogy. This brings us to identifying the scoffers who were asking, "Where is the promise of His coming?" (2 Peter 3:3). Peter was describing the scoffers of his day who were scoffing at what Jesus had predicted in the Olivet Discourse and elsewhere during His ministry, that He would return in judgment before their generation passed away.

---

37. See chapter 10 of this book.

The fact is, the New Testament writers, including Peter (1 Pet. 1:20; 4:7), taught that Jesus would return "shortly" (Rev. 1:1, 3; 22:10), before the last apostle died (John 21:18-24; Matt. 16:27-28),[38] within a generation (Matt. 24:34), because the time was "near" for them (James 5:7-9; Rev. 1:3), and the old covenant was "near to disappear" (Heb. 8:13). Peter wrote, "The end of all things is at hand" (1 Pet. 4:7). What he described in that verse must have applied to what we read in 2 Peter 3. The "coming" mentioned by New Testament writers was a "coming" in judgment, not a physical coming like Jesus' incarnation, but like the predicted comings that resulted in judgments by God as described by Old Testament prophets (e.g., Isa. 19:1; Micah 1:2-4; Zeph. 1:6, 14).

The judgment coming that the New Testament describes was leveled against Israel in the period leading up to the temple's destruction in AD 70 (Matt. 22:1-14). It was this prophesied event that bred a generation of prophetic scoffers because three decades had passed with no change in Israel's situation. The temple was still standing, stone upon stone (24:2), when the scoffers began to ridicule the earlier prediction made by Jesus. In fact, the rebuilt temple was more beautiful than ever.

The scoffing done by Peter's skeptics makes sense only if a particular time frame—their generation—was in view. Around AD 30, when Jesus sat upon the Mount of Olives (24:1-3), He prophesied what would happen before their generation passed away (24:34). By the time Peter wrote his letter, that 40-year generation was coming to an end and the temple was still standing. As a result, these scoffers questioned the prediction that "not one stone **here** will be left upon another" (24:2) and **"this generation** will not pass away until all these things take place" (24:34). Life in Jerusalem was going on as it had been, just like before the flood. There was no perceived threat to the temple, and the Roman Empire and its army had not made any overtures to do battle with the Jews (Luke 21:10; 19:43), so some people began to ridicule Jesus' prediction like many liberals do today and thereby question the reliability of Jesus as a prophet and the integrity of the Bible. These were the "false teachers" who were introducing "destructive heresies, even denying

38. See chapter 17 of this book.

the Master who bought them, bringing swift destruction on themselves" (2 Pet. 2:1; cp. 2 Thess. 2:10).

The people Peter accused of being "scoffers" were enemies of Jesus and the gospel and were alive when Peter and Jude wrote their letters. Jude writes:

> But you, beloved, ought to remember the words that were spoken beforehand by the apostles of our Lord Jesus Christ, that they were saying to you, "In the last time there will be mockers, following after their own ungodly lusts." These **are** [present tense] the **ones who cause** [present tense] divisions, worldly-minded, devoid of the Spirit (Jude 17-19).

When are/were the "last times"? The writer to the Hebrews defines the phrase for us as "these last days" (Heb. 1:1-2), that is, the days in which he was writing his epistle. Peter confirms this when he notes, "For He was foreknown before the foundation of the world but **has appeared in these last times** for the sake of **you**" (1 Pet. 1:20) at what was the "consummation of the ages" (Heb. 9:26). Peter's "in the last time" (1 Pet. 1:5) and "in these last times" (1:20) described the same timeframe. The following is from an 18th century work:

> [God did not] cease till he made a final End and Dissolution of the Jewish Oeconomy [economy], which St. Peter calls the End of all things (I Pet. iv. 7) and St. James, the Coming of the Lord (Jam. v. 8) and which our Saviour calls the Coming of the Son of Man (Mat. xiv. 27, 28) the last of which verses may probably be an Allusion to the Roman Eagle, which was the Ensign of the Roman Empire.[39]

Notice Jude's audience reference: "these are the ones who are hidden reefs in **your** love feasts" (1:12), and "these **are** the ones causing [present active participle] divisions" (v. 19). Jude is describing the mockers in his day. Paul had warned the Ephesian church that "savage wolves" would come in among them, "not sparing the flock ... speaking perverse things, to draw away the disciples after them" (Acts 20:29-30;

---

39. John Home, *The Scripture History of the Jews, and Their Republick*, 2 vols. (London: 1737), 303.

cp. Jude 1:4; Gal. 2:4; 2 Tim. 3:6; 2 Pet. 2:1). John mentions Diotrephes who "does not accept what we say" (2 John 9).

There's a big difference between a "scoffer" who rejects God's Word outright and someone who argues for an alternative interpretation using sound biblical arguments by interpreting the time words and stated audience used by the Bible writers as accurate. A person who disagrees with modern-day prophetic speculation is not a "scoffer," especially when there have been centuries of failed attempts at predicting the certainty of the end.

Second Peter 3 links "scoffers" (v. 3 in KJV; "mockers" in NASB) with "the last days" (v. 3), "the promise of His coming" (v. 4), the "day of the Lord" (v. 10), and the passing away of the "heavens" and the "earth" (v. 10). As has been pointed out, "last days" is not code for events leading up either to an event called the "rapture of the church" or a future physical coming. Gordon Clark comments:

> "The last days," which so many people think refers to what is still future at the end of this age, clearly means the time of Peter himself. I John 2:18 says it is, in his day, *the last hour*. Acts 2:17 quoted Joel as predicting the last days as the lifetime of Peter.... Peter obviously means his own time.[40]

There are other passages such as, "as **you** see the day drawing near" (Heb. 10:25; also 1 John 2:18), "upon whom the ends of the ages **have come**" (1 Cor. 10:11), and the storing up of their treasure in "the last days" (James 5:3) not "for" the last days. The question is, the last days of what? The last days of the old covenant with its stone temple, blood sacrifices, and earthly sinful and temporary human priesthood, the theme of the book of Hebrews.

Scoffers aren't new. A similar story is found in the Old Testament that is comparable to Jesus' description of the destruction of Jerusalem that He prophesied in the Olivet Discourse in the Gospels and the description of the scoffers of their day mentioned by Peter and Jude:

> Furthermore, all the officials of the priests and the people were very unfaithful following all the abominations of the nations; and they defiled the house of the Lord which He had sanctified

---

40. Gordon H. Clark, *II Peter: A Short Commentary* (Nutley, NJ: Presbyterian and Reformed, 1975), 64.

in Jerusalem. The Lord, the God of their fathers, sent word to them again and again by His messengers, because He had compassion on His people and on His dwelling place; **but they continually mocked the messengers of God, despised His words and scoffed at His prophets**, until the wrath of the Lord arose against His people, until there was no remedy. Therefore, He brought up against them the king of the Chaldeans who slew their young men with the sword in the house of their sanctuary, and had no compassion on young man or virgin, old man or infirm; He gave them all into his hand. All the articles of the house of God, great and small, and the treasures of the house of the Lord, and the treasures of the king and of his officers, he brought them all to Babylon. Then they burned the house of God and broke down the wall of Jerusalem and burned all its fortified buildings with fire and destroyed all its valuable articles. Those who had escaped from the sword he carried away to Babylon; and they were servants to him and to his sons until the rule of the kingdom of Persia, to fulfill the word of the Lord by the mouth of Jeremiah, until the land had enjoyed its Sabbaths. All the days of its desolation it kept sabbath until seventy years were complete (2 Chron. 36:14-21).

The mockers had called into question the prophecies of the prophets about the soon coming judgment on Judah. Their generation would see it come to pass, not some distant generation. James said as much:

Therefore be patient, brothers *and sisters,* until the coming of the Lord. The farmer waits for the precious produce of the soil, being patient about it, until it gets the early and late rains. You too be patient; strengthen your hearts, **for the coming of the Lord is near.** Do not complain, brothers, against one another, so that you may not be judged; **behold, the Judge is standing right at the doors** [Matt. 24:33] (James 5:7-9).

Near for those to whom James wrote his letter. It's not the age of the earth but the end of planet earth that really matters. Is it going to end in a meltdown? Is that meltdown near? According to premillennialists, the dissolution of the heavens and earth doesn't happen until the end of the thousand years in Revelation 20.

# CHAPTER 21

# Should We Still
# Be Celebrating the
# Lord's Supper?

S ince I've been studying eschatology, there has been a great deal of
pushback. First it came from dispensationalists. This was expected
since it's where I spent most of my time and effort. It's the dominant
view today. In fact, it's dominated the prophetic landscape for nearly
200 years. End-time thinking, and prophetic prognostication goes back
further as Francis X. Gumerlock demonstrates in his book *The Day and
the Hour.*

Eschatology of Hal Lindsey's *The Late Great Planet Earth,* the Left
Behind series, books and sermons by Chuck Smith have done social,
political, and cultural damage with claims that Jesus was going to
return within a certain time frame (1948-1988), that we are (were) the
"terminal generation," and signs are everywhere that the rapture is
just around the corner even though the so-called rapture is said to be
an event not preceded by signs. (See my book *Ten Popular Prophecy
Myths Exposed and Answered*) Since we are said to be living at the
end of prophetic history, so the theory goes, what we see happening
in our world today is a prophetic inevitability. As a result, the world is
a sinking ship, and you would never rearrange the deckchairs on the
*Titanic.* You would be looking for an escape or David Jeremiah's "Great
Disappearance" called the "rapture of the Church."

The main factor in these studies comes down to the timing of the
coming of the Lord. Is it exclusively a future event? Was it an event that
took place before that first-century church generation passed away in
AD 70 with the destruction of the temple and the end of the attendant
Old Covenant system (Matt. 24:3). Or are there two comings? One in
that first generation (Matt. 24:34) and a coming yet to take place?

The evidence for a soon coming of Jesus to that first generation of believers (to the Jew first) is overwhelming (e.g., Matt. 10:23; 16:27-28; 24-25; Mark 13; Luke 17 and 21; John 21:22). For example:

> Be patient, then, brothers, **until the Lord's coming**. See how the farmer awaits the precious fruit of the soil—how patient he is for the fall and spring rains. You, too, be patient and strengthen your hearts, **because the Lord's coming is near**. Do not complain about one another, brothers, so that you will not be judged. Look, **the Judge is standing at the door!** (James 5:7-9)

When the Lord came as promised, was it now for James' reader to stop being altogether patient?

Peter described it as "the end of all things is **near**" (1 Pet. 4:7). Earlier in his epistle he wrote that Jesus "has appeared in **these last times for the sake of you**" (1:20). Their time was the "last times," covenantally speaking, "upon whom the ends of the ages have come" (1 Cor. 10:11). Such time markers fill the New Testament. The book of Revelation begins and ends by stating "for the time is near" (1:3; 22:10).

This is when it gets interesting. In 1 Corinthians 11:23-26 we find the following:

> For I received from the Lord that which I also delivered to you, that the Lord Jesus, on the night when He was betrayed, took bread; and when He had given thanks, He broke it and said, "This is My body, which is for you; do this in remembrance of Me." In the same way He also took the cup after supper, saying, "This cup is the new covenant in My blood; do this, as often as you drink it, in remembrance of Me." For as often as you eat this bread and drink the cup, **you proclaim the Lord's death until He comes**.

We find the Lord's Supper mentioned in Matthew 26:26-30; Mark 14:22-26; and Luke 22:19-20. There is no mention of Jesus' coming in these Gospel accounts about the Lord's Supper. Jesus states, "This cup is **the new covenant** in my blood" (Luke 22:20).

Take note of "until He comes" in 1 Corinthians 11:26. The argument goes like this: If Jesus already came, then why do we still observe the Lord's Supper" or, "If you say Jesus already came, then are saying we shouldn't celebrate the Lord's Supper?" Notice what the passage does **not** say: "Eat this bread and drink the cup ... **until He comes.**" The logic of reading it this way could mean that since Jesus came in their generation (e.g., Matt. 10:23; 16:27-28; 24:30), there is no longer a requirement or reason to celebrate the Lord's Supper. The verb καταγγέλλετε (*katangellete*) is a present indicative ("you show"), not an imperative ("show!").[1] Their celebrating the Lord's Supper proclaimed Jesus' death. There is no command to celebrate the Lord's Supper only until Jesus' comes. This is a misstatement of the text and changes its entire meaning.

Jesus was the Passover Lamb. He shed His blood for His people. The shedding of blood is no longer required. Jesus inaugurated a "new covenant." Jesus' shed blood did it once for all time. Bread (representing His body broken for us) and wine (representing His blood shed for us) are a feast, not a sacrificial meal. On the cross Jesus said, "It is finished" (John 19:28-30). To practice the Lord's Supper unworthily brought temporal judgment, being "guilty of the body and blood of the Lord" (1 Cor. 11:27; see Heb. 6:6; 10:29). To whom is Paul applying this warning? John Lightfoot comments:

> Not all Christians, that walked not exactly according to the gospel rule...; but of those, that relapse and apostatize from the gospel of Judaism.... For when any, professing the gospel, so declined to Judaism [that is, reverted back to Judaism], that he put the blood of Christ in subordination to the Passover, and acknowledged nothing more in it, that was acknowledged in the blood of a lamb, and other sacrifices,—namely, that they were a mere commemoration and nothing else,— oh! How did he vilify that blood of the eternal covenant! He is 'guilty of the blood of the Lord,' who assents to the shedding of his blood, and gives his vote to his death, as inflicted for a 'mere shadow,' and nothing else;—which they [the Judaizers] did.

As a result, they "ate and drank judgment to themselves" (v. 29). It was a warning like what the Jews of Jesus' day were given (Matt. 21-25) about the coming judgment on the temple and nation of Israel. See James

---

1. Frederic Louis Godet, *Commentary on First Corinthians* (Grand Rapids, MI: Kregel, [1899] 1977), 590.

Jordan's commentary *Matthew 23-25* published by American Vision. The Judaizers were a major threat to the church. They were the New Testament's antichrists (1 John 2:18, 22; 4:1-3; 2 John 7).

But what about the phrase "until He comes"? What "coming" is Paul describing? He's describing the coming that the entire New Testament said was near (see above passages). There is no indication that 1 Corinthians 11:26 refers to any other coming. But why "until He comes" in judgment against Jerusalem that puts an end to the Old Covenant system? When Jesus prophesied that He would come and tear down the temple stone by stone, it was a warning. If anyone continued to hold on to the cold, lifeless, and sterile stones of the temple and relied on earthly priests and animal sacrifices to atone for sin (Heb. 11), they would bring judgment down on themselves. This is why Jesus warned them to abandon the temple and city of Jerusalem and flee to escape God's judgment (Matt. 24:16-20).

> But when **you see** Jerusalem surrounded by armies, then recognize that **her desolation is near**. Then those who are in Judea must flee to the mountains, and those who are inside the city must leave, and those who are in the country must not enter the city; because **these are days of punishment**, so that all things which have been written will be fulfilled. Woe to those women who are pregnant, and to those who are nursing babies in those days; for there will be great distress upon the land, and **wrath to this people**; and they will fall by the edge of the sword, and will be led captive into all the nations; and Jerusalem will be trampled underfoot by the Gentiles until the times of the Gentiles are fulfilled (Luke 21:20-24; Matt. 24:16).

Celebrating the Lord's Supper week after week served as a testimony that the Jerusalem above (Gal. 4:25-26), the heavenly Zion (Heb. 12:22-24), was the **eternal** city, not the land-based city. Notice what Paul writes to the Thessalonians, a city where the Jews "formed a mob" that led to Paul and Silas fleeing to Berea (Acts 17:1-10).

> For the word of the Lord has sounded forth **from you**, not only in Macedonia and Achaia, but in every place your faith toward God has gone out, so that we have no need to say anything. For they themselves report about us as to the

kind of reception we had with you, and how you turned to God from idols to serve a living and true God, and **to wait for His Son from heaven**, whom He raised from the dead, *that is,* **Jesus who rescues us from the wrath to come** [a wrath that John the Baptist said was about to [*mellō*] come for that generation: Luke 3:7] (1 Thess. 1:8-10).

Those who diminished the finished work of Christ and turned back to some form of Judaism would be judged in their own bodies (1 Cor. 11:30-34). We find something similar in 2 Thessalonians 1:

[W]e ourselves speak proudly of you among the churches of God for your perseverance and faith **in the midst of all your persecutions and afflictions which you endure**. This is a plain indication of God's righteous judgment so that you will be considered worthy of the kingdom of God, for which you indeed are suffering. For after all **it is only right for God to repay with affliction those who afflict you**, and to give relief to you who are afflicted, along with us, **when the Lord Jesus will be revealed from heaven with His mighty angels in flaming fire** [Matt. 16:27-28], dealing out retribution to those who do not know God, and to those who do not obey the gospel of our Lord Jesus. These people will pay the penalty of eternal destruction, away from the presence of the Lord and from the glory of His power, **when He comes to be glorified among His saints on that day**, and to be marveled at among all who have believed—because our testimony to you was believed (vv. 3-10).

Again, Paul is not describing some distant coming and retribution. Who was persecuting and afflicting them? "[F]or **you** also endured the same suffering at the hands of **your** own countrymen, even as they [the churches in Judea] did from the Jews.... With the result that they always fill up the measure of their sins. But wrath has come upon them to the utmost" (2:14-16; also Matt. 23:32; Acts 7:51-53). Paul did not describe a distant future coming of Jesus.

Some critics get hung up on the use of the word "until" as if it means once that coming takes place, there is no longer any need for the Lord's Supper. The use of "until" does not mean a full stop, because at the heart of the Lord's Supper is the proclamation of the Lord's death (1 Cor. 11:26). That remains a constant reminder throughout the generations. After the judgment of Jerusalem, the Judaizers were essentially done away with as well as the symbol of the Old Covenant, the physical temple. But the proclamation of the Lord's death and the reality of the new covenant are still needed as the Lord's Supper was originally given (Matt 26:26-30; Mark 14:22-26; and Luke 22:19-20).

"Until" is not a full-stop indicator in 1 Corinthians 15:25 ("For He must reign **until** He has put all His enemies under His feet") otherwise we have an obvious contradiction. Jesus' reign is eternal. It does not stop when all His enemies are under His feet:

- [Jesus] will be great and will be called the Son of the Most High; and the Lord God will give Him the throne of His father David; and He will reign over the house of Jacob forever, and **His kingdom will have no end** (Luke 1:32-33).

- Then to Him was given dominion and glory and a kingdom, That all peoples, nations, and languages should serve Him. **His dominion is an everlasting dominion,** Which shall not pass away, **And His kingdom the one Which shall not be destroyed** (Dan. 7:14).

- But to the Son He says: **"Your throne, O God, is forever and ever;** A scepter of righteousness is the scepter **of Your Kingdom"** (Heb. 1:8).

What is not eternal is the Old Covenant: "In that He says, 'A new covenant,' He has made the first obsolete. Now what is becoming obsolete and growing old is ready to vanish away" (Heb. 8:13). Jesus' kingdom does not come to an end even though the word "until" is used in 1 Corinthians 15:25.

Consider this from Stephen's testimony to his fellow Jews: "But as the time of the promise which God had assured to Abraham was approaching, the people increased and multiplied in Egypt, **until** ANOTHER KING AROSE OVER EGYPT WHO DID NOT KNOW JOSEPH" (Acts 7:17-18). Did Israel stop multiplying when this new king arose? Not at all. He tried to stop them from multiplying by afflicting them with taskmasters. "But the more the taskmasters afflicted them, **the**

**more they multiplied** and the more they spread out, so that they were in dread of the sons of Israel" (Ex. 1:8-10). Not to be deterred in his tyranny, the king commanded the midwives to kill the male Israelite children at birth.

The use of "until" (ἄχρι οὗ/achri ou) in Acts 7:18 does not mean a full stop, and the same is true when "until" (ἄχρι οὗ) is used in 1 Corinthians 15:25 and when "until" (ἄχρι οὗ) is used in 1 Corinthians 11:26. Consider the following:

> We can do no better than to present here a condensation of the argument of Dr. [Israel] Warren in his work, *The Parousia of Christ*, pages 102-105. The passage does not deny that the coming of Christ was near, but is founded on that very fact, which is affirmed and reiterated all through this epistle; and so the objection lies against Paul himself, and not against the theory we are endeavoring to uphold. But there exists no inconsistency. The phrase "till" or "until," ἄχρι οὗ, while specifying a time unto which something is continued, does by no means imply that its continuance then ceases. The children of Israel increased in Egypt "till another king arose," etc.; but did they not increase afterward also? (Acts vii, 17, 18.) "Until the law sin was in the world;" was it not here also after the law was given? (Rom. v, 13.) "That which ye have, hold fast till I come" (Rev. ii, 25). Here is a case exactly in point. Here is the very same phrase precisely, and used under much the same circumstances. Did Christ mean that the church at Thyatira was not to be faithful after he came? No more can we suppose that Paul meant that the church at Corinth was not to celebrate the Lord's Supper after Christ came.

> But they were to live continually with the watchword in their mouths, "*Maran atha*," "The Lord cometh," or, is coming, and do all things in view of this event, which was hastening on rapidly. So the eucharist was to be partaken of in view of Christ's coming, and not as a secular feast. "*Ye* do show forth the Lord's death till he come." They were the very ones who were to solemnly perform this behest of Christ, for they were the ones who might live to see him appear. But whence would the Corinthian church after A. D. 70, and whence do we in A.

D. 1900 [and beyond], derive the obligation to observe this ordinance? From the command of Christ: "Take, eat; this is my body. Drink ye all of this, for this is my blood." All Christians are to observe it as a memorial of their Lord, as a witness of Christ's death, and as a means of fellowship with one another, and of communion with the Lord, while here in the flesh.[2]

The time markers in the New Testament, including 1 Corinthians are unmistakable:

- I thank my God always concerning you for the grace of God which was given to **you** by Christ Jesus, that **you** were enriched in everything by Him in all utterance and all knowledge, even as the testimony of Christ was confirmed in **you**, so that you come short in no gift, **eagerly waiting for the revelation of our Lord Jesus Christ,** who will also **confirm you to the end**, that **you** may be blameless in **the day of our Lord Jesus Christ** (1 Cor. 1:4-8).

- But this I say, brethren, **the time is short**, so that **from now on** even those who have wives should be as though they had none, those who weep as though they did not weep, those who rejoice as though they did not rejoice, those who buy as though they did not possess, and those who use this world as not misusing it. For the form of this world **is passing away** (1 Cor. 7:29-31; see 1 Peter 4:7).

- Now all these things happened to them [Israel] as examples, and they were written **for our admonition, upon whom the ends of the ages have come** (1 Cor. 10:11).

The use of "until He comes" in 1 Corinthians 11:26 needs to be understood in the full context of the New Testament (see above). The use of "come" can't be interpreted in isolation as an independent proof text. It's sad that this is the way Bible interpretation is often done today. Moses Stuart explained the process this way:

---

2. William S. Urmy, *Christ Came Again: The Parousia of Christ a Past Event, the Kingdom of Christ a Present Fact, with a Consistent Eschatology* (New York: Eaton & Mains, 1900), 199-200.

In very many cases, the *first* thing has been to study theology, the *second*, to read the Bible, in order to find proofs of what has already been adopted as matter of belief.[3]

What was true in Stuart's day is often true today.

---

3. From Notes by Stuart in his edition of Johann August Ernesti's *Elements of Interpretation* (Andover: Flagg and Gould, 1822), 75.

# CHAPTER 22

# Putting It All Together

You don't need to be Bible scholar or seminary graduate to read and study the Bible. What you do need to do is pay attention to what the Bible says and doesn't say. When I was a very new Christian in 1973, I attended a Tuesday night get together called The Green House in Fort Lauderdale, Florida. It was a complimentary ministry of Coral Ridge Presbyterian Church. It was a place where young people could attend with a more relaxed atmosphere compared to the more formal Coral Ridge. The teaching at the Green House was as solid as you would get at Coral Ridge.

First time visitors, no matter who they were or their background, heard the gospel in a separate class. There was great fellowship and Bible study and even a free meal. It was held in the home of Rennie and Virginia Schmidt. It was Virginia who encouraged me to go to seminary.

One young man impressed me with his knowledge of the Bible. His name is Neal Ganzel who is a pastor of a church in Florida. At that time, I didn't know much about the Bible, but I wanted to learn. So, I asked Neal how he was so knowledgeable. He said, "I use a concordance."

There was no internet in those days. If you wanted to cross reference passages, you used either *Strong's Concordance* or *Young's Analytical Concordance*. Young's *Concordance* has been revised and updated over the years. Strong's and Young's are big fat books, but they were necessary if you wanted to study the Bible unencumbered by interpretive systems. If you wanted to know how many times and where a word is found in the KJV, all you needed to do was check out the concordance. Strong's *Concordance* included a Hebrew and Greek dictionary linked to its own numbering system. For example, three Greek words are translated "world": 165 (*aiōn*/age), 3625 (*oikoumenē*/inhabited earth, known world), and 2889 (*kosmos*/world). This is how the list looks in the concordance where *w* stands for "world," the verse where it's located, and the dictionary number where the definitions are found:

coming, and the end of the *w*......................Mt. 24:3        165
Shall be preached in all the *w*....................Mt. 24:15        3625
Beginning of the *w* to this time..................Mt. 24:21        2889

Although these different words are translated "world" in the KJV and some other translations, each Greek word can have a distinct meaning that does not make them synonyms. Notice that in Matthew 24:14 and Luke 2:1, the Greek word *oikoumenē* is used, number 3625 using Strong's *Concordance* numbering system.[1] Knowing this offers some help as to why Jesus used *oikoumenē* in Matthew 24:14, the only time in Matthew's Gospel that *oikoumenē* is used since Jesus was describing upcoming events for that generation (24:34) that were decidedly local (24:14-20).

*Young's Analytical Concordance* takes a different approach. It took Robert Young around 40 years to complete his work that included three years of typesetting. Under the word "World," as translated in the KJV, each specific Greek word has its own category listed. For example, in the case of the Greek word *oikoumenē* there is a list of 14 entries. Young does not include Luke 21:26 in his list because the KJV translates *oikoumenē* as "earth." His *Concise Critical Commentary on the Holy Bible* includes this comment on 21:26: "thinking about the things coming upon the (Jewish) world...," an obvious description of what was local and limited by geography:

---

1. STRONGS G3625:

οἰκουμένη, οἰκουμένης, ἡ (feminine of the present passive participle from οἰκέω (namely, γῆ; cf. Winers Grammar, § 64, 5; Buttmann, § 123, 8));

**1. the inhabited earth;**

a. in Greek writings often **the portion of the earth inhabited by the Greeks**, in distinction from the lands of the barbarians, cf. Passow, ii., p. 415a; (Liddell and Scott, under the word, I.).

b. in the Greek authors who wrote about Roman affairs (like the Latin *orbis terrarum*) equivalent to **the Roman empire**: so πᾶσα ἡ οἰκουμένη contextually equivalent to all the subjects of this empire, Luke 2:1.

c. **the whole inhabited earth, the world** (so in (Hyperides, Eux. 42 (probably Liddell and Scott)) the Sept. for לֵבֵב and אֶרֶץ): Luke 4:5; Luke 21:26; Acts 24:5; Romans 10:18; Revelation 16:14; Hebrews 1:6 (πᾶσα ἡ οἰκουμένη, Josephus, b. j. 7, 3, 3); ὅλη ἡ οἰκουμένη, Matthew 24:14; Acts 11:28 (in the same sense Josephus, Antiquities 8, 13, 4 πᾶσα ἡ οἰκουμένη; cf. Bleek, Erklär. d. drei ersten Evv. i., p. 68); by metonymy, **the inhabitants of the earth, men**: Acts 17:6, 31 (Psalm 9:9); ; ἡ οἰκουμένη ὅλη, all mankind, Revelation 3:10; Revelation 12:9.

10. *Habitable earth or land, οἰκουμένη oikoumenē*

Matt 24.14 preached in all the world for a witness

Luke 2.1 a decree .. that all the world should be ta.

4.5 showed .. him all the kingdoms of the w.

Acts 11.28 the great dearth [famine] throughout all the world

17.6 These that have turned the world upside

17.31 in the which he will judge the world in

19.27 whom all Asia and the world worshippeth

24.5 among all the Jews throughout the world

Anyone studying eschatology who does not deal with how the NT uses specific words related to the topic is being dishonest and is letting a predetermined system interpret Scripture. The average Christian does not know anything about these Greek word differences of what lexicons and Bible dictionaries say. For example, the following is from Thayer's Greek Lexicon on *oikoumenē*:

1. the inhabited earth;

*a.* in Greek writings often the portion of the earth inhabited by the Greeks, in distinction from the lands of the barbarians, cf. Passow, ii., p. 415a; (Liddell and Scott, under the word, I.).

*b.* in the Greek authors who wrote about Roman affairs (like the Latinorbis terrarum) equivalent to the Roman empire: so πᾶσα ἡ οἰκουμένη [all the οἰκουμένη] contextually equivalent to all the subjects of this empire, Luke 2:1.

In *A Greek-English Lexicon* compiled by Henry George Liddell and Robert Scott we find the following:

I. οἰκουμένη, (sc. γῆ), ἡ, *inhabited region,*...; then the Greek world, opp. barbarian lands, ... = the inhabited world (including non-Greek lands, as Ethiopia, India, Scythia), as opp. possibly uninhabited regions, ... = our world (= Asia, Libya, Europe);

II. the Roman world, ... Acts 17.6, 24.5, ...

The following is from Otto Flender's article on "οἰκουμένη" in *The New International Dictionary of New Testament Theology* (1:518-519), Colin Brown, General Editor.

> [*Οἰκουμένη*] means the inhabited (earth) and was used (a) from Dem[osthenes] (4th cent. B.C.) on for the world inhabited by the Greeks in contrast to those lands inhabited by "barbarians"; (b) from Aristot[le], (4th cent. B.C.) on for the inhabited world, including the barbarian lands, i.e., settled, as opposed to unsettled; 9c) the Roman period (since the conquest of the East in the 2nd cent. B.C.) for the *imperium Romanum*—lands under Roman rule. In other words, what had originally been a geographical and cultural concept had become a political concept in the Roman period. The Emperor Nero was entitled *sōtēr* (saviour) and *euergetēs* (benefactor) of the οἰκουμένη....

> The LXX uses the word 46 times ... Throughout, the word means the inhabited world....

> οἰκουμένη is found 15 times in the NT, mainly in Luke (8 times) and Rev. (3 times). It is used generally as in Hel[lenistic] popular speech meaning the inhabited world.... [But] the political and imperial usage predominate[s] [based on] Lk. 2:1. The Emperor Augustus ordered a census of the whole οἰκουμένη, i.e. that is, the territories over which he ruled.... In Acts 17:6 the preaching of the apostles is attacked as a political crime directed against the Emperor by men "who have turned the οἰκουμένη upside down." Similarly in Acts 19:27 and 24:5 Paul is called a causer of trouble in the οἰκουμένη. In the latter passage he is accused of it before the roman governor.

Below is a response I gave to a Facebook post about Matthew 24. Audience relevance is important. Who are the "you" throughout the chapter? There was an audience who heard what Jesus said. For example, when Jesus said, "**you** will be hearing of wars and rumors of wars," who were the "you"? When Jesus said, "they will deliver **you** up to tribulation, and will kill **you**," who were the "you"? They were the same "you" mentioned in Matthew 10:17 and 30 (see Acts 5:40; 22:19; 26:11; 2 Cor. 11:24-26). Jesus was not referring to a distant future audience. Put yourself in the place of those who heard Jesus. As someone in that audience, would **you** have thought that the use of "you" meant someone else in another time? The capstone is what Jesus said in Matthew 24:33: "so, **you** too, when **you** see all these things, recognize that He [or **it**] is near, at the door." Is the second "you" different from the first "you"? If we know the first use of "you," we can know the meaning of the second use of "you." They are the same "you."

Here is my initial response that begins with an important question:

**Chris** Who are the "you" in Matthew 24? They were the ones in Jesus' audience. The judgment was local and could be escaped on foot. Flat roofs. Cloaks. Sabbath regulation. First-century fulfillment before their generation passed away.

**Chris responded with the following:**

"Um, no."

Matthew 24:14 NKJV—"And this gospel of the kingdom will be preached in all the world as a witness to all the nations, and then the end will come."

Here was my final response:

Um, yes. "And this gospel of the kingdom will be preached in all the *oikoumenē* [not *kosmos*] as a witness to all the nations, and then the end will come." The end of what? The "end of the age" as the NKJV translates the Greek word αἰῶνος/*aiōnos*. The original KJV translates αἰῶνος as "world" (24:3). Was the gospel preached to all the *oikoumenē* before that generation passed away? It was. How do we know? Because the Bible tells us it was. *Oikoumenē* is used in Luke 2:1 and refers to the then known world or the political boundary of the Roman Empire. Rome could only tax its Empire. The famine in Acts 11:28 was not global, again, "world" = *oikoumenē*.

Check out Romans 1:8 where the Greek word *kosmos* is used: "First, I thank my God through Jesus Christ for you all, that your faith is spoken of throughout the whole world." See Colossians 1:6 and 1:23: "if indeed you continue in the faith, grounded and steadfast, and are not moved away from the hope of the gospel which you heard, which was preached to every creature under heaven, of which I, Paul, became a minister" (v. 23).

You might want to look at 1 Timothy 3:16: "And without controversy great is the mystery of godliness: God was manifested in the flesh, justified in the Spirit, / Seen by angels, / Preached among the Gentiles, / Believed on in the world [kosmos], / Received up in glory." Paul goes so far as to say, "But NOW [the gospel] is made manifest, and by the scriptures of the prophets, according to the commandment of the everlasting God, made known to ALL NATIONS for the obedience of faith" (Rom. 16:25).

The same interpretive approach should be taken with the Greek word "antichrist." If some prophecy "experts" are to be believed, THE antichrist is all over the Bible. In reality, the word "antichrist" only appears in four verses and is specific in its definition, number, and time of appearance:

*Young's Analytical Concordance* includes the following on the word **"ANTI-CHRIST"** found in only four New Testament passages:

An opponent of Christ, ἀντίχριστος *antichristos*.

1 Jo. 2.18 antichrist shall come .. are there many a[ntichrists].

2.22 He is antichrist, that denieth the Father

4.3 this is that (spirit) of antichrist, whereof

2 Jo. 7 This is a deceiver and an antichrist

When people on Facebook write about the supposed coming end-time antichrist, I ask these four questions:

Could you (1) reference the verses where the word "antichrist" is found, (2) define antichrist by using the Bible's definition, (3) identify the number of antichrists, the time of their appearing, and (4) explain how these describe a yet future prophetic figure? Here's what the Bible says and doesn't say about antichrists:

1. "Antichrist is primarily a Christian term based on interpretation of passages in the New Testament, in which the term 'antichrist' occurs five times in 1 John and 2 John (Greek: ἀντίχριστος, *antichristos*), once in plural form and four times in the singular."

2. An antichrist is a "liar . . . who denies that Jesus is the Christ" and "denies the Father and the Son" (1 John 2:22; cf. 2 John 7). It's most likely that the antichrists were first-century Jews who did not believe that Jesus was God in human flesh (cf. Rev. 2:9; 3:9). They were not political leaders and did not possess preternatural powers.

3. There were many antichrists (1 John 2:18).

4. Antichrists had already "gone out into the world" when John wrote his second epistle (2 John 7).

5. Earlier John had written that "even now many antichrists have appeared; from this we know that it is the last hour" (1 John 2:18). The "last hour" is most likely a reference to the events surrounding the destruction of Jerusalem that took place in AD 70.

6. The book of Revelation does not use the word antichrist which seems odd since it's during this future time that we're told THE antichrist will oversee the rebuilding of another temple, make a covenant with the Jews, and break that covenant, events the last book of the Bible do not mention.

7. Revelation 2:9 and 3:9 use the phrase "synagogue of Satan" most like a reference to the word "antichrists."

Antichrist theorists will argue the Bible describes a "composite" antichrist: "the son of destruction" and "the man of lawlessness" (2 Thess. 2:3), "the prince who is to come" (Dan. 9:26), "the little horn" (Dan. 7:8; 8:9), "the beast"—there are two of them—(Rev. 13:1, 11), and several other biblical characters rolled into one. But based on the Bible's definition, number, and timing of the antichrists of John's day, the composite antichrist argument does not work. The exception may be with the man of lawlessness in 2 Thessalonians 2. (See my book *Last Days Madness* for a two-chapter study of 2 Thessalonians 2 and Appendix C of this book).

# APPENDIX A

# John Lightfoot's Commentary on Mark 9:1

*Ver. 1:* τὴν βασιλείαν τοῦ Θεοῦ ἐληλυθυῖαν ἐν δυνάμει. [*tēn basileian tou theou elēluthuian en dunamei*] *The kingdom of God coming in power.* In Matthew, it is *the Son of man coming in his kingdom.* The coming of Christ in his vengeance and power to destroy the unbelieving and most wicked nation of the Jews is expressed under these forms of speech. Hence the day of judgment and vengeance:

I. It is called "the great and terrible day of the Lord," Acts 2:20; 2 Thessalonians 2:2;3.

II. It is described as "the end of the world," Jeremiah 4:27; Matthew 24:29; etc.

III. In that phrase, "in the last times," Isaiah 2:2; Acts 2:17; 1 Timothy 4:1; 2 Peter 3:3; that is, in the last times of that city and dispensation.

IV. Thence, the beginning of the "new world," Isaiah 65:17; 2 Peter 3:13.

V. The vengeance of Christ upon that nation is described as his "coming," John 21:22; Hebrews 10:37; his "coming in the clouds," Revelation 1:7; "in glory with the angels," Matthew 24:30; etc.

VI. It is described as the 'enthroning of Christ, and his twelve apostles judging the twelve tribes of Israel,' Matthew 19:28; Luke 22:30.

# Various Intimations of a Speedy Coming of Christ Were Fulfilled in the Beginning of the Gospel Age[1]

These are expressed principally by the words ἐγγύς and ταχύ in the Revelation, and ἐγγίζω in the Gospels and Epistles. I shall exhibit a few examples: —

Matt. 3:2; 4:17; 10:7: "The kingdom of heaven is at hand" — ἤγγικεν.

Matt. 26:45: "The hour is at hand" — ἤγγικεν.

Mark 1:15; Luke 10:9, 11: "The kingdom of God is at hand" — ἤγγικεν.

Mark 14:42: "He that betrayeth me is at hand" — ἤγγικεν.

Luke 16:8: "The time draweth near" — ἤγγικεν

Luke 21:20: "The desolation thereof" (of Jerusalem)" is nigh" — ἤγγικεν.

Rom. 13:12: "The day is at hand"— ἤγγικεν.

Heb. 10:25: "Ye see the day approaching" — ἐγγίζουσαν.

James 5:8: "The coming of the Lord draweth nigh" — ἤγγικεν.

---

1. James Glasgow, *The Apocalypse: Translated and Expounded* (Edinburgh: T&T Clark, 1872), 59-60.

1 Pet. 4:7: "The end of all" (Πάντων — of the spiritually dead in the previous verse) "is at hand" — ἤγγικεν.

Matt. 26:18: "My time is at hand" — ἐγγύς.

Luke 21:31: "The kingdom of God is nigh at hand" — ἐγγύς.

Phil. 4:5: "The Lord is at hand" — ἐγγύς.

Rev. 1:3; 22:10: "The time is at hand" — ἐγγύς.

The examples now given relate principally to time; but the words in more than forty instances refer to place and denote immediate contiguity.

## So ταχύ and cognates may be exemplified:

Luke 14:21: "Go out quickly into the streets" — ταχέως.

Luke 16:6: "Sit down quickly" — ταχέως.

John 11:31: "She rose up hastily [quickly]" — ταχέως.

1 Cor. 4:19: "I will come to you shortly." — ταχέως

2 Thess. 2:2: "That ye be not soon (ταχέως) shaken" — ταχέως.

2 Pet. 1:14: "Shortly (ταχινή) I must put off this tabernacle."

John 13:27: "That thou doest, do quickly" — τάχιον.

Acts 12:7: "Rise up quickly" — ἐν τάχει.

Rom. 16:20: "God shall bruise Satan under your feet shortly" — ἐν τάχει.

Matt. 28:7: "Go quickly (ταχύ) and tell His disciples." — ἐν τάχει.

John 11:29: "She rose quickly" — ταχύ.

Rev. 1:1; 22:6: "Things which must shortly come to pass" — ἐν τάχει.

Rev. 2:16: "I will come to Pergamos quickly" — ταχύ — in the Neronian persecution.

Rev. 3:11: "I come quickly" — ταχύ: viz. on Jerusalem.

Rev. 11:14: "The third woe cometh quickly" — ταχύ — in three and a half years.

Rev. 22:7, 12, 20: "I come quickly" — ταχύ.

# Johann Christian Schoettgen's *Commentary on 2 Thessalonians 2*[1]

## Introduction

In researching for my book *Last Days Madness* I came across a range of opinions on popular prophetic texts, especially the identity of the Man of Lawlessness in 2 Thessalonians 2. As one would expect, the commentators were either preterists or futurists. Preterists place the fulfillment of Paul's prophecy under the inspiration of the Holy Spirit before the destruction of Jerusalem in AD 70 and identify the Man of Lawlessness as Israel's religious leaders. Futurists, and this would include historicists, claim the Man of Lawlessness is either the Roman Pontiff, the position of most of the Reformers, or a yet to be revealed religious-political figure, typically described as the Antichrist.

While I found some helpful expositions of 2 Thessalonians 2, the most beneficial was a Latin discussion of the passage written by Johann Christian Schoettgen (1687-1751), a German New Testament scholar and philologist, who completed a Latin commentary on the New Testament begun by the English Hebraist scholar Rev. John Lightfoot (1602-1675). Lightfoot's four-volume commentary was originally published between 1658 and 1674. It was translated into English and published in four

---

1. The full title reads, *Johann Christian Schoettgen's Hebraic and Talmudic Background on the Entire New Testament [Horae Ebraicae et Talmudicae in universum Novum Testamentum] Supplemented by The Background of John Lightfoot on the Historical Books With the Epistles and the Apocalypse Similarly Illustrated. Also Included are Select Discussions on Sacred Theology, and Indices of Scripture References, Significant Words and Important Topics* (1733): http://goo.gl/auAwzV

Translated from Latin by N.E. Barry Hofstetter (1958-2022). Mr. Barry Hofstetter earned four degrees: B.A. in Ancient Studies from the University of Maryland; M.A. in Classical Languages (Greek and Latin) from the Ohio State University; the M.Div and Th.M (New Testament) from Westminster Theological Seminary. He taught Latin at the high school, college, and graduate level as well as Theological Bibliography at WTS.

volumes in 1859.[2] Lightfoot is noteworthy, not only for his voluminous writings[3] but for his participation in the Westminster Assembly (1643-1649) that produced the Westminster Confession and Larger and Shorter Catechisms.[4]

A study of Lightfoot's *Commentary* led me to investigate whether he wrote anything on 2 Thessalonians 2. Since his *Commentary* stressed the importance of applying several eschatological texts to the destruction of Jerusalem in AD 70 based on the gospel accounts, I wanted to know how Lightfoot interpreted 2 Thessalonians 2. A brief exposition appears in volume three of his *Whole Works* where he concludes, according to verse 7, "'The mystery of iniquity was already working,' when the apostle wrote this Epistle, which cannot possibly be understood but of the Jewish nation; and so it is explained again and again' [1 John 2:18; 4:3; 2 John 7]."[5]

Schoettgen's Latin commentary offers a full exposition of 2 Thessalonians 2 that is in keeping with Lightfoot's interpretive methods. It, too, is preterist. As far as I know, the following is the first English translation of this section of Schoettgen's Latin exposition.

## Translator's Note

In keeping with most commentators of this period and consonant with the scope of this commentary, Schoettgen frequently cites Greek, Hebrew, and Aramaic sources. In many instances, the citation adds little, and I have simply ignored the reference and rendered Schoettgen's Latin translation. In other cases, his argument depends on some nuance in the original language, in which case I have either supplied an explanatory note or transliterated the term(s) and given a translation in addition to Schoettgen's. All scripture verses are translated directly from the Greek text as cited by Schoettgen.

---

2. This work has been republished as John Lightfoot, *A Commentary on the New Testament from the Talmud and Hebraica: Matthew—1 Corinthians* (Peabody, MA: Hendrickson Publishers, [1859] 1989).

3. *The Whole Works of the Rev. John Lightfoot*, ed. John Rogers Pitman, 13 vols. (London: J.F. Dove, 1822).

4. William M. Hetherington, *History of the Westminster Assembly of Divines* (Edmonton, AB Canada: Still Water Revival Books, [1856] 1993).

5. *The Whole Works of the Rev. John Lightfoot*, 232.

## Verse 1: "Concerning the coming of our Lord"

Already it was determined from the prior epistle that the Thessalonians were curious to learn about the time of judgment against the perverse Jews. They seem to have finally asked the Apostle through a letter, to receive a response directly from him. Although he was reluctant to discuss this in the earlier letter, nevertheless moved by their prayers he is a bit more eager to explain these judgments here. While many of the protestant theologians desire that the western Antichrist (that is the Roman Pontiff, to whom I shall never deny that many of these things pertain) be described in this passage, nevertheless, if the text is rightly related to the circumstance, then the apostle speaks of such a matter as was at that time immediate, and which the Thessalonians believed was able to affect their own lives. If indeed he spoke concerning affairs which would take place after a great interval of time, he would have had no need to warn them in verse 2 not to believe others who preached otherwise. Why should it be of equal concern to them what ought to happen after ten centuries? Indeed, he so speaks now concerning this judgment, because, since it would happen in a short time, it would be of interest first to the Jews, and then especially to the Gentiles who had been converted. Further in verse 6 the apostle says that the Thessalonians knew whatever it was that impedes and holds back the revelation of the Antichrist. And indeed, the Thessalonians were not able to know those reasons, which would impede the Roman Pontiff and his revelation, since at that time there was no bishop of Rome, or if there had been his power would have been very small, so that in no way could he have aspired to any dominance.

Indeed, about this Antichrist, concerning whom Paul has spoken, I understand that he intends Pharisaic and Rabbinic Judaism, not Judaism itself, which God wanted to be buried with honor as a religion established by himself. But, as I have said, he means the Judaism of the Rabbis, which surely deserves the name of "antichristianism." Who resists Christ more, who resists the apostles more than the Pharisees, the Rabbis, the Scribes, those learned in the Law, in Judea and outside it? It was necessary that these be destroyed since their malice would continually increase until the end of the Jewish Republic.

Nevertheless, I do not wish to altogether exclude the Pontiff and the Roman clergy, since, as the sons of the Philosophers say, those who agree on the third point effectively share the same name. Therefore, since most of these details which the Apostle here explains pertain also to the Roman Pontiff, surely in a clear sense he is called by us "Antichrist," whatever the Pontiffs here might yelp. And in the same sense, this phraseology is biblical, that the Roman Pontiff is the Antichrist, and that the impious, who live today, are pronounced under God's judgment, although the names of the impious alive today are not included in the Sacred Writing. But the details are better established by the exegesis of the individual items.

"Coming" (Gk. παρουσίας) refers to the judgment against the Jews according to the custom of the Old Testament Scriptures. Judges 5:14 says, "Behold, the Lord comes with myriads of his holy ones." Revelation 22:12: "Behold, I come quickly, and my reward with me." We shall not compare the rather numerous references. Also pertinent here is the term "Maranatha" (Our Lord Comes), which contains nothing else than the threat of divine judgment.

## "and our gathering together to Him"

While these words do indeed seem to deal with the second coming of Christ, this interpretation is not consonant with the context, and so they admit of a different sense. Without a doubt, the Greek ἐπισυναγωγῆς [episunageins] refers to the collection of the church under the earlier manifestation of God's presence, as in Matthew 23:37.[6] Although truly by the work of the Apostles many first from the Jews, and then from the Gentiles were gathered to Christ, nevertheless the false apostles and Rabbis returned many again into error. Certainly, since for so long a time the judgments between the Jewish republic and the Pharisees were greatly different, some among them began to vacillate. But after that final judgment of Christ we all, says the Apostle, shall finally be led to Christ, finally, our constancy in the Christian Religion will be confirmed.

In the same fashion, the Church has been dispersed under the Papacy, but by the ministry of Luther and the other Reformers, it has been returned to its former glory.

6. Also, Matthew 24:31.

## Verse 2: "shaken from the mind"

From the same mind, surely, which Paul formed in them through the teaching of the Gospel. The Rabbis and the Pharisees were deeply involved in that, as in Gal 1:6 and various passages in the Book of Acts.

## "Neither through the Spirit"

By Spirit (Gk. Πνεύματος/*pneumatos*) is meant the Spirit of Prophecy. It should be noted that the Rabbis and false apostles very often wrote letters edited under the name of Paul, in which they interspersed their own comments. For this reason, Paul found it necessary to confirm his letters with his own personal signature.

Among other things, they produced false prophecies, apocalypses, and visions in which they portrayed the Apostle as refuting the very things which he had taught here. Such Apocalypses of Paul, J. A. Fabricius records in his work on the *Apocryphal New Testament*[7] and following. And while someone wishes to establish those which are put forth there as rather more recent, (and we do not strongly oppose that position), nevertheless more of this kind were able to be produced in the apostolic period which today, even as the rest, do not fully survive. Certainly, the plain sense of the Apostle's words scarcely permits us to believe otherwise.

## "Nor through a word"

To understand "word" (Gk. Λόγου/*logou*) as "history" or "sermon" seems equally good options to me. I have taught above at the reference to the epistle to the Galatians[8] that the evangelical history was falsely presented under the name of Paul. If therefore entire false books were composed, how much more is it credible that his sermons were corrupted and interpolated?

## "Nor through a letter"

From this passage, we see that rather many spurious letters were attributed to the Apostle in ancient times. The words "as though through us" support this interpretation. Part of the material is introduced here,

---

7. Joseph Alberto Fabricio, *Codex Apocryphus Novi Testamenti*, 4 vols. (Hamburg, Germany: Christianum Herold, 1743), 943: https://bit.ly/3U8fELH

8. This citation is earlier in the commentary than the translated text.

but especially that which concerns the instigation of judgments on the Jewish Republic.

## "had come"

That time would happen in the very near future, which in the mind of the Apostle was substantially different from the present.

## Verse 3: "because unless he come"

The syntax is elliptical, and the subject of the clause must be supplied: the judgments will not be revealed until the apostasy is first made manifest.

## "apostasy"

Surely the defection of the Pharisees, not from sound doctrine, for this is something which had happened long ago and was soundly true even before the time of Christ. Rather, that singular and notable rebellion is indicated which the Jews, at the instigation of the Pharisees and Rabbis, had begun against the Power of Rome.

## "Man of Sin"[9]

Not one individual is meant by this term, but all the Pharisees, Rabbis, and experts in the law who are worthy of this title, since not only have they sinned but they have also caused other "transgressors" to sin. They had taught men to transgress the divine precepts so that their traditions remained intact. Indeed, they committed that very sin against the Holy Spirit, since they defamed the divine miracles of Christ with blasphemies, although in him were met all the most exacting criteria for the Messiah, and conscience indeed convicted them. Nevertheless, they were unwilling to lay aside their own authority and prostrate themselves before so abject a man. Furthermore, their entire life was one continual sin, since through that entire period of time they thought

---

9. Schoettgen includes a list of references from the Scriptures and Rabbinic writings in which he gives the Latin, Greek, Hebrew, and Aramaic terms behind "Man of Sin." While these citations do not substantially contribute to his argumentation, I include the Scripture references for the interested reader: Proverbs 6:12 and Isaiah 55:7.

of nothing else except how they might cast off the yoke of Rome, once rebellion had been stirred up.

The same must be said of the Roman Pontiff, under which type must be understood not simply one individual, but the majority of the Pontiffs, and not they alone, but the entire Roman clergy. Their entire life, yesterday and today, is nothing except sin, something which is excellently demonstrated from the history of the church.

## "The Son of Destruction"

In Hebrew there occurs the term *benim mishchatim* (מַשְׁחִיתִם בָּנִים Is. 1:4)[10] which marvelously illuminates the usage here. It notes by the use of the Hiphil conjugation that such people not only destroy themselves but also hasten others to ruin. Indeed, we might prove the truth of this metonymy[11] from this, that the Pharisees and Rabbis caused many to perish. Christ upbraids them because they cross land and see to make a proselyte, who as a result becomes a far worse son of hell than they (Matt. 23:15). We omit more examples for the sake of brevity, since the depravity of the Pharisees is obscure to no one of us. Furthermore, the Apostle declares that in the future there are among the Jews those who would hasten destruction both for themselves and others. And clearly, so that we may move on, history has proved the outcome of this prediction. With a will, as it were, the entire Jewish nation sought its own ruin. Josephus confirms this in *The Jewish War* 6.36: "It was God who condemned the entire people and turned all the way of salvation into destruction."[12] The passage concerning Simon at 7.7 also supports this.

The Roman Pontiff is deservedly called the son of destruction, who, by his skillful cheats, has kept the laity from reading the divine word and condemned innumerable souls to perdition; and (let me not say)

---

10. Alas, sinful nation / People weighed down with iniquity / Offspring of evildoers / **Sons who act corruptly!** / They have abandoned the LORD / They have despised the Holy One of Israel / They have turned away from Him.

11. Latin *denominatio* refers to using the name of one object for another. In the context of the sentence, Schoettgen means that although the terminology in Isaiah does not literally refer to the Pharisees and Rabbis, it nevertheless describes them perfectly.

12. I render the sense of the quotation; Schoettgen partially quotes the Greek and provides a Latin translation.

by his cruelty and tyranny has destroyed the earthly life and bodies of many more.

## Verse 4: "the one who resists, etc."

The Pharisees and Rabbis cared too little for God and his worship but were extremely fervent of their own prestige and that of their traditions. They report such things of themselves to the eternal shame of themselves and their own. In the Bava Metzia[13] section 59.2 after the Pharisees have disputed in various ways about their tradition, they thus go on.[14] Indeed Gameliel, himself a Pharisee, but whose heart was made from better stuff, was unwilling to "fight against God" (Acts 5:39). But his colleagues and successors were not ashamed to fight with the immortal gods after the fashion of the Titans.[15]

They especially dared to extol themselves against God in the time of the siege of Jerusalem, when they committed many crimes, so that even Josephus called his own people "godless," in *The Jewish War* 6 and 4.18.

Furthermore, when the Apostle here speaks concerning those who go by the name of the gods, I think that he means the magistracy, which in the Sacred Scriptures it is well known that it is called by the name of the gods.[16] Josephus, himself a Pharisee, testifies (in *The Jewish War* 1.5.1, Rufinus's version) that the Pharisees sometimes gave tenuous reverence to this.[17]

We do not need to spend much time here concerning the Pontiff and the Roman clergy. It is well known that certain of them held the

---

13. "Bava Metzia (Talmudic Aramaic: אבב אעיצמ, 'The Middle Gate') is the second of the first three Talmudic tractates in the order of Nezikin ('Damages'), the other two being Bava Kamma and Bava Batra. Originally all three formed a single tractate called *Nezikin* (torts or injuries), each *Bava* being a Part or subdivision. Bava Metzia discusses civil matters such as property law and usury. It also examines one's obligations to guard lost property that have been found, or property explicitly entrusted to him."

14. Following is a list of citations from the Rabbinic writings designed to illustrate that the Rabbis consistently disagree with the plain sense of God's word, and so resist God. We move on to Schoettgen's conclusion.

15. In Greek mythology, the Titans fought with the gods, whom the fates had ordained to rule heaven and earth. The Titans lost and were destroyed or eternally punished (such as Atlas, condemned to support the earth on his shoulders).

16. Schoettgen refers to the fact that the officials in Israel were sometimes referred to as *elohim*, the same term which is used of God (cf. Ps. 82:1).

17. Schoettgen follows with the quotation from Josephus.

Gospel of Christ to be a fable and abominated the Sacred Scripture, since it spoiled the purity of the Roman style. Indeed, the Roman Pontiff is a rebel against emperors and other kings, whence it is sufficiently well considered that the very same thing was indicated by the apostle. However, we are unwilling to be more comprehensive in application to the Roman Pontiff, since others have treated this sufficiently elsewhere.

## "or worship"

The Hebrew *aburah* denotes the divine cult. To this, and particularly to the external, the Pharisees wished to appear most devoted. But let one who would learn of them more accurately know that they only observed the divine cult in so far as it agreed with their own formulations and traditions. I call as my witness the entire Talmud, in which they take great pains to do nothing else except advance their own empty chatter, so that, after they have thought out their insipid distinctions, they treat their vain ceremonies as divine ordinances. But concerning the inner worship of God there was clearly among them a deep silence.

## "into the temple of God as though God"

By the temple of God is surely meant the temple in Jerusalem. In it the Pharisees sat, since at first they were the assessors of the great Sanhedrin, which was originally the *lishkat hagazit*, the "room of the cut stone." That room was situated on the southern side of the temple, as the Codex Midoth agrees. Afterward, when they were exiled from there, its place was *habeth bahar*, "in the mountain," or more precisely "to the hill of the temple," and indeed *behanawiot*, in the booths.[18] We do not cite more examples but refer the reader to the writers on the Sanhedrin, who are rather many. In this temple of God, therefore, the Pharisees sat as God, for they were judges, *elohim*, who spoke justice in the name of God. Indeed the Pharisees abused their divine authority for their own convenience, greed, and ambition.

At that time the Pharisees had many in the priesthood, and sometimes through cheats and bribery aspired to the dignity of the High Priest. For in the last times there was no one High Priest, but many, who in the New Testament are most often joined with the Pharisees,

---

18. Latin *taberna*, which can refer to any small dwelling, including a tent or booth.

and furthermore, since they were involved in common business, it is credible that they cultivated the same sect. Sitting in the temple of God, these High Priests believed that they filled the place of God, and so persuaded the people of whatever seemed useful to themselves. They interpreted Scripture, not from the mind of God, but from their own, and so again abused their authority.

## Verse 6: "that which restrains"

"That which delays this judgment for a little while." The following verse speaks of "the one who restrains," "that one who delays the matter,"[19] and who first must be taken out of the midst. It is not easy to say who is understood. Perhaps not unreasonably one could surmise that it refers to the Christians, who by their prayers had put off the matter for some time, until, warned by a divine oracle, they had quit Jerusalem and repaired to Pella.

## Verse 7: "The mystery of lawlessness"

This is "evil doctrine" itself, cf. "the mystery of godliness," "the doctrine of true religion," 1 Tim. 3:16. Sohar Genesis. section 12: "It is necessary, that a man join himself to those who believe in one God and so separate himself from the mystery of evil." Sohar Exodus. section 64:254: "There is a time given to love God, and there is another time given, which is the mystery of strange gods (i.e., of the worship of idols) by which a man is known to hate God, as though his heart were not moved."

## Verse 8: "will remove by the Spirit of his mouth"

A certain power must be understood which was more than human, and by which the pride of the Pharisees, together with the whole republic of the Jews, was destroyed. Not by word alone does one overcome or take from the midst unless he is in accord with God himself, or those who are equipped by him with divine authority. Thus, the Midrash records concerning Moses (Jalkut Simeon part I section 52.3) where an Israelite, Dathen, whom the Jews had set up, thus says to Moses "Do you really say this to kill me?" Then these words are added: "They have

---

19. The Greek is respectively to *katechon* (neuter) and *ho katechon* (masculine).

prophesied this concerning themselves, for he (Moses) overwhelmed them with his word." Rasche annotates these words at Exodus 2:14, since it was well known that Moses killed the Egyptian.

We need not adduce other examples by way of advice, except this, here in the appropriate place, as it were: namely that Titus himself, when Jerusalem was defeated, understood this. When the neighboring peoples offered him the crown, so that he would be well adorned for his triumphal march, he replied that he was unworthy of this honor, for he had not accomplished this of himself, but submitted his hands to God manifesting his wrath.[20] So strongly was Jerusalem fortified that the enemy held back for rather long, and so numerous the people, that they could not have conquered them without great difficulty, unless God so disposed of everything that the truth of those predictions would remain steadfast.

## "he will destroy"

He will so destroy, that nothing would survive. The entire Pharisaic movement would be "null and void,"[21] without effect. Although the Jews showed great power in restoring their republic and the Pharisees had erected centers of study in various ancient cities, including Babylon, Tiberias, Sora, Nehardea, and Pombeditha, nevertheless all their works were in vain. Although among themselves they often incubated dogmas and traditions, they nevertheless could never propagate other peoples. Therefore we may rightly call Judaism a corpse, whose bones lie scattered, and whose life and soul is bereft (Matt 24:28).

## "by the manifestation of his presence"

"Manifestation" (Gk. ἐπιφανείᾳ) and "presence" (Gk. παρουσίας) though in other places used as synonyms, here differ somewhat in sense. For *epiphaneia* denotes clear splendor, just as *epiphanes*[22] denotes noble, excellent, clear. Therefore, by reason of hendiadys[23] *epiphaneiates parousias* [the manifestation of his presence] is his *parousia epiphanes*

---

20. Again, Schoettgen cites the Greek and then translates accurately into Latin.

21. Greek *argos, aergos*.

22. The corresponding adjective.

23. Schoettgen uses the actual Greek for the term. *Hendiadys* is literally "one through two" and is used when one noun modifies another as though an adjective.

[manifest presence]. "His coming, which will occur clearly before the eyes of all," his visible majesty and splendor no one will be able to deny.

## Verse 9: "whose"

Surely "the man of lawlessness," concerning whom the preceding verse treats. The construction here must be referred to the farther, not the nearer antecedent.

## "according to the work of Satan"

That many Jews had some commerce with Satan the Jews, who speak for themselves, are witnesses. Clearly, they appointed no member to the Sanhedrin unless he had precise knowledge of the magic arts. No one could truly learn these unless Satan was his professor. Sanhedrin section 17.1 R. Johanen said: "No one is chosen to be a member of the Sanhedrin except men of outstanding stature, wise, handsome, mature, *Uba 'ali keshaphim*[24] and skilled in magic, also knowledgeable in the language of the Septuagint." These same things are repeated in Menachoth section 65.1 where Raschius adds the case to be established from this principle, that, if perhaps a magician put out his fire by his arts, they nevertheless are able to execute him in some other way. As though God, who had ordered that sorcerers should be rooted out and destroyed, deprived of life, would not know, or would not be present for those who truly keep his commandments. More examples of this kind occur in Eifenmengerus, whom we shall not copy here.

Impudently enough they rave that holy men knew sorcery so that no one would charge them with the crime of practicing such arts. So they teach that Abraham taught sorcery to his sons born of Ketura, and they understood it through such offerings, by which he dismissed them having been taught by himself and his son Isaac. Thus they abundantly reference the commerce of Solomon with Asmodeus in the Gittin Tractate. There is no need to cite it here, since Edzardus and Eifenmengerus have it in Latin and German, and the Jews themselves in their own writings and language.

---

24. Literally, "masters of sorcery." See Gideon Bohak, *Ancient Jewish Magic: A History* (New York: Cambridge University Press, 2008), 367. "The word *keshaphim* is associated in 2 K. 9:22 with the 'harlotries of Jezebel' (*zenûnê 'izebhel*), i.e., Phoenician idolatry."

Furthermore, to those who confess it a certain type of demon was given, which they call "Jewish." Sohar Numer, section 104.413 "I determine that king Asmodeus and all his family are Jewish devils." These, therefore, are the teachers of the Rabbis. How else would they know the many things that they advance about devils, their distinguishing characteristics and secrets, unless they had not been taught by the Devil himself? Clearly God did not reveal these things to them. But even if many of their traditions are incredible (as can be discerned from the indices of Eifenmengerus), they nonetheless indict themselves, since we judge them by their own confession. We advance nothing at present concerning the practice of the Cabala, which plainly consists of traffic with unclean spirits. Therefore also Christ, in John 8:44 in this sense called the Devil the "father of the Jews," that is, their teacher, who impelled them to every sort of evil.

## "every kind of false miracle, sign, and wonders"

With Satan as their resource, first the Pharisees, and then other antichrists were able to perform miracles, which were understood as *dunameis* (δυνάμεις),[25] and then also produce signs. For the Savior himself predicted that they would produce great signs and wonders, Matt 24:24. Many such things the Jews offer concerning their own feats, that they have eradicated mountains and trees, healed the sick, and such like, concerning which we are unwilling to treat at length.

## Verse 10: "the trickery of evil"

This is "evil trickery." The Pharisees labored especially hard at deceiving others. Hence elsewhere the Apostle says that they suppress the truth by their lies, Rom 1:25. Even more ignorant people (who afterward perished for eternity) attempted to cover up the divine truth of the Messiah's coming.

## "they did not receive the love of the truth"

Quite often I have wondered why it happened that the Pharisees and Rabbis, whom we cannot deny individually have every faculty of

---

25. One of the Greek terms for miraculous events. The Vulgate, in keeping with Jerome's literalistic agenda, translates *virtutes*.

reason, collectively did not recognize the truth of Christ as the present Messiah. Certainly they had the knowledge of Scripture, nor could they be ignorant of the present time of the Messianic advent. Nor is there any doubt that a few of their colleagues who believed in Christ (we know only Nicodemus and Josephus) spoke with the rest concerning this affair. There is no doubt that they did, since the Talmudic scholars themselves, in the Tractate Sanhedrin chapter 11, dispute concerning the various interpretations of the Messianic advent, from which we may produce various arguments against the Jews themselves. However, most of them were unwilling to accept the truth even so, since to this point for a sufficiently long time they had believed otherwise, and had taught others. They were afraid that their authority would be diminished, if they changed their mind, for they had come to a rather mature, indeed even decrepit age, and they had been admonished by a Teacher who was much younger.

I am not able to forget that this same Pharisaism rules among certain of our own learned men right up to this very day. A learned man knows the truth and it is his duty to pursue and love it, whether it is discovered and promoted by ourselves or others. But reality itself teaches that today is far otherwise. Many are found who do not love the truth, but propose something which is convenient to their own agenda, far too admiring of their own inventions. Others, who are able to count rather more years, put forth certain common opinions according to the custom of their ancestors, just as they received them. They begrudge those upon whom God graciously bestows better and then contradict them. Not all learned men so deny themselves that they are willing to say that they have insufficient understanding, even should they be corrected by others. Hence they are imitators of the Pharisees (although they will deny it) in suppressing the truth, and persecuting others.

## Verse 11: "Working of Error"

Clearly the errors in the Jewish tribe produced such deep roots that they are not easily able to be dug out. There is no one, who knows the Jews even a little, who does not testify concerning their noted obstinacy. Hence it is with difficulty that their conversion occurs. In those times, when the republic verged on destruction, they were so stubborn in their plans that the nobles of the Pharisees were open to be easily led by them into destruction.

## Verse 15: "the traditions"

In other places the Apostle better opposes the Pharisaic traditions, especially those which he had set forth either in writing or by word of mouth. See above at 1 Cor 11:23.

# Other Books by Gary DeMar

*God and Government:*
*A Bible, Historical, and*
*Constitutional Perspective*

*Last Days Madness:*
*Obsession of the Modern Church*

*Ruler of the Nations*

*America's Christian History:*
*The Untold Story*

*Surviving College Successfully*

*The Reduction of Christianity:*
*A Biblical Response to Dave Hunt*

*The Debate Over Christian*
*Reconstruction*

*Christian Reconstruction: What*
*It Is. What It Isn't. (with Gary*
*North)*

*To Pledge Allegiance:*
*A New World in View*

*To Pledge Allegiance:*
*Reformation to Colonization*

*To Pledge Allegiance:*
*On the Road to Independence*

*War of the Worldviews*

*Is Jesus Coming Soon?*

*Left Behind:*
*Separating Fact from Fiction*

*Thinking Straight in a Crooked*
*World: A Christian Defense*
*Manual*

*The Case for America's Christian*
*Heritage*

*The Early Church and the End of*
*the World*

*Liberty at Risk:*
*Exposing the Politics of Plunder*

*Whoever Controls the Schools*
*Rules the World*

*Memory Mechanics:*
*How to Memorize Anything*

*The Gog and Magog End-Time*
*Alliance*

*The Case for America's Christian*
*Heritage*

*Myths, Lies, & Half-Truths*

*10 Prophecy Myths Exposed and*
*Answered*

*Identifying the Real Last Days*
*Scoffers*

*Wars and Rumors of Wars*

*The Rapture and the Fig Tree*
*Generation*